الاستنباط من البحر العميق

AL- ISTINBĀTU MIN AL BAHRI AL A'MÌQ

DROPS FROM THE DEEP OCEAN

REFLECTIONS ON THE QUR'AN

Fadl and Rahmah of Allah ﷻ in Guidance

with a focus on

▶ **Contemporary Renderings**
▶ **Psychological Explorations**
▶ **Western Discourses**
▶ **Lexical Analysis**

VOLUME 2

Dr. M. Yunus Kumek

Address to the Islamic Religious Scholars & Philosophers

Medina House
publishing

Cover Photo by Y. Kumek, Alexandria, Egypt, January 12, 2019.

Medina House*
publishing

www.medinahouse.org
170 Manhattan Ave, Po. Box 63
New York 14215
contact@medinahouse.org

Published in the United States of America.

Table of Contents
VOLUME 2

VOLUME 2

Sûrah An'âm

[1]¹

الْحَمْدُ لِلّهِ الَّذِي خَلَقَ السَّمَاوَاتِ وَالأَرْضَ وَجَعَلَ الظُّلُمَاتِ وَالنُّورَ ثُمَّ الَّذِينَ كَفَرُواْ بِرَبِّهِم يَعْدِلُونَ

The name of this Sûrah is An'am, meaning blessings coming, right after the Sûrah named "Maidah", "the food trays", as one of the blessings, possibly, as Allah (‎ﷻ) always knows the best. The Sûrah teaches us, to thank Allah ‎ﷻ for all the nimah's, by starting "Alhamdulillah lazi....", as the Sûrah name is ana'am, the bounties. There are five prayers in a day and there are five surahs in the Qurān that start with Alhamdullillah: Sûrah Fātiha, Ana'am, Kahf, Saba and Fātir. It is also interesting to note that there are things humans take as granted but Allah ‎ﷻ reminds the person to recognize that true hamd, appreciation is only for Allah ‎ﷻ. For example:

الْحَمْدُ لِلّهِ رَبِّ الْعَالَمِينَ {الفاتحة/2}	General Hamd for everything.
ضَرْلأَاوَ تِاوَامَسَّلا قَلَخَ يذِلَّا لِلّهِ دُمْحَلْا رَوُنُّلاوَ تِامُلُظُّلا لَعَجَوَ (Sûrah ana'am 1)	Hamd to for the creation of skies and the earth. Hamd for the making of light and darkness.
الْحَمْدُ لِلّهِ الَّذِي أَنزَلَ عَلَى عَبْدِهِ الْكِتَابَ وَلَمْ يَجْعَل لَّهُ عِوَجَا {الكهف/1} (Sûrah kahf 1)	Hamd for the Qurān. Hamd for making the Qurān Perfect.
يِفِ امَوَ تِاوَامَسَّلا يِف امَ هُلَ يذِلَّا لِلّهِ دُمْحَلْا قِرْخِلأْا يِف دُمْحَلْا هُلَوَ ضِرْلأَْا (Sûrah saba 1)	Hamd for the Ownership and Control of Allah ‎ﷻ of everything in the skies, and on the earth Hamd for all the blessings given in the afterlife.
الْحَمْدُ لِلّهِ فَاطِرِ السَّمَاوَاتِ وَالأَرْضِ جَاعِلِ الْمَلائِكَةِ رُسُلاً (Sûrah Fātir 1)	Hamd for the origination of the skies and earth. Hamd for making angels regulating all the affairs as the messengers of Allah ‎ﷻ.

---

1. 6:1 ALL PRAISE is due to God, who has created the heavens and the earth, and brought into being deep darkness as well as light: and yet, those who are bent on denying the truth regard other powers as their Sustainer's equals!

As one can realize the skies and the earth are big nimah, and bounty from Allah ﷻ. For many years, humans are trying to find in the space a similar system like earth and sky but no sign of existence similar or comparable to ours. This simply can show that the earth and skies are big blessings for humans as their habitat. It is important to pay attention to words خَلَقَ[2] and فَاطِر[3] used for the skies and earth. The word جَعَلَ[4] is used for another blessing of giving a quality and purpose after their initial creation. For example, after the creation of earth and sky, zulumāt and Nûr are given as a quality to give purpose with جَعَلَ. Allah ﷻ sent the Qurān and made it perfect with جَعَلَ. Allah ﷻ created angels and gave them the responsibility of arranging all the affairs of natural and humanly engagements to prevent chaos with جَعَلَ, الله اعلم.

And after all the blessings, bounties, nimahs, the people still don't recognize and equate other things as their god, as the remaining of the verse says, "summa allazina kafaru bi Rabbihim ya'dilun."

[12 & 54][5]

قُل لِّمَن مَّا فِي السَّمَاوَاتِ وَالأَرْضِ قُل لِّلَّهِ كَتَبَ عَلَى نَفْسِهِ الرَّحْمَةَ لَيَجْمَعَنَّكُمْ إِلَى يَوْم الْقِيَامَةِ لاَ رَيْبَ فِيهِ الَّذِينَ خَسِرُواْ أَنفُسَهُمْ فَهُمْ لاَ يُؤْمِنُونَ {الأنعام/12}

وَإِذَا جَاءكَ الَّذِينَ يُؤْمِنُونَ بِآيَاتِنَا فَقُلْ سَلاَمٌ عَلَيْكُمْ كَتَبَ رَبُّكُمْ عَلَى نَفْسِهِ الرَّحْمَةَ أَنَّهُ مَن عَمِلَ مِنكُمْ سُوءًا بِجَهَالَةٍ ثُمَّ تَابَ مِن بَعْدِهِ وَأَصْلَحَ فَأَنَّهُ غَفُورٌ رَّحِيمٌ {الأنعام/54}

SubhanAllah, Allah ﷻ is telling us that Allah ﷻ is treating us and will treat us with Rahmah, Mercy, Caring and Love. Therefore, when one looks at different wrong constructions of people about the Creator and how over time, the books or scriptures have been changed or altered by people.

It is always important to review the unchanged scripture, the Qurān in these discussions to know who Allah ﷻ truly and correctly is. In the same Sūrah of Sūrah Ena'ām, Allah ﷻ mentions the word rahmah in the 12th ayah. Yet, a special rahmah including with the general can be signified with the additional phrase of رَبُّكُمْ[6] in ayah 54. This can be similar to the classical discussions on بِسْمِ اللهِ الرَّحْمَنِ الرَّحِيمِ that the name of Allah ﷻ as Rahmān is general which means rahmah for all, but the name of Allah ﷻ as Rahìm is special rahmah of Allah ﷻ in the dunya and akhirah for the appreciators, the believers, الله اعلم.

[7]قَدْ نَعْلَمُ إِنَّهُ لَيَحْزُنُكَ الَّذِي يَقُولُونَ فَإِنَّهُمْ لاَ يُكَذِّبُونَكَ وَلَكِنَّ الظَّالِمِينَ بِآيَاتِ اللهِ [33-44] يَجْحَدُونَ{الأنعام/33} وَلَقَدْ كُذِّبَتْ رُسُلٌ مِّن قَبْلِكَ فَصَبَرُواْ عَلَى مَا كُذِّبُواْ وَأُوذُواْ حَتَّى أَتَاهُمْ نَصْرُنَا وَلاَ مُبَدِّلَ لِكَلِمَاتِ اللهِ وَلَقَدْ جَاءكَ مِن نَّبَإِ الْمُرْسَلِينَ {الأنعام/34} وَإِن كَانَ كَبُرَ عَلَيْكَ إِعْرَاضُهُمْ فَإِنِ اسْتَطَعْتَ أَن تَبْتَغِيَ نَفَقًا فِي الأَرْضِ أَوْ سُلَّمًا فِي السَّمَاء فَتَأْتِيَهُم بِآيَةٍ وَلَوْ شَاء اللهُ لَجَمَعَهُمْ عَلَى الْهُدَى فَلاَ تَكُونَنَّ مِنَ الْجَاهِلِينَ {الأنعام/35} إِنَّمَا يَسْتَجِيبُ الَّذِينَ يَسْمَعُونَ وَالْمَوْتَى يَبْعَثُهُمُ اللهُ ثُمَّ إِلَيْهِ يُرْجَعُونَ {الأنعام/36} وَقَالُواْ لَوْلاَ نُزِّلَ عَلَيْهِ آيَةٌ مِّن رَّبِّهِ قُلْ إِنَّ اللهَ قَادِرٌ عَلَى أَن يُنَزِّلٍ آيَةً وَلَكِنَّ أَكْثَرَهُمْ لاَ يَعْلَمُونَ {الأنعام/37} وَمَا مِن دَآبَّةٍ فِي الأَرْضِ وَلاَ طَائِرٍ يَطِيرُ بِجَنَاحَيْهِ إِلاَّ أُمَمٌ أَمْثَالُكُم مَّا فَرَّطْنَا فِي الكِتَابِ مِن

---

6. Your Lord.

7. 6:33 We know that you, [O Muhammad], are saddened by what they say. And indeed, they do not call you untruthful, but it is the verses of Allah that the wrongdoers reject. 6:34 And certainly were messengers denied before you, but they were patient over the denial, and they were harmed until Our victory came to them. And none can alter the words [i.e., decrees] of Allah. And there has certainly come to you some information about the [previous] messengers. 6:35 And if their evasion is difficult for you, then if you are able to seek a tunnel into the earth or a stairway into the sky to bring them a sign, [then do so]. But if Allah had willed, He would have united them upon guidance. So never be of the ignorant. 6:36 Only those who hear will respond. But the dead—Allah will resurrect them; then to Him they will be returned. 6:37 And they say, "Why has a sign not been sent down to him from his Lord?" Say, "Indeed, Allah is Able to send down a sign, but most of them do not know." 6:38 And there is no creature on [or within] the earth or bird that flies with its wings except [that they are] communities like you. We have not neglected in the Register a thing. Then unto their Lord they will be gathered. 6:39 But those who deny Our verses are deaf and dumb within darknesses. Whomever Allah wills—He leaves astray; and whomever He wills—He puts him on a straight path. 6:40 Say, "Have you considered: if there came to you the punishment of Allah or there came to you the Hour—is it other than Allah you would invoke, if you should be truthful?" 6:41 No, it is Him [alone] you would invoke, and He would remove that for which you invoked Him if He willed, and you would forget what you associate [with Him]. 6:42 And We have already sent [messengers] to nations before you, [O Muhammad]; then We seized them with poverty and hardship that perhaps they might humble themselves [to Us]. 6:43 Then why, when Our punishment came to them, did they not humble themselves? But their hearts became hardened, and Satan made attractive to them that which they were doing. 6:44 So when they forgot that by which they had been reminded, We opened to them the doors of every [good] thing until, when they rejoiced in that which they were given, We seized them suddenly, and they were [then] in despair.

شَيْءٍ ثُمَّ إِلَى رَبِّهِمْ يُحْشَرُونَ {الأنعام/38} وَالَّذِينَ كَذَّبُواْ بِآيَاتِنَا صُمٌّ وَبُكْمٌ فِي الظُّلُمَاتِ مَن يَشَإِ اللّهُ يُضْلِلْهُ وَمَن يَشَأْ يَجْعَلْهُ عَلَى صِرَاطٍ مُّسْتَقِيمٍ {الأنعام/39} قُلْ أَرَأَيْتُكُم إِنْ أَتَاكُمْ عَذَابُ اللّهِ أَوْ أَتَتْكُمُ السَّاعَةُ أَغَيْرَ اللّهِ تَدْعُونَ إِن كُنتُمْ صَادِقِينَ {الأنعام/40} بَلْ إِيَّاهُ تَدْعُونَ فَيَكْشِفُ مَا تَدْعُونَ إِلَيْهِ إِنْ شَاء وَتَنسَوْنَ مَا تُشْرِكُونَ {الأنعام/41} وَلَقَدْ أَرْسَلنَآ إِلَى أُمَمٍ مِّن قَبْلِكَ فَأَخَذْنَاهُمْ بِالْبَأْسَاء وَالضَّرَّاء لَعَلَّهُمْ يَتَضَرَّعُونَ {الأنعام/42} فَلَوْلا إِذْ جَاءهُمْ بَأْسُنَا تَضَرَّعُواْ وَلَكِن قَسَتْ قُلُوبُهُمْ وَزَيَّنَ لَهُمُ الشَّيْطَانُ مَا كَانُواْ يَعْمَلُونَ {الأنعام/43} فَلَمَّا نَسُواْ مَا ذُكِّرُواْ بِهِ فَتَحْنَا عَلَيْهِمْ أَبْوَابَ كُلِّ شَيْءٍ حَتَّى إِذَا فَرِحُواْ بِمَا أُوتُواْ أَخَذْنَاهُم بَغْتَةً فَإِذَا هُم مُّبْلِسُونَ {الأنعام/44}

The above ayahs mention the concern of Rasulullah ﷺ about teaching the people about genuine knowledge and belief in Allah ﷻ. Rasulullah ﷺ embodies the responsibility of the Prophethood and messengership. The feeling of this responsibility was at such a high level that Allah ﷻ relieves and comforts the Prophet ﷺ. Allah ﷻ gives the reasons and presents examples from the past to the Prophet صلى الله عليه وسلم and to the believers who have this high goal of telling people truly about Allah ﷻ. In this case, the true believers have this concern similar to their Prophet ﷺ. Allah ﷻ mentions that if you happen to bring the miracles that they want, they still will not believe in Allah ﷻ because Allah ﷻ in reality knows the reason of their rejection but the Prophet may not know. Therefore, one should understand the context of the statement is فَلاَ تَكُونَنَّ مِنَ الْجَاهِلِينَ[8]. In this context, Allah ﷻ mentions that if Allah ﷻ wants they can be all on the guidance as mentioned وَلَوْ شَاء اللّهُ لَجَمَعَهُمْ[9] عَلَى الْهُدَى. In this phrase, لَجَمَعَهُمْ can signify by force. In other words, it is not the free choice of people but by force. In other words, a person cannot be forced to believe in and appreciate Allah ﷻ as mentioned with the phrase of لَجَمَعَهُمْ[10]. Therefore, the free choice is essential for a person. If the person is not interested to listen, think and appreciate, it can be similar to a spiritually dead person as mentioned in إِنَّمَا يَسْتَجِيبُ الَّذِينَ[11] يَسْمَعُونَ وَالْمَوْتَى. They can still argue uselessly and say وَقَالُواْ لَوْلاَ نُزِّلَ عَلَيْهِ[12] آيَةٌ مِّن رَّبِّهِ قُلْ إِنَّ اللّهَ قَادِرٌ عَلَى أَن يُنَزِّلٍ آيَةً وَلَكِنَّ أَكْثَرَهُمْ لاَ يَعْلَمُونَ. Here, the point is bringing an ayah. If Allah ﷻ wants then Allah ﷻ can bring and show miracles to them and they may be forced to believe. The problem here

---

8. So never be of the ignorant.
9. But if Allah had willed, He would have united them upon guidance.
10. He would have united them.
11. Only those who hear will respond. But the dead.
12. And they say, "Why has a sign not been sent down to him from his Lord?" Say, "Indeed, Allah is Able to send down a sign, but most of them do not know."

seems to be their attitude. Because there are already a lot of ayahs and signs around such as ¹³وَمَا مِن دَآبَّةٍ فِي الأَرْضِ وَلاَ طَائِرٍ يَطِيرُ بِجَنَاحَيْهِ إِلَّا أُمَمٌ أَمْثَالُكُم. They don't see those but act like مَّا فَرَّطْنَا فِي الكِتَابِ مِن شَيْءٍ ثُمَّ إِلَى رَبِّهِمْ يُحْشَرُونَ a dead person as mentioned before and now: وَالَّذِينَ كَذَّبُواْ بِآيَاتِنَا صُمٌّ وَبُكْمٌ فِي ﴾الأنعام/39﴿ ¹⁴الظُّلُمَاتِ مَن يَشَإِ اللّهُ يُضْلِلْهُ وَمَن يَشَأْ يَجْعَلْهُ عَلَى صِرَاطٍ مُّسْتَقِيم. After this logical discussion, another logical discussion is about the unknowns and uncertainties that a person may face such as calamities or disasters: قُلْ أَرَأَيْتُكُم إِنْ أَتَاكُمْ عَذَابُ اللّهِ أَوْ أَتَتْكُمُ السَّاعَةُ أَغَيْرَ اللّهِ تَدْعُونَ إِن كُنتُمْ صَادِقِينَ¹⁵ ﴾الأنعام/40﴿ بَلْ إِيَّاهُ تَدْعُونَ فَيَكْشِفُ مَا تَدْعُونَ إِلَيْهِ إِنْ شَاء وَتَنسَوْنَ مَا تُشْرِكُونَ¹⁶ ﴾الأنعام/41﴿ In this case, who does the person ask help from? Allah ﷻ gives opportunities people to think and appreciate about Allah ﷻ in the times of difficulty. This happened before وَلَقَدْ أَرْسَلنَآ إِلَى أُمَمٍ مِّن قَبْلِكَ فَأَخَذْنَاهُمْ بِالْبَأْسَاء وَالضَّرَّاء لَعَلَّهُمْ ﴾الأنعام/42﴿ ¹⁷يَتَضَرَّعُونَ and is happening now. The reality is فَلَوْلا إِذْ جَاءهُمْ their بَأْسُنَا تَضَرَّعُواْ وَلَكِن قَسَتْ قُلُوبُهُمْ وَزَيَّنَ لَهُمُ الشَّيْطَانُ مَا كَانُواْ يَعْمَلُونَ¹⁸ ﴾الأنعام/43﴿ hearts and their nafs, themselves were not interested as an attitude and once that was the case, their friend shaytan helped to ease this path for them. Then, what happened? فَلَمَّا نَسُواْ مَا ذُكِّرُواْ بِهِ فَتَحْنَا عَلَيْهِمْ أَبْوَابَ كُلِّ شَيْءٍ حَتَّى إِذَا فَرِحُواْ بِمَا أُوتُواْ أَخَذْنَاهُم بَغْتَةً فَإِذَا هُم مُّبْلِسُونَ¹⁹ ﴾الأنعام/44﴿

Allah opened and created the ways what they wanted to do: wealth, oppression, fun and dunya, everything in the world. But one day, the time was and will be over and they died and their lifestyles left the traces of sadness as a memory. This is mentioned as فَقُطِعَ دَابِرُ الْقَوْمِ الَّذِينَ ظَلَمُواْ وَالْحَمْدُ لِلّهِ رَبِّ الْعَالَمِينَ²⁰ ﴾الأنعام/45﴿.

---

13. And there is no creature on [or within] the earth or bird that flies with its wings except [that they are] communities like you. We have not neglected in the Register a thing. Then unto their Lord they will be gathered.

14. But those who deny Our verses are deaf and dumb within darknesses. Whomever Allah wills—He leaves astray; and whomever He wills—He puts him on a straight path.

15. Say, "Have you considered: if there came to you the punishment of Allah or there came to you the Hour—is it other than Allah you would invoke, if you should be truthful?"

16. No, it is Him [alone] you would invoke, and He would remove that for which you invoked Him if He willed, and you would forget what you associate [with Him].

17. And We have already sent [messengers] to nations before you, [O Muhammad]; then We seized them with poverty and hardship that perhaps they might humble themselves [to Us].

18. 43 Then why, when Our punishment came to them, did they not humble themselves? But their hearts became hardened, and Satan made attractive to them that which they were doing.

19. So when they forgot that by which they had been reminded, We opened to them the doors of every [good] thing until, when they rejoiced in that which they were given, We seized them suddenly, and they were [then] in despair.

20. So the people that committed wrong were eliminated. And ☒praise to Allah, Lord of the worlds. ☒

And, remember, all the Hamd, true Appreciation belongs to Allah even though the self-oppressors did not implement and recognize this in their lives.

[59]²¹

وَعِندَهُ مَفَاتِحُ الْغَيْبِ لاَ يَعْلَمُهَا إِلاَّ هُوَ وَيَعْلَمُ مَا فِي الْبَرِّ وَالْبَحْرِ وَمَا تَسْقُطُ مِن وَرَقَةٍ إِلاَّ يَعْلَمُهَا وَلاَ حَبَّةٍ فِي ظُلُمَاتِ الأَرْضِ وَلاَ رَطْبٍ وَلاَ يَابِسٍ إِلاَّ فِي كِتَابٍ مُّبِينٍ

In this verse, according to some scholars, the expression وَلَا رَطْبٍ وَلَا يَابِسٍ²² إِلاَّ فِي كِتَابٍ مُّبِينٍ can mean that the Qurān implicitly or explicitly contains all the knowledge for all the sciences, for all the past and future events.

[81-83]²³

وَكَيْفَ أَخَافُ مَا أَشْرَكْتُمْ وَلاَ تَخَافُونَ أَنَّكُمْ أَشْرَكْتُم بِاللّهِ مَا لَمْ يُنَزِّلْ بِهِ عَلَيْكُمْ سُلْطَانًا فَأَيُّ الْفَرِيقَيْنِ أَحَقُّ بِالأَمْنِ إِن كُنتُمْ تَعْلَمُونَ {الأنعام/81}

وَتِلْكَ حُجَّتُنَا آتَيْنَاهَا إِبْرَاهِيمَ عَلَى قَوْمِهِ نَرْفَعُ دَرَجَاتٍ مَّن نَّشَاء إِنَّ رَبَّكَ حَكِيمٌ عَلِيمٌ {الأنعام/83}

One can review the logical engagements of the messengers of Allah ﷻ in the Qurān with their people to convince them for the belief in tawhid. One can also realize that these reasoning discourses were also inspired and revealed to them from Allah ﷻ as mentioned in وَتِلْكَ حُجَّتُنَا آتَيْنَاهَا إِبْرَاهِيمَ, الله اعلم. In other words, Allah ﷻ teaches the anbiya how to engage with their people through logic and reasoning. For humans, one of the primary tools of choice or decision making is through reasoning, الله اعلم.

---

21. (6:59) And with Him are the keys of the unseen; none knows them except Him. And He knows what is on the land and in the sea. Not a leaf falls but that He knows it. And no grain is there within the darknesses of the earth and no moist or dry [thing] but that it is [written] in a clear record. ▨
22. And no moist or dry [thing] but that it is [written] in a clear record.
23. 6:81 And how should I fear what you associate while you do not fear that you have associated with Allah that for which He has not sent down to you any authority? So which of the two parties has more right to security, if you should know?" 6:82 They who believe and do not mix their belief with injustice—those will have security, and they are [rightly] guided. 6:83 And that was Our [conclusive] argument which We gave Abraham against his people. We raise by degrees whom We will. Indeed, your Lord is Wise and Knowing. ▨

[125]²⁴

فَمَن يُرِدِ اللّهُ أَن يَهْدِيَهُ يَشْرَحْ صَدْرَهُ لِلإِسْلاَمِ وَمَن يُرِدْ أَن يُضِلَّهُ يَجْعَلْ صَدْرَهُ ضَيِّقًا حَرَجًا كَأَنَّمَا يَصَّعَّدُ فِي السَّمَاء كَذَلِكَ يَجْعَلُ اللّهُ الرِّجْسَ عَلَى الَّذِينَ لاَ يُؤْمِنُونَ {الأنعام/125}

There are three key words in this ayah that also reveal themselves in other parts of the Qurān. These key words are: لِلإِسْلاَمِ²⁵, صَدْرَهُ²⁶, يَشْرَحْ²⁵, and . The classical translations of صدر is chest. One can look at the word sadr صدر how it is used in the Qurān such as كِتَابٌ أُنزِلَ إِلَيْكَ فَلاَ يَكُن فِي صَدْرِكَ حَرَجٌ مِّنْهُ لِتُنذِرَ بِهِ وَذِكْرَى لِلْمُؤْمِنِينَ²⁷{الأعراف/2}.

It is interesting to note that the word صدر is used with the شرح, for example {الشرح/1}²⁸ أَلَمْ نَشْرَحْ لَكَ صَدْرَكَ, or {طه/25}²⁹ قَالَ رَبِّ اشْرَحْ لِي صَدْرِي.

Sometimes this word صدر is used with the word ضَائِقٌ³⁰ almost opposite of شرح such as فَلَعَلَّكَ تَارِكٌ بَعْضَ مَا يُوحَى إِلَيْكَ وَضَائِقٌ بِهِ صَدْرُكَ أَن يَقُولُواْ لَوْلاَ أُنزِلَ عَلَيْهِ كَنزٌ أَوْ جَاء مَعَهُ مَلَكٌ إِنَّمَا أَنتَ نَذِيرٌ وَاللّهُ عَلَى كُلِّ شَيْءٍ وَكِيلٌ {هود/12}³¹, or

وَلَقَدْ نَعْلَمُ أَنَّكَ يَضِيقُ صَدْرُكَ بِمَا يَقُولُونَ ³²{الحجر/97}

صَدْرَهُ ضَيِّقًا حَرَجًا كَأَنَّمَا يَصَّعَّدُ فِي السَّمَاء كَذَلِكَ يَجْعَلُ اللّهُ الرِّجْسَ عَلَى الَّذِينَ لاَ يُؤْمِنُونَ ³³{الأنعام/125}

One may see that there is the expansion and contraction of chest with both يَشْرَحْ صَدْرَهُ³⁴ and يَضِيقُ صَدْرُكَ³⁵ in the above renderings.

Another key word, that is used with صدر is Islam. This can have a meaning that Islam is the external frame work as the chest being external

---

24. 6:125 So whoever Allah wants to guide—He expands his breast to [contain] Islam; and whoever He wants to misguide—He makes his breast tight and constricted as though he were climbing into the sky. Thus does Allah place defilement upon those who do not believe.
25. Expand.
26. His breasts.
27. [This is] a Book revealed to you, [O Muhammad]—so let there not be in your breast distress therefrom—that you may warn thereby and as a reminder to the believers.
28. Did We not expand for you, [O Muhammad], your breast? ⊠
29. [Moses] said, "My Lord, expand [i.e., relax] for me my breast [with assurance].
30. Constrained.
31. Then would you possibly leave [out] some of what is revealed to you, or is your breast constrained by it because they say, "Why has there not been sent down to him a treasure or come with him an angel?" But you are only a warner. And Allah is Disposer of all things.
32. And We already know that your breast is constrained by what they say.
33. He makes his breast tight and constricted as though he were climbing into the sky. Thus does Allah place defilement upon those who do not believe. ⊠
34. Expand his breast.
35. Make his breast tight.

frame of the heart. Another ayah to allude to this notion is اللَّهُ شَرَحَ أَفَمَن[36] صَدْرَهُ لِلْإِسْلَامِ فَهُوَ عَلَى نُورٍ مِّن رَّبِّهِ فَوَيْلٌ لِّلْقَاسِيَةِ قُلُوبُهُم مِّن ذِكْرِ اللَّهِ أُوْلَئِكَ فِي ضَلَالٍ مُبِينٍ {الزمر/22}

In the cases of person's Islam, it is from the Fadl and Rahmah of Allah 🕮 is that one can see the ayahs اللَّهُ صَدْرَهُ لِلْإِسْلَامِ[37], قَالَ رَبِّ اشْرَحْ لِي صَدْرِي {طه/25}[38], or {الشرح/1}[39] أَلَمْ نَشْرَحْ لَكَ صَدْرَكَ, explicitly mentions that is from Allah 🕮. In the opposite case, opening oneself to kufr or being in the state of contraction of heart is due to person's kasb, acquirement, as mentioned: مَن كَفَرَ بِاللَّهِ مِن بَعْدِ إِيمَانِهِ إِلَّا مَنْ أُكْرِهَ وَقَلْبُهُ مُطْمَئِنٌّ بِالْإِيمَانِ وَلَكِن مَّن شَرَحَ بِالْكُفْرِ صَدْرًا فَعَلَيْهِمْ غَضَبٌ مِّنَ اللَّهِ وَلَهُمْ عَذَابٌ عَظِيمٌ[40] {النحل/106}

The word qalb, heart is used with the word dhikr. The essence of Islam is dhikr. In this perspective, the coupling occurs between the chest and heart, Islam and dhikr. The chest is the external frame of the heart. Islam is the external frame of the dhikr. Therefore, Islam and chest can be at the same level, representing the external aspects. Heart and dhikr can be at the same level representing the essence. One can review the ayah اتْلُ مَا أُوحِيَ إِلَيْكَ مِنَ الْكِتَابِ وَأَقِمِ الصَّلَاةَ إِنَّ الصَّلَاةَ تَنْهَى عَنِ الْفَحْشَاءِ وَالْمُنكَرِ وَلَذِكْرُ اللَّهِ أَكْبَرُ وَاللَّهُ يَعْلَمُ مَا تَصْنَعُونَ[41] {العنكبوت/54} if the teachings of Islam such as salah is the external frame, then the dhikr is the essence.

The real dhikr occurs at the heart as many of the ayahs of the Qurān allude to this: الَّذِينَ إِذَا ذُكِرَ اللَّهُ وَجِلَتْ قُلُوبُهُمْ وَالصَّابِرِينَ عَلَى مَا أَصَابَهُمْ وَالْمُقِيمِي الصَّلَاةِ وَمِمَّا رَزَقْنَاهُمْ يُنفِقُونَ[42] {الحج/35}

الَّذِينَ آمَنُواْ وَتَطْمَئِنُّ قُلُوبُهُم بِذِكْرِ اللَّهِ أَلاَ بِذِكْرِ اللَّهِ تَطْمَئِنُّ الْقُلُوبُ[43] {الرعد/28}

Both the frame, external and internal are necessary, similar to the soul and its need of the body, الله اعلم.

---

36. So is one whose breast Allah has expanded to [accept] Islam and he is upon [i.e., guided by] a light from his Lord [like one whose heart rejects it]? Then woe to those whose hearts are hardened against the remembrance of Allah. Those are in manifest error.
37. So is one whose breast Allah has expanded to [accept] Islam.
38. [Moses] said, "My Lord, expand [i.e., relax] for me my breast [with assurance]."
39. Did We not expand for you, [O Muhammad], your breast?
40. Whoever disbelieves in [i.e., denies] Allah after his belief... except for one who is forced [to renounce his religion] while his heart is secure in faith. But those who [willingly] open their breasts to disbelief, upon them is wrath from Allah, and for them is a great punishment.
41. Recite, [O Muhammad], what has been revealed to you of the Book and establish prayer. Indeed, prayer prohibits immorality and wrongdoing, and the remembrance of Allah is greater. And Allah knows that which you do. ▨
42. Who, when Allah is mentioned, their hearts are fearful, and [to] the patient over what has afflicted them, and the establishers of prayer and those who spend from what We have provided them.
43. Those who have believed and whose hearts are assured by the remembrance of Allah. Unquestionably, by the remembrance of Allah hearts are assured." ▨

8

Sûrah A'rāf

[16]⁴⁴

قَالَ فَبِمَا أَغْوَيْتَنِي لأَقْعُدَنَّ لَهُمْ صِرَاطَكَ الْمُسْتَقِيمَ {الأعراف/16}

This is the blame of shaytan which shows the concept of evil that when a person does something bad, the person does not take any blame on oneself but blames God. The same story has been happening like shaytan did in the beginning of all creation. On the other hand, when Adam as and the true believers and appreciators of Allah ﷻ, make a mistake, they immediately repent and ask forgiveness.

[19-20]⁴⁵

وَيَا آدَمُ اسْكُنْ أَنتَ وَزَوْجُكَ الْجَنَّةَ فَكُلاَ مِنْ حَيْثُ شِئْتُمَا وَلاَ تَقْرَبَا هَذِهِ الشَّجَرَةَ فَتَكُونَا مِنَ الظَّالِمِينَ {الأعراف/19} فَوَسْوَسَ لَهُمَا الشَّيْطَانُ لِيُبْدِيَ لَهُمَا مَا وُورِيَ عَنْهُمَا مِن سَوْءَاتِهِمَا وَقَالَ مَا نَهَاكُمَا رَبُّكُمَا عَنْ هَذِهِ الشَّجَرَةِ إِلاَّ أَن تَكُونَا مَلَكَيْنِ أَوْ تَكُونَا مِنَ الْخَالِدِينَ {الأعراف/20}

When the person is prohibited from doing something, the temptation or waswasa of human nature or tendency makes the person incline towards this prohibited item. It is natural or normal to fall into sin, error, something harmful even though one can instruct the person or a child the harmful outcomes of this engagement. As mentioned by the Prophet (26) (صلى الله عليه وسلم) (hadith# 2499) & (20) (hadith#2451), the normalization of this concept that it is normal to make mistakes, sins or errors but the best one is the person who accepts their mistake and turns to Allah ﷻ with repentance and humbleness as exemplified by Adam as. So, this approach can be important in both adult and childhood education, the emphasis of normalization of making mistakes but the

---

44. (7:16) [Whereupon Iblis] said: "Now that Thou hast thwarted me, I shall most certainly lie in ambush for them all along Thy straight way,
45. 7:19 And "O Adam, dwell, you and your wife, in Paradise and eat from wherever you will but do not approach this tree, lest you be among the wrongdoers." 7:20 But Satan whispered to them to make apparent to them that which was concealed from them of their private parts. He said, "Your Lord did not forbid you this tree except that you become angels or become the immortal."

most important thing is to ask forgiveness from Allah ﷻ and connecting to Allah ﷻ again and again. The methodology of not being perfect as a human being should be normalized yet, the teaching of what to do if one makes a mistake in childhood and adult education is critical as the next step.

[21-23][46]

وَقَاسَمَهُمَا إِنِّي لَكُمَا لَمِنَ النَّاصِحِينَ {الأعراف/21} فَدَلَّاهُمَا بِغُرُورٍ فَلَمَّا ذَاقَا الشَّجَرَةَ بَدَتْ لَهُمَا سَوْءَاتُهُمَا وَطَفِقَا يَخْصِفَانِ عَلَيْهِمَا مِن وَرَقِ الْجَنَّةِ وَنَادَاهُمَا رَبُّهُمَا أَلَمْ أَنْهَكُمَا عَن تِلْكُمَا الشَّجَرَةِ وَأَقُل لَّكُمَا إِنَّ الشَّيْطَانَ لَكُمَا عَدُوٌّ مُّبِينٌ {الأعراف/22} قَالاَ رَبَّنَا ظَلَمْنَا أَنفُسَنَا وَإِن لَّمْ تَغْفِرْ لَنَا وَتَرْحَمْنَا لَنَكُونَنَّ مِنَ الْخَاسِرِينَ

As seen in the above ayah, for Shaytan, it is not easy to make zalla to Adam as. The Shaytan swore and Adam as did not know that a being or creation of God can swear on the name of Allah ﷻ about saying the truth but yet then still can lie as shaytan did. Also as another possibility that Adam as could have forgotten the command of Allah ﷻ not to approach that tree, as the name of the human is al-insān, the one who forgets, الله اعلم. Again, the role model attitude of Adam as and our mother Hawwa as comes as

قَالاَ رَبَّنَا ظَلَمْنَا أَنفُسَنَا وَإِن لَّمْ تَغْفِرْ لَنَا وَتَرْحَمْنَا لَنَكُونَنَّ مِنَ الْخَاسِرِينَ [47]

This should be the approach to learn and to teach in the relationship with Allah ﷻ. The approach is resetting one's position with the Creator, Rabbul Alamin, and asking forgiveness.

One can see possibly that Adam as may have wanted to worship like angels and forget the prohibition of Allah ﷻ about the tree when فَوَسْوَسَ إِلَيْهِ الشَّيْطَانُ قَالَ يَا آدَمُ هَلْ أَدُلُّكَ عَلَى شَجَرَةِ الْخُلْدِ وَمُلْكٍ لَّا يَبْلَى [48] {طه/120}

---

46. 7:21 And he swore unto them, "Verily, I am of those who wish you well indeed!" (22)—and thus he led them on with deluding thoughts. But as soon as the two had tasted [the fruit] of the tree, they became conscious of their nakedness; and they began to cover themselves with pieced-together leaves from the garden. And their Sustainer called unto them: "Did I not forbid that tree unto you and tell you, 'Verily, Satan is your open foe'?"
7:23 The two replied: "O our Sustainer! We have sinned against ourselves—and unless Thou grant us forgiveness and bestow Thy mercy upon us, we shall most certainly be lost!"
47. The two replied: "O our Sustainer! We have sinned against ourselves—and unless Thou grant us forgiveness and bestow Thy mercy upon us, we shall most certainly be lost!"
48. Then Satan whispered to him; he said, "O Adam, shall I direct you to the tree of eternity and possession that will not deteriorate?"

The Desire of Being What You are Not: Adam and Shaytan as Angels

It is interesting to note that there is something appealing about being an angel. Shaytan was a jinn but wanted to be like angels as mentioned وَإِذْ قُلْنَا لِلْمَلَائِكَةِ اسْجُدُوا لِآدَمَ فَسَجَدُوا إِلَّا إِبْلِيسَ كَانَ مِنَ الْجِنِّ فَفَسَقَ عَنْ أَمْرِ رَبِّهِ أَفَتَتَّخِذُونَهُ وَذُرِّيَّتَهُ أَوْلِيَاءَ مِن دُونِي وَهُمْ لَكُمْ عَدُوٌّ بِئْسَ لِلظَّالِمِينَ بَدَلاً [49] {الكهف/50}. Adam as was a human being but wanted possibly to be like an angel as mentioned وَقَالَ مَا نَهَاكُمَا رَبُّكُمَا عَنْ هَذِهِ الشَّجَرَةِ إِلَّا أَن تَكُونَا مَلَكَيْنِ أَوْ تَكُونَا مِنَ الْخَالِدِينَ [50] {الأعراف/20}.

In both above cases, one can see that either angels have very appealing features or there is another reason that we don't know.

Yet, the test and trial is to be pleased with what and how Allah ﷻ created this being. In other words, if Allah ﷻ created a being as a human, jinn, man, woman, black or white, the person should be pleased with Allah ﷻ's choice with a form or dress of creation. This shows an attitude of ridah, acceptance humbleness, humility and submission to Allah ﷻ as the word muslim in Arabic entails. This is a notion not as an identity tag but as the essential trait of all creation. In this perspective, all the creation has the noble title of a'bd, worshipper of Allah ﷻ. However, when a creation is not pleased in which dress, form or species that Allah ﷻ has created, then this is a sign of an implicit or explicit ingratitude to Allah ﷻ. Therefore, shukr and hamd as a gratitude and thankfulness to Allah ﷻ is the essence of imān. Gaflah, heedlessnes, denial and the desire who or what you are not is the essence of kufr.

Yet, Allah ﷻ still gives the person what they ask for. For example, shaytan was permitted to be with angels and be with them. Yet, when everyone in the gathering received the order to respect the new creation of Allah ﷻ, Adam as, as وَإِذْ قُلْنَا لِلْمَلَائِكَةِ اسْجُدُوا لِآدَمَ فَسَجَدُوا إِلَّا إِبْلِيسَ كَانَ مِنَ الْجِنِّ فَفَسَقَ عَنْ أَمْرِ رَبِّهِ أَفَتَتَّخِذُونَهُ وَذُرِّيَّتَهُ أَوْلِيَاءَ مِن دُونِي وَهُمْ لَكُمْ عَدُوٌّ بِئْسَ لِلظَّالِمِينَ بَدَلاً {الكهف/50}, shaytan couldn't handle maintaining this company of angels. Because, angels submitted to Allah ﷻ and yet, Shaytan showed a trait that was hidden in him for a longtime. It could have been better for shaytan to be humble, and accept who he was and stayed with his other fellow

---

49. And [mention] when We said to the angels, "Prostrate to Adam," and they prostrated, except for Iblees. He was of the jinn and departed from [i.e., disobeyed] the command of his Lord. Then will you take him and his descendants as allies other than Me while they are enemies to you? Wretched it is for the wrongdoers as an exchange.

50. But Satan whispered to them to make apparent to them that which was concealed from them of their private parts. He said, "Your Lord did not forbid you this tree except that you become angels or become of the immortal."

beings, jinns, if he was not going to disobey Allah ﷻ when he received the same order with angels, الله اعلم. Or, it could have been best to still keep the company of angels but ask forgiveness after his disobedient position, الله اعلم.

On the other hand, when shaytan tricked Adam as with a similar tool to instill Adam as to be like angels, then, when Adam as realized his mistake, he immediately asked tawbah and forgiveness and still maintained his position with Allah الله اعلم, ﷻ.

[27]⁵¹

{ يَا بَنِي آدَمَ لاَ يَفْتِنَنَّكُمُ الشَّيْطَانُ كَمَا أَخْرَجَ أَبَوَيْكُم مِّنَ الْجَنَّةِ يَنزِعُ عَنْهُمَا لِبَاسَهُمَا لِيُرِيَهُمَا سَوْءَاتِهِمَا إِنَّهُ يَرَاكُمْ هُوَ وَقَبِيلُهُ مِنْ حَيْثُ لاَ تَرَوْنَهُمْ إِنَّا جَعَلْنَا الشَّيَاطِينَ أَوْلِيَاء لِلَّذِينَ لاَ يُؤْمِنُونَ {الأعراف/27}

It is interesting to review above ayahs in the context of its emotional feelings. For example, if someone comes and lies and deceives one's mother and father and makes them lose their home, and comfort. This person would not really like this deceiver but probably dislike and hate him or her. Similarly, a person can have more affinity and closeness with Adam as with the above verse when Allah ﷻ mentions يَا بَنِي آدَمَ لَا يَفْتِنَنَّكُمُ⁵² الشَّيْطَانُ كَمَا أَخْرَجَ أَبَوَيْكُم مِّنَ الْجَنَّةِ. In addition, this deceiver also swears that he or she would do the same to the later generations or offspring of Adam, although one may not want to be in that position, then shaytan really becomes an enemy at a personal level as mentioned يَا أَيُّهَا النَّاسُ كُلُواْ مِمَّا فِي الأَرْضِ حَلاَلاً طَيِّباً وَلاَ تَتَّبِعُواْ خُطُوَاتِ الشَّيْطَانِ إِنَّهُ لَكُمْ عَدُوٌّ مُّبِينٌ⁵³{البقرة/168}.

---

51. (7:27) O children of Adam! Do not allow Satan to seduce you in the same way as he caused your ancestors to be driven out of the garden: he deprived them of their garment [of God-consciousness] in order to make them aware of their nakedness. Verily, he and his tribe are lying in wait for you where you cannot perceive them! Verily, We have placed [all manner of] satanic forces near unto those who do not [truly] believe;

52. O children of Adam! Do not allow Satan to seduce you in the same way as he caused your ancestors to be driven out of the garden.

53. O mankind, eat from whatever is on earth [that is] lawful and good and do not follow the footsteps of Satan. Indeed, he is to you a clear enemy. ⌧

[31]⁵⁴

يَا بَنِي آدَمَ خُذُواْ زِينَتَكُمْ عِندَ كُلِّ مَسْجِدٍ وكُلُواْ وَاشْرَبُواْ وَلاَ تُسْرِفُواْ إِنَّهُ لاَ يُحِبُّ الْمُسْرِفِينَ
{الأعراف/31}

The expression يَا بَنِي آدَمَ⁵⁵does not refer only to the believers but to everyone. It is interesting because one can expect only believers or Muslims would go to masjids. However, this can allude to the importance of inviting people to the masjids for showing the ethnography of what and how are the prayers and people's engagement during the prayers are. Everyone can fulfil their spiritual needs through different means along with their needs of eating and drinking as mentioned in وكُلُواْ⁵⁶ وَاشْرَبُوا. In this case, spiritual needs can be fulfilled in the masjids. In this perspective, invitation of others to taste this spiritual engagement in the masjids can be important.

In this perspective, there are limits in eating and drinking as mentioned in لاَ يُحِبُّ الْمُسْرِفِينَ⁵⁷ but there are no limits in spiritual engagements of heart and mind as this can be mentioned as خُذُواْ زِينَتَكُمْ⁵⁸. Here, the word زِينَتَكُمْ⁵⁹ can refer to the valuables of diamond and gold which can represent one's prayers, crying, sujuds, rukus, duas, dhikrs and other learning and experiential dispositions. Because masjids have the sole and main purpose of these for their purpose of establishment but not engaging in other activities primarily. Other activities can be secondary. The word زِينَتَكُمْ for a woman can mean to dress up and beatify for her husband. The word زِينَتَكُمْ for a man can have the same beatification. However, a person can beatify oneself through prayers, crying, sujuds, rukus, duas, dhikrs and other learning and experiential dispositions in one's relationship with Allah ﷻ.

Therefore, people who are not familiar with these valuables can observe and witness, perhaps experience those by inviting them in the masjids as mentioned in this ayah.

---

54. O children of Adam, take your adornment [i.e., wear your clothing] at every masjid, and eat and drink, but be not excessive. Indeed, He likes not those who commit excess. ⌧
55. O children of Adam.
56. And eat and drink.
57. He likes not those who commit excess.
58. Take your adornment [i.e., wear your clothing].
59. Your adornments.

In the classical interpretations of this verse, the word زِينَتَكُم is understood as wearing one's best and cleanest clothes in the places of worship, masjids. Also, there can be a similar order in the previous scriptures as Christians make the habit of going to churches with their best clothes, الله اعلم.

[96-99]⁶⁰

وَلَوْ أَنَّ أَهْلَ الْقُرَى آمَنُواْ وَاتَّقَواْ لَفَتَحْنَا عَلَيْهِم بَرَكَاتٍ مِّنَ السَّمَاء وَالأَرْضِ وَلَكِن كَذَّبُواْ فَأَخَذْنَاهُم بِمَا كَانُواْ يَكْسِبُونَ {الأعراف/96}

أَفَأَمِنَ أَهْلُ الْقُرَى أَن يَأْتِيَهُمْ بَأْسُنَا بَيَاتاً وَهُمْ نَآئِمُونَ {الأعراف/97} أَوَ أَمِنَ أَهْلُ الْقُرَى أَن يَأْتِيَهُمْ بَأْسُنَا ضُحًى وَهُمْ يَلْعَبُونَ {الأعراف/98} أَفَأَمِنُواْ مَكْرَ اللّهِ فَلاَ يَأْمَنُ مَكْرَ اللّهِ إِلاَّ الْقَوْمُ الْخَاسِرُونَ {الأعراف/99}

Although one can review above ayahs for the people who don't believe in Allah ﷻ, but a believer should take heed from them as well. In this perspective, it would be interesting to think the ayahs from its opposite. For example, أَفَأَمِنَ أَهْلُ الْقُرَى أَن يَأْتِيَهُمْ بَأْسُنَا بَيَاتاً وَهُمْ نَآئِمُونَ {الأعراف/97}, the people who are sleeping all night can be considered in gaflah. So, to avoid from a possible bad outcome as mentioned as بَأْسُنَا⁶¹, one should at least use portion of the night for the remembrance of Allah ﷻ. Similarly, أَوَ أَمِنَ أَهْلُ الْقُرَى أَن يَأْتِيَهُمْ بَأْسُنَا ضُحًى وَهُمْ يَلْعَبُونَ⁶², a person is fresh in the day time with energy. Everything can be considered a fake play except remembrance of Allah ﷻ with how this person uses their energy. To avoid again بَأْسُنَا, the person should at least use the portion of the day for the remembrance of Allah ﷻ. In both cases, to avoid مَكْرَ⁶³, any possible

---

60. 7:96 Yet if the people of those communities had but attained to faith and been conscious of Us, We would indeed have opened up for them blessings out of heaven and earth: but they gave the lie to the truth—and so We took them to task through what they [themselves] had been doing."
7:97 Can, then, the people of any community ever feel secure that Our punishment will not come upon them by night, while they are asleep? (7:98) Why, can the people of any community ever feel secure that Our punishment will not come upon them in broad daylight, while they are engaged in (worldly] play? (7:99) Can they, then, ever feel secure from God's deep devising? But none feels secure from God's deep devising save people who are [already] lost.
61. Our punishment.
62. Why, can the people of any community ever feel secure that Our punishment will not come upon them in broad daylight, while they are engaged in (worldly] play?
63. Deep devising.

trial and tests, iqamatu salah can be the main remedy. Yet, for the elect more can be expected, الله اعلم.

[121-127]⁶⁴

قَالُواْ آمَنَّا بِرَبِّ الْعَالَمِينَ {الأعراف/121} رَبِّ مُوسَى وَهَارُونَ {الأعراف/122} قَالَ فِرْعَوْنُ آمَنتُم بِهِ قَبْلَ أَن آذَنَ لَكُمْ إِنَّ هَذَا لَمَكْرٌ مَّكَرْتُمُوهُ فِي الْمَدِينَةِ لِتُخْرِجُواْ مِنْهَا أَهْلَهَا فَسَوْفَ تَعْلَمُونَ {الأعراف/123} لأُقَطِّعَنَّ أَيْدِيَكُمْ وَأَرْجُلَكُم مِّنْ خِلافٍ ثُمَّ لأُصَلِّبَنَّكُمْ أَجْمَعِينَ {الأعراف/124} قَالُواْ إِنَّا إِلَى رَبِّنَا مُنقَلِبُونَ {الأعراف/125} وَمَا تَنقِمُ مِنَّا إِلاَّ أَنْ آمَنَّا بِآيَاتِ رَبِّنَا لَمَّا جَاءتْنَا رَبَّنَا أَفْرِغْ عَلَيْنَا صَبْرًا وَتَوَفَّنَا مُسْلِمِينَ {الأعراف/126} وَقَالَ الْمَلأُ مِن قَوْمِ فِرْعَوْنَ أَتَذَرُ مُوسَى وَقَوْمَهُ لِيُفْسِدُواْ فِي الأَرْضِ وَيَذَرَكَ وَآلِهَتَكَ قَالَ سَنُقَتِّلُ أَبْنَاءهُمْ وَنَسْتَحْيِي نِسَاءهُمْ وَإِنَّا فَوْقَهُمْ قَاهِرُونَ {الأعراف/127}

Above is interesting to analyze the reply of the magicians in وَمَا تَنقِمُ مِنَّا إِلاَّ أَنْ آمَنَّا بِآيَاتِ رَبِّنَا لَمَّا جَاءتْنَا رَبَّنَا أَفْرِغْ عَلَيْنَا صَبْرًا وَتَوَفَّنَا مُسْلِمِينَ {الأعراف/126}.

- ► The magicians made a deal with Firawn right before the meeting with Musa as that they would be rewarded and be in close companion of Firawn if they won.

- ► Yet, after seeing the miracles, they declared the faith and imān to Allah ﷻ.

- ► Then, Firawn threatened them with torturous killing and he claimed that it was a preplanned plot of Musa as with magicians against Firawn.

- ► With all these abrupt and immediate scary and horrifying changes happening, the magicians have a very rational and calm statement as وَمَا تَنقِمُ مِنَّا إِلاَّ أَنْ آمَنَّا بِآيَاتِ رَبِّنَا لَمَّا جَاءتْنَا رَبَّنَا أَفْرِغْ عَلَيْنَا صَبْرًا وَتَوَفَّنَا مُسْلِمِينَ {الأعراف/126}.

---

64. (121) [and] exclaiming: "We have come to believe in the Sustainer of all the worlds, (7:122) the Sustainer of Moses and Aaron!" (7:123) Said Pharaoh: "Have you come to believe in him91 ere I have given you permission? Behold, this is indeed a plot which you have cunningly devised in this [my] city in order to drive out its people hence! But in time you shall come to know, [my revenge]: (7:124) most certainly shall I cut off your hands and your feet in great numbers, because of [your] perverseness, and then I shall most certainly crucify you, in great numbers, all together!"7:125 They answered: "Verily, unto our Sustainer do we turn—(7:126) for thou takest vengeance on us only because we have come to believe in our Sustainer's messages as soon as they came to us. O our Sustainer! Shower us with patience in adversity, and make us die as men who have surrendered themselves unto Thee!"
7:127 And the great ones among Pharaoh's people said: "Wilt thou allow Moses and his people to spread corruption on earth, and to [cause thy people to] forsake thee and thy gods?" [Pharaoh] replied: "We shall slay their sons in great numbers and shall spare [only] their women: for, verily, we h.old sway over them!"

I think one can realize a similar type of sakina in the fresh imān of magicians with Musa's as rational arguments with Firawn when he was sent by Allah ﷻ to invite him to imān, to believe in Rabbul Alamin. Second, the magicians' statement was also very similar to the believer, mumin min al-i Firawn, as mentioned وَقَالَ رَجُلٌ مُّؤْمِنٌ مِّنْ آلِ فِرْعَوْنَ يَكْتُمُ إِيمَانَهُ أَتَقْتُلُونَ رَجُلًا أَن يَقُولَ رَبِّيَ اللَّهُ وَقَدْ جَاءكُم بِالْبَيِّنَاتِ مِن رَّبِّكُمْ وَإِن يَكُ كَاذِبًا فَعَلَيْهِ كَذِبُهُ وَإِن يَكُ صَادِقًا يُصِبْكُم بَعْضُ الَّذِي يَعِدُكُمْ إِنَّ اللَّهَ لَا يَهْدِي مَنْ هُوَ مُسْرِفٌ كَذَّابٌ {غافِر/28}[65]
This can be also similar sakina granted to him at the fearful situations.

Third, Allah ﷻ shows examples how the discourses of invitation of others to the religion or dawah in these examples that one should appeal to one's basic mind and reason with nice words. Fourth, one can see that how a person or people are punished with the Just attribute of Allah ﷻ that at multiple incidents there were people appealing to the mind and reason of the person, Firawn, but the person still turned away, الله اعلم.

[143][66]

وَلَمَّا جَاء مُوسَى لِمِيقَاتِنَا وَكَلَّمَهُ رَبُّهُ قَالَ رَبِّ أَرِنِي أَنظُرْ إِلَيْكَ قَالَ لَن تَرَانِي وَلَكِنِ انظُرْ إِلَى الْجَبَلِ فَإِنِ اسْتَقَرَّ مَكَانَهُ فَسَوْفَ تَرَانِي فَلَمَّا تَجَلَّى رَبُّهُ لِلْجَبَلِ جَعَلَهُ دَكًّا وَخَرَّ موسَى صَعِقًا فَلَمَّا أَفَاقَ قَالَ سُبْحَانَكَ تُبْتُ إِلَيْكَ وَأَنَاْ أَوَّلُ الْمُؤْمِنِينَ {الأعراف/143}

Musa as, one of the ulul azm Prophets of Allah ﷻ, wants to see Allah ﷻ and then his human faculties even does not endure when he looks at a tajalli on a mountain. Mountain crunches into pieces and Musa as faints. This is a human reality with the encounters of Divine Reality, Rabbul Alamin.

This human reality can also show itself at the encounters of the person with the Qurān. When the person dives into the ocean of the Qurān, sometimes human mind, all physical, emotional and spiritual faculties of a person can explode. The person can faint similar to Musa as or even die if the person really embodies the khushu of communicating and reading the Kalām of Allah ﷻ. Since, most of us are in the state

---

65. And a believing man from the family of Pharaoh who concealed his faith said, "Do you kill a man [merely] because he says, 'My Lord is Allah' while he has brought you clear proofs from your Lord? And if he should be lying, then upon him is [the consequence of] his lie; but if he should be truthful, there will strike you some of what he promises you. Indeed, Allah does not guide one who is a transgressor and a liar.

66. 7:143 And when Moses came [to Mount Sinai] at the time set by Us, and his Sustainer spoke unto him, he said: "O my Sustainer! Show [Thyself] unto me, so that I might behold Thee!"

of ghaflah, heedlessness, we may not feel this embodiment. Yet, there are reports and narrations who died or fainted while they were in their embodiment of the Qurān (34).

On the other hand, to relax the person's faculties while engaging genuinely with the Qurān, the hadith follows as a model human representation of the Divine teachings. While being engaged with Hadith, with the teachings of the Prophet صلى الله عليه وسلم similar to a calming breeze, the person feels again the full realization of a being a human, such as eating, drinking, going to a market, having a spouse etc. All these and other human discourses emerge. As the Qurān also presents this reality that if Allah ﷻ sends angels as a messenger on earth then, they would be also in a human form. So, accepting our reality as a human is the first step as suggested and advised in the Qurān by Allah ﷻ. Thus, the human messengers fulfill this notion of a model human being, living among people but delivering guidance from Allah ﷻ.

One can also realize this notion of Azamah in Kabah while visiting Makkah compared to human renderings of calm breezes while staying in Madinah with the Prophet ﷺ. "Visiting" and "staying" are the key words in the former statement. The arrogant pious can sometimes forget while being in the presence of Azamah with Allah ﷻ. Shaytan can be one example. The Prophet صلى الله عليه وسلم constantly declares his humanness yet increases the maiyyah, the companionship with Allah ﷻ. At one pole, there is shaytan losing and forgetting who he is as the creation of Allah ﷻ. At another pole, there is the Prophet صلى الله عليه وسلم maintaining relationship with Allah ﷻ but in full realization of his humanness and his being the creation of Allah ﷻ with full humbleness and gratitude.

In addition to the above discussion, the word saiqa, صَعِقًا, is also interesting to research as a separate topic in this ayah. On can review this word in the Qurān for example:

وَخَرَّ موسَى صَعِقًا فَلَمَّا أَفَاقَ قَالَ سُبْحَانَكَ تُبْتُ إِلَيْكَ وَأَنَا أَوَّلُ الْمُؤْمِنِينَ ⁶⁷{الأعراف/143}

وَنُفِخَ فِي الصُّورِ فَصَعِقَ مَن فِي السَّمَاوَاتِ وَمَن فِي الْأَرْضِ إِلَّا مَن شَاء اللَّهُ ثُمَّ نُفِخَ فِيهِ أُخْرَى فَإِذَا هُم قِيَامٌ يَنظُرُونَ ⁶⁸{الزمر/68}

---

67. And Moses fell unconscious. And when he awoke, he said, "Exalted are You! I have repented to You, and I am the first of the believers."
68. And the Horn will be blown, and whoever is in the heavens and whoever is on the earth will fall dead except whom Allah جل جلاله wills. Then it will be blown again, and at once they will be standing, looking on.

فَذَرْهُمْ حَتَّى يُلَاقُوا يَوْمَهُمُ الَّذِي فِيهِ يُصْعَقُونَ ⁶⁹ {الطور/45}

There is a threshold time and point for everyone and all the creation for realization of Real Reality and for realization of who they are as creations. In this perspective, the ayah فَذَرْهُمْ حَتَّى يُلَاقُوا يَوْمَهُمُ الَّذِي فِيهِ يُصْعَقُونَ {الطور/45} alludes to the ones who are far from this realization. Then, the ayah وَنُفِخَ فِي الصُّورِ فَصَعِقَ مَن فِي السَّمَاوَاتِ وَمَن فِي الْأَرْضِ إِلَّا مَن شَاءَ اللَّهُ ثُمَّ نُفِخَ فِيهِ أُخْرَى فَإِذَا هُم قِيَامٌ يَنظُرُونَ {الزمر/68} alludes of this realization for all creation. Lastly, for the ones who are close to Allah ﷻ, such as the prophets and the awliya of Allah ﷻ, this realization can happen on the earth with different qualities and quantities according to their level as mentioned in the ayah وَخَرَّ موسَى صَعِقًا فَلَمَّا أَفَاقَ قَالَ سُبْحَانَكَ تُبْتُ إِلَيْكَ وَأَنَا أَوَّلُ الْمُؤْمِنِينَ {الأعراف/143} الله اعلم.

Sûrah Anfâl

[24]⁷⁰

يَا أَيُّهَا الَّذِينَ أَمَنُوا اسْتَجِيبُوا لِلَّهِ وَلِلرَّسُولِ إِذَا دَعَاكُمْ لِمَا يُحْيِيكُمْ وَاعْلَمُوا أَنَّ اللَّهَ يَحُولُ بَيْنَ الْمَرْءِ وَقَلْبِهِ وَأَنَّهُ إِلَيْهِ تُحْشَرُونَ (24)

Sûrah Kahf

وَاصْبِرْ نَفْسَكَ مَعَ الَّذِينَ يَدْعُونَ رَبَّهُم بِالْغَدُوةِ وَالْعَشِيِّ يُرِيدُونَ وَجْهَهُ وَلَا تَعْدُ عَيْنَاكَ عَنْهُمْ تُرِيدُ زِينَةَ الْحَيوةِ الدُّنْيَا وَلَا تُطِعْ مَنْ أَغْفَلْنَا قَلْبَهُ عَن ذِكْرِنَا وَاتَّبَعَ هَوَاهُ وَكَانَ أَمْرُهُ فُرُطًا (28)⁷¹

Sûrah Shuârah

إِلَّا مَنْ أَتَى اللَّهَ بِقَلْبٍ سَلِيمٍ (89)⁷²

---

69. So leave them until they meet their Day in which they will be struck insensible.
70. 8:24 O you who have attained to faith! Respond to the call of God and the Apostle whenever he calls you unto that which will give you life; and know that God intervenes between man and [the desires of] his heart, and that unto Him you shall be gathered. (8:25) And beware of that temptation to evil which does not befall only those among you who are bent on denying the truth, to the exclusion of others; and know that God is severe in retribution.
71. And keep yourself patient [by being] with those who call upon their Lord in the morning and the evening, seeking His countenance. And let not your eyes pass beyond them, desiring adornments of the worldly life, and do not obey one whose heart We have made heedless of Our remembrance and who follows his desire and whose affair is ever [in] neglect.
72. But only one who comes to Allah جل جلاله with a sound heart."

Sûrah Ahzāb

يَا نِسَاءَ النَّبِيِّ لَسْتُنَّ كَأَحَدٍ مِنَ النِّسَاءِ اِنِ اتَّقَيْتُنَّ فَلَا تَخْضَعْنَ بِالْقَوْلِ فَيَطْمَعَ الَّذِي فِي قَلْبِهِ مَرَضٌ وَقُلْنَ قَوْلًا مَعْرُوفًا[73] (32)

Sûrah Ghāfir

اَلَّذِينَ يُجَادِلُونَ فِي اَيَاتِ اللهِ بِغَيْرِ سُلْطَانٍ اَتَيهُمْ كَبُرَ مَقْتًا عِنْدَ اللهِ وَعِنْدَ الَّذِينَ اَمَنُوْا كَذَلِكَ يَطْبَعُ اللهُ عَلَى كُلِّ قَلْبِ مُتَكَبِّرٍ جَبَّارٍ[74] (35)

Sûrah Shûrah

اَمْ يَقُولُونَ افْتَرَى عَلَى اللهِ كَذِبًا فَاِنْ يَشَا اللهُ يَخْتِمْ عَلَى قَلْبِكَ وَيَمْحُ اللهُ الْبَاطِلَ وَيُحِقُّ الْحَقَّ بِكَلِمَاتِهٖ اِنَّهُ عَلِيمٌ بِذَاتِ الصُّدُورِ[75] (24)

Sûrah Jathiyah

اَفَرَاَيْتَ مَنِ اتَّخَذَ اِلَهَهُ هَوٰيهُ وَاَضَلَّهُ اللهُ عَلَى عِلْمٍ وَخَتَمَ عَلَى سَمْعِهِ وَقَلْبِهِ وَجَعَلَ عَلَى بَصَرِهِ غِشَاوَةً فَمَنْ يَهْدِيهِ مِنْ بَعْدِ اللهِ اَفَلَا تَذَكَّرُونَ[76] (23)

Sûrah Qāf

مَنْ خَشِيَ الرَّحْمٰنَ بِالْغَيْبِ وَجَاءَ بِقَلْبٍ مُنِيبٍ[77] (33)

Sûrah Dhariyāt

اِنَّ فِي ذٰلِكَ لَذِكْرَى لِمَنْ كَانَ لَهُ قَلْبٌ اَوْ اَلْقَى السَّمْعَ وَهُوَ شَهِيدٌ[78] (37)

---

73. O wives of the Prophet, you are not like anyone among women. If you fear Allah جل جلاله, then do not be soft in speech [to men], lest he in whose heart is disease should covet, but speak with appropriate speech.

74. Those who dispute concerning the signs of Allah جل جلاله without an authority having come to them—great is hatred [of them] in the sight of Allah جل جلاله and in the sight of those who have believed. Thus does Allah seal over every heart [belonging to] an arrogant tyrant.

75. Or do they say, "He has invented about Allah جل جلاله a lie"? But if Allah جل جلاله willed, He could seal over your heart. And Allah جل جلاله eliminates falsehood and establishes the truth by His words. Indeed, He is Knowing of that within the breasts.

76. Have you seen he who has taken as his god his [own] desire, and Allah جل جلاله has sent him astray due to knowledge and has set a seal upon his hearing and his heart and put over his vision a veil? So who will guide him after Allah جل جلاله? Then will you not be reminded?

77. Who feared the Most Merciful unseen and came with a heart returning [in repentance].

78. And We left therein a sign for those who fear the painful punishment.

Sûrah Taghābun

مَّا أَصَابَ مِنْ مُصِيبَةٍ إِلَّا بِإِذْنِ اللَّهِ وَمَنْ يُؤْمِنْ بِاللَّهِ يَهْدِ قَلْبَهُ وَاللَّهُ بِكُلِّ شَيْءٍ عَلِيمٌ (11) [79]

As one can review some of the above ayahs about qalb, one can see that the gist of everything happens at the level of qalb. Allah ﷻ can change the state of one's qalb depending on one's kasb, acquirement, choice, free will execution and attitude as mentioned in this Sûrah as

يَا أَيُّهَا الَّذِينَ آمَنُوا اسْتَجِيبُوا لِلَّهِ وَلِلرَّسُولِ إِذَا دَعَاكُمْ لِمَا يُحْيِيكُمْ وَاعْلَمُوا أَنَّ اللَّهَ يَحُولُ بَيْنَ الْمَرْءِ وَقَلْبِهِ وَأَنَّهُ إِلَيْهِ تُحْشَرُونَ (24) [80]

For the person, it is important to detach the heart from everything but Allah ﷻ. Therefore, in the field of tasawwuf, there are a lot systematic methodologies developed to implement this notion of detachment and cleaning. For example, constant muraqaba means continuous looking and monitoring of one's own heart spiritually. The ideal state of heart is called qalbun salim as mentioned in Sûrah Shuarah 89) [81] أَتَى اللَّهَ بِقَلْبٍ سَلِيمٍ.

So, the term qalbun salim, a state of heart detached from all the ill and diseased feelings but only filled with the pleasure of Allah ﷻ. This is the state mentioned for a person like Ibrahim as. This is a person who lives his or her life and dies, to meet with Allah ﷻ in this state.

As the person looks at something or hears something, immediately feelings are formed in one's heart. In life it is very difficult, to first diagnose and then to filter one's feelings and emotions. These could be positive or negative feelings. Negative ones could be the diseased feelings of superiority, arrogance, judgment, ungratefulness etc. So, one can engage with dhikr to remove the effect of these negative feelings. Yet, if the dhikr is not internalized, the effect of dhikr can be limited in fulfilling for the level of qalbun salim. In this perspective, the scholars of the internal sciences developed the practice of minimum talk, sleep and eating. So that one can increase and be as much as in muraqaba,

---

79. No disaster strikes except by permission of Allah جل جلاله. And whoever believes in Allah جل جلاله—He will guide his heart. And Allah جل جلاله is Knowing of all things.

80. O you who have believed, respond to Allah جل جلاله and to the Messenger when he calls you to that which gives you life. And know that Allah جل جلاله intervenes between a man and his heart and that to Him you will be gathered.

81. But only one who comes to Allah جل جلاله with a sound heart."

constant monitoring of the heart. When all those three, sleeping, talking and eating are done in excess they decrease the moments of muraqaba.

In other words, one should be at all times connected to his or her heart for monitoring. One can call this ihsān as the person does this to be fully aware that Allah ﷻ is constantly watching the person. Or, the person does it in order to detach them from everything except Allah ﷻ. Therefore, the gist of dhikrs such as La ilaha illa Allah or SubhanAllah in their true implication help to achieve this state of qalbun salim[82].

In this state, the person naturally smiles like Rasulullah ﷺ because the person is in the true state of sakina, happiness and falāh. The smiling, gentle, kind treatment becomes fitrah of the person similar to Rasulullah ﷺ.

One can also review the ayahs of khatm, sealing of heart as mentioned for munafiqûn and other cases why and when it happens. If the person fills the heart with everything except with Allah ﷻ then this heart dies, and it is sealed. The expected for humans' spiritual journey is the opposite: emptying the heart from everything except Allah ﷻ. Below are examples and reasons of this khatm:

Sûrah Ghāfir

اَلَّذِينَ يُجَادِلُونَ فِي اٰيَاتِ اللّٰهِ بِغَيْرِ سُلْطَانٍ اَتٰيهُمْ كَبُرَ مَقْتًا عِنْدَ اللّٰهِ وَعِنْدَ الَّذِينَ اٰمَنُواۤ كَذٰلِكَ يَطْبَعُ اللّٰهُ عَلٰى كُلِّ قَلْبِ مُتَكَبِّرٍ جَبَّارٍ (35)[83]

Sûrah Shûrah

اَمْ يَقُولُونَ افْتَرٰى عَلَى اللّٰهِ كَذِبًا فَاِنْ يَشَاِ اللّٰهُ يَخْتِمْ عَلٰى قَلْبِكَ وَيَمْحُ اللّٰهُ الْبَاطِلَ وَيُحِقُّ الْحَقَّ بِكَلِمَاتِهٖ اِنَّهُ عَلِيمٌ بِذَاتِ الصُّدُورِ (24)[84]

---

82. A sound heart.

83. Those who dispute concerning the signs of Allah جل جلاله without an authority having come to them—great is hatred [of them] in the sight of Allah جل جلاله and in the sight of those who have believed. Thus does Allah جل جلاله seal over every heart [belonging to] an arrogant tyrant.

84. Or do they say, "He has invented about Allah جل جلاله a lie"? But if Allah جل جلاله willed, He could seal over your heart. And Allah جل جلاله eliminates falsehood and establishes the truth by His words. Indeed, He is Knowing of that within the breasts.

Sûrah Jāsiyah

أَفَرَأَيْتَ مَنِ اتَّخَذَ إِلَهَهُ هَوَاهُ وَأَضَلَّهُ اللهُ عَلَى عِلْمٍ وَخَتَمَ عَلَى سَمْعِهِ وَقَلْبِهِ وَجَعَلَ عَلَى
بَصَرِهِ غِشَاوَةً فَمَنْ يَهْدِيهِ مِنْ بَعْدِ اللهِ أَفَلَا تَذَكَّرُونَ [85](23)

A believer can also have diseased heart as mentioned in Sûrah Ahzab:

يَا نِسَاءَ النَّبِيِّ لَسْتُنَّ كَأَحَدٍ مِنَ النِّسَاءِ إِنِ اتَّقَيْتُنَّ فَلَا تَخْضَعْنَ بِالْقَوْلِ فَيَطْمَعَ الَّذِي فِي قَلْبِهِ
مَرَضٌ وَقُلْنَ قَوْلًا مَعْرُوفًا [86](32)

Emptying the heart can mean removing all the crude and detailed ill feelings with istighfār. Then, when the heart is empty at this point then, putting fully inside Allah ﷻ is possible. In all this process of emptying, discharging and charging, Allah ﷻ helps the person.

In this purification process, the first step is to believe in Allah ﷻ as mentioned in Sûrah Tagābun:

مَنْ يُؤْمِنْ بِاللهِ يَهْدِ قَلْبَهُ وَاللهُ بِكُلِّ شَيْءٍ عَلِيمٌ [87]

Then, one feels the notion of qalbun salim when the person starts doing things only and solely for Allah ﷻ without the interference or presence of people as mentioned in Sûrah Qāf 33:

مَنْ خَشِيَ الرَّحْمَنَ بِالْغَيْبِ وَجَاءَ بِقَلْبٍ مُنِيبٍ [88]

Finally, one can realize this critical state of heart as mentioned that Allah ﷻ can change the state of the heart depending on the disposition of the person يَا أَيُّهَا الَّذِينَ آمَنُوا اسْتَجِيبُوا لِلَّهِ وَلِلرَّسُولِ إِذَا دَعَاكُمْ لِمَا يُحْيِيكُمْ وَاعْلَمُوا أَنَّ اللهَ يَحُولُ
بَيْنَ الْمَرْءِ وَقَلْبِهِ وَأَنَّهُ إِلَيْهِ تُحْشَرُونَ [89](24)

This state of the heart makes the person happy in this dunya and akhirah or stressed, miserable, and fearful.

---

85. Have you seen he who has taken as his god his [own] desire, and Allah جل جلاله has sent him astray due to knowledge and has set a seal upon his hearing and his heart and put over his vision a veil? So who will guide him after Allah جل جلاله? Then will you not be reminded?
86. O wives of the Prophet, you are not like anyone among women. If you fear Allah جل جلاله, then do not be soft in speech [to men], lest he in whose heart is disease should covet, but speak with appropriate speech.
87. And whoever believes in Allah جل جلاله—He will guide his heart. And Allah جل جلاله is Knowing of all things.
88. Who feared the Most Merciful unseen and came with a heart returning [in repentance].
89. O you who have believed, respond to Allah جل جلاله and to the Messenger when he calls you to that which gives you life. And know that Allah جل جلاله intervenes between a man and his heart and that to Him you will be gathered.

9

Sûrah A'râf

[157-158][90]

{ الَّذِينَ يَتَّبِعُونَ الرَّسُولَ **النَّبِيَّ الأُمِّيَّ** الَّذِي يَجِدُونَهُ مَكْتُوبًا عِندَهُمْ فِي التَّوْرَاةِ وَالإِنجِيلِ يَأْمُرُهُم بِالْمَعْرُوفِ وَيَنْهَاهُمْ عَنِ الْمُنكَرِ وَيُحِلُّ لَهُمُ الطَّيِّبَاتِ وَيُحَرِّمُ عَلَيْهِمُ الْخَبَائِثَ وَيَضَعُ عَنْهُمْ إِصْرَهُمْ وَالأَغْلاَلَ الَّتِي كَانَتْ عَلَيْهِمْ فَالَّذِينَ آمَنُواْ بِهِ وَعَزَّرُوهُ وَنَصَرُوهُ وَاتَّبَعُواْ النُّورَ الَّذِيَ أُنزِلَ مَعَهُ أُوْلَئِكَ هُمُ الْمُفْلِحُونَ {الأعراف/157} قُلْ يَا أَيُّهَا النَّاسُ إِنِّي رَسُولُ اللهِ إِلَيْكُمْ جَمِيعًا الَّذِي لَهُ مُلْكُ السَّمَاوَاتِ وَالأَرْضِ لا إِلَهَ إِلاَّ هُوَ يُحْيِي وَيُمِيتُ فَآمِنُواْ بِاللهِ وَرَسُولِهِ **النَّبِيِّ الأُمِّيِّ** الَّذِي يُؤْمِنُ بِاللهِ وَكَلِمَاتِهِ وَاتَّبِعُوهُ لَعَلَّكُمْ تَهْتَدُونَ {الأعراف/158}

It is interesting to note the word النَّبِيِّ الأُمِّيِّ[91]_that the position of the Prophet ﷺ is emphasized that the Prophet ﷺ was ummi. This word can mean that the Prophet ﷺ does not know how to write or read that the Prophet ﷺ did not use the other scriptures, as some of the mustashriqûn or orientalists can bring arguments. In other contexts, the expression النَّبِيِّ الأُمِّيِّ can also mean that the pure, cherishing and nurturing like a mother, conclusive, inclusive, and the universal Prophet ﷺ that overviews and includes all the teachings of the previous scriptures and the prophets in his teachings ﷺ. This expression also is present in the verses below:

الَّذِينَ يَتَّبِعُونَ رَسُولَ **النَّبِيَّ الأُمِّيَّ** الَّذِي يَجِدُونَهُ مَكْتُوبًا عِندَهُمْ فِي التَّوْرَاةِ وَالإِنجِيلِ يَأْمُرُهُم بِالْمَعْرُوفِ وَيَنْهَاهُمْ عَنِ الْمُنكَرِ وَيُحِلُّ لَهُمُ الطَّيِّبَاتِ وَيُحَرِّمُ عَلَيْهِمُ الْخَبَائِثَ وَيَضَعُ عَنْهُمْ إِصْرَهُمْ وَالأَغْلاَلَ الَّتِي كَانَتْ عَلَيْهِمْ فَالَّذِينَ آمَنُواْ بِهِ وَعَزَّرُوهُ وَنَصَرُوهُ وَاتَّبَعُواْ النُّورَ الَّذِيَ أُنزِلَ مَعَهُ أُوْلَئِكَ هُمُ الْمُفْلِحُونَ {الأعراف/157}

---

90. 7:157 Those who follow the Messenger, the unlettered prophet, whom they find written [i.e., mentioned] in what they have of the Torah and the Gospel, who enjoins upon them what is right and forbids them what is wrong and makes lawful for them the good things and prohibits for them the evil and relieves them of their burden and the shackles which were upon them. So they who have believed in him, honored him, supported him and followed the light which was sent down with him—it is those who will be the successful. 7:158 Say, [O Muúammad], "O mankind, indeed I am the Messenger of Allah جل جلاله to you all, [from Him] to whom belongs the dominion of the heavens and the earth. There is no deity except Him; He gives life and causes death." So believe in Allah جل جلاله and His Messenger, the unlettered prophet, who believes in Allah جل جلاله and His words, and follow him that you may be guided.
91. The unlettered prophet.

They find this fact about the Prophet صلى الله عليه وسلم in their books.

قُلْ يَا أَيُّهَا النَّاسُ إِنِّي رَسُولُ اللَّهِ إِلَيْكُمْ جَمِيعًا الَّذِي لَهُ مُلْكُ السَّمَاوَاتِ وَالأَرْضِ لا إِلَهَ
إِلاَّ هُوَ يُحْيِي وَيُمِيتُ فَآمِنُواْ بِاللَّهِ وَرَسُولِهِ **النَّبِيِّ الأُمِّيِّ** الَّذِي يُؤْمِنُ بِاللَّهِ وَكَلِمَاتِهِ وَاتَّبِعُوهُ
لَعَلَّكُمْ تَهْتَدُونَ {الأعراف/158}

In the above ayah, the ayah starts with a general expression addressing to all human beings to show the universality of the Prophet ﷺ.

هُوَ الَّذِي بَعَثَ فِي الأُمِّيِّينَ رَسُولًا مِّنْهُمْ يَتْلُو عَلَيْهِمْ آيَاتِهِ وَيُزَكِّيهِمْ وَيُعَلِّمُهُمُ الْكِتَابَ
وَالْحِكْمَةَ وَإِن كَانُوا مِن قَبْلُ لَفِي ضَلالٍ مُّبِينٍ [92]{الجمعة/2} وَآخَرِينَ مِنْهُمْ لَمَّا يَلْحَقُوا
بِهِمْ وَهُوَ الْعَزِيزُ الْحَكِيمُ [93]{الجمعة/3}

The above ayah normalizes this case of النَّبِيِّ الأُمِّيِّ[94] within its cultural context specifically but with a general purpose and wisdom from Allah ﷻ as well.

---

92. It is He who has sent among the unlettered [Arabs] a Messenger from themselves reciting to them His verses and purifying them and teaching them the Book [i.e., the Qurān] and wisdom [i.e., the sunnah]—although they were before in clear error

93. And [to] others of them who have not yet joined them. And He is the Exalted in Might, the Wise.

94. The unlettered prophet.

11

Sûrah Tawbah

[61]⁹⁵

وَمِنْهُمُ الَّذِينَ يُؤْذُونَ النَّبِيَّ وَيَقُولُونَ هُوَ أُذُنٌ قُلْ أُذُنُ خَيْرٍ لَّكُمْ يُؤْمِنُ بِاللَّهِ وَيُؤْمِنُ لِلْمُؤْمِنِينَ
وَرَحْمَةٌ لِّلَّذِينَ آمَنُواْ مِنكُمْ وَالَّذِينَ يُؤْذُونَ رَسُولَ اللَّهِ لَهُمْ عَذَابٌ أَلِيمٌ {التوبة/61}

It is interesting the word أُذُنٌ⁹⁶ in our current discourses of life. The word in its possible and technical sense can allude to the concept of spying for different purposes. In its applicability, when there is a group of people who may tend to do work together, the group leader tends often in public formal or informal venues to be asserted as a person working for others or spying. Identifying the leaders in this perspective looks like a common phenomenon that happened before and is happening today. From another perspective at a reflective point of the social incidents, if a person or group is blaming others to be spying there is always the possibility of this action performed by this group or individuals of claimants. The ayah mentions the concept of positive monitoring for public interest as a possibility with the word أُذُنُ خَيْرٍ⁹⁷. In this sense, negative or destructive spying is discouraged but positive monitoring for everyone's interest with justice without oppression is a possible practice, الله اعلم.

---

95. 9:61 AND AMONG those [enemies of the truth] there are such as malign the Prophet by saying, "He is all ear. Say: "[Yes,] he is all ear, [listening] to what is good for you!87 He believes in God, and trusts the believers, and is [a manifestation of God's] grace towards such of you as have [truly] attained to faith. And as for those who malign God's Apostle—grievous suffering awaits them [in the life to come]!"
96. All ear.
97. [Yes,] he is all ear, [listening] to what is good.

[122]⁹⁸

وَمَا كَانَ الْمُؤْمِنُونَ لِيَنفِرُواْ كَآفَّةً فَلَوْلاَ نَفَرَ مِن كُلِّ فِرْقَةٍ مِّنْهُمْ طَآئِفَةٌ لِّيَتَفَقَّهُواْ فِي الدِّينِ وَلِيُنذِرُواْ قَوْمَهُمْ إِذَا رَجَعُواْ إِلَيْهِمْ لَعَلَّهُمْ يَحْذَرُونَ {التوبة/122}

The above ayah can also signify the need for the interpretation of the teachings according to time and place. In other words, the main, asil, of the teachings of the religion does not change. But, the people of Allah ﷻ, the scholars need to bring the reviving principles of the religion depending on the spiritual diseases of the time, generations and places. In this perspective, the teachings of the religions are not only the legal laws but at that time, if there are different influences due to various reasons from different places, the scholars should present these teachings in a reviving format like Imam Ghazali rh. For example, Imam Ghazali at his time mainly worked on the influences of the Islamic teachings from the Greek philosophy. He presented the teachings of the religion with the format or framework of these influences so that the people were clear but not confused.

In this perspective, especially at our time, the Cognitive Behavioral Education with Therapy (CBET) similar to CBT (Cognitive Behavioral Therapy) from the Islamic practice can be important. In other words, the قتل, qital or jihād, concept now replaces itself with the logical, genuine and practical discourses to persuade the people and to remove these diseases in the minds and hearts. One can call this as CBET of the Qurān and the Sunnah. As some of my scholars used to call "Quranic Operatic System", OS with the Qurān in people's mind. In other words, one of the contemporary scholars (36) used to ask this question: "how did the Qurān make a huge change in sahabas' minds and hearts? Why does this change not exist at our time? How can we contemporize this original motivation for our time?"

---

98. And it is not for the believers to go forth [to battle] all at once. For there should separate from every division of them a group [remaining] to obtain understanding in the religion and warn their people when they return to them that they might be cautious.

Sûrah Yûnus

وَمِنْهُم مَّن يَسْتَمِعُونَ إِلَيْكَ أَفَأَنتَ تُسْمِعُ الصُّمَّ وَلَوْ كَانُواْ لاَ يَعْقِلُونَ {يونس/42}

وَمِنهُم مَّن يَنظُرُ إِلَيْكَ أَفَأَنتَ تَهْدِي الْعُمْيَ وَلَوْ كَانُواْ لاَ يُبْصِرُونَ {يونس/43}

[42-43][99]

These two ayahs are very interesting to analyze. When one analyzes them initially, there are some very remarkable perspectives. We will inshAllah bring their analysis later in order to benefit from them further with the Tawfik of Allah 12.☙

Sûrah Hûd

It is interesting to view in the previous chapter in Sûrah Yûnus, there were some prophets mentioned. In this Sûrah, the cases of the prophets continue with more details and examples. One can look at the relationship of messengership, nubuwwah as its frame work is explained in Sûrah Yûnus. Then, it is more detailed in Sûrah Hûd, الله اعلم.

[3][100]

وَأَنِ اسْتَغْفِرُواْ رَبَّكُمْ ثُمَّ تُوبُواْ إِلَيْهِ يُمَتِّعْكُم مَّتَاعًا حَسَنًا إِلَى أَجَلٍ مُسَمًّى وَيُؤْتِ كُلَّ ذِي فَضْلٍ فَضْلَهُ وَإِن تَوَلَّوْاْ فَإِنِّيَ أَخَافُ عَلَيْكُمْ عَذَابَ يَوْمٍ كَبِيرٍ {هود/3}

The relations between istighfâr, tawbah and having a life with afiyah is mentioned. Here, the key expression in this Sûrah is اسْتَغْفِرُواْ رَبَّكُمْ ثُمَّ[101] تُوبُواْ إِلَيْهِ. When one analyzes the rest of the Sûrah one can realize as:

---

99. 10:42 And there are among them such as (pretend to] listen to thee: but canst thou cause the deaf to hearken even though they will not use their reason? (10:43) And there are among them such as [pretend to] look towards thee: but canst thou show the right way to the blind even though they cannot see?
100. (11:3) Ask your Sustainer to forgive you your sins, and then turn towards Him in repentance—[whereupon] He will grant you a goodly enjoyment of life [in this world] until a term set [by Him is fulfilled]; and [in the life to come] He will bestow upon everyone possessed of merit [a full reward for] his merit. But if you turn away, then, verily, I dread for you the suffering [which is bound to befall you] on that awesome Day!
101. Ask your Sustainer to forgive you your sins, and then turn towards Him in repentance.

وَيَا قَوْمِ اسْتَغْفِرُواْ رَبَّكُمْ ثُمَّ تُوبُواْ إِلَيْهِ يُرْسِلِ السَّمَاء عَلَيْكُم مِّدْرَارًا وَيَزِدْكُمْ قُوَّةً إِلَى قُوَّتِكُمْ وَلاَ تَتَوَلَّوْاْ مُجْرِمِينَ {هود/52} 102

فَاسْتَغْفِرُوهُ ثُمَّ تُوبُواْ إِلَيْهِ إِنَّ رَبِّي قَرِيبٌ مُّجِيبٌ {هود/61} 103

وَاسْتَغْفِرُواْ رَبَّكُمْ ثُمَّ تُوبُواْ إِلَيْهِ إِنَّ رَبِّي رَحِيمٌ وَدُودٌ {هود/90} 104

In this perspective, the key word اسْتَغْفِرِ[105] can be analyzed. In this word, the first three letters اسْتَ can mean the desire, the need, the position, or the realizing of a person accepting his or her mistakes, evils, sins, or the engagements of acts that displeases Allah. In other words, the person can say: "Oh Allah جل جلاله, I accept and I realize that I did this evil, I did this sin, I did this mistake, I shamefully did this act that displeases You although You were with me at that time. I accept it oh Allah جل جلاله. Please forgive me." The last part "please forgive me" can allude to the remaining part of the word of غْفِر.

One can understand that the first position is to realize who you are and what you did. Therefore, in the fields of tasawwuf it is emphasized constantly that the teaching of knowing yourself can take the person to knowledge about Allah.

Then, the word ثُمَّ[106] can allude that there is a gap between istighfār and tawba. This may mean الله اعلم that the real position of tawbah can be gained by embodying istighfār over time. The expression تُوبُواْ إِلَيْهِ[107] can indicate that once the person embodies istighfār then, this is the real position of going to Allah, being with Allah, and pleasing Allah.

After all these discourses, one can have some possible idea, why the Prophet mentioned about Sûrah Hûd that this Sûrah made him old (26). In its true sense, the Prophet understands what those commands and ayahs mean in terms of istighfār, and tawbah with the responsibilities of being a human in one's relationship to Allah as well

---

102. And O my people, ask forgiveness of your Lord and then repent to Him. He will send [rain from] the sky upon you in showers and increase you in strength [added] to your strength. And do not turn away, [being] criminals."
103. So ask forgiveness of Him and then repent to Him. Indeed, my Lord is near and responsive."
104. And ask forgiveness of your Lord and then repent to Him. Indeed, my Lord is Merciful and Affectionate."
105. Ask forgiveness.
106. Then.
107. Repent to him.

as his ﷺ responsibilities as the messenger to deliver what he embodies to others, الله اعلم.

[47-48]¹⁰⁸

قَالَ رَبِّ إِنِّي أَعُوذُ بِكَ أَنْ أَسْأَلَكَ مَا لَيْسَ لِي بِهِ عِلْمٌ وَإِلاَّ تَغْفِرْ لِي وَتَرْحَمْنِي أَكُن مِّنَ الْخَاسِرِينَ {هود/47} قِيلَ يَا نُوحُ اهْبِطْ بِسَلاَمٍ مِّنَّا وَبَرَكَاتٍ عَلَيْكَ وَعَلَى أُمَمٍ مِّمَّن مَّعَكَ وَأُمَمٌ سَنُمَتِّعُهُمْ ثُمَّ يَمَسُّهُم مِّنَّا عَذَابٌ أَلِيمٌ {هود/48}

Here is a perfect example of a believer. Immediately, when Nûh as understands without knowing and realizing that he asked something that was not in the boundaries of pleasure of Allah ﷻ, then he immediately resets himself. This reminds the real position of a believer as mentioned by the Prophet ﷺ to be like a tree bending with the wind and coming back to his or her original position (3) (9). This is also mentioned in Sûrah Fath [29:48]. In this perspective, resetting oneself constantly and coming back to the original, expected and natural position of fitrah through istighfâr, tawba and asking forgiveness from Rabbul Alamin is the first nature of a believer.

In this perspective, we are constantly being engaged with verbal, physical and even thought and idea related engagements throughout the day that displeases Allah ﷻ. Therefore, realizing this disposition is the key. Coming in front of Allah ﷻ with dua, prayer, salah and revealing the truth as

"Oh Allah جل جلاله, I again came to your door with a lot of sins, evils, oppressions, the things that I displeased You. You are still giving me the air I can breathe, the food I can eat, the eyes I can see, the ears I can hear and all other endless nimahs. I don't deserve it but You are the Source of Fadl and Rahmah. I normally deserve all the punishments but You are the Source of Fadl and Rahmah. With this, I am so shameful of myself with all Your bounties on

---

108. 11:47 Said [Noah]: "O my Sustainer! Verily, I seek refuge with Thee from [ever again] asking of Thee anything whereof I cannot have any knowledge! For unless Thou grant me forgiveness and bestow Thy mercy upon me, I shall be among the lost!"
11:48 [Thereupon] the word was spoken: "O Noah! Disembark in peace from Us, and with [Our] blessings upon thee as well as upon the people [who are with thee, and the righteous ones that will spring from thee and] from those who are with thee. But [as for the unrighteous] folk [that will spring from you]—We shall allow them to enjoy life [for a little while], and then there will befall them grievous suffering from Us."

me. Please forgive me. I need You. I love You. I cannot do without You. You ar-Rahmān, ar-Rahìm. Thank you for all your bounties although I don't deserve. All the Hamd is for You in reality. Please forgive me. Make me one of the ones in Jannah without any hasab with Your Fadl and Rahmah. Always give me an easy and good life in this dunya and akhirah with Your Fadl and Rahmah although I don't deserve it. You are Arhamu Rahimin, You are At-Tawwab. [109]

"اللهم صلى على سيدنا محمد".

On the other hand, munāfiq or kāfir, has the stance of "I don't care". Or, they try to find reasons for all the encounters and be in the modes of argumentation, rejection, ingratitude, heedlessness, distraction, unawareness of one's true self, and etc. In this position, a person lives all their life like this, then at one point when he or she cannot bear the pains of reality, he or she gets knocked down like a tree as the Prophet صلى الله عليه وسلم mentions (26) but cannot get up and cannot be alive any more. "Oh Allah جل جلاله, protect us from being in this situation, Amìn."

[113][110]

وَ لاَ تَرْكَنُواْ إِلَى الَّذِينَ ظَلَمُواْ فَتَمَسَّكُمُ النَّارُ وَمَا لَكُم مِّن دُونِ اللّهِ مِنْ أَوْلِيَاء ثُمَّ لاَ تُنصَرُونَ {هود/113}

Kasb can be translated into English with the word of acquirement. In other words, the person makes intention and inclination to acquire an action. The seed of acquirement is inclination and intention. In another perspective, one can also consider checking one's inclinations towards injustice or justice or fairness. Because, as stated in the ayah, the inclinations can transform into acquirements. One can see this approach of inclination in the phrase وَلَا تَرْكَنُواْ[111] that one should check one's heart and mind when there is an oppression where the person stands or feels towards.

---

109. Oh Allah جل جلاله, send blessings on our master Muhammad ﷺ.
110. (11:113)And do not incline towards, nor rely upon, those who are bent on evildoing lest the fire [of the hereafter] touch you: for [then] you would have none to protect you from God, nor would you ever be succoured [by Him].
111. And do not incline towards.

13

Sûrah Yûsuf

Yûsuf as first singled out by his brothers. Then, he was singled out in the well. Then, he was singled out in the house that he was enslaved. Then, he was in the prison as a place where everyone is singled out. In all these cases, one can view that Yûsuf as shows an example of a life span not taking anyone as a friend, company, and trust except Allah ﷻ. He experiences and lives it from childhood, to youth and to the old age. One can say that the children are vulnerable if they don't have protection or guardian. Here is a case that shows how Allah ﷻ can be the best guardian of a person from childhood to adulthood. Similarly, in the cases of orphanage, one can assume that no one is taking care of this child, but in reality Allah ﷻ is the Real Guardian, taking caring of all orphans, children and everyone, الله اعلم.

[36-40][112]

وَدَخَلَ مَعَهُ السِّجْنَ فَتَيَانِ قَالَ أَحَدُهُمَا إِنِّي أَرَانِي أَعْصِرُ خَمْرًا وَقَالَ الآخَرُ إِنِّي أَرَانِي أَحْمِلُ فَوْقَ رَأْسِي خُبْزًا تَأْكُلُ الطَّيْرُ مِنْهُ نَبِّئْنَا بِتَأْوِيلِهِ إِنَّا نَرَاكَ مِنَ الْمُحْسِنِينَ {يوسف/36} قَالَ لاَ يَأْتِيكُمَا طَعَامٌ تُرْزَقَانِهِ إِلاَّ نَبَّأْتُكُمَا بِتَأْوِيلِهِ قَبْلَ أَن يَأْتِيكُمَا ذَلِكُمَا مِمَّا عَلَّمَنِي رَبِّي

---

112. 12:36 NOW two young men happened to go to prison at the same time as Joseph. One of them said: "Behold, I saw myself [in a dream] pressing wine." And the other said: "Behold, I saw myself [in a dream] carrying bread on my head, and birds were eating thereof." [And both entreated Joseph:] "Let us know the real meaning of this! Verily, we see that thou art one of those who know well [how to interpret dreams]." 12:37 [Joseph] answered: "Ere there comes unto you the meal which you are [daily] fed, I shall have informed you of the real meaning of your dreams, [so that you might know what is to come] before it comes unto you: for this is [part] of the knowledge which my Sustainer has imparted to me. "Behold, I have left behind me the ways of people who do not believe in God, and who persistently refuse to acknowledge the truth of the life to come; (12:38) and I follow the creed of my forefathers Abraham, Isaac and Jacob. It is not conceivable that we should [be allowed to] ascribe divinity to aught beside God: this is [an outcome] of God's bounty unto us and unto all mankind—but most people are ungrateful.
12:39 "O my companions in imprisonment! Which is more reasonable:[belief in the existence of numerous divine] lords, each of them different from the other—or [in] the One God, who holds absolute sway over all that exists?
12:40 "All that you worship instead of God is nothing but [empty] names which you have invented42—you and your forefathers—[and] for which God has bestowed no warrant from on high. Judgment [as to what is right and what is wrong] rests with God alone—[and] He has ordained that you should worship nought but Him: this is the [one] ever-true faith; but most people know it not.

إِنِّي تَرَكْتُ مِلَّةَ قَوْمٍ لاَّ يُؤْمِنُونَ بِاللّهِ وَهُم بِالآخِرَةِ هُمْ كَافِرُونَ {يوسف/37} وَاتَّبَعْتُ
مِلَّةَ آبَآئِي إِبْرَاهِيمَ وَإِسْحَقَ وَيَعْقُوبَ مَا كَانَ لَنَا أَن نُّشْرِكَ بِاللّهِ مِن شَيْءٍ ذَلِكَ مِن فَضْلِ
اللّهِ عَلَيْنَا وَعَلَى النَّاسِ وَلَكِنَّ أَكْثَرَ النَّاسِ لاَ يَشْكُرُونَ {يوسف/38} يَا صَاحِبَيِ السِّجْنِ
أَأَرْبَابٌ مُّتَفَرِّقُونَ خَيْرٌ أَمِ اللّهُ الْوَاحِدُ الْقَهَّارُ {يوسف/39} مَا تَعْبُدُونَ مِن دُونِهِ إِلاَّ أَسْمَاء
سَمَّيْتُمُوهَا أَنتُمْ وَآبَآؤُكُم مَّا أَنزَلَ اللّهُ بِهَا مِن سُلْطَانٍ إِنِ الْحُكْمُ إِلاَّ لِلّهِ أَمَرَ أَلاَّ تَعْبُدُواْ إِلاَّ
إِيَّاهُ ذَلِكَ الدِّينُ الْقَيِّمُ وَلَكِنَّ أَكْثَرَ النَّاسِ لاَ يَعْلَمُونَ {يوسف/40}

It is important review above ayahs for the methods of tabligh that Yûsuf as demonstrates. One should remember that all the Prophets come to challenge the values of their time regarding disbelief, injustice and immoral acts. In this perspective, above words and themes chosen by Yûsuf as can also reflect the required context of that time and place. As the Qurān is universal, we can also find the above methodology of tabligh useful and beneficial to implement at any time including our times, depending on the context and the person. For example, why the Names of Allah ﷻ الْوَاحِدُ الْقَهَّارُ were chosen in the above ayahs. This can be an example of contextualization of the situation, time, and space.

[55-58][113]

وَكَذَلِكَ مَكَّنِّا لِيُوسُفَ فِي الأَرْضِ يَتَبَوَّأُ مِنْهَا حَيْثُ يَشَاء نُصِيبُ بِرَحْمَتِنَا مَن نَّشَاء وَلاَ
نُضِيعُ أَجْرَ الْمُحْسِنِينَ {يوسف/56}

Sometimes, in the works of deen, we become so ambitious and unknowingly possibly indulge in shirk. In the sense that sometimes, asking positions for the benefit of deen can very easily hiding itself under arrogance, riya, and other shirk diseases. In this regard, Allah ﷻ mentions the reality of getting positions as وَكَذَلِكَ مَكَّنِّا لِيُوسُفَ فِي الأَرْضِ. So, if the person is really sincere Allah ﷻ can enable those cases. The person may just show a tiny inclination as part of the free will as قَالَ اجْعَلْنِي عَلَى خَزَائِنِ الأَرْضِ إِنِّي حَفِيظٌ عَلِيمٌ {يوسف/55} as only with the verbal discourse of Yûsuf as as mentioned in this ayah.

---

113. (12:55) [Joseph] replied: "Place in my charge the store-houses of the land; behold, I shall be a good and knowing keeper. 12:56 (56) And thus We established Joseph securely in the land [of Egypt]: he had full mastery over it, [doing] whatever he willed. [Thus do] We cause Our grace to alight upon whomever We will; and We do not fail to requite the doers of good. (12:57) But in the eyes of those who have attained to faith and have always been conscious of Us, a reward in the life to come is a far greater good [than any reward in this world].12:58 AND [after some years,] Joseph's brothers came [to Egypt] and presented themselves before him: and he knew them [at once], whereas they did not recognize him.

In some cases, there may not be even any verbal discourse but it could be a thought, a feeling or nothing yet, the Mashiyyah, Divine Will, of Allah ﷻ as mentioned in وَجَاء إِخْوَةُ يُوسُفَ فَدَخَلُواْ عَلَيْهِ فَعَرَفَهُمْ وَهُمْ لَهُ مُنكِرُونَ {يوسف/58}[114] when Yûsuf as's brothers came from nowhere with the plan of Allah ﷻ. Did Yûsuf as want to get back to them? الله اعلم, as the Prophet of Allah ﷺ, we would say no. Yet, still Allah ﷻ takes care of everything for the person.

One can see also this in the example of Musa as as mentioned

إِذْ أَوْحَيْنَا إِلَى أُمِّكَ مَا يُوحَى {طه/38}[115] أَنِ اقْذِفِيهِ فِي التَّابُوتِ فَاقْذِفِيهِ فِي الْيَمِّ فَلْيُلْقِهِ الْيَمُّ بِالسَّاحِلِ يَأْخُذْهُ عَدُوٌّ لِّي وَعَدُوٌّ لَّهُ وَأَلْقَيْتُ عَلَيْكَ مَحَبَّةً مِّنِّي وَلِتُصْنَعَ عَلَى عَيْنِي {طه/39}[116] إِذْ تَمْشِي أُخْتُكَ فَتَقُولُ هَلْ أَدُلُّكُمْ عَلَى مَن يَكْفُلُهُ فَرَجَعْنَاكَ إِلَى أُمِّكَ كَيْ تَقَرَّ عَيْنُهَا وَلَا تَحْزَنَ وَقَتَلْتَ نَفْسًا فَنَجَّيْنَاكَ مِنَ الْغَمِّ وَفَتَنَّاكَ فُتُونًا فَلَبِثْتَ سِنِينَ فِي أَهْلِ مَدْيَنَ ثُمَّ جِئْتَ عَلَى قَدَرٍ يَا مُوسَى [117]{طه/40}

This can show that a person really should focus on their relationship with Allah ﷻ then Allah ﷻ takes care of everything and makes everything easy, wonderous, pleasant and joyful. The person can be in Jannah in this world before going there after death, inshAllah. Even that Jannah after death becomes much better as mentioned وَلَأَجْرُ الآخِرَةِ خَيْرٌ لِّلَّذِينَ آمَنُواْ وَكَانُواْ يَتَّقُونَ [118]{يوسف/57}

One should not forget that when things may go in the way that the person wants or desires but still the person is not safe from istidraj or makr of Allah ﷻ. Therefore, Yûsuf as asks dying as a Muslim due to this uncertainty as mentioned [119]أَنتَ وَلِيِّي فِي الدُّنْيَا وَالآخِرَةِ تَوَفَّنِي مُسْلِمًا وَأَلْحِقْنِي بِالصَّالِحِينَ {يوسف/101}, الله اعلم.

---

114. AND [after some years,] Joseph's brothers came [to Egypt] and presented themselves before him: and he knew them [at once], whereas they did not recognize him.

115. When We inspired to your mother what We inspired.

116. [Saying], 'Cast him into the chest and cast it into the river, and the river will throw it onto the bank; there will take him an enemy to Me and an enemy to him.' And I bestowed upon you love from Me776 that you would be brought up under My eye [i.e., observation and care].

117. [And We favored you] when your sister went and said, 'Shall I direct you to someone who will be responsible for him?' So We restored you to your mother that she might be content and not grieve. And you killed someone, but We saved you from retaliation and tried you with a [severe] trial. And you remained [some] years among the people of Madyan. Then you came [here] at the decreed time, O Moses.

118. And the reward of the Hereafter is better for those who believed and were fearing Allah جل جلاله.

119. My Lord, You have given me [something] of sovereignty and taught me of the interpretation of dreams. Creator of the heavens and earth, You are my protector in this world and the Hereafter. Cause me to die a Muslim and join me with the righteous."

[77-79]¹²⁰

{ قَالُواْ إِن يَسْرِقْ فَقَدْ سَرَقَ أَخٌ لَّهُ مِن قَبْلُ فَأَسَرَّهَا يُوسُفُ فِي نَفْسِهِ وَلَمْ يُبْدِهَا لَهُمْ قَالَ
أَنتُمْ شَرٌّ مَّكَانًا وَاللَّهُ أَعْلَمُ بِمَا تَصِفُونَ {يوسف/77} قَالُواْ يَا أَيُّهَا الْعَزِيزُ إِنَّ لَهُ أَبًا شَيْخًا
كَبِيرًا فَخُذْ أَحَدَنَا مَكَانَهُ إِنَّا نَرَاكَ مِنَ الْمُحْسِنِينَ {يوسف/78} قَالَ مَعَاذَ اللَّهِ أَن نَّأْخُذَ إِلاَّ
مَن وَجَدْنَا مَتَاعَنَا عِندَهُ إِنَّا إِذًا لَّظَالِمُونَ {يوسف/79}

The Qurān gives the inner feelings of the person. In this case, the Qurān mentions Yûsuf as inner feelings as فَأَسَرَّهَا يُوسُفُ فِي نَفْسِهِ وَلَمْ يُبْدِهَا لَهُمْ قَالَ أَنتُمْ شَرٌّ مَّكَانًا وَاللَّهُ أَعْلَمُ بِمَا تَصِفُونَ {يوسف/77}. SubhanAllah ﷻ, this is another proof about the Qurān is the Haqq, the truth that who can know the self-dialogue and inner feelings of the person other than the person, and Allah ﷻ. Here, Allah ﷻ mentions the inner feelings of Yûsuf as which are not known to anyone.

قَالَ مَعَاذَ اللَّهِ أَن نَّأْخُذَ إِلاَّ مَن وَجَدْنَا مَتَاعَنَا عِندَهُ إِنَّا إِذًا لَّظَالِمُونَ {يوسف/79}

Another teaching comes to implement justice even though the person can feel sad and have softness, and compassion for others. Yûsuf as needs to act firm in order to get to the point of teaching a lesson to them, SubhanAllah. This can be also related to acting similarly with discipline and firmness with the other groups although the person can be soft in real life. The Qurān uses the word أشدّ or أغلظ for this firmness as in Sûrah Fath for the kuffar, الله اعلم.

---

120. (12:77) [As soon as the cup came to light out of Benjamin's bag, the brothers] exclaimed: "If he has stolen-well, a brother of his used to steal aforetime!" Thereupon Joseph said to himself, without revealing his thought to them: "You are far worse in this respect, and God is fully aware of what you are saying." 12:78 They said: "O thou great one! Behold, he has a father, a very old man: detain, therefore, one of us in his stead. Verily, we see that thou art a doer of good!"
12:79 He answered: "May God preserve us from [the sin of] detaining any other than him with whom we have found our property—for then, behold, we would indeed be evildoers!"

[80 & 10]¹²¹

فَلَمَّا اسْتَيْأَسُواْ مِنْهُ خَلَصُواْ نَجِيًّا قَالَ كَبِيرُهُمْ أَلَمْ تَعْلَمُواْ أَنَّ أَبَاكُمْ قَدْ أَخَذَ عَلَيْكُم مَّوْثِقًا مِّنَ اللّهِ وَمِن قَبْلُ مَا فَرَّطتُمْ فِي يُوسُفَ فَلَنْ أَبْرَحَ الأَرْضَ حَتَّىَ يَأْذَنَ لِي أَبِي أَوْ يَحْكُمَ اللّهُ لِي وَهُوَ خَيْرُ الْحَاكِمِينَ {يوسف/80}

{ قَالَ قَآئِلٌ مَّنْهُمْ لاَ تَقْتُلُواْ يُوسُفَ وَأَلْقُوهُ فِي غَيَابَةِ الْجُبِّ يَلْتَقِطْهُ بَعْضُ السَّيَّارَةِ إِن كُنتُمْ فَاعِلِينَ ¹²²{يوسف/10}

When one analyzes the two expressions قَالَ كَبِيرُهُمْ¹²³ and قَالَ قَآئِلٌ مَّنْهُمْ¹²⁴ as mentioned in the above two ayahs, قَالَ قَآئِلٌ مَّنْهُمْ can show that this person suggests a relative evil or relative good in its context. When they were planning to kill them this person at least gave a suggestion better than what the other brothers were planning to do. It was still bad but relatively good. Therefore, it received the mention rank in the Qurān as قَالَ قَآئِلٌ مَّنْهُمْ. Compared to the later case as in قَالَ كَبِيرُهُمْ, there is a specific mention of the person because this person did self-accountability and made a correct statement. Therefore, this was recognized and mentioned with more specificity as قَالَ كَبِيرُهُمْ.

Another possibility is that Allah ☀ teaches us the adab of hiding people's faults as mentioned with the expression قَالَ قَآئِلٌ مَّنْهُمْ, although there is a relative good in it but not a full good. On the other hand, when there is a benefit and complete goodness in an engagement, as in this case of the attitude of self-accountability, then there is an encouragement in the Qurān by giving details about who this person was as mentioned in قَالَ كَبِيرُهُمْ. اﷲ اعلم

---

121. (12:80) And so, when they lost all hope of [moving] him, they withdrew to take counsel [among themselves]. The eldest of them said: "Do you not remember that your father has bound you by a solemn pledge before God—and how, before that, you had failed with regard to Joseph? Hence, I shall not depart from this land till my father gives me leave or God passes judgment in my favour: for He is the best of all judges. 12:10 Another of them said: "Do not slay Joseph, but—rather—if you must do something—cast him into the dark depths of this well, [whence] some caravan may pick him up."

122. Said a speaker among them, "Do not kill Joseph but throw him into the bottom of the well; some travelers will pick him up—if you would do [something]." ⌧

123. The eldest [brother] said.

124. Said a speaker among them.

[90]¹²⁵

{ قَالُواْ أَإِنَّكَ لَأَنتَ يُوسُفُ قَالَ أَنَاْ يُوسُفُ وَهَذَا أَخِي قَدْ مَنَّ اللّهُ عَلَيْنَا إِنَّهُ مَن يَتَّقِ وَيِصْبِرْ
فَإِنَّ اللّهَ لاَ يُضِيعُ أَجْرَ الْمُحْسِنِينَ {يوسف/90}

In the above verse, there are some key concepts:

► قَدْ مَنَّ اللّهُ عَلَيْنَا: Allah ﷻ gives all the good, Al-Mannan. Don't think that it is from me, as a human being. Don't elevate me.

► إِنَّهُ مَن يَتَّقِ وَيِصْبِرْ: The key to any achievement is having the respect, and appreciation of Allah ﷻ with patience. Do not blame for any evil or bad by saying: Why Allah ﷻ gave this to me? But be patient, keep and continue with your taqwa of Allah ﷻ.

[100]¹²⁶

وَرَفَعَ أَبَوَيْهِ عَلَى الْعَرْشِ وَخَرُّواْ لَهُ سُجَّدًا وَقَالَ يَا أَبَتِ هَذَا تَأْوِيلُ رُؤْيَايَ مِن قَبْلُ قَدْ
جَعَلَهَا رَبِّي حَقًّا وَقَدْ أَحْسَنَ بَي إِذْ أَخْرَجَنِي مِنَ السِّجْنِ وَجَاء بِكُم مِّنَ الْبَدْوِ مِن بَعْدِ
أَن نَّزغَ الشَّيْطَانُ بَيْنِي وَبَيْنَ إِخْوَتِي إِنَّ رَبِّي لَطِيفٌ لِّمَا يَشَاء إِنَّهُ هُوَ الْعَلِيمُ الْحَكِيمُ
{يوسف/100}

After all their evil, Yûsuf as does not blame them but the Shaytan أَنّ¹²⁷ نَّزغَ الشَّيْطَانُ بَيْنِي وَبَيْنَ إِخْوَتِي. This is the notion practically shown by a Prophet of Allah ﷺ as a role model about how one should implement the evil, the theodicy in one's life. If it happened to anyone else, the person would have blamed and said to them "you ruined all my life, etc." which is the reality in the case of Yûsuf as but Yûsuf as a role model shows how to rely on Allah ﷻ and makes tawakkul and sees and understands

---

125. (12:90) They exclaimed: "Why—is it indeed thou who art Joseph?" He answered: "I am Joseph, and this is my brother. God has indeed been gracious unto us. Verily, if one is conscious of Him and patient in adversity—behold, God does not fail to requite the doers of good!"
126. 12:100 And he raised his parents to the highest place of honour; and they [all] fell down before Him, prostrating themselves in adoration. Thereupon [Joseph] said: "O my father! This is the real meaning of my dream of long ago, which my Sustainer has made come true. And He was indeed good to me when He freed me from the prison, and [when] He brought you [all unto me] from the desert after Satan had sown discord between me and my brothers. Verily, my Sustainer is unfathomable in [the way He brings about] whatever He wills: verily, He alone is all-knowing, truly wise!"
127. After Satan had sown discord between me and my brothers.

all the internal meanings of the ugly incidents which one can call evil, SubhanAllah.

اللهم جعلنا من الذين يتبعون الحق[128]

امين

[101][129]

رَبِّ قَدْ آتَيْتَنِي مِنَ الْمُلْكِ وَعَلَّمْتَنِي مِن تَأْوِيلِ الْأَحَادِيثِ فَاطِرَ السَّمَاوَاتِ وَالْأَرْضِ أَنتَ وَلِيِّي فِي الدُّنْيَا وَالْآخِرَةِ تَوَفَّنِي مُسْلِمًا وَأَلْحِقْنِي بِالصَّالِحِينَ {يوسف/101}

It is extremely difficult to maintain the balance of the qalb when the people are showing tawajjuh towards the person in worldly and akhirah related matters. Therefore, some of the awliya did not want to be known and always tried to protect the level of unknown identity in their books, in their engagements of inviting people to the deen and in engagement of other good deeds. Because, recognition by people brings another difficulty of self-control in tazkiyatul nafs that the person constantly needs to hammer his or her nafs in reality about these achievements that they are not from the person but from Allah ﷻ. Some of the awliya tried to maintain this normalness and sameness among people to eliminate this type of burden of tazkiyatul nafs. If sometimes people realized their difference in piety, then they got so much disturbed and disgusted about themselves due to the possibility of riyā or shirk on the path of Allah جل جلاله and putting another level of burden of tazkiyatul nafs on their weak shoulders. Some awliya immediately left these places, towns, and even mosques that they used to attend when people started talking about their piety. One can always be at a higher level of "I don't care or I am not affected," but I don't know if this is practically possible if there is no protection from Allah ﷻ against the evils of one's nafs and shaytan.

If one thinks the point that Yûsuf as reached that it was a triumph in worldly matters as he as had the power, authority and position. He had also the position at another level being a prophet, son of a prophet

---

128. O Allah جل جلاله, make us from among those who follow the truth. Amìn.
129. 12:101 "O my Sustainer! Thou hast indeed bestowed upon me something of power, and hast imparted unto me some knowledge of the inner meaning of happenings. Originator of the heavens and the earth! Thou art near unto me in this world and in the life to come: let me die as one who has surrendered himself unto Thee, and make me one with the righteous!"

and then showing a very perfect level of kindness and forgiveness to his brothers after going through long lasting difficulties due his brother's makr, zulm, oppression and evil towards him. Yet, at this position, Yûsuf as is worried about keeping this high state of being a true Muslim and mumin until he dies and even dying with this state as mentioned in تَوَفَّنِي

مُسْلِمًا وَأَلْحِقْنِي بِالصَّالِحِينَ [130] {يوسف/101}.

In this ayah, there are some key words and concepts mentioned:

1. رَبِّ قَدْ آتَيْتَنِي مِنَ الْمُلْكِ وَعَلَّمْتَنِي مِن تَأْوِيلِ

    Allah gave everything to Yûsuf as: the position being the minister of the country and knowledge, i'lm. So, Yûsuf as is not claiming any ownership with these but giving to the Real Owner. Every good is given to the person from Allah , Al-Mannan. Therefore, don't claim any ownership in any good. It is a lie and kufr. If there is any good it is given from Allah .

2. أَنتَ وَلِيِّي فِي الدُّنْيَا وَالآخِرَةِ

    The Prophet Yûsuf as is teaching us the secret of how to achieve the results even in the most difficult and worst situations. The secret is only having Allah as the Waliyy. The Waliyy is the Real Friend, the Protector, the One Who is all the time with the person, the One who takes care of the Person, the One the person will go back to eventually and meet. This is true in this world and after death.

3. تَوَفَّنِي مُسْلِمًا وَأَلْحِقْنِي بِالصَّالِحِينَ

    The person does not have any guarantee of their state of dying. Although the person can live a very pious life but can die in a contrary state. The opposite is true as well. If Yûsuf as, as the Prophet of Allah , is making dua to Allah for that, how about us?

---

130. Cause me to die a Muslim and join me with the righteous." ⌧

Sûrah Ibrāhim

As the previous Sûrah concentrates on Yûsuf as taking Allah as waliyy, another embodiment of being Khalil, the Friend of Allah is Ibrahim as. This Sûrah has this name of Ibrahim as after the Sûrah named after Yûsuf as.

[1-3][131]

الَر كِتَابٌ أَنزَلْنَاهُ إِلَيْكَ لِتُخْرِجَ النَّاسَ مِنَ الظُّلُمَاتِ إِلَى النُّورِ بِإِذْنِ رَبِّهِمْ إِلَى صِرَاطِ
الْعَزِيزِ الْحَمِيدِ {إبراهيم/1} اللّهِ الَّذِي لَهُ مَا فِي السَّمَاوَاتِ وَمَا فِي الأَرْضِ وَوَيْلٌ لِّلْكَافِرِينَ
مِنْ عَذَابٍ شَدِيدٍ {إبراهيم/2} الَّذِينَ يَسْتَحِبُّونَ الْحَيَاةَ الدُّنْيَا عَلَى الآخِرَةِ وَيَصُدُّونَ عَن
سَبِيلِ اللّهِ وَيَبْغُونَهَا عِوَجًا أُوْلَئِكَ فِي ضَلاَلٍ بَعِيدٍ {إبراهيم/3}

One can realize that the main purpose of the Qurān is to take people from darknesses of kufr to the lights of imān. Therefore, if one is squeezed and contracted spiritually, being in anxiety, distress or nervousness, the Qurān takes the person out of those dark states to the light of imān. One of the check points of having the Nûr of imān or not for the person can be if he or she wants to meet with Allah or not. In other words, does one prefer akhirah over dunya?

---

131. 14:1 Alif. Lam. Ra. A DIVINE WRIT [is this a revelation] which We have bestowed upon thee from on high in order that thou might bring forth all mankind, by their Sustainer's leave, out of the depths of darkness into the light: onto the way that leads to the Almighty, the One to whom all praise is due—(14:2) to God, unto whom all that is in the heavens and all that is on earth belongs. But woe unto those who deny the truth: for suffering severe (14:3) awaits those who choose the life of this world as the sole object of their love, preferring it to [all thought of] the life to come, and who turn others away from the path of God and try to make it appear crooked. Such as these have indeed gone far astray!

14

Sûrah Hijr

[45-48]¹³²

إِنَّ الْمُتَّقِينَ فِي جَنَّاتٍ وَعُيُونٍ {الحجر/45} ادْخُلُوهَا بِسَلَامٍ آمِنِينَ {الحجر/46} وَنَزَعْنَا
مَا فِي صُدُورِهِم مِّنْ غِلٍّ إِخْوَانًا عَلَى سُرُرٍ مُّتَقَابِلِينَ {الحجر/47} لَا يَمَسُّهُمْ فِيهَا نَصَبٌ
وَمَا هُم مِّنْهَا بِمُخْرَجِينَ {الحجر/48}

In this ayah, the existence of غِلّ, ill feelings of one to another is acknowledged. In other words, the default of life's struggle in one's own self is performed through the process of tazkiya, to remove and positivize the ill-feel feelings in one's heart, and, in other words, to transform these negative feelings to the positive ones. Yet, Allah ﷻ mentions that if there are some still left then غِلّ وَنَزَعْنَا مَا فِي صُدُورِهِم مِّنْ, they will be taken out in Jannah with the fadl, and rahmah of Allah ﷻ.

Another feeling that can come to a person's mind is the fear of disappearance of a nimah. Especially, when a person is situated in all pleasures and places of Jannah, one can ask "are we going to lose them?" This fear can put the person in agony and not enjoying these pleasures. Then, Allah ﷻ mentions as وَمَا هُم مِّنْهَا بِمُخْرَجِينَ, that they won't be deported, kicked out, expelled, and thrown out from these ni'mahs, inshAllah.

[71-72]¹³³

قَالَ هَٰؤُلَاء بَنَاتِي إِن كُنتُمْ فَاعِلِينَ {الحجر/71}

لَعَمْرُكَ إِنَّهُمْ لَفِي سَكْرَتِهِمْ يَعْمَهُونَ {الحجر/72}

It is interesting to focus on the word سَكَر how it is used here and other parts of the Qurān and how it is borrowed in different fields such as

---

132. 15:45 VERILY, those who are conscious of God [shall find themselves in the hereafter] amidst gardens and springs, (15:46) [having been received with the greeting,] "Enter here in peace, secure!" (15:47) And [by then] We shall have removed whatever unworthy thoughts or feelings may have been [lingering] in their breasts, [and they shall rest] as brethren, facing one another [in love] upon thrones of happiness. (48) No weariness shall ever touch them in this [state of bliss], and never shall they have to forgo it.
133. 15:71 [Lot] said: "[Take instead] these daughters of mine, if you must do [whatever you intend to do]!" (15:72) [But the angels spoke thus:] "As thou livest, [O Lot, they will not listen to thee:] behold, in their delirium [of lust] they are but blindly stumbling to and fro!"

tasawwuf or in legal rulings such as وَمِن ثَمَرَاتِ النَّخِيلِ وَالأَعْنَابِ تَتَّخِذُونَ مِنْهُ
سَكَرًا وَرِزْقًا حَسَنًا إِنَّ فِي ذَلِكَ لآيَةً لِّقَوْمٍ يَعْقِلُونَ 134{النحل/67}.

In this case, with the context of Lût as's qawm, people are in a state of delusion due to their urges, and desires they want to do what they want to do in a blind state as mentioned يَعْمَهُونَ135. This notion is explicitly mentioned also in لَقَالُواْ إِنَّمَا سُكِّرَتْ أَبْصَارُنَا بَلْ نَحْنُ قَوْمٌ مَّسْحُورُونَ 136{الحجر/15}. The expression is presented with both words eyes and the word sakr as سُكِّرَتْ أَبْصَارُنَا137.

It is interesting to control one's urges such as anger, lust or others. They can possibly make the person blind if the person does not control or gauge them in positive and permissible ways as Lût as mentions قَالَ هَؤُلاء بَنَاتِي إِن كُنتُمْ فَاعِلِينَ 138{الحجر/71}.

One can see that at the cases or states of sakr, the person cannot differentiate right from wrong or blurriness as mentioned with the words of blindness or eyes. Another time that puts the person of an utmost mixture of delusion, confusion, or blindness is at the time of death as mentioned وَجَاءتْ سَكْرَةُ الْمَوْتِ بِالْحَقِّ ذَلِكَ مَا كُنتَ مِنْهُ تَحِيدُ 139{ق/19}.

Sûrah Nahl

[74-76]140

فَلاَ تَضْرِبُواْ لِلّهِ الأَمْثَالَ إِنَّ اللّهَ يَعْلَمُ وَأَنتُمْ لاَ تَعْلَمُونَ {النحل/74}

---

134. Cause me to die a Muslim and join me with the righteous."
135. They are but blindly stumbling to and fro.
136. They would say, "Our eyes have only been dazzled. Rather, we are a people affected by magic."
137. Our eyes have only been dazzled.
138. [Lot] said, "These are my daughters –if you would be doers [of lawful marriage]."
139. And the intoxication of death will bring the truth; that is what you were trying to avoid.
140. 16:74 Hence, do not coin any similitudes for God!84 Verily, God knows [all], whereas you have no [real] knowledge.
16:75 God propounds [to you] the parable of [two men] a man enslaved, unable to do anything of his own accord, and a [free] man upon whom We have bestowed goodly sustenance [as a gift] from Ourselves, so that he can spend thereof [at will, both] secretly and openly. Can these [two] be deemed equal? All praise is due to God [alone]: but most of them do not understand it.
16:76 And God propounds [to you] the parable of two [other] men—one of them dumb, unable to do anything of his own accord, and a sheer burden on his master: to whichever task the latter directs him, he accomplishes no good. Can such a one be considered the equal of [a wise man] who enjoins the doing of what is right and himself follows a straight way?

ضَرَبَ اللّهُ مَثَلاً عَبْدًا مَّمْلُوكًا لاَّ يَقْدِرُ عَلَى شَيْءٍ وَمَن رَّزَقْنَاهُ مِنَّا رِزْقًا حَسَنًا فَهُوَ يُنفِقُ
مِنْهُ سِرًّا وَجَهْرًا هَلْ يَسْتَوُونَ الْحَمْدُ لِلّهِ بَلْ أَكْثَرُهُمْ لاَ يَعْلَمُونَ {النحل/75} وَضَرَبَ اللّهُ
مَثَلاً رَّجُلَيْنِ أَحَدُهُمَا أَبْكَمُ لاَ يَقْدِرُ عَلَىَ شَيْءٍ وَهُوَ كَلٌّ عَلَى مَوْلاهُ أَيْنَمَا يُوَجِّههُ لاَ يَأْتِ
بِخَيْرٍ هَلْ يَسْتَوِي هُوَ وَمَن يَأْمُرُ بِالْعَدْلِ وَهُوَ عَلَى صِرَاطٍ مُّسْتَقِيمٍ {النحل/76}

The above ayahs 75 and 76 are very rich in their possible representation and meanings as Allah ﷻ mentions لاَ تَضْرِبُواْ لِلّهِ الأَمْثَالَ إِنَّ اللّهَ يَعْلَمُ وَأَنتُمْ لاَ تَعْلَمُونَ [141] {النحل/74}. If one analyses the ayahs 75 and 76 there could be very different representations and possibilities that can emerge as different meanings. As an usûl, methodology, one should first refer to the hadith and understanding of sahabah and salaf in the understandings of all the ayahs including these.

In one perspective, these ayahs can refer to the free-will of a person that if used correctly is a blessing for the person from Allah ﷻ.

In another perspective, in child education when one reviews the contemporary discussions about enabling the children or discovering each child's individual potential, the above ayahs can allude to the possibilities of this enablement. One can consider the traditional upbringing of a child with micromanagement of the children by disabling their existing potentials. Oppositely, one can find the current approaches of liberal ideas in child education as the extreme approach of the lack of guidance. As a balance, guidance and enablement which would help the person to discover their abilities with free choice can be suggested in these verses. However, the fruitful products of this guidance can be checked if this person or child becomes a contributor to the society as mentioned يُنفِقُ مِنْهُ سِرًّا وَجَهْرًا [142]. Or, the person becomes a burden on the family, or society without these self-discoveries of one's potential as [143] أَحَدُهُمَا أَبْكَمُ لَا يَقْدِرُ عَلَىَ شَيْءٍ وَهُوَ كَلٌّ عَلَى مَوْلاهُ, الله اعلم

---

141. Hence, do not coin any similitudes for God! Verily, God knows [all], whereas you have no [real] knowledge.
142. So that he can spend thereof [at will, both] secretly and openly.
143. One of them dumb,86 unable to do anything of his own accord, and a sheer burden on his master.

15

Sûrah Isrã

[24]¹⁴⁴

وَاخْفِضْ لَهُمَا جَنَاحَ الذُّلِّ مِنَ الرَّحْمَةِ وَقُل رَّبِّ ارْحَمْهُمَا كَمَا رَبَّيَانِي صَغِيرًا
{الإسراء/24}

Allah ﷻ teaches us the etiquettes of different engagements and the etiquettes of making dua. In this case, the teaching is about how to make dua to Allah ﷻ about one's parents as رَّبِّ ارْحَمْهُمَا كَمَا رَبَّيَانِي صَغِيرًا¹⁴⁵. In my experience of different Muslim communities, I witnessed especially the Muslims from Bangladesh frequently making this dua, MashAllah which is an example of teaching of the Qurān being accepted and practiced by the masses in public. Unfortunately, it is not the case for all the teachings of the Qurān and Sunnah being publicly practiced, but, yet one becomes happy when witnesses at least some of these teachings being present.

This dua رَّبِّ ارْحَمْهُمَا كَمَا رَبَّيَانِي صَغِيرًا is very interesting in its choice of words which are very correlative and meaningful in parent and children relationship. Parent children relationship is a cyclic relationship. One can become either a parent, or a children or both. Experiential knowledge and relevance of this dua is for everyone without any exceptions.

When one analyzes the chosen words in رَبَّيَانِي كَمَا ارْحَمْهُمَا رَّبِّ صَغِيرًا, there are the motifs of correlation and parallelism, love, caring, mercy, upbringing, taking care, vulnerability, and helplessness in the relationship of children and parents. The roles can be switched. In other words, in an older age, a child can be like a parent for his or her parents if this child remembers it. The word كَمَا suggests this parallelism between the child and parent. As parents expected to have rahmah on their children, similar attitude is expected, when a parent especially gets older and weaker, from the child as the child now becomes stronger.

---

144. (24) and spread over them humbly the wings of thy tenderness, and say: "O my Sustainer! Bestow Thy grace upon them, even as they cherished and reared me when I was a child!"

145. O my Sustainer! Bestow Thy grace upon them, even as they cherished and reared me when I was a child!"

[32]¹⁴⁶

{وَلاَ تَقْرَبُواْ الزِّنَى إِنَّهُ كَانَ فَاحِشَةً وَسَاء سَبِيلاً {الإسراء/32}

It is important to realize that Allah ﷻ mentions to us how one can start
falling into sin, something that is against human nature as instructed by
Allah ﷻ. In this case, the starting point can be the eyes or thoughts. If
one normalizes looking at the haram and does not become disturbed,
then, the next step can be the physical touch and the last step can be the
actual haram itself as mentioned by the Prophet 3) ﷺ). A person should,
therefore, have an inner disturbance with each possible sin. His or her
imān should make this person uncomfortable if the person is engaged
with something that Allah ﷻ is not pleased with. Losing this discomfort
or disturbance can be a major loss or degradation in one's relationship
with Allah ﷻ.

[106-109]¹⁴⁷

وَقُرْآنًا فَرَقْنَاهُ لِتَقْرَأَهُ عَلَى النَّاسِ عَلَى مُكْثٍ وَنَزَّلْنَاهُ تَنزِيلاً {الإسراء/106} قُلْ آمِنُواْ
بِهِ أَوْ لاَ تُؤْمِنُواْ إِنَّ الَّذِينَ أُوتُواْ الْعِلْمَ مِن قَبْلِهِ إِذَا يُتْلَى عَلَيْهِمْ يَخِرُّونَ لِلأَذْقَانِ سُجَّدًا
{الإسراء/107} وَيَقُولُونَ سُبْحَانَ رَبِّنَا إِن كَانَ وَعْدُ رَبِّنَا لَمَفْعُولاً {الإسراء/108}

وَيَخِرُّونَ لِلأَذْقَانِ يَبْكُونَ وَيَزِيدُهُمْ خُشُوعًا {الإسراء/109} (سجدة مستحبة)

Difference between Subhan Allah and Subhan Rabbina

> Subhan Allah is the divine phrase that signifies one's starting
and beginning genuine relationship with Allah ﷻ. Here, the
lafzu Mubarak, Allah is used because, in a general usage a
person who is not truly or fully in practice can use this phrase
to establish relationship with Allah ﷻ. Or, it could be in the

---

146. 17:32 And do not commit adultery"—for, behold, it is an abomination and an evil way.
147. (17:106) [bearing] a discourse which We have gradually unfolded, so that thou might
read it out to mankind by stages, seeing that We have bestowed it from on high step by step,
as [one] revelation. 17:107 Say: "Believe in it or do not believe." Behold, those who are already
endowed with [innate] knowledge fall down upon their faces in prostration as soon as this
[divine writ] is conveyed unto them, (17:108) and say, "Limitless in His glory is our Sustainer!
Verily, our Sustainer's promise has been fulfilled!" 17:109 And so they fall down upon their
faces, weeping, and [their consciousness of God's grace] increases their humility.

language that someone can use it for an exclamation mark that the person may not fully internalize the meaning just as a sound of astonishment similar to "oh my God" in English. At this level, this is still valuable and important and appreciated by Allah 🌸.

▶ Once, the person goes beyond the first stage to the second stage of prayer, with full intention, reading the surahs from the Qurān, this person is assumed that he or she is already on the journey of establishing relationship with Allah 🌸. In this perspective, Allah 🌸lets from the Divine Fadl and Mercy, the Rabb attribute. Then, the expression Subhan Allah transforms at a personal embodiment level and becomes the rope as the connection point from general to specific as Subhan Rabbiya Al-Azeem at the Ruku and Subhan Rabbiya Al-A'la at the prostration. In these positions, the person should know that the person already entered into the house and he or she is not saying Subhan Allah but Subhan Rabbiya Al-Azeem or Al-A'la. At this state and position, the traveler should maintain the highest caution and adab of presence with Allah 🌸with ihsān, the perfect union, being in the presence of Allah 🌸. For example, before the person starts praying, he or she can be considered outside the house. As soon as this person starts praying, he or she is not outside anymore but inside the house now by being in the prayer. In other words, the person is at the Divine Presence now with Allah 🌸and talking to Allah 🌸.

▶ Once the person leaves the house, as an outsider as if saying good bye, the person says SubhanAllah 33 times as a dhikr or tasbih as a way of greeting and leaving the house.

اللّٰهم جعلنا منهم امين

Sûrah Kahf

Some of the central themes of this Sûrah are tests, trials and patience.

[1][148]

الْحَمْدُ لِلَّهِ الَّذِي أَنزَلَ عَلَى عَبْدِهِ الْكِتَابَ وَلَمْ يَجْعَل لَّهُ عِوَجَا {الكهف/1}

عَلَى عَبْدِهِ is used to specify the hass, specificity, on Rasulullah ﷺ and general, the amm, for every one as mentioned by Baqhawi (37).

In another perspective, one should realize that it is a nimah for every individual to realize that the Qurãn is a blessing for everyone. Therefore, the expression عَلَى عَبْدِهِ[149] is mentioned to specify that for each person the Qurãn is a huge blessing in one's personal life. As the person can make shukr, hamd and show gratitude and thankfulness to Allah ﷻ for one's health, wealth and welfare in one's life, one should also really show a similar or more gratitude, thankfulness, shukr and hamd for the Qurãn from Rabbul Alamin. One can appreciate the Qurãn more if the person acquires the knowledge about the current situation of prior scriptures sent by Allah ﷻ. In the scholarship of these scriptures, there is no similar discussion of authenticity compared to the established authenticity of the Qurãn (37). When a person is not comfortable reading a text whether if it is revealed by God or not, the person can easily be turned off before even starting to read about it. Therefore, it is not surprising to find other religious followers being turned off their religion and changing and seeking for other religions that would have more authentic texts from Allah ﷻ. The logic or intellect necessitates this disposition.

It is Sunnah to read this chapter every Friday. One of the reasons could be to remind the person that there is a reason for everything happening. In other words, the Western understanding of theodicy can alienate some people from Allah ﷻ. Therefore, when a Muslim reads this Sûrah every Friday, it is a reminder on a regular basis that there are meanings of the evil-seeming incidents happening constantly and that we don't understand their real meanings. The story of the Moses as and

---

148. 18:1 ALL PRAISE is due to God, who has bestowed. this divine writ from on high upon His servant, and has not allowed any deviousness to obscure its meaning:
149. Upon His Servant.

Khidr destroys this negative understanding of theodicy which alienates people from the religion and God.

[10]¹⁵⁰

The first example of the trial, test and patience is with the incident of kahf, cave and the youth. The importance of youth is also mentioned with the word الْفِتْيَةُ¹⁵¹ that most of the time the spirit of youth can handle challenges compared to the people who are spiritually worn out. There are a lot of old aged people who are spiritually fresh and there are a lot of young people who are spiritually old. There are a lot of writings on the concept of fityah or futuwwah in tasawwuf which some people translate as chivalry. Another key word in this ayah is rasdh.

إِذْ أَوَى الْفِتْيَةُ إِلَى الْكَهْفِ فَقَالُوا رَبَّنَا آتِنَا مِن لَّدُنكَ رَحْمَةً وَهَيِّئْ لَنَا مِنْ أَمْرِنَا رَشَدًا {الكهف/10}

[18]¹⁵²

وَكَذَلِكَ بَعَثْنَاهُمْ لِيَتَسَاءلُوا بَيْنَهُمْ قَالَ قَائِلٌ مِّنْهُمْ كَمْ لَبِثْتُمْ قَالُوا لَبِثْنَا يَوْمًا أَوْ بَعْضَ يَوْمٍ قَالُوا رَبُّكُمْ أَعْلَمُ بِمَا لَبِثْتُمْ فَابْعَثُوا أَحَدَكُم بِوَرِقِكُمْ هَذِهِ إِلَى الْمَدِينَةِ فَلْيَنظُرْ أَيُّهَا أَزْكَى طَعَامًا فَلْيَأْتِكُم بِرِزْقٍ مِّنْهُ وَلْيَتَلَطَّفْ وَلَا يُشْعِرَنَّ بِكُمْ أَحَدًا {الكهف/19}

Allah ﷻ shows if one is patient, then Allah ﷻ gives them victory. The above example is a case where it is first proved the people themselves, as well as the people around them, and the generations after and until the yawmul qiyamah as mentioned in the Qurān.

---

150. 18:10 When those youths took refuge in the cave, they prayed: "O our Sustainer! Bestow on us grace from Thyself, and endow us, whatever our [outward] condition, with consciousness of what is right!"
151. Youth.
152. (18:18) And thou wouldst have thought that they were awake, whereas they lay asleep. And We caused them to turn over repeatedly, now to the right, now to the left; and their dog [lay] on the threshold, its forepaws outstretched.

[20][153]

{ إِنَّهُمْ إِن يَظْهَرُوا عَلَيْكُمْ يَرْجُمُوكُمْ أَوْ يُعِيدُوكُمْ فِي مِلَّتِهِمْ وَلَن تُفْلِحُوا إِذًا أَبَدًا {الكهف/20} }

But, still the reality of the potential evil and jealousy of humans can be present. Therefore, caution and prudence are some of the means of making dua, prayer, and asking protection from Allah ﷻ.

[21][154]

وَكَذَلِكَ أَعْثَرْنَا عَلَيْهِمْ لِيَعْلَمُوا أَنَّ وَعْدَ اللَّهِ حَقٌّ وَأَنَّ السَّاعَةَ لَا رَيْبَ فِيهَا إِذْ يَتَنَازَعُونَ بَيْنَهُمْ أَمْرَهُمْ فَقَالُوا ابْنُوا عَلَيْهِم بُنْيَانًا رَّبُّهُمْ أَعْلَمُ بِهِمْ قَالَ الَّذِينَ غَلَبُوا عَلَى أَمْرِهِمْ لَنَتَّخِذَنَّ عَلَيْهِم مَّسْجِدًا {الكهف/21}

And the case of Allah ﷻ's promise, لِيَعْلَمُوا أَنَّ وَعْدَ اللَّهِ حَقٌّ [155], is mentioned that the patient ones inshAllah will be the ones who will be in success and in victory with the wa'd[156] of Allah. This is witnessed with other generations as mentioned وَكَذَلِكَ أَعْثَرْنَا عَلَيْهِم[157].

[28][158]

وَاصْبِرْ نَفْسَكَ مَعَ الَّذِينَ يَدْعُونَ رَبَّهُم بِالْغَدَاةِ وَالْعَشِيِّ يُرِيدُونَ وَجْهَهُ وَلَا تَعْدُ عَيْنَاكَ عَنْهُمْ تُرِيدُ زِينَةَ الْحَيَاةِ الدُّنْيَا وَلَا تُطِعْ مَنْ أَغْفَلْنَا قَلْبَهُ عَن ذِكْرِنَا وَاتَّبَعَ هَوَاهُ وَكَانَ أَمْرُهُ فُرُطًا {الكهف/28}

---

153. (18:20) for, behold, if they should come to know of you, they might stone you to death or force you back to their faith—in which case you would never attain to any good!"
154. 18:21 AND IN THIS way have We drawn [people's] attention to their story, so that they might know—whenever they debate among themselves as to what happened to those [Men of the Cave]—that God's promise [of resurrection] is true, and that there can be no doubt as to [the coming of] the Last Hour. And so, some [people] said: "Erect a building in their memory; God knows best what happened to them."
Said they whose opinion prevailed in the end: "Indeed, we must surely raise a house of worship in their memory!"
155. That God's promise [of resurrection] is true.
156. Promise.
157. AND IN THIS way have We drawn [people's] attention to their story.
158. (18:28) And contain thyself in patience by the side of all who at morn and at evening invoke their Sustainer, seeking His countenance, and let not thine eyes pass beyond them in quest of the beauties of this world's life; and pay no heed to any whose heart We have rendered heedless of all remembrance of Us because he had always followed [only] his own desires, abandoning all that is good and true.

The central theme of Sabr, patience comes as (baraat istidlal) here. It can be easier to implement patience when one is with the people of Allah ﷻ (wali) who are constantly in ibadah as mentioned by وَاصْبِرْ نَفْسَكَ[159] مَعَ الَّذِينَ يَدْعُونَ رَبَّهُم بِالْغَدَاةِ وَالْعَشِيِّ يُرِيدُونَ وَجْهَهُ وَلَا تَعْدُ عَيْنَاكَ عَنْهُمْ. During the times of grief, it is important not to focus on the loss or the source of grief but on the discourses and relationship with the wali of Allah ﷻ as mentioned by وَلَا تَعْدُ عَيْنَاكَ عَنْهُمْ[160], even do not take your eyes from the people of Allah ﷻ. Because most of the time people agree that patience is a virtue but they don't know how to practice it. Therefore, one of the practical suggestions of this ayah is that when the person is with the ones who are close to Allah ﷻ then it will be easier and help the person to be patient. The ayah is mentioning if the person loses something and he or she can view others as enjoying their lives. The person should not be trapped with others' worldly achievements and positions as mentioned by عَنْهُمْ تُرِيدُ زِينَةَ الْحَيَاةِ الدُّنْيَا وَلاَ تُطِعْ مَنْ أَغْفَلْنَا قَلْبَهُ عَن ذِكْرِنَا وَاتَّبَعَ هَوَاهُ وَكَانَ أَمْرُهُ[161] فُرُطًا. In reality, their product can be futile, such as oppression and evil as mentioned by فُرُطًا[162].

[30][163]

إِنَّ الَّذِينَ آمَنُوا وَعَمِلُوا الصَّالِحَاتِ إِنَّا لَا نُضِيعُ أَجْرَ مَنْ أَحْسَنَ عَمَلًا {الكهف/30} أُوْلَئِكَ لَهُمْ جَنَّاتُ عَدْنٍ تَجْرِي مِن تَحْتِهِمُ الْأَنْهَارُ يُحَلَّوْنَ فِيهَا مِنْ أَسَاوِرَ مِن ذَهَبٍ وَيَلْبَسُونَ ثِيَابًا خُضْرًا مِّن سُندُسٍ وَإِسْتَبْرَقٍ مُّتَّكِئِينَ فِيهَا عَلَى الْأَرَائِكِ نِعْمَ الثَّوَابُ وَحَسُنَتْ مُرْتَفَقًا {الكهف/31}

At the time of loss or grief, the importance of imān and the rewards prepared by Allah ﷻ for the patient ones can be emphasized as mentioned in the above case.

---

159. And contain thyself in patience by the side of all who at morn and at evening invoke their Sustainer, seeking His countenance, and let not thine eyes pass beyond them.
160. And let not thine eyes pass beyond them.
161. Beyond them in quest of the beauties of this world's life; and pay no heed to any whose heart We have rendered heedless of all remembrance of Us because he had always followed [only] his own desires, abandoning all that is good and true.
162. Good and true.
163. 18:30 [But,] behold, as for those who attain to faith and do righteous deeds—verily, We do not fail to requite any who persevere in doing good.

[31-34]¹⁶⁴

وَاضْرِبْ لَهُم مَّثَلًا رَّجُلَيْنِ جَعَلْنَا لِأَحَدِهِمَا جَنَّتَيْنِ مِنْ أَعْنَابٍ وَحَفَفْنَاهُمَا بِنَخْلٍ وَجَعَلْنَا بَيْنَهُمَا زَرْعًا {الكهف/32} كِلْتَا الْجَنَّتَيْنِ آتَتْ أُكُلَهَا وَلَمْ تَظْلِم مِّنْهُ شَيْئًا وَفَجَّرْنَا خِلَالَهُمَا نَهَرًا {الكهف/33} وَكَانَ لَهُ ثَمَرٌ فَقَالَ لِصَاحِبِهِ وَهُوَ يُحَاوِرُهُ أَنَا أَكْثَرُ مِنكَ مَالًا وَأَعَزُّ نَفَرًا {الكهف/34}

Now, the cases are presented. First, the case of two individuals: one is respected with position and wealth in the society and the other is miskin, poor, having no position and not respected. Their outcomes are presented.

[43-44]¹⁶⁵

وَلَمْ تَكُن لَّهُ فِئَةٌ يَنصُرُونَهُ مِن دُونِ اللَّهِ وَمَا كَانَ مُنتَصِرًا {الكهف/43} هُنَالِكَ الْوَلَايَةُ لِلَّهِ الْحَقِّ هُوَ خَيْرٌ ثَوَابًا وَخَيْرٌ عُقْبًا {الكهف/44}

---

164. (18:31) theirs shall be gardens of perpetual bliss—[gardens] through which running waters flow—wherein they will be adorned with bracelets of gold and will wear green garments of silk and brocade, [and] wherein upon couches they will recline: how excellent a recompense, and how goodly a place to rest! 18:32 AND PROPOUND unto them the parable of two men, upon one of whom We had bestowed two vinyards, and surrounded them with date-palms, and placed a field of grain in-between. (18:33) Each of the two gardens yielded its produce and never failed therein in any way, for We had caused a stream to gush forth in the midst of each of them. (18:34) And so [the man] had fruit in abundance. And [one day] he said to his friend, bandying words with him, "More wealth have I than thou, and mightier am I as regards [the number and power of my] followers!" 18:35 And having [thus] sinned against himself, he entered his garden, saying, "I do not think that this will ever perish! (18:36) And neither do I think that the Last Hour will ever come. But even if [it should come, and] I am brought before my Sustainer, I will surely find something even better than this as [my last] resort!" 18:37 And his friend answered him in the course of their argument: "Wilt thou blaspheme against Him who has created thee out of dust,44 and then out of a drop of sperm, and in the end has fashioned thee into a [complete] man? (18:38) But as for myself, [I know that] He is God, my Sustainer; and I cannot attribute divine powers to any but my Sustainer." 18:39 And [he continued:] "Alas, if thou hadst but said, on entering thy garden, 'Whatever God wills [shall come to pass, for] there is no power save with God!' Although, as thou seest, I have less wealth and offspring than thou, (18:40) yet it may well be that my Sustainer will give me something better than thy garden—just as He may let loose a calamity out of heaven upon this [thy garden], so that it becomes a heap of barren dust (18:41) or its water sinks deep into the ground, so that thou wilt never be able to find it again!" 18:42 And [thus it happened:] his fruitful gardens were encompassed [by ruin], and there he was, wringing his hands over all that he had spent on that which now lay waste, with its trellises caved in; and he could but say, "Oh, would that I had not attributed divine powers to any but my Sustainer!" (18:43)—for now he had nought47 to succour him in God's stead, nor could he succour himself.
165. (18:43)—For now he had nought to succour him in God's stead, nor could he succour himself. 18:44 For thus it is: all protective power belongs to God alone, the True One. He is the best to grant ecompense, and the best to determine what is to be.

When there is a problem, we tend to seek people's help. Then, most or all the time the problem gets worse and we get in depressive states. Then, overtime, as a nima'h from Allah ﷻ, we start forgetting the magnitude of initial effects of this problem, as al-insān means the one who forgets. Then, the effect of this problem fades. On the other hand, if the person takes another route when the problem happens, that is, to run to Allah ﷻ to solve, to beg and to cry, then, the person can transform this evil-seeming incident into a very fruitful opportunity. One can really have an opportunity to use and make an advantage of this evil-seeming incident. Yet, there are very few who have this approach. Today's increasing number of mental clinics can be proof of this although they are needed for the ones who don't know how to transform these evil-seeming incidents to an opportunity of a mental and heart boost making the person self-dependent, confident, and strong with reliance on Allah ﷻ. Rather, the person becomes dependent on the medicine, these clinics and humans.

The real friend, waliyy is always Allah ﷻ. It is expected that the person should realize this at all times: at the end, during and before of all trials, losses, gains, in good health and wealth as mentioned هُنَالِكَ[166] الْوَلَايَةُ لِلَّهِ الْحَقِّ هُوَ خَيْرٌ ثَوَابًا وَخَيْرٌ عُقْبًا.

[45][167]

{ وَاضْرِبْ لَهُم مَّثَلَ الْحَيَاةِ الدُّنْيَا كَمَاء أَنزَلْنَاهُ مِنَ السَّمَاء فَاخْتَلَطَ بِهِ نَبَاتُ الْأَرْضِ فَأَصْبَحَ هَشِيمًا تَذْرُوهُ الرِّيَاحُ وَكَانَ اللَّهُ عَلَى كُلِّ شَيْءٍ مُّقْتَدِرًا {الكهف/45}

Then, the case of these false attachments, position, wealth, and status are presented as the garbage of the world. It can be trashed at any time by Allah ﷻ as mentioned with وَكَانَ اللَّهُ عَلَى كُلِّ شَيْءٍ مُّقْتَدِرًا.

---

166. For thus it is: all protective power belongs to God alone, the True One. He is the best to grant ecompense, and the best to determine what is to be.
167. 18:45 AND PROPOUND unto them the parable of the life of this world: [it is] like the water which We send down from the skies, and which is absorbed by the plants of the earth: but [in time] they turn into dry stubble which the winds blow freely about. And it is God [alone] who determines all things.

[46][168]

الْمَالُ وَالْبَنُونَ زِينَةُ الْحَيَاةِ الدُّنْيَا وَالْبَاقِيَاتُ الصَّالِحَاتُ خَيْرٌ عِندَ رَبِّكَ ثَوَابًا وَخَيْرٌ أَمَلًا
{الكهف/46}

Other examples of attachments and problems are presented but then always the good work gets the points and rewards from Allah ﷻ as mentioned in the above verse.

[50][169]

[50]وَإِذْ قُلْنَا لِلْمَلَائِكَةِ اسْجُدُوا لِآدَمَ فَسَجَدُوا إِلَّا إِبْلِيسَ كَانَ مِنَ الْجِنِّ فَفَسَقَ عَنْ أَمْرِ رَبِّهِ أَفَتَتَّخِذُونَهُ وَذُرِّيَّتَهُ أَوْلِيَاءَ مِن دُونِي وَهُمْ

لَكُمْ عَدُوٌّ بِئْسَ لِلظَّالِمِينَ بَدَلَ

Also, in this chapter it is interesting to note that when people don't appreciate God and follow the evil, and the chief of it, Satan, Allah ﷻ reminds humans of this expected genuine relationship between the person and the Real Giver, Allah ﷻ. How can one not appreciate Allah (ﷻ) if this person does not recognize the Creator and follow the evils as represented and monumentalized with the word "Satan" or "Shaytan", as mentioned in the above verse 50?

---

168. (18:46) Wealth and children are an adornment of this, world's life: but good deeds, the fruit whereof endures forever, are of far greater merit in thy Sustainer's sight, and a far better source of hope.
169. 18:50 AND [remember that] when We told the angels, "Prostrate yourselves before Adam," they all prostrated themselves, save Iblis: he [too] was one of those invisible beings, but then he turned away from his Sustainer's command. Will you, then, take him and his cohorts for (your), masters instead of Me, although they are your foe? How vile an exchange on the evildoers' part!

[60-82]¹⁷⁰

وَإِذْ قَالَ مُوسَى لِفَتَاهُ لَا أَبْرَحُ حَتَّى أَبْلُغَ مَجْمَعَ الْبَحْرَيْنِ أَوْ أَمْضِيَ حُقُبًا {الكهف/60} فَلَمَّا بَلَغَا مَجْمَعَ بَيْنِهِمَا نَسِيَا حُوتَهُمَا فَاتَّخَذَ سَبِيلَهُ فِي الْبَحْرِ سَرَبًا {الكهف/61}

فَلَمَّا جَاوَزَا قَالَ لِفَتَاهُ آتِنَا غَدَاءنَا لَقَدْ لَقِينَا مِن سَفَرِنَا هَذَا نَصَبًا {الكهف/62} قَالَ أَرَأَيْتَ إِذْ أَوَيْنَا إِلَى الصَّخْرَةِ فَإِنِّي نَسِيتُ الْحُوتَ وَمَا أَنسَانِيهُ إِلَّا الشَّيْطَانُ أَنْ أَذْكُرَهُ وَاتَّخَذَ سَبِيلَهُ فِي الْبَحْرِ عَجَبًا {الكهف/63} قَالَ ذَلِكَ مَا كُنَّا نَبْغِ فَارْتَدَّا عَلَى آثَارِهِمَا قَصَصًا {الكهف/64} فَوَجَدَا عَبْدًا مِّنْ عِبَادِنَا آتَيْنَاهُ رَحْمَةً مِنْ عِندِنَا وَعَلَّمْنَاهُ مِن لَّدُنَّا عِلْمًا {الكهف/65}

Now, the real case of patience and the batin, unseen realities for the evil-seeming incidents reveal themselves. Now, an elect Prophet of Allah ﷻ, Musa as, cannot fully rationalize these evil-seeming incidents. With the a'sa, the staff of patience, one can see the difficulty of the reality of patience in evil-seeming incidents as part of the test and trials. Musa as was famous for carrying a staff.

This is another knowledge, i'lm ladunn, gained and given by Allah ﷻ. This i'lm ladun is given to an agent or messenger of Allah ﷻ, the Khidr as, who are not visible all the time but visible sometimes. This is internal knowledge given by Allah جل جلاله as the i'lm-ladunn.

---

170. 18:60 AND LO! , [In the course of his wanderings,] Moses said to his servant: "I shall not give up until I reach the junction of the two seas, even if I [have to] spend untold years [in my quest]!" 18:61
But when they reached the junction between the two [seas], they forgot all about their fish, and it took its way into the sea and disappeared from sight. (18:62) And after the two had walked some distance, [Moses] said to his servant: "Bring us our mid-day meal; we have indeed suffered hardship on this [day of] our journey!"
18:63 Said [the servant]: "Wouldst thou believe it? When we betook ourselves to that rock for a rest, behold, I forgot about the fish—and none but Satan made me thus forget it!—and it took its way into the sea!

[64-82][171]

قَالَ أَرَأَيْتَ إِذْ أَوَيْنَا إِلَى الصَّخْرَةِ فَإِنِّي نَسِيتُ الْحُوتَ وَمَا أَنسَانِيهُ إِلَّا الشَّيْطَانُ أَنْ أَذْكُرَهُ
وَاتَّخَذَ سَبِيلَهُ فِي الْبَحْرِ عَجَبًا {الكهف/63} قَالَ ذَلِكَ مَا كُنَّا نَبْغِ فَارْتَدَّا عَلَى آثَارِهِمَا
قَصَصًا {الكهف/64}

The adab of Yusha as is seen when something evil bad happens it is
important to blame the shaytan and the nafs as mentioned with وَمَا[172]
أَنسَانِيهُ إِلَّا الشَّيْطَانُ أَنْ أَذْكُرَهُ.

___

171. 18:64 [Moses] exclaimed: "That [was the place] which we were seeking!" And the two
turned back, retracing their footsetps, (18:65) and found one of Our servants, on whom We
had bestowed grace from Ourselves and unto whom We had imparted knowledge [issuing]
from Ourselves. (18:66) Moses said unto him: "May I follow thee on the understanding that
thou wilt impart to me something of that consciousness of what is right which has been
imparted to thee?" 18:67 [The other] answered: "Behold, thou wilt never be able to have
patience with me—(18:68) for how couldst thou be patient about something that thou canst
not comprehend within the compass of (thy) experience?" 18:69 Replied [Moses]: "Thou wilt
find me patient, if God so wills; and I shall not disobey thee in anything!" (18:70) Said [the
sage]: "Well, then, if thou art to follow me, do not question me about aught [that I may do]
until I myself give thee an account thereof." 18:71 And so the two went on their way, till [they
reached the seashore; and] when they disembarked from the boat [that had ferried them
across], the sage made a hole in it—[whereupon Moses exclaimed: "Hast thou made a hole
in it in order to drown the people who may be [travelling] in it? Indeed, thou hast done a
grievous thing!" (18:72) He replied: "Did I not tell thee that thou wilt never be able to have
patience with me?" (18:73) Said [Moses]: "Take me not to task for my having forgotten [myself],
and be not hard on me on account of what I have done!" (18:74) And so the two went on, till,
when they met a young man, [the sage] slew him—(whereupon Moses exclaimed: "Hast thou
slain an innocent human being without [his having taken] another man's life? Indeed, thou
hast done a terrible thing!" 18:75 He replied: "Did I not tell thee that thou wilt never be able to
have patience with me?" (18:76) Said [Moses]: "If, after this, I should ever question thee, keep
me not in thy company: [for by] now thou hast heard enough excuses from me." (18:77) And
so the two went on, till, when they came upon some village people, they asked them for food;
but those [people] refused them all hospitality. And they saw in that (village) a wall which was
on the point of tumbling down, and [the sage] rebuilt it [whereupon Moses said: "Hadst thou
so wished, surely thou couldst [at least] have obtained some payment for it?" 18:78 [The sage]
replied: "This is the parting of ways between me and thee. [And now] I shall let thee know
the real meaning of all [those events] that thou wert unable to bear with patience: (18:79) "As
for that boat, it belonged to some needy people who toiled upon the sea—and I desired to
damage it because (I knew that) behind them was a king who is wont to seize every boat by
brute force. 18:80 "And as for that young man, his parents were [true] believers—whereas we
had every reason to fear that he would bring bitter grief upon them by [his] overweening
wickedness and denial of all truth: (18:81) and so we desired that their Sustainer grant them
in his stead [a child] of greater purity than him, and closer [to them] in loving tenderness.
18:82 "And as for that wall, it belonged to two orphan boys [living] in the town, and beneath
it was [buried] a treasure belonging to them [by right]. Now their father had been a righteous
man, and so thy Sustainer willed it that when they come of age they should bring forth their
treasure by thy Sustainer's grace. "And I did not do (any of) this of my own accord: this is the
real meaning of all [those events] that thou wert unable to bear with patience."
172. And none but Satan made me thus forget it!

[65-66]

فَوَجَدَا عَبْدًا مِّنْ عِبَادِنَا آتَيْنَاهُ رَحْمَةً مِنْ عِندِنَا وَعَلَّمْنَاهُ مِن لَّدُنَّا عِلْمًا {الكهف/65} قَالَ لَهُ مُوسَى هَلْ أَتَّبِعُكَ عَلَى أَن تُعَلِّمَنِ مِمَّا عُلِّمْتَ رُشْدًا {الكهف/66}

In the above verses, one can review the existence of different types of sciences, I'lm as mentioned with the expression وَعَلَّمْنَاهُ مِن لَّدُنَّا عِلْمًا[173]. This can show that even the great Prophet of Allah ﷺ do not know certain sciences. This can bring a perspective that to accept everyone that there can be some perspectives and knowledge that Allah ﷺ gave to each person. What they are good at can be different and we can learn from them as Musa as mentions[174] قَالَ لَهُ مُوسَى هَلْ أَتَّبِعُكَ عَلَى أَن تُعَلِّمَنِ مِمَّا عُلِّمْتَ رُشْدًا. So, the question is not being jealous of what people know as knowledge. Or, it is not position of "I know everything" but accepting that the person is in need of learning with humbleness and humility from others. In natural sciences, social sciences, or in spiritual sciences of heart and mind, one can always seek the knowledge with the position of learning even though he or she can be called an expert. If it is not someone's field of specialization, then it deserves more attention to learn from what the person does not know.

[67][175]

قَالَ إِنَّكَ لَن تَسْتَطِيعَ مَعِيَ صَبْرًا {الكهف/67}

The repeated key expression against evil is patience. Explicitly, it is repeated in the verses for a reason that it is not easy to be patient.

[68][176]

It is difficult to be patient because our human intellect requires reasoning and when we can't, then this point is alluded as

وَكَيْفَ تَصْبِرُ عَلَى مَا لَمْ تُحِطْ بِهِ خُبْرًا {الكهف/68}

---

173. We had bestowed grace from Ourselves and unto whom We had imparted knowledge [issuing] from Ourselves.
174. Moses said unto him: "May I follow thee on the understanding that thou wilt impart to me something of that consciousness of what is right which has been imparted to thee?"
175. [The other] answered: "Behold, thou wilt never be able to have patience with me.
176. For how could thou be patient about something that thou canst not comprehend within the compass of (thy) experience?"

[79]¹⁷⁷

أَمَّا السَّفِينَةُ فَكَانَتْ لِمَسَاكِينَ يَعْمَلُونَ فِي الْبَحْرِ فَأَرَدتُّ أَنْ أَعِيبَهَا وَكَانَ وَرَاءهُم مَّلِكٌ يَأْخُذُ كُلَّ سَفِينَةٍ غَصْبًا

The first case of evil, a group of miskin, good people and ready to be oppressed by an oppressor and Allah ﷻ sends Khidr to perform an evil-seeming incident to protect them from a bigger evil with a small evil-seeming incident. So, Allah ﷻ is protecting and it is important to be patient.

It is important to realize the adab with Allah ﷻ in the expressions of Khidr as. The sigah in فَأَرَدتُّ is mutakallim that Khidr as takes the blame on himself as mentioned فَأَرَدتُّ أَنْ أَعِيبَهَا. The adab with Allah ﷻ requires not to render anything bad, evil or unpleasant with Allah ﷻ.

[80-81]¹⁷⁸

وَأَمَّا الْغُلَامُ فَكَانَ أَبَوَاهُ مُؤْمِنَيْنِ فَخَشِينَا أَن يُرْهِقَهُمَا طُغْيَانًا وَكُفْرًا {الكهف/80} فَأَرَدْنَا أَن يُبْدِلَهُمَا رَبُّهُمَا خَيْرًا مِّنْهُ زَكَاةً وَأَقْرَبَ رُحْمًا {الكهف/81}

The second case of evil-seeming incident is about the loss of our attachments such as things related with wealth, children, job, or position even though it can seem that we may not deserve to lose them. But, Allah ﷻ teaches that the inner reality that Allah ﷻ gives the person better than what he or she loses if the person is patient and still carries gratitude for Allah ﷻ. Then, the person can still maintain a close relationship with Allah ﷻ. At the end, the person can receive something better than what the person has before inshaAllah.

It is again important to realize the adab with Allah ﷻ in the expressions of Khidr as. The sigah in فَأَرَدْنَا is mutakallim plural that taking the life of someone is not a pleasant action. The adab with Allah ﷻ requires not to render anything unpleasant with Allah ﷻ. Therefore, Allah ﷻ creates

---

177. As for that boat, it belonged to some needy people who toiled upon the sea—and I desired to damage it because [I knew that] behind them was a king who is wont to seize every boat by brute force.
178. 18:80 "And as for that young man, his parents were [true] believers—whereas we had every reason to fear that he would bring bitter grief upon them by [his] overweening wickedness and denial of all truth: (18:81) and so we desired that their Sustainer grant them in his stead [a child] of greater purity than him, and closer [to them] in loving tenderness.

the means for the death of people. Yet, everything happens with the Mashiyyah of Allah ﷻ.

[82]¹⁷⁹

وَأَمَّا الْجِدَارُ فَكَانَ لِغُلَامَيْنِ يَتِيمَيْنِ فِي الْمَدِينَةِ وَكَانَ تَحْتَهُ كَنزٌ لَّهُمَا وَكَانَ أَبُوهُمَا صَالِحًا فَأَرَادَ رَبُّكَ أَنْ يَبْلُغَا أَشُدَّهُمَا وَيَسْتَخْرِجَا كَنزَهُمَا رَحْمَةً مِّن رَّبِّكَ وَمَا فَعَلْتُهُ عَنْ أَمْرِي ذَلِكَ تَأْوِيلُ مَا لَمْ تَسْطِع عَّلَيْهِ صَبْرًا {الكهف/82}

The third case of evil-seeming incident is that we feel so sad about a case that the person is helpless such as a child, or people being in war that our mercy is so high that, astagfirullah, we think and question about the mercy of Allah ﷻ. But Allah ﷻ takes care of everything and plans as the Best Planner and as the Most Merciful as mentioned in the above ayah. Allah ﷻ gives the real ability and empowerment. One should remember that the person or agent is not the real implicit or explicit doer as mentioned by وَمَا فَعَلْتُهُ عَنْ أَمْرِي ذَلِكَ تَأْوِيلُ مَا لَمْ تَسْطِع عَّلَيْهِ صَبْرٌ ¹⁸⁰

The siga فَأَرَادَ رَبُّكَ¹⁸¹ mentions the direct interference of Allah ﷻ. As this is the case of an orphan, there is an indication that Allah ﷻ directly takes care of the needs of the orphans without any means. One can also remember the hadith of Rasulullah ﷺ that the person who raises an orphan will be very close to Rasulullah 3) ﷺ).

[83]¹⁸²

The next case is another agent or Prophet of Allah ﷻ, Zulqarnayn, but this time acting explicitly and has a position and strength to prevent evil in the society.

---

179. 18:82 "And as for that wall, it belonged to two orphan boys [living] in the town, and beneath it was [buried] a treasure belonging to them [by right]. Now their father had been a righteous man, and so thy Sustainer willed it that when they come of age they should bring forth their treasure by thy Sustainer's grace. "And I did not do (any of) this of my own accord: this is the real meaning of all [those events] that thou wert unable to bear with patience."
180. And I did not do (any of) this of my own accord: this is the real meaning of all [those events] that thou wert unable to bear with patience.
181. So thy Sustainer willed it.
182. 18:83 AND THEY will ask thee about the Two-Horned One. Say: "I will convey unto you something by which he ought to be remembered."

[84]¹⁸³

إِنَّا مَكَّنَّا لَهُ فِي الْأَرْضِ وَآتَيْنَاهُ مِن كُلِّ شَيْءٍ سَبَبًا {الكهف/84}

Allah ﷻ gives the real ability to the person or agent. They are not the real implicit or explicit doers as mentioned by this verse.

[85-88]¹⁸⁴

{ حَتَّى إِذَا بَلَغَ مَغْرِبَ الشَّمْسِ وَجَدَهَا تَغْرُبُ فِي عَيْنٍ حَمِئَةٍ وَوَجَدَ عِندَهَا قَوْمًا قُلْنَا يَا ذَا الْقَرْنَيْنِ إِمَّا أَن تُعَذِّبَ وَإِمَّا أَن تَتَّخِذَ فِيهِمْ حُسْنًا {الكهف/86} قَالَ أَمَّا مَن ظَلَمَ فَسَوْفَ نُعَذِّبُهُ ثُمَّ يُرَدُّ إِلَى رَبِّهِ فَيُعَذِّبُهُ عَذَابًا نُّكْرًا {الكهف/87} وَأَمَّا مَنْ آمَنَ وَعَمِلَ صَالِحًا فَلَهُ جَزَاءً الْحُسْنَى وَسَنَقُولُ لَهُ مِنْ أَمْرِنَا يُسْرًا {الكهف/88}

The first case is evil done openly as mentioned by the sun in the dirt... وَجَدَهَا تَغْرُبُ فِي عَيْنٍ حَمِئَةٍ¹⁸⁵. Allah ﷻ sends Zulqarnayn as to establish justice and to remove evil and oppression.

The second case of removing evil is removing life difficulties.

The third case is preventing evil of people oppressing others, والله اعلم.

If one compares the two cases of Khidr as and Zulqarnayn rh both are dealing and addressing the evil. In the cases of Khidr as , he is the special agent addressing and protecting the weak in a mysterious and unknown way to humans. The humans judge externally about these cases and they consider them as evil but they don't know that an agent of Allah ﷻ, Khidr as works to protect these weak people from evil and oppression.

In the second case, people are again weak but they encounter a figure of justice, a powerful human like Zulqarnayn as as the agent of Allah ﷻ. The people in this case see that the evil is prevented by someone and that they can externally judge that Allah ﷻ sends someone to help them. One

---

183. 18:84 Behold, We established him securely on earth, and endowed him with [the knowledge of] the right means to achieve anything [that he might set out to achieve]; (18:85) and so he chose the right means [in whatever he did]."

184. 18:86 Until, when he reached the setting of the sun [i.e., the west], he found it [as if] setting in a spring of dark mud, and he found near it a people. We [i.e., Allah جلاله] said, "O Dhul-Qarnayn, either you punish [them] or else adopt among them [a way of] goodness." 18:87 He said, "As for one who wrongs, we will punish him. Then he will be returned to his Lord, and He will punish him with a terrible punishment [i.e., Hellfire]. 18:88 But as for one who believes and does righteousness, he will have a reward of the best [i.e., Paradise], and we [i.e., Dhul-Qarnayn] will speak to him from our command with ease."

185. He found it [as if] setting in a spring of dark mud.

should note that Zul Qarnayn as constantly mentions that he is the agent of Allah ﷻ and acting with the help and empowerment of Allah ﷻ.

In both cases, Allah ﷻ helps humans and intervenes and prevents the evil. Now, the test or trial in all these cases are the attitude and perspectives of the person. Does the person blame Allah ﷻ in the first case astagfirullah, au'zu billah like we hear a lot? Or, does the person say Allah ﷻ sees me, watches me and takes care of me? Unfortunately, we don't hear this perspective much but only a few times. So, this is the real test and trial. Believing and trusting in Allah ﷻ in both cases of the visible and invisible seeming evil incidents is the key, الله اعلم.

إِنَّا مَكَّنَّا لَهُ فِي الْأَرْضِ وَآتَيْنَاهُ مِن كُلِّ شَيْءٍ سَبَبًا [186] {الكهف/84}

فَأَتْبَعَ سَبَبًا [187] {الكهف/85}

ثُمَّ أَتْبَعَ سَبَبًا {الكهف/89}

ثُمَّ أَتْبَعَ سَبَبًا {الكهف/92}

There are two critical words here سَبَبًا[188] and أَتْبَعَ[189]. The words sabab can show that Allah ﷻ created the reasons, causality and the relation between cause and effect. When the person understands this and follows as mentioned in أَتْبَعَ, then, the case of success can come in our world dimensions of causality. Here, it is specifically mentioned that Zulqarnayn follows the reasons, sabab, created by Allah ﷻ to achieve a goal.

The realm of Khidr as shows the opposite of this case as the human causality is no more valid. But, the Cause of all Causes, Allah ﷻ, Musabbabul Asbab has the authority of everything, allows, approves or disapproves.

---

186. Indeed, We established him upon the earth, and We gave him to everything a way [i.e., means].
187. So he followed a way.
188. A way.
189. Followed.

16

Sûrah Maryam

[39]¹⁹⁰

{مريم/39} وَأَنذِرْهُمْ يَوْمَ الْحَسْرَةِ إِذْ قُضِيَ الْأَمْرُ وَهُمْ فِي غَفْلَةٍ وَهُمْ لَا يُؤْمِنُونَ

It is important to analyze the word غَفْلَةٍ and its appearance in the Qurān. It may mean that there are facts that exist, but the person cannot be aware of. The person acts carelessly and he or she does not see, realize and embody them in one's life. For example, when a person really thinks about one's physical body, it really feels scary, awesome and disabling. In the sense that, for example, a person eats food but he or she is not in control of what is happening inside the body. The person does not know what is happening in his or her blood veins, cells, under his or her skin. This tafakkur, or reflection can put the person really in a position of losing one's mind if the person does not follow the teachings of Allah ﷻ about the essence of who we are. There should be an effort to break the rusts of غَفْلَةٍ¹⁹¹, carelessness or heedlessness. In the Oxford dictionary, the word carelessness is defined as (21):" not giving sufficient attention or thought" for avoiding harm or errors from something. The above ayah exactly mentions this as وَأَنذِرْهُمْ يَوْمَ الْحَسْرَةِ إِذْ قُضِيَ الْأَمْرُ وَهُمْ فِي غَفْلَةٍ that "warn them that they can give sufficient attention and thought so that they can avoid the harms, errors and problems in the Day of Self-Blame. People will be in blame mode in that Day so warn them now."

This word is present with different and similar meanings as :

{الأنبياء/1} اقْتَرَبَ لِلنَّاسِ حِسَابُهُمْ وَهُمْ فِي غَفْلَةٍ مَّعْرِضُونَ ¹⁹²

{ق/22} لَقَدْ كُنتَ فِي غَفْلَةٍ مِّنْ هَذَا فَكَشَفْنَا عَنكَ غِطَاءَكَ فَبَصَرُكَ الْيَوْمَ حَدِيدٌ ¹⁹³

---

190. (19:39) Hence, warn them of [the coming of] the Day of Regrets, when everything will have been decided—for as yet they are heedless, and they do not believe [in it].
191. Heedlessness.
192. [The time of] their account has approached for the people, while they are in heedlessness turning away.
193. [It will be said], "You were certainly in unmindfulness of this, and We have removed from you your cover, so your sight, this Day, is sharp."

Here is the case when the person accepts this fact:

وَاقْتَرَبَ الْوَعْدُ الْحَقُّ فَإِذَا هِيَ شَاخِصَةٌ أَبْصَارُ الَّذِينَ كَفَرُوا يَا وَيْلَنَا قَدْ كُنَّا فِي غَفْلَةٍ مِّنْ هَذَا بَلْ كُنَّا ظَالِمِينَ 194{الأنبياء/97}

In the below case:

وَاصْبِرْ نَفْسَكَ مَعَ الَّذِينَ يَدْعُونَ رَبَّهُم بِالْغَدَاةِ وَالْعَشِيِّ يُرِيدُونَ وَجْهَهُ وَلَا تَعْدُ عَيْنَاكَ عَنْهُمْ تُرِيدُ زِينَةَ الْحَيَاةِ الدُّنْيَا وَلَا تُطِعْ مَنْ أَغْفَلْنَا قَلْبَهُ عَن ذِكْرِنَا وَاتَّبَعَ هَوَاهُ وَكَانَ أَمْرُهُ فُرُطًا {الكهف/28}

When the person is in gaflah, then he or she follows his or her desires as mentioned وَلَا تُطِعْ مَنْ أَغْفَلْنَا قَلْبَهُ عَن ذِكْرِنَا وَاتَّبَعَ هَوَاهُ.

Another word important word to analyze is غَمْرَةٍ as mentioned below. فَذَرْهُمْ فِي غَمْرَتِهِمْ حَتَّى حِينٍ 195{المؤمنون/54}

بَلْ قُلُوبُهُمْ فِي غَمْرَةٍ مِّنْ هَذَا وَلَهُمْ أَعْمَالٌ مِن دُونِ ذَلِكَ هُمْ لَهَا عَامِلُونَ 196{المؤمنون/63}

الَّذِينَ هُمْ فِي غَمْرَةٍ سَاهُونَ {الذاريات/11}

We will inshAllah bring their analysis later in order to benefit from them further with the Tawfik of Allah ﷻ.

Sûrah Tāha

[17]197

وَمَا تِلْكَ بِيَمِينِكَ يَا مُوسَى

[18]198

قَالَ هِيَ عَصَايَ أَتَوَكَّأُ عَلَيْهَا وَأَهُشُّ بِهَا عَلَى غَنَمِي وَلِيَ فِيهَا مَآرِبُ أُخْرَى

---

194. And [when] the true promise [i.e., the resurrection] has approached; then suddenly the eyes of those who disbelieved will be staring [in horror, while they say], "O woe to us; we had been unmindful of this; rather, we were wrongdoers."
195. So leave them in their confusion for a time.
196. But their hearts are covered with confusion over this, and they have [evil] deeds besides that [i.e., disbelief] which they are doing.
197. (20:17) "Now, what is this in thy right hand, O Moses?"
198. 20:18 He answered: "It is my staff; I lean on it; and with it I beat down leaves for my sheep; and [many] other uses have I for it."

Allah ☙ is teaching Musa (as) not to make tawakkul, اًأَتَوَكَّأ[199], anything external other than Allah ☙. In this case, the external can be the staff for Musa as to rely on. The only Being truly trusted and relied on is Allah ☙. Internally, Allah ☙ is teaching that there is nothing to make tawakkul upon, except Allah ☙. The following verse mentions this:

22[200]

وَاضْمُمْ يَدَكَ إِلَى جَنَاحِكَ تَخْرُجْ بَيْضَاء مِنْ غَيْرِ سُوءٍ آيَةً أُخْرَى

Another reliance point in this case is the hand of a person. Since, someone's hand is the tool that a person can rely on to do an action or work. When a person gets signals from his or her heart or mind, the executing organ is the hand. When Musa as understands this, to reach this level of tawakkul, he (as) makes dua to Allah ☙ and says:

25[201]

قَالَ رَبِّ اشْرَحْ لِي صَدْرِي

which can translate as "Oh, Allah ☙, to reach that level of internal and external reliance, not to make reliance on anything except You, not to make any tawakkul except you, Oh Allah ☙, please open my chest and heart."

[83-84][202]

وَمَا أَعْجَلَكَ عَن قَوْمِكَ يَا مُوسَى {طه/83} قَالَ هُمْ أُولَاء عَلَى أَثَرِي وَعَجِلْتُ إِلَيْكَ رَبِّ لِتَرْضَى {طه/84}

قَالَ فَإِنَّا قَدْ فَتَنَّا قَوْمَكَ مِن بَعْدِكَ وَأَضَلَّهُمُ السَّامِرِيُّ[203] {طه/85}

---

199. Lean on.
200. (20:22) "Now place thy hand within thy armpit: it will come forth [shining] white, without blemish, as another sign [of Our grace],
201. 20:25 Said [Moses]: "O my Sustainer! Open up my heart [to Thy light],
202. 20:83 [AND GOD SAID:] "Now what has caused thee, O Moses, to leave thy people behind in so great a haste?" (20:84) He answered: "They are treading in my footsteps while I have hastened unto Thee, O my Sustainer, so that Thou might be well-pleased [with me]."
203. [Allah جل جلاله] said, "But indeed, We have tried your people after you [departed], and the Sāmiri has led them astray."

Allah ﷻ knows everything. The questions directed by Allah ﷻ for us to learn and to reveal the batin or the true reality of the incidents that humans are not aware of because they are limited and they act and judge with the apparent.

In this case, besides the apparent meanings as mentioned in the tafasir, the expression وَمَا أَعْجَلَكَ عَن قَوْمِكَ can allude to the difficult balance between one's responsibilities towards others and the desire and rush to spend time with Allah ﷻ as mentioned وَعَجِلْتُ إِلَيْكَ رَبِّ لِتَرْضَى {طه/84}[204]. If this balance is missed, sometimes a test or trial can hit the person as the next ayah mentions قَالَ فَإِنَّا قَدْ فَتَنَّا قَوْمَكَ مِن بَعْدِكَ وَأَضَلَّهُمُ السَّامِرِيُّ{طه/85}.

Another example for this can be the case of Jurayj as mentioned by the Prophet 9) ﷺ). Jurayj (rh) was in deep desire to spend time with Allah ﷻ in worship but yet he happened to overlook the call of his mother when she called him. Then, as it is mentioned in the hadith that there was a test and a trial for Jurayj (rh). In both cases of Musa as and Jurayj rh, Allah ﷻ helped them and made them pass the test because they both desired Allah ﷻ above everything. Yet, both incidents teach us the case of balance to minimize the tests and trials in our lives, الله أعلم.

[120][205]

فَوَسْوَسَ إِلَيْهِ الشَّيْطَانُ قَالَ يَا آدَمُ هَلْ أَدُلُّكَ عَلَى شَجَرَةِ الْخُلْدِ وَمُلْكٍ لَّا يَبْلَى {طه/120}

وَيَا آدَمُ اسْكُنْ أَنتَ وَزَوْجُكَ الْجَنَّةَ فَكُلاَ مِنْ حَيْثُ شِئْتُمَا وَلاَ تَقْرَبَا هَذِهِ الشَّجَرَةَ فَتَكُونَا مِنَ الظَّالِمِينَ {الأعراف/19}[206] فَوَسْوَسَ لَهُمَا الشَّيْطَانُ لِيُبْدِيَ لَهُمَا مَا وُورِيَ عَنْهُمَا مِن سَوْءَاتِهِمَا وَقَالَ مَا نَهَاكُمَا رَبُّكُمَا عَنْ هَذِهِ الشَّجَرَةِ إِلاَّ أَن تَكُونَا مَلَكَيْنِ أَوْ تَكُونَا مِنَ الْخَالِدِينَ {الأعراف/20}[207]

When the person is prohibited from doing something, the temptation or waswasa of human nature or tendency makes the person incline towards it. It is natural or normal to fall into sin, error, something harmful even though one can instruct and warn a person or a child the harmful

---

204. And I hastened to You, my Lord, that You be pleased."
205. 20:120 But Satan whispered unto him, saying: "O Adam! Shall I lead thee to the tree of life eternal; and [thus] to a kingdom that will never decay?"
206. And "O Adam, dwell, you and your wife, in Paradise and eat from wherever you will but do not approach this tree, lest you be among the wrongdoers."
207. But Satan whispered to them to make apparent to them that which was concealed from them of their private parts. He said, "Your Lord did not forbid you this tree except that you become angels or become the immortal."

outcomes of this engagement. As mentioned by the Prophet صلى الله عليه
وسلم (26), there is the normalization of this concept that it is normal to
make mistakes, sins or errors but the best one is the one who accepts one's
mistake and turns to Allah ﷻ with inabah, repentance and humbleness as
exemplified by Adam as. So, this approach can be important in both adult
and child education, the emphasis of teaching the notion of normalizing
the mistakes but then the most important thing is to ask forgiveness from
Allah ﷻ and to connect again and again. The methodology of not being a
perfect human being should come first but the teaching of what to do if
one makes a mistake in childhood and adult education is paramount[208].

وَقَاسَمَهُمَا إِنِّي لَكُمَا لَمِنَ النَّاصِحِينَ لأعراف/21} فَدَلَّاهُمَا بِغُرُور فَلَمَّا ذَاقَا الشَّجَرَةَ بَدَتْ
لَهُمَا سَوْءَاتُهُمَا وَطَفِقَا يَخْصِفَانِ عَلَيْهِمَا مِن وَرَقِ الْجَنَّةِ وَنَادَاهُمَا رَبُّهُمَا أَلَمْ أَنْهَكُمَا عَن
تِلْكُمَا الشَّجَرَةِ وَأَقُل لَّكُمَا إِنَّ الشَّيْطَآنَ لَكُمَا عَدُوٌّ مُبِين {لأعراف/22} قَالاَ رَبَّنَا ظَلَمْنَا
أَنفُسَنَا وَإِن لَّمْ تَغْفِرْ لَنَا وَتَرْحَمْنَا لَنَكُونَنَّ مِنَ الْخَاسِرِينَ

As seen in the above ayah, for Shaytan, it is not easy to make zalla of
Adam as. Shaytan was swearing and Adam as did not know a possible
being or creation who would be swearing and yet at the same time
possibly lying. Possibly, Adam as could have forgotten the command of
Allah ﷻ that he should not have approached to that tree, as the name of
the human is al-insān, the one who forgets, الله اعلم. Again, the role model
attitude of Adam as and our mother Hawwa as reveals itself as below:

قَالاَ رَبَّنَا ظَلَمْنَا أَنفُسَنَا وَإِن لَّمْ تَغْفِرْ لَنَا وَتَرْحَمْنَا لَنَكُونَنَّ مِنَ الْخَاسِرِينَ

This should be the approach to learn and to teach in the relationship
with Allah ﷻ. The approach is resetting one's position with the Creator,
Rabbul Alamin, and asking forgiveness.

One can see possibly that Adam as may have wanted to worship like
angels and forget the prohibition of Allah ﷻ about that the tree when
فَوَسْوَسَ إِلَيْهِ الشَّيْطَانُ قَالَ يَا آدَمُ هَلْ أَدُلُّكَ عَلَى شَجَرَةِ الْخُلْدِ وَمُلْكٍ لَّا يَبْلَى {طه/120}[209]

---

208. And he swore [by Allah جل جلاله] to them, "Indeed, I am to you from among the sincere
advisors." So he made them fall, through deception. And when they tasted of the tree, their
private parts became apparent to them, and they began to fasten together over themselves
from the leaves of Paradise. And their Lord called to them, "Did I not forbid you from that
tree and tell you that Satan is to you a clear enemy?" They said, "Our Lord, we have wronged
ourselves, and if You do not forgive us and have mercy upon us, we will surely be among the
losers."

209. Then Satan whispered to him; he said, "O Adam, shall I direct you to the tree of eternity
and possession that will not deteriorate?"

[130]²¹⁰

{ فَاصْبِرْ عَلَى مَا يَقُولُونَ وَسَبِّحْ بِحَمْدِ رَبِّكَ قَبْلَ طُلُوعِ الشَّمْسِ وَقَبْلَ غُرُوبِهَا وَمِنْ آنَاءِ اللَّيْلِ فَسَبِّحْ وَأَطْرَافَ النَّهَارِ لَعَلَّكَ تَرْضَى {طه/130} }

The pleasure of Allah ﷻ comes with Sabr. Similarly, one can review the ayah

فَاصْبِرْ عَلَى مَا يَقُولُونَ وَسَبِّحْ بِحَمْدِ رَبِّكَ قَبْلَ طُلُوعِ الشَّمْسِ وَقَبْلَ الْغُرُوبِ {ق/39}²¹¹.

The importance and easiness in the application of patience can be achieved if and when a person engages oneself with dhikr, tasbih with hamd before sunrise and sunset. These may be the times when a person can embody the power of patience if the person engages herself or himself with remembrance of Allah ﷻ especially around these times of the day. In a broader perspective, the effect of قَبْلَ طُلُوعٍ²¹² can continue all day and the effect of وَقَبْلَ الْغُرُوبِ²¹³ can continue all night, الله اعلم.

In other words, the sabr is easy to implement with the engagement of oneself with refreshing breezes of dhikr, Qurān and prayers. It is very difficult to implement sabr if one is not engaged with those. Other engagements can help the person as well but as soon as the engagement is over the person can feel the pain. But, in the case of salah, the Qurān, and the duas and hadith from al-Habib, Rasulullah ﷺ, the engagement with them does not only feel better but the person at the same time has the power to have stamina for later times. The person can realize here the discussions of an active patience but not a depressive one. In other words, these engagements build up and strengthen one's spiritual power and stamina as one builds up muscles by physical training through different fitness strategies.

---

210. (20:130) Hence, bear with patience whatever they [who deny the truth] may say, and extol thy Sustainer's limitless glory and praise Him before the rising of the sun and before its setting; and extol His glory, too, during some of the hours of the night as well as during the hours of the day, so that thou might attain to happiness.

211. So be patient, [O Muhammad], over what they say and exalt [Allah جل جلاله] with praise of your Lord before the rising of the sun and before its setting.

212. Before the rising [of the sun].

213. And before its setting.

17

Sûrah Anbiyã

[10][214]

{الأنبياء/10} لَقَدْ أَنزَلْنَا إِلَيْكُمْ كِتَابًا فِيهِ ذِكْرُكُمْ أَفَلَا تَعْقِلُونَ

In the expression لَقَدْ أَنزَلْنَا إِلَيْكُمْ[215] , the word إِلَيْكُمْ[216] can show the personal relevance of each person with the Qurān as if the Qurān is revealed to him or her. In its formal language of revelation, the Qurān is revealed to the Prophet صلى الله عليه وسلم with the proposition علي instead of الى. In other words, علي indicates the Qurān being revealed to the main and essential source, to Rasulullah ﷺ. Then, in the resulting effects, the reflections of this initial source is coming on the heart of each individual.

[35][217]

{الأنبياء/35} كُلُّ نَفْسٍ ذَائِقَةُ الْمَوْتِ وَنَبْلُوكُم بِالشَّرِّ وَالْخَيْرِ فِتْنَةً وَإِلَيْنَا تُرْجَعُونَ

{العنكبوت/57}[218] كُلُّ نَفْسٍ ذَائِقَةُ الْمَوْتِ ثُمَّ إِلَيْنَا تُرْجَعُونَ

It is interesting in the above ayahs that death is mentioned with the word ذَائِقَة, to taste. In this perspective, death is not something to be scared of as humans fear and depressed, but as presented here, it can be something to be the opposite as mentioned in its wording, الله اعلم.

[87][219]

وَذَا النُّونِ إِذ ذَهَبَ مُغَاضِبًا فَظَنَّ أَن لَّن نَّقْدِرَ عَلَيْهِ فَنَادَى فِي الظُّلُمَاتِ أَن لَّا إِلَهَ إِلَّا أَنتَ سُبْحَانَكَ إِنِّي كُنتُ مِنَ الظَّالِمِينَ (87)

---

214. 21:10 [O MEN!] We have now bestowed upon you from on high a divine writ containing all that you ought to bear in mind: will you not, then, use your reason?
215. [O MEN!] We have now bestowed upon you.
216. Upon you.
217. 21:35 Every human being is bound to taste death; and We test you [all] through the bad and the good [things of life] by way of trial: and unto Us you all must return.
218. Every soul will taste death. Then to Us will you be returned.
219. 21:87 AND [remember] him of the great fish—when he went off in wrath, thinking that We had no power over him! But then he cried out in the deep darkness [of his distress]: "There is no deity save Thee! Limitless art Thou in Thy glory! Verily, I have done wrong!"

One can ask what makes the dua of Yûnus as so special? In the expression, لَا إِلَهَ إِلَّا أَنْتَ سُبْحَانَكَ إِنِّي كُنْتُ مِنَ الظَّالِمِينَ[220], the first part is the tawhid with لَا إِلَهَ إِلَّا أَنْتَ, then tanzih and tasbih with سُبْحَانَكَ and then the position of the person as a being of nothing and at the same time oppressing oneself constantly in reality as with the expression إِنِّي كُنْتُ مِنَ الظَّالِمِينَ. All the oppressions can be removed with the Tawfik of Allah .

[92][221]

إِنَّ هَذِهِ أُمَّتُكُمْ أُمَّةً وَاحِدَةً وَأَنَا رَبُّكُمْ فَاعْبُدُونِ {الأنبياء/92}

This is a very universal and inclusive verse that each time one reads it, one can reset who one's ummah is and one can imagine that collectively we are in front of our Rabb, Rabbul Alamin, Allah , , Azza wa Jal, Ar-Rahmān, Ar-Rahìm. Because in the previous ayahs, Allah mentions all the anbiya with their names as the name of this Sûrah is Sûrah anbiya. Therefore, this ayah becomes very conclusive, inclusive and universal as إِنَّ هَذِهِ أُمَّتُكُمْ أُمَّةً وَاحِدَةً وَأَنَا رَبُّكُمْ فَاعْبُدُونِ

Then, Allah puts in perspectives who the real ummah and the Creator is. Then, this true ummah, in their essence and core are the prophets, role models and real khalifahs represent as this ummah, the pure, true and genuine agents to follow. Once the person establishes this perspective, one can establish the tawhid and the ubudiyah. Most of the people accept Allah in tawhid, uluhiyah and rububiyah. But, then, they worship and practice wrong and not genuine things. In reality, this should also follow along with the true worship and practice in religion. As the Qurān addresses different problems of imān as some have issues with uluhiyah and some with rububiyah and some with ubudiyah. In its true sense as the Prophet mentions, a Muslim can have still remnants of these three problems internally or implicitly but not externally or explicitly as in the case of riya, showing off mentioned by the Prophet similar to a black ant walking in the dark (12). This can be an implicit shirk. It may be very difficult to detect it. In this perspective, one can review the meanings of the true ubudiyah to Allah in the Qurān around word of ubudiyah that is mentioned in different verses. For example,

---

220. There is no deity save Thee! Limitless art Thou in Thy glory! Verily, I have done wrong.
221. 21:92 VERILY, [O you who believe in Me,] this community of yours is one single community, since I am the Sustainer of you all: worship, then, Me [alone]!

يَا عِبَادِيَ الَّذِينَ آمَنُوا إِنَّ أَرْضِي وَاسِعَةٌ فَإِيَّايَ فَاعْبُدُونِ ²²²{العنكبوت/56} كُلُّ نَفْسٍ
ذَائِقَةُ الْمَوْتِ ثُمَّ إِلَيْنَا تُرْجَعُونَ ²²³{العنكبوت/57}

The above verses engage people with the excuse of leaving their worship to Allah ﷻ due to different reasons of difficulties in practicing one's religion in a specific location. Allah ﷻ reminds them to leave that place as the life is short and one should keep this in perspective and stay focused.

إِنَّا أَنزَلْنَا إِلَيْكَ الْكِتَابَ بِالْحَقِّ فَاعْبُدِ اللَّهَ مُخْلِصًا لَّهُ الدِّينَ ²²⁴{الزمر/2}

قُلْ إِنِّي أُمِرْتُ أَنْ أَعْبُدَ اللَّهَ مُخْلِصًا لَّهُ الدِّينَ ²²⁵{الزمر/11} وَأُمِرْتُ لِأَنْ أَكُونَ أَوَّلَ
الْمُسْلِمِينَ ²²⁶{الزمر/12} قُلْ إِنِّي أَخَافُ إِنْ عَصَيْتُ رَبِّي عَذَابَ يَوْمٍ عَظِيمٍ ²²⁷{الزمر/13}
قُلِ اللَّهَ أَعْبُدُ مُخْلِصًا لَّهُ دِينِي ²²⁸{الزمر/14} فَاعْبُدُوا مَا شِئْتُم مِّن دُونِهِ قُلْ إِنَّ الْخَاسِرِينَ
الَّذِينَ خَسِرُوا أَنفُسَهُمْ وَأَهْلِيهِمْ يَوْمَ الْقِيَامَةِ أَلَا ذَٰلِكَ هُوَ الْخُسْرَانُ الْمُبِينُ ²²⁹{الزمر/15}

The above verses show the true and sincere worship, ubudiyah to Allah ﷻ. There is no true and pure tawhid when one includes other partners implicitly or explicitly in ubudiyah, uluhiyah or rububiyyah.

بَلِ اللَّهَ فَاعْبُدْ وَكُن مِّنَ الشَّاكِرِينَ {الزمر/٦٦} وَمَا قَدَرُوا اللَّهَ حَقَّ قَدْرِهِ وَالْأَرْضُ
جَمِيعًا قَبْضَتُهُ يَوْمَ الْقِيَامَةِ وَالسَّمَاوَاتُ مَطْوِيَّاتٌ بِيَمِينِهِ سُبْحَانَهُ وَتَعَالَىٰ عَمَّا يُشْرِكُونَ
{الزمر/٦٧}

---

222. O My servants who have believed, indeed My earth is spacious, so worship only Me.
223. Every soul will taste death. Then to Us will you be returned.
224. Indeed, We have sent down to you the Book, [O Muhammad], in truth. So worship Allah جل جلاله, [being] sincere to Him in religion.
225. Say, [O Muhammad], "Indeed, I have been commanded to worship Allah جل جلاله, [being] sincere to Him in religion.
226. And I have been commanded to be the first [among you] of the Muslims."
227. Say, "Indeed I fear, if I should disobey my Lord, the punishment of a tremendous Day."
228. Say, "Allah جل جلاله [alone] do I worship, sincere to Him in my religion.
229. So worship what you will besides Him." Say, "Indeed, the losers are the ones who will lose themselves and their families on the Day of Resurrection. Unquestionably, that is the manifest loss."

[230]The above verse mentions the relationship between worship, ubududiyah and appreciation and shukr. By not making ibadah to Allah ﷻ, humans really don't appreciate Allah ﷻ. What a loss on their part!

{ وَلَمَّا جَاءَ عِيسَى بِالْبَيِّنَاتِ قَالَ قَدْ جِئْتُكُم بِالْحِكْمَةِ وَلِأُبَيِّنَ لَكُم بَعْضَ الَّذِي تَخْتَلِفُونَ فِيهِ فَاتَّقُوا اللَّهَ وَأَطِيعُونِ 231{الزخرف/63} إِنَّ اللَّهَ هُوَ رَبِّي وَرَبُّكُمْ فَاعْبُدُوهُ هَذَا صِرَاطٌ مُّسْتَقِيمٌ 232{الزخرف/64} فَاخْتَلَفَ الْأَحْزَابُ مِن بَيْنِهِمْ فَوَيْلٌ لِّلَّذِينَ ظَلَمُوا مِنْ عَذَابِ يَوْمٍ أَلِيمٍ 233{الزخرف/56} }

Above, in Sûrah Zukhruf is an interesting case, Allah ﷻ mentions the case of Isa as. Isa as orders his followers to worship Allah ﷻ Who is the Creator of both Isa as and all humans as mentioned in the ayah. Then, it mentions فَاخْتَلَفَ الْأَحْزَابُ مِن بَيْنِهِمْ [234] can show the Christians' perspective as a problem on rububiyah, and ubududiyah in this verse but also with Uluhiyah as mentioned in other verses.

وَإِنَّ اللَّهَ رَبِّي وَرَبُّكُمْ فَاعْبُدُوهُ هَذَا صِرَاطٌ مُّسْتَقِيمٌ 235{مريم/36}

The above mentions the true correct path, sirat mustaqim is with the true worship of Allah ﷻ. Both go hand in hand. In other words, amal and imān are together.

رَبُّ السَّمَاوَاتِ وَالْأَرْضِ وَمَا بَيْنَهُمَا فَاعْبُدْهُ وَاصْطَبِرْ لِعِبَادَتِهِ هَلْ تَعْلَمُ لَهُ سَمِيًّا 236{مريم/65}

---

230. Rather, worship [only] Allah جل جلاله and be among the grateful.
They have not appraised Allah جل جلاله with true appraisal, while the earth entirely will be [within] His grip on the Day of Resurrection, and the heavens will be folded in His right hand. Exalted is He and high above what they associate with Him.
231. And when Jesus brought clear proofs, he said, "I have come to you with wisdom [i.e., prophethood] and to make clear to you some of that over which you differ, so fear Allah جل جلاله and obey me.
232. Indeed, Allah جل جلاله is my Lord and your Lord, so worship Him. This is a straight path."
233. But the denominations from among them differed [and separated], so woe to those who have wronged from the punishment of a painful Day.
234. But the denominations from among them differed [and separated].
235. [Jesus said], "And indeed, Allah جل جلاله is my Lord and your Lord, so worship Him. That is a straight path."
236. Lord of the heavens and the earth and whatever is between them—so worship Him and have patience for His worship. Do you know of any similarity to Him?"

The above shows why one should worship to Allah ﷻ with full tawhid. Tawhid has rububiyah[237], uluhiyah[238], and ubudiyah[239]. In other words, first establishing the true tawhid in rububiyah to know who takes care of everything in the universe. Then, this should be the reason why one should have the true tawhid with ubudiyah, worship only Allah ﷻ. Tawhid in uluhiyah necessitates recognizing explicitly one Creator as a creed. In all cases, one recognizes the Oneness of Allah ﷻ in the creed of belief as the tawhid in uluhiyah, the Oneness of Allah ﷻ as the care taker of everything in the universe as the tawhid in rububiyah, and reflecting this Oneness of Allah ﷻ in the worship and worshipping only to Allah ﷻ alone but nothing else as the tawhid in ubudiyah. When this is all accomplished then the sincere belief without any partners to Allah ﷻ can be embodied in oneself. This can be called ikhlas.

$$ \{14/طه\}^{240} \ إِنَّنِي أَنَا اللَّهُ لَا إِلَهَ إِلَّا أَنَا فَاعْبُدْنِي وَأَقِمِ الصَّلَاةَ لِذِكْرِي $$

Again, after one knows the true tawhid in uluhiyah, then this should lead to immediately tawhid in ubudiyah, that the person should worship only Allah ﷻ. The highest form of worship is the salah for showing tawhid in ubudiyah. The reason, outcome and the fruit of all ubudiyah is dhikr of Allah ﷻ. In other words, dhikr is being always in the presence of Allah ﷻ. The true dhikr is ihsan at all the times in one's life as mentioned by Hadith Jibril (3).

$$ \{25/الأنبياء\}^{241} \ وَمَا أَرْسَلْنَا مِن قَبْلِكَ مِن رَّسُولٍ إِلَّا نُوحِي إِلَيْهِ أَنَّهُ لَا إِلَهَ إِلَّا أَنَا فَاعْبُدُونِ $$

As mentioned in the above ayah, these teachings are not something new. As very meaningfully mentioned by Allah ﷻ in the Sûrah of anbiya that Allah ﷻ send at different times the same message with different messengers that the Creator is one and everyone should recognize this truly and worship Allah ﷻ purely and solely with ikhlas.

---

237. Lordship.
238. Realm of power.
239. Servanthood.
240. Indeed, I am Allah جل جلاله. There is no deity except Me, so worship Me and establish prayer for My remembrance.
241. And We sent not before you any messenger except that We revealed to him that, "There is no deity except Me, so worship Me."

إِنَّ رَبَّكُمُ اللّهُ الَّذِي خَلَقَ السَّمَاوَاتِ وَالأَرْضَ فِي سِتَّةِ أَيَّامٍ ثُمَّ اسْتَوَى عَلَى الْعَرْشِ يُدَبِّرُ الأَمْرَ مَا مِن شَفِيعٍ إِلاَّ مِن بَعْدِ إِذْنِهِ ذَلِكُمُ اللّهُ رَبُّكُمْ فَاعْبُدُوهُ أَفَلاَ تَذَكَّرُونَ 242 {يونس/3}

The above ayah can be translated as "After all these signs of rububiyah and uluhiyah, why don't you worship to Allah ﷻ? Don't you think?"

وَلِلّهِ غَيْبُ السَّمَاوَاتِ وَالأَرْضِ وَإِلَيْهِ يُرْجَعُ الأَمْرُ كُلُّهُ فَاعْبُدْهُ وَتَوَكَّلْ عَلَيْهِ وَمَا رَبُّكَ بِغَافِلٍ عَمَّا تَعْمَلُونَ 243 {هود/123}

After this, if they don't worship, and recognize Allah ﷻ, you worship and make tawakkul to Allah ﷻ. Allah ﷻ knows all the realities of unseen, the future, their end. Don't worry Allah ﷻ is All Aware of with their heedlessness.

[108]²⁴⁴

قُلْ إِنَّمَا يُوحَى إِلَيَّ أَنَّمَا إِلَهُكُمْ إِلَهٌ وَاحِدٌ فَهَلْ أَنتُم مُّسْلِمُونَ {الأنبياء/108}

Allah ﷻ in the Qurān gives different avenues, paths and approaches in one's personal spiritual journey so that the person can grab one and say that "I believe in and appreciate Allah ﷻ." Above is one of the discourses or paths, after going through all different possibilities explaining to us, Allah ﷻ instructs the Prophet ﷺ to say that finally : "I am being instructed that Your Creator is One." After this are you going to believe?

The expression فَهَلْ أَنتُم²⁴⁵ can be a position of all possible paths, and discourses presented and after all this "Are you not going to follow? Are you not going to be appreciative? Are you not going to leave the evil and your bad habits? Such as:

---

242. Indeed, your Lord is Allah جل جلاله, who created the heavens and the earth in six days and then established Himself above the Throne, arranging the matter [of His creation]. There is no intercessor except after His permission. That is Allah جل جلاله, your Lord, so worship Him. Then will you not remember?

243. And to Allah جل جلاله belong the unseen [aspects] of the heavens and the earth and to Him will be returned the matter, all of it, so worship Him and rely upon Him. And your Lord is not unaware of that which you do.

244. (21:108) Say: "It has but been revealed unto me103 that your God is the One and Only God: will you, then, surrender yourselves unto Him?"

245. Will you, then.

فَإِن لَّمْ يَسْتَجِيبُواْ لَكُمْ فَاعْلَمُواْ أَنَّمَا أُنزِلِ بِعِلْمِ اللَّهِ وَأَن لاَّ إِلَهَ إِلاَّ هُوَ <u>فَهَلْ أَنتُم مُّسْلِمُونَ</u>
{هود/14}[246]

وَعَلَّمْنَاهُ صَنْعَةَ لَبُوسٍ لَّكُمْ لِتُحْصِنَكُم مِّن بَأْسِكُمْ <u>فَهَلْ أَنتُمْ</u> شَاكِرُونَ[247]{الأنبياء/80}

إِنَّمَا يُرِيدُ الشَّيْطَانُ أَن يُوقِعَ بَيْنَكُمُ الْعَدَاوَةَ وَالْبَغْضَاء فِي الْخَمْرِ وَالْمَيْسِرِ وَيَصُدَّكُمْ عَن
ذِكْرِ اللَّهِ وَعَنِ الصَّلاَةِ <u>فَهَلْ أَنتُم مُّنتَهُونَ</u>[248] {المائدة/91}

Sûrah Hajj

[1-2][249]

يَا أَيُّهَا النَّاسُ اتَّقُوا رَبَّكُمْ إِنَّ زَلْزَلَةَ السَّاعَةِ شَيْءٌ عَظِيمٌ {الحج/1} يَوْمَ تَرَوْنَهَا تَذْهَلُ
كُلُّ مُرْضِعَةٍ عَمَّا أَرْضَعَتْ وَتَضَعُ كُلُّ ذَاتِ حَمْلٍ حَمْلَهَا وَتَرَى النَّاسَ سُكَارَى وَمَا هُم
بِسُكَارَى وَلَكِنَّ عَذَابَ اللَّهِ شَدِيدٌ {الحج/2}

The name of this Sûrah is Hajj. The first verses of the Sûrah depict the
End of Time and the Day of Judgment. The rituals of hajj according to
some scholars also depicts the End of Time and the Day of Judgment.

---

246. And if they do not respond to you—then know that it [i.e., the Qurān] was revealed with
the knowledge of Allah جل جلاله and that there is no deity except Him. Then, would you [not]
be Muslims?
247. And We taught him the fashioning of coats of armor to protect you from your [enemy in]
battle. So will you then be grateful?
248. Satan only wants to cause between you animosity and hatred through intoxicants and
gambling and to avert you from the remembrance of Allah جل جلاله and from prayer. So will
you not desist?
249. 22:1 O MEN! Be conscious of your Sustainer: for, verily, the violent convulsion of the
Last Hour will be an awesome thing! (22:2) On the Day when you behold it, every woman
that feeds a child at her breast will utterly forget her nursling, and every woman heavy with
child will bring forth her burden [before her time]; and it will seem to thee that all mankind
is drunk, although they will not be drunk—but vehement will be [their dread of] God's
chastisement.

[30-38]²⁵⁰

ذَلِكَ وَمَن يُعَظِّمْ حُرُمَاتِ اللَّهِ فَهُوَ خَيْرٌ لَّهُ عِندَ رَبِّهِ وَأُحِلَّتْ لَكُمُ الْأَنْعَامُ إِلَّا مَا يُتْلَى عَلَيْكُمْ فَاجْتَنِبُوا الرِّجْسَ مِنَ الْأَوْثَانِ وَاجْتَنِبُوا قَوْلَ الزُّورِ {الحج/30}

حُنَفَاء لِلَّهِ غَيْرَ مُشْرِكِينَ بِهِ وَمَن يُشْرِكْ بِاللَّهِ فَكَأَنَّمَا خَرَّ مِنَ السَّمَاء فَتَخْطَفُهُ الطَّيْرُ أَوْ تَهْوِي بِهِ الرِّيحُ فِي مَكَانٍ سَحِيقٍ {الحج/31} ذَلِكَ وَمَن يُعَظِّمْ شَعَائِرَ اللَّهِ فَإِنَّهَا مِن تَقْوَى الْقُلُوبِ {الحج/32} لَكُمْ فِيهَا مَنَافِعُ إِلَى أَجَلٍ مُّسَمًّى ثُمَّ مَحِلُّهَا إِلَى الْبَيْتِ الْعَتِيقِ {الحج/33} وَلِكُلِّ أُمَّةٍ جَعَلْنَا مَنسَكًا لِيَذْكُرُوا اسْمَ اللَّهِ عَلَى مَا رَزَقَهُم مِّن بَهِيمَةِ الْأَنْعَامِ فَإِلَهُكُمْ إِلَهٌ وَاحِدٌ فَلَهُ أَسْلِمُوا وَبَشِّرِ الْمُخْبِتِينَ {الحج/34} الَّذِينَ إِذَا ذُكِرَ اللَّهُ وَجِلَتْ قُلُوبُهُمْ وَالصَّابِرِينَ عَلَى مَا أَصَابَهُمْ وَالْمُقِيمِي الصَّلَاةِ وَمِمَّا رَزَقْنَاهُمْ يُنفِقُونَ {الحج/35} وَالْبُدْنَ جَعَلْنَاهَا لَكُم مِّن شَعَائِرِ اللَّهِ لَكُمْ فِيهَا خَيْرٌ فَاذْكُرُوا اسْمَ اللَّهِ عَلَيْهَا صَوَافَّ فَإِذَا وَجَبَتْ جُنُوبُهَا فَكُلُوا مِنْهَا وَأَطْعِمُوا الْقَانِعَ وَالْمُعْتَرَّ كَذَلِكَ سَخَّرْنَاهَا لَكُمْ لَعَلَّكُمْ تَشْكُرُونَ {الحج/36} لَن يَنَالَ اللَّهَ لُحُومُهَا وَلَا دِمَاؤُهَا وَلَكِن يَنَالُهُ التَّقْوَى مِنكُمْ كَذَلِكَ سَخَّرَهَا لَكُمْ لِتُكَبِّرُوا اللَّهَ عَلَى مَا هَدَاكُمْ وَبَشِّرِ الْمُحْسِنِينَ {الحج/37} إِنَّ اللَّهَ يُدَافِعُ عَنِ الَّذِينَ آمَنُوا إِنَّ اللَّهَ لَا يُحِبُّ كُلَّ خَوَّانٍ كَفُورٍ {الحج/38}

The above ayahs are very interesting and dense. One can review the history of world religions, and why Allah ﷻ has constantly sent religions

---

250. 30.That [has been commanded], and whoever honors the sacred ordinances of Allah جل جلاله —it is best for him in the sight of his Lord. And permitted to you are the grazing livestock, except what is recited to you. So avoid the uncleanliness of idols and avoid false statement. 31.Inclining [only] to Allah جل جلاله, not associating [anything] with Him. And he who associates with Allah جل جلاله —it is as though he had fallen from the sky and was snatched by the birds or the wind carried him down into a remote place. 32. That [is so]. And whoever honors the symbols [i.e., rites] of Allah جل جلاله —indeed, it is from the piety of hearts. 33. For you therein [i.e., the animals marked for sacrifice] are benefits for a specified term then their place of sacrifice is at the ancient House. 34. And for all religion We have appointed a rite [of sacrifice] that they may mention the name of Allah جل جلاله over what He has provided for them of [sacrificial] animals. For your god is one God, so to Him submit. And, [O Muhammad], give good tidings to the humble [before their Lord].35. Who, when Allah جل جلاله is mentioned, their hearts are fearful, and [to] the patient over what has afflicted them, and the establishers of prayer and those who spend from what We have provided them.36. And the camels and cattle We have appointed for you as among the symbols [i.e., rites] of Allah جل جلاله; for you therein is good. So mention the name of Allah جل جلاله upon them when lined up [for sacrifice]; and when they are [lifeless] on their sides, then eat from them and feed the needy [who does not seek aid] and the beggar. Thus have We subjected them to you that you may be grateful. 37. Their meat will not reach Allah جل جلاله, nor will their blood, but what reaches Him is piety from you. Thus have We subjected them to you that you may glorify Allah for that [to] which He has guided you; and give good tidings to the doers of good. 38. Indeed, Allah جل جلاله defends those who have believed. Indeed, Allah جل جلاله does not like everyone treacherous and ungrateful.

in their relationship around the key words and concepts of حُرُمَاتِ اللهِ,
شَعَائِرَ اللهِ[251], and مَنسَكًا[252].

One can see the possible human reality of being in a physical and
material world. Allah ﷻ accordingly sends some حُرُمَاتِ اللهِ, شَعَائِرَ اللهِ, and
مَنسَكًا in order to transform this human concrete or positivist thinking of
materialism into a genuine unlimited engagement of a true relationship
with One and Only Creator. In other words, Allah ﷻ mentions that these
are only sacred or holy symbols designated by Allah ﷻ. So, one should
understand their true value and place but not go beyond this symbolism.

For example, there are interpretations about the Kabah. When
people are gathered around the Kabah, it can be a symbolism of
Jannah, Heaven, when people will see Allah ﷻ which would be most
the pleasurable time in Heaven. As one can relate a lot of narrations
about the feelings of Azamah, greatness and awe, as one visits Makkah at
Haram looking at the Kabah hearing the Qurān in prayer recitation. The
feelings of azamah, awe, majesty, grandeur can be a tiny sample of when
the person is going to see Allah ﷻ in Jannah. Or, the gathering of people
around the Kabah can be a representation of people gathered in front of
Allah ﷻ and in the Judgment Day. The angels are present as well in the
Judgment Day as mentioned in Sûrah Fajr of the ayah 22. The people are
in their simple sheet clothes representing with detachments from all the
world both during the Hajj and in the Day of Judgment.

In all the engagements of belief, the transgression and false approaches
can occur in the over-cross of the boundaries of symbolism. In other
words, one cannot reach to the essence if there is no understanding of
literal versus figurative. Oppositely, one can approximate to the true
essence if the knowledge of boundaries is clear and distinctive. This
is especially true in the spiritual journeys and in the relationship with
Allah ﷻ within the realms and tools of the human mind and experience.

Allah ﷻ in the life of human history has sent the same message. This
is also mentioned here حُنَفَاء لِلَّهِ[253], and حُنَفَاء لِّلَّهِ غَيْرَ مُشْرِكِينَ بِهِ[254].

---

251. Anyone who honors the symbols set up by God.
252. A rite [of sacrifice].
253. Inclining [only] to Allah جل جلاله.
254. Inclining [only] to Allah جل جلاله, not associating [anything] with Him.

So, the true perspective is that accepting the teachings from Allah ﷻ with submission as a Muslim. Islam can mean to imply the main literal meanings that believing in Allah ﷻ purely as Allah ﷻ is One and Unique. At the same time, due to human needs of physicality or materiality in the world, Allah ﷻ orders humans to perform rituals which has sacred symbols as mentioned حُرُمَاتِ اللهِ, شَعَائِرَ اللهِ, and مَنسَكًا. But, in this practice, one should not attach divinity to these symbols and not make shirk but always be constantly حُنَفَاء لِلهِ غَيْرَ مُشْرِكِينَ بِه.

The practices of worshipping to the golden calf, picture depictions, or sculptures representing divinity are some examples of over crossing the boundaries of this physical or material engagements of humans. In these ayahs, Allah ﷻ underlines not making shirk with over crossing the boundaries as emphasized with the expressions حُنَفَاء لِلهِ, حُنَفَاء لِلهِ غَيْرَ, and مُشْرِكِينَ بِه. Yet, at the same time respecting the signs or symbols that are designated by Allah ﷻ as mentioned شَعَائِرَ اللهِ, حُرُمَاتِ اللهِ, and.

If one looks at Buddhism, there is the concept of sacrifice for their sacred ones or deities. If one looks at Judaism there is the concept of sacrifice. If one looks at Hinduism, there is the concept of sacrifice. There is the symbolic cleanliness with water or rivers. So, one can view and understand, when symbols are replaced with the essence.

In this perspective, Allah ﷻ is reminding to have respect to those symbols but without making shirk in other words taking the figurative as literal. It is highly possible that Allah ﷻ has sent similar messages for previous people but today we name them as different religions. The question is about the preservation of symbolism versus the essence. It is easy to be deviated from the original teachings. Therefore, as one final reminder to protect the essence, Allah ﷻ sent Islam and the Prophet ﷺ, as rahmatan lil alamin.

Muslims have this teaching clearly in the Qurān and in hadith and Sunnah of the Prophet ﷺ. But, in its small scale, Muslims have the possibilities of falling into shirk due to this symbolism versus essence. The Prophet صلى الله عليه وسلم mentions this categorically as small and big shirk. In this perspective, constant detachment and purification of the imān through salah, prayers, dhikr and istighfar are the key elements to safeguard one's imān in order not to do shirk.

Another interesting part in the below ayah

وَلِكُلِّ أُمَّةٍ جَعَلْنَا مَنسَكًا لِيَذْكُرُوا اسْمَ اللَّهِ عَلَى مَا رَزَقَهُم مِّن بَهِيمَةِ الْأَنْعَامِ فَإِلَهُكُمْ إِلَهٌ وَاحِدٌ فَلَهُ أَسْلِمُوا وَبَشِّرِ الْمُخْبِتِينَ 255 {الحج/34}

is the normalization of the notion of مَنسَكًا. This may have different symbolism of ibadah but in their essence, it is expected that all are for One and Unique Creator, Allah ﷺ but not making shirk. The normalization comes with the phrase وَلِكُلِّ أُمَّةٍ جَعَلْنَا مَنسَكًا256. Allah ﷺ sends possible symbolisms for all the ummahs, 18 الله اعلم

18

Sûrah Muminûn

[2] & [9]257

الَّذِينَ هُمْ فِي صَلَاتِهِمْ خَاشِعُونَ {المؤمنون/2}
وَالَّذِينَ هُمْ عَلَى صَلَوَاتِهِمْ يُحَافِظُونَ {المؤمنون/9}

If one can review above two verses that follow in the same Sûrah but separated by a few ayahs, one can see the similar but different discourses. The first one can signify a personal account in prayers, in nawafil especially increasing the husu' as mentioned in فِي صَلَاتِهِمْ خَاشِعُونَ258. The husu' is expressed with the harf jar فِي as if transfusing in the soul of the salah, prayer.

When the word salatihim, صَلَاتِهِم compared to salawatihim, صَلَوَاتِهِمْ259. which may signify the praying with jamah with continuation as mentioned yuhafizuun, يُحَافِظُونَ260. The harf jar عَلَى is mentioned to continue five prayers with jamaah as a requirement with the condition

---

255. And for all religion We have appointed a rite [of sacrifice] that they may mention the name of Allah جل جلاله over what He has provided for them of [sacrificial] animals. For your god is one God, so to Him submit. And, [O Muhammad], give good tidings to the humble [before their Lord].

256. And for all religion We have appointed a rite [of sacrifice].

257. (23:2) Those who humble themselves in their prayer.(23:9) And who guard their prayers [from all worldly intent].

258. Humble themselves in their prayer.

259. Their prayer.

260. Those who guard.

of submission, to follow the guidelines and rules of the sacred law, the
Qurān and the hadith.

[12-14]²⁶¹

وَلَقَدْ خَلَقْنَا الْإِنْسَانَ مِنْ سُلَالَةٍ مِنْ طِينٍ (١٢) ثُمَّ جَعَلْنَاهُ نُطْفَةً فِي قَرَارٍ مَكِينٍ (١٣) ثُمَّ
خَلَقْنَا النُّطْفَةَ عَلَقَةً فَخَلَقْنَا الْعَلَقَةَ مُضْغَةً فَخَلَقْنَا الْمُضْغَةَ عِظَامًا فَكَسَوْنَا الْعِظَامَ لَحْمًا ثُمَّ
أَنْشَأْنَاهُ خَلْقًا آخَرَ فَتَبَارَكَ اللهُ أَحْسَنُ الْخَالِقِينَ (١٤)

After the perfect creation process and creation order presented in the
above ayahs, then one is expected to say (25)فَتَبَارَكَ اللهُ أَحْسَنُ الْخَالِقِينَ²⁶² after
witnessing this perfection in the creation.

In the expression فَكَسَوْنَا الْعِظَامَ لَحْمًا²⁶³, the body of a person has a
similitude of a dress with the word فَكَسَوْنَا²⁶⁴. The Prophet ﷺ uses the same
word for making dua for wearing a new dress as اللهم لك الحمد انت كسوتنه²⁶⁵
اسالك خير ما صنع له. In this perspective, one can view the body similar to
a dress. When a person dies, Allah ﷻ can make him wear another dress
in the grave, in the Day of Judgement, in the places of punishment or in
Heaven. So, the body serves as a secondary purpose for a human. Yet,
most of the people bring the arguments of bodily destructions as the
termination and extinction of a person. This shows the obstruction of
people at the external but not going to the essence, الله اعلم.

One can clearly see the Prophet ﷺ shows the practical application of
the Qurān in the Sunnah. As one of the narrations show the Prophet صلى
الله عليه وسلم used to add the expression فَتَبَارَكَ اللهُ أَحْسَنُ الْخَالِقِينَ ²⁶⁶while he was
making his sujud (9) (534).

---

261. 9:12 And certainly did We create man from an extract of clay. 9:13 Then We placed him
as a sperm-drop⁴ in a firm lodging [i.e., the womb]. 9:14 Then We made the sperm-drop into
a clinging clot, and We made the clot into a lump [of flesh], and We made [from] the lump,
bones, and We covered the bones with flesh; then We developed him into another creation.
So blessed is Allah جل جلاله, the best of creators.
262. So blessed is Allah جل جلاله, the best of creators.
263. And We covered the bones.
264. We covered.
265. O Allah جل جلاله, praise be to Thee! as Thou hast clothed me with it, I ask Thee for its good
and the good of that for which it was made.
266. So blessed is Allah جل جلاله, the best of creators.

[15-16]²⁶⁷

ثُمَّ إِنَّكُمْ بَعْدَ ذَلِكَ لَمَيِّتُونَ {المؤمنون/15} ثُمَّ إِنَّكُمْ يَوْمَ الْقِيَامَةِ تُبْعَثُونَ {المؤمنون/16}

The word لَمَيِّتُونَ has a ta'kid, emphasis which can signify many deaths such as spiritual deaths although the person has a physical death. In addition, it can signify the death of all the creation except the Al-Baki, Allah ﷻ. Then, the word تُبْعَثُونَ without takid can have only one hashr and accountability in front of Allah اعلم الله, ﷻ.

[17]²⁶⁸

وَلَقَدْ خَلَقْنَا فَوْقَكُمْ سَبْعَ طَرَائِقَ وَمَا كُنَّا عَنِ الْخَلْقِ غَافِلِينَ {المؤمنون/17}

Sometimes when humans make scientific discoveries about different layers in the sky, atmosphere or in the space, they may feel self-sufficient and arrogant as if they can do anything without interference and knowledge of Allah ﷻ. Then, Allah ﷻ reminds to this effect that Allah ﷻ created everything, وَلَقَدْ خَلَقْنَا فَوْقَكُمْ سَبْعَ طَرَا²⁶⁹. Allah ﷻ gave opportunity humans to discover the creation. Allah ﷻ constantly watches about the creation as mentioned in this ayah, وَمَا كُنَّا عَنِ الْخَلْقِ غَافِلِينَ. One can relate this ayah with the Western understandings of deity and why the people get alienated due to some of these wrong conceptions and constructions.

[18]²⁷⁰

وَأَنزَلْنَا مِنَ السَّمَاءِ مَاءً بِقَدَرٍ فَأَسْكَنَّاهُ فِي الْأَرْضِ وَإِنَّا عَلَى ذَهَابٍ بِهِ لَقَادِرُونَ {المؤمنون/18}

The word فَأَسْكَنَّاهُ can allude to the fact that when rain comes gushing it can be a punishment as it can cause flood and destruction. As it seeps

---

267. 23:15 And then, behold! after all this, you are destined to die; (23:16) and then, behold! you shall be raised from the dead on Resurrection Day.
268. (23:17) And, indeed, We have created above you seven [celestial] orbits;7 and never are We unmindful of [any aspect of Our] creation.
269. And, indeed, We have created above you seven [celestial] orbits.
270. (23:18) And We send down water from the skies in accordance with a measure [set by Us], and then We cause it to lodge in the earth: but, behold, We are most certainly able to withdraw this [blessing]!

through the earth calmly and swiftly as the word فَأَسْكَنَّاهُ can also indicate then, it is a Rahmah from Allah ﷻ. Similar understanding can be for wind. So, one can realize each item can be a ni'mah or a destruction for the person. Children, spouse, food, anger, etc. can be some other examples. Everything that we ecounter can have a dual identity. In this regard, even if the person does not have a genuine intention and humbleness for guidance, the Qurān can be a destruction for them as mentioned in the Qurān.

[20][271]

وَشَجَرَةً تَخْرُجُ مِن طُورِ سَيْنَاء تَنبُتُ بِالدُّهْنِ وَصِبْغٍ لِّلْآكِلِينَ {المؤمنون/20}

One of the possible renderings of the above ayah is olive and olive oil. So, eating both of them are encouraged, الله اعلم.

[27][272]

فَأَوْحَيْنَا إِلَيْهِ أَنِ اصْنَعِ الْفُلْكَ بِأَعْيُنِنَا وَوَحْيِنَا فَإِذَا جَاء أَمْرُنَا وَفَارَ التَّنُّورُ فَاسْلُكْ فِيهَا مِن كُلٍّ زَوْجَيْنِ اثْنَيْنِ وَأَهْلَكَ إِلَّا مَن سَبَقَ عَلَيْهِ الْقَوْلُ مِنْهُمْ وَلَا تُخَاطِبْنِي فِي الَّذِينَ ظَلَمُوا إِنَّهُم مُّغْرَقُونَ {المؤمنون/27}

It is interesting to analyze the case with the expression وَلاَ تُخَاطِبْنِي فِي[273] الَّذِينَ ظَلَمُو when Nûh as asks about his son. Then, the case of Ibrahim as قَدْ كَانَتْ لَكُمْ أُسْوَةٌ حَسَنَةٌ فِي إِبْرَاهِيمَ وَالَّذِينَ مَعَهُ إِذْ قَالُوا لِقَوْمِهِمْ إِنَّا بُرَاء مِنكُمْ وَمِمَّا تَعْبُدُونَ مِن دُونِ اللَّهِ كَفَرْنَا بِكُمْ وَبَدَا بَيْنَنَا وَبَيْنَكُمُ الْعَدَاوَةُ وَالْبَغْضَاء أَبَدًا حَتَّى تُؤْمِنُوا بِاللَّهِ وَحْدَهُ إِلَّا قَوْلَ إِبْرَاهِيمَ لِأَبِيهِ لَأَسْتَغْفِرَنَّ لَكَ وَمَا أَمْلِكُ لَكَ مِنَ اللَّهِ مِن شَيْءٍ رَّبَّنَا عَلَيْكَ تَوَكَّلْنَا وَإِلَيْكَ أَنَبْنَا وَإِلَيْكَ

---

271. (23:20) as well as a tree that issues from [the lands adjoining] Mount Sinai, yielding oil and relish for all to eat.

272. (23:27) Thereupon We inspired him thus: "Build, under Our eyes12 and according to Our inspiration, the ark [that shall save thee and those who follow thee]. And when Our judgment comes to pass, and waters gush forth in torrents over the face of the earth, place on board of this [ark] one pair of each [kind of animal] of either sex, as well as thy family—excepting those on whom sentence has already been passed —; and do not appeal to Me [any more] in behalf of those who are bent on evildoing—for, behold, they are destined to be drowned!

273. And do not appeal to Me [any more] in behalf of those who are bent on evildoing.

إِلاَّ قَوْلَ إِبْرَاهِيمَ لِأَبِيهِ لَأَسْتَغْفِرَنَّ لَكَ وَمَا. ²⁷⁴الْمَصِيرُ {٤/الممتحنة} where the expression. وَمَا
أَمْلِكُ لَكَ مِنَ اللهِ مِن شَيْءٍ رَّبَّنَا عَلَيْكَ تَوَكَّلْنَا. And also, the case of

فَلَمَّا ذَهَبَ عَنْ إِبْرَاهِيمَ الرَّوْعُ وَجَاءتْهُ الْبُشْرَى يُجَادِلُنَا فِي قَوْمِ لُوطٍ{هود/٧٤}²⁷⁵ إِنَّ
إِبْرَاهِيمَ لَحَلِيمٌ أَوَّاهٌ مُنِيبٌ {هود/٧٥}²⁷⁶ يَا إِبْرَاهِيمُ أَعْرِضْ عَنْ هَذَا إِنَّهُ قَدْ جَاء أَمْرُ رَبِّكَ
وَإِنَّهُمْ آتِيهِمْ عَذَابٌ غَيْرُ مَرْدُودٍ {هود/٧٦}²⁷⁷.

In all above cases, there is the qada of Allah ﷻ but the messengers and anbiya can approach with their disposition possibly due to knowing what the qada of Allah ﷻ is.

In the case of Nûh as, the request of the saving of his son and the expression وَلاَ تُخَاطِبْنِي فِي الَّذِينَ ظَلَمُو ²⁷⁸ that الله اعلم, that Nûh as was directly communicating with Allah ﷻ. In the case of Ibrahim as with Lut as, Ibrahim as is communication with the angels. Sometimes, communicating through means as in the case of shafah can have a lenient position in acceptance and treatment. In other words, Allah ﷻ can forgive people due to the Prophet ﷺ in the akhirah but not if the people themselves asks, الله اعلم. In the case of Ibrahim as asking about his father, Ibrahim as puts also his position that وَمَا أَمْلِكُ لَكَ مِنَ اللَّه مِن شَيْءٍ ²⁷⁹ رَّبَّنَا عَلَيْكَ تَوَكَّلْنَا he asks but he doesn't know the qada and Ridah of Allah, ﷻ الله اعلم. This also can show the levels of the Prophets as well that Ibrahim as can be at a higher level than Nûh as as the above expressions in the ayahs may reflect, الله اعلم.

On another perspective, the expression وَلاَ تُخَاطِبْنِي²⁸⁰can show that when a person makes dua to Allah ﷻ then, Allah ﷻ responds to each person. In the case of Nûh as, Allah ﷻ shows us that as the Prophet, Nûh

274. There has already been for you an excellent pattern in Abraham and those with him, when they said to their people, "Indeed, we are disassociated from you and from whatever you worship other than Allah جل جلاله. We have denied you, and there has appeared between us and you animosity and hatred forever until you believe in Allah جل جلاله alone"—except for the saying of Abraham to his father, "I will surely ask forgiveness for you, but I have not [power to do] for you anything against Allah جل جلاله. Our Lord, upon You we have relied, and to You we have returned, and to You is the destination.
275. And when the fright had left Abraham and the good tidings had reached him, he began to argue [i.e., plead] with Us concerning the people of Lot.
276. Indeed, Abraham was forbearing, grieving and [frequently] returning [to Allah جل جلاله].
277. [The angels said], "O Abraham, give up this [plea]. Indeed, the command of your Lord has come, and indeed, there will reach them a punishment that cannot be repelled."
278. And do not appeal to Me [any more] in behalf of those who are bent on evildoing.
279. But I have not [power to do] for you anything against Allah جل جلاله. Our Lord, upon You we have relied.
280. And do not appeal to Me [any more].

as immediately receives the response. For others, there is the response if the person knows and understands it. In other words, Allah ﷻ always but always answers, and corresponds to all sincere duas of people.

In another perspective, since Allah ﷻ answers all the duas then, one should keep etiquette and adab with Allah ﷻ while making dua and asking from Allah ﷻ. The expression وَلَا تُخَاطِبْنِي shows that if a person is given a high value by Allah ﷻ that when he or she calls Allah ﷻ, then Allah ﷻ immediately answers. In this case, the person should use this ability wisely with adab and be thankful a lot for this nimah of Allah ﷻ. In other words, Allah ﷻ's answer and correspondence of all duas itself is a huge nimah and potential for a person. [28]²⁸¹

فَإِذَا اسْتَوَيْتَ أَنتَ وَمَن مَّعَكَ عَلَى الْفُلْكِ فَقُلِ الْحَمْدُ لِلَّهِ الَّذِي نَجَّانَا مِنَ الْقَوْمِ الظَّالِمِينَ
{المؤمنون/28}

According to the teaching of this ayah, when a person is saved by Allah ﷻ from an oppressor, or any type of oppression, difficulty or calamity then, the person should make hamd to Allah ﷻ as mentioned as فَقُلِ الْحَمْدُ لِلَّهِ الَّذِي نَجَّانَا مِنَ الْقَوْمِ الظَّالِمِينَ²⁸².

[51]²⁸³

يَا أَيُّهَا الرُّسُلُ كُلُوا مِنَ الطَّيِّبَاتِ وَاعْمَلُوا صَالِحًا إِنِّي بِمَا تَعْمَلُونَ عَلِيمٌ {المؤمنون/51}

The relationship of eating clean and healthy with doing good work is mentioned in this ayah. It doesn't say halal but tayyib. At one perspective, it is already default for the prophets to eat halal. So, halal is not mentioned because it is already there. At an above level, among halal items, the tayyib is suggested for the ones who are close to Allah ﷻ. In our understanding, today's healthy, organic, and non-GMO food can be under this category of tayyib, الله اعلم. Tayyib at another level can be the food cooked by a pious person of Allah ﷻ who makes dhikr constantly

---

281. 23:28 "And as soon as thou and those who are with thee are settled in the ark, say: 'All praise is due to God, who has saved us from those evildoing folk!' (23:29) "And say: 'O my Sustainer! Cause me to reach a destination blessed [by Thee]—for Thou art the best to show man how to reach his [true] destination!'"
282. Say: 'All praise is due to God.
283. 23:51 O YOU APOSTLES! Partake of the good things of life, and do righteous deeds: verily, I have full knowledge of all that you do.

before, during or after cooking. There is an effect of both the ingredients of the food and who cooked it and how it was cooked.

[58][284]

وَالَّذِينَ هُم بِآيَاتِ رَبِّهِمْ يُؤْمِنُونَ {المؤمنون/58}

When there are the signs of Allah ﷻ if a person recognize them and believes them, then this person can attain one of the qualities of a believer. Some of the main signs are the Qurān, the Prophet ﷺ and the other internal and external signs sent by Allah ﷻ in each person's lifespan. This notion is also expressed in [285] سَنُرِيهِمْ آيَاتِنَا فِي الْآفَاقِ وَفِي أَنفُسِهِمْ حَتَّى يَتَبَيَّنَ لَهُمْ أَنَّهُ الْحَقُّ أَوَلَمْ يَكْفِ بِرَبِّكَ أَنَّهُ عَلَى كُلِّ شَيْءٍ شَهِيدٌ {فصلت/53}. In other words, there is constant shower of ayahs of Allah ﷻ coming to the person daily. If the person is an attitude of carelessness, negligence and heedlessness then the person cannot attain to the true quality of a believer, الله اعلم.

[72][286]

أَمْ تَسْأَلُهُمْ خَرْجًا فَخَرَاجُ رَبِّكَ خَيْرٌ وَهُوَ خَيْرُ الرَّازِقِينَ {المؤمنون/72}

In the works of dawah, sometimes, the person is disappointed, fired from his duties and forced to leave his residence. In all these engagements, the person may have frustrations. In this ayah, Allah ﷻ reminds and consoles with the expression فَخَرَاجُ رَبِّكَ خَيْرٌ وَهُوَ خَيْرُ الرَّازِقِينَ that the person should really turn away from the worldly causes to the Real Cause, Allah ﷻ.

---

284. (23:58) and who believe in their Sustainer's messages,
285. We will show them Our signs in the horizons and within themselves until it becomes clear to them that it is the truth.
286. 22:72 As it is, whenever Our messages are conveyed unto them in all their clarity, thou canst perceive utter repugnance on the faces of those who are bent on denying the truth: they would almost assault those who convey Our messages unto them! Say: "Shall I, then, tell you of something worse than what you feel at present? It is the fire [of the hereafter] that God has promised to those who are bent on denying the truth: and how vile a journey's end!"

[75-78]²⁸⁷

وَلَوْ رَحِمْنَاهُمْ وَكَشَفْنَا مَا بِهِم مِّن ضُرٍّ لَّلَجُّوا فِي طُغْيَانِهِمْ يَعْمَهُونَ ﴿المؤمنون/75﴾ وَلَقَدْ أَخَذْنَاهُم بِالْعَذَابِ فَمَا اسْتَكَانُوا لِرَبِّهِمْ وَمَا يَتَضَرَّعُونَ ﴿المؤمنون/76﴾

حَتَّى إِذَا فَتَحْنَا عَلَيْهِم بَابًا ذَا عَذَابٍ شَدِيدٍ إِذَا هُمْ فِيهِ مُبْلِسُونَ ﴿المؤمنون/77﴾ وَهُوَ الَّذِي أَنشَأَ لَكُمُ السَّمْعَ وَالْأَبْصَارَ وَالْأَفْئِدَةَ قَلِيلًا مَّا تَشْكُرُونَ ﴿المؤمنون/78﴾

It is important to note that when a person is affiliated with evil-seeming incidents, the wisdom behind is to make the person go back to Allah ﷻ, ask forgiveness and use this as an opportunity to establish a proper and genuine relationship as mentioned as يَتَضَرَّعُونَ²⁸⁸. Therefore, a person can witness some people in pain and difficulty but in reality this can be blessing for this person and sometimes for others. It can be blessing sometimes for others that if these people don't have this difficulty, then they may tend to cause fasad for other people. It can be blessing for the person that it may make the person to be always in need of Allah ﷻ but when this difficulty or evil-seeming incident is removed, then he or she may become again arrogant, or heedless, الله اعلم.

One can review three levels of evil-seeming incidents 1) ضُرّ (2 لْعَذَاب 3) عَذَابٍ شَدِيد.

In all cases, the corresponding dispositions are 1) فَمَا (2 طُغْيَانِهِمْ, اسْتَكَانُوا لِرَبِّهِمْ وَمَا يَتَضَرَّعُونَ, and 3) مُبْلِسُونَ. From here, one can analyze that a minor difficulty, ضُرّ, is given to a person so that he or she stops their evil renderings, طُغْيَانِهِمْ, their spoiled, careless and heedless positions in one's relationship with Allah ﷻ. If this still continues and the person does not have a genuine relationship with Allah ﷻ with humbleness and

287. (22:75) [In His almightiness,] God chooses message-bearers from among the angels as well as from among men. But, behold, God [alone] is all-hearing, all-seeing: (22:76) [whereas their knowledge is limited,] He knows all that lies open before them and all that is hidden from them—for all things go back to God [as their source]. 22:77 O YOU who have attained to faith! Bow down and prostrate yourselves, and worship your Sustainer [alone], and do good, so that you might attain to a happy state! (22:78) And strive hard in God's cause with all the striving that is due to Him: it is He who has elected you [to carry His message], and has laid no hardship on you in [anything that pertains to] religion, [and made you follow] the creed of your forefather Abraham. It is He who has named you—in bygone times as well as in this [divine writ]—"those who have surrendered themselves to God", so that the Apostle might bear witness to the truth before you, and that you might bear witness to it before all mankind. Thus, be constant in prayer, and render the purifying dues, and hold fast unto God. He is your Lord Supreme: and how excellent is this Lord Supreme, and how excellent this Giver of Succour!
288. And all that is hidden from them.

humility, a problem or calamity, العذاب, can hit the person that the person now is expected to go back to Allah ﷺ and find solace by making dua and repentance as the word استكانوا is from the word sukun. One can see that it is just one hardship as mentioned with marifah, العذاب. Lastly, if this still doesn't work then the person is affected by series of serious tribulations, عَذَابٍ شَدِيد as mentioned nakirah. Yet, in this case, the person becomes hopeless and still does not go back to Allah ﷺ and does not embody the trait of being grateful for the bounties of Allah ﷺ. As the following ayah mentions the true expected disposition of the person in all discourses is that to embody the trait of being تَشْكُرُونَ, being grateful and thankful to Allah ﷺ when the statement قَلِيلًا مَّا تَشْكُرُونَ follows in the next ayah, الله اعلم.

عفو و العافيتة في الدني و الأخرة²⁸⁹ اللهم ان اسالك

[91-100]²⁹⁰

{ مَا اتَّخَذَ اللَّهُ مِن وَلَدٍ وَمَا كَانَ مَعَهُ مِنْ إِلَهٍ إِذًا لَّذَهَبَ كُلُّ إِلَهٍ بِمَا خَلَقَ وَلَعَلَا بَعْضُهُمْ عَلَى بَعْضٍ سُبْحَانَ اللَّهِ عَمَّا يَصِفُونَ {المؤمنون/91} عَالِمِ الْغَيْبِ وَالشَّهَادَةِ فَتَعَالَى عَمَّا يُشْرِكُونَ {المؤمنون/92} قُل رَّبِّ إِمَّا تُرِيَنِّي مَا يُوعَدُونَ {المؤمنون/93} رَبِّ فَلَا

---

289. O Allah, I ask for your pardon and well-being in this life and in the hereafter.

290. (23:91) Never did God take unto Himself any offspring, nor has there ever been any deity side by side with Him: [for, had there been any,] lo! each deity would surely have stood apart [from the others] in whatever it had created, and they would surely have [tried to] overcome one another! Limitless in His glory is God, [far] above anything that men may devise by way of definition, (23:92) knowing all that is beyond the reach of a created being's perception as well as all that can be witnessed by a creature's senses or mind and, hence, sublimely exalted is He above anything to which they may ascribe a share in His divinity!

23:93 SAY: "O my Sustainer! If it be Thy will to let me witness [the fulfilment of] whatever they [who blaspheme against Thee] have been promised [to suffer]—(23:94) do not, O my Sustainer, let me be one of those evildoing folk!" 23:95 [Pray thus—] for, behold, We are most certainly able to let thee witness [the fulfilment, even in this world, of] whatever We promise them! (23:96) [But whatever they may say or do,] repel the evil [which they commit] with something that is better: We are fully aware of what they attribute [to Us].23:97 And say: "O my Sustainer! I seek refuge with Thee from the promptings of all evil impulses; (23:98) and I seek refuge with Thee, O my Sustainer, lest they come near unto me!"

23:99 [AS FOR THOSE who will not believe in the life to come, they go on lying to themselves] until, when death approaches any of them, he prays: "O my Sustainer! Let me return, let me return [to life], (23:100) so that I might act righteously in whatever I have failed [aforetime]!" Nay, it is indeed but a [meaningless] word that he utters: for behind those [who leave the world] there is a barrier [of death] until the Day when all will be raised from the dead! 23:101 Then, when the trumpet [of resurrection] is blown, no ties of kinship will on that Day prevail among them, and neither will they ask about one another.

تَجْعَلْنِي فِي الْقَوْمِ الظَّالِمِينَ {المؤمنون/94} وَإِنَّا عَلَى أَن نُّرِيَكَ مَا نَعِدُهُمْ لَقَادِرُونَ
{المؤمنون/95} ادْفَعْ بِالَّتِي هِيَ أَحْسَنُ السَّيِّئَةَ نَحْنُ أَعْلَمُ بِمَا يَصِفُونَ {المؤمنون/96}
وَقُل رَّبِّ أَعُوذُ بِكَ مِنْ هَمَزَاتِ الشَّيَاطِينِ {المؤمنون/97} وَأَعُوذُ بِكَ رَبِّ أَن يَحْضُرُونِ
{المؤمنون/98} حَتَّى إِذَا جَاءَ أَحَدَهُمُ الْمَوْتُ قَالَ رَبِّ ارْجِعُونِ {المؤمنون/99} لَعَلِّي
أَعْمَلُ صَالِحًا فِيمَا تَرَكْتُ كَلَّا إِنَّهَا كَلِمَةٌ هُوَ قَائِلُهَا وَمِن وَرَائِهِم بَرْزَخٌ إِلَى يَوْمِ يُبْعَثُونَ
{المؤمنون/100}

In this Sûrah and as well as many other places of the Qurān al Karim, there are key words such as عَمَّا يَصِفُونَ[291] and عَمَّا يُشْرِكُونَ[292] for understanding the human limits. These expressions constantly repeat and there is a reason due to constant human inclinations of wrong renderings about Allah ﷻ, the Exalted. If a person does not have boundaries of adab of thoughts, and emotions that humans are limited creations like others then, it is very easy to mentally and emotionally wander around in prohibited poisonous wrong and dark lands similar to black holes in outer space. In this regard, the dhikr سُبْحَانَ اللهِ constantly reminds this to the person. These erroneous wanderings also require constant istighfār as well. Therefore, knowing what you have from the Qurān and Sunnah and acting on it, is the key as the Prophet ﷺ advises about the beneficial knowledge, i'lm (20) (hadith #4048). These are the main areas where philosophers and some Western affected Muslims have possible issues to lack of: 1)adab with Allah, 2) knowing one's limits as humans in this relationship, 3) not accepting and submitting and surrendering themselves fully to the diamond and perfect teachings of the Qurān and Sunnah.

[93-95]

قُل رَّبِّ إِمَّا تُرِيَنِّي مَا يُوعَدُونَ {المؤمنون/93} رَبِّ فَلَا تَجْعَلْنِي فِي الْقَوْمِ الظَّالِمِينَ
{المؤمنون/94} وَإِنَّا عَلَى أَن نُّرِيَكَ مَا نَعِدُهُمْ لَقَادِرُونَ {المؤمنون/95}

The above set of ayahs are very interesting to focus on. Allah ﷻ teaches Rasulullah ﷺ and the following generations of Muslims with the word قُل what one should do in the cases of nifāq or zulm, especially if there are possibilities of the Divine recompenses for these evil engagements. So, it is important to ask and make dua to Allah ﷻ not to be among the

---

291. Of what they attribute [to Us].
292. A share in His divinity!

people who are being punished as mentioned قُل رَّبِّ إِمَّا تُرِيَنِّي مَا يُوعَدُونَ
{المؤمنون/93} رَبِّ فَلَا تَجْعَلْنِي فِي الْقَوْمِ الظَّالِمِينَ {المؤمنون/94}.

Then, the interesting part is how can the Prophet ﷺ or believers witness the punishment when they are not with them? In this case, the word عَلَى can signify something the person uses as a means or a tool to know, to watch and to understand. In this case, the word عَلَى can symbolize for example something similar to live TV or live internet broadcasting tools or means that people can witness the events while they are not in the places of occurrences or incidents. Definitely, this is just an example. Allah ﷻ can do anything without any means or tools beyond our imagination because today we have these technological tools that we possibly can understand and realize better what the Qurān can possibly refer, الله اعلم.

[96-98]

ادْفَعْ بِالَّتِي هِيَ أَحْسَنُ السَّيِّئَةَ نَحْنُ أَعْلَمُ بِمَا يَصِفُونَ {المؤمنون/96} وَقُل رَّبِّ أَعُوذُ بِكَ
مِنْ هَمَزَاتِ الشَّيَاطِينِ {المؤمنون/97} وَأَعُوذُ بِكَ رَبِّ أَن يَحْضُرُونِ {المؤمنون/98}

When a person of imān interacts with other groups for dawah and tabligh, there is always possibility of uncomfortable, improper and unsuitable topics to be discussed about religion and about the behaviors how they are presented and communicated. In these engagements, a person can feel the effect of these dirty styles and disgusting discourses especially when one compares it with the sweetness of imān. To avoid from these sickening and unpleasant feelings, the person should constantly and humbly read and ask from Rabbul Alamin the following duas as thought by Rabbul A'lamin that [293] رَّبِّ أَعُوذُ بِكَ مِنْ هَمَزَاتِ الشَّيَاطِينِ and [294] وَأَعُوذُ بِكَ رَبِّ and أَن يَحْضُرُونِ so that Allah ﷻ protects this person from their evil effects. One should always also weigh the tradeoffs of these involvements or engagements. Sometimes, it is better to avoid not to engage or join in these types of meetings if there is not much benefit but mostly possible harms. Especially, if a person deals with arrogant attitudes of mind but not humble and true humility attitudes of being a human in front of

---

293. O my Sustainer! I seek refuge with Thee from the promptings of all evil impulses.
294. I seek refuge with Thee, O my Sustainer, lest they come near unto me!

Allah ﷻ. Then, things can become fruitless and arguments can become useless but harmful for the person unfortunately.

[112-114][295]

قَالَ كَمْ لَبِثْتُمْ فِي الْأَرْضِ عَدَدَ سِنِينَ {المؤمنون/112} قَالُوا لَبِثْنَا يَوْمًا أَوْ بَعْضَ يَوْمٍ فَاسْأَلِ الْعَادِّينَ {المؤمنون/113} قَالَ إِن لَّبِثْتُمْ إِلَّا قَلِيلًا لَّوْ أَنَّكُمْ كُنتُمْ تَعْلَمُونَ {المؤمنون/114}

The importance of knowing that a person lives a short life and accordingly taking advantage of this life is reminded us in this ayah.

[117-118][296]

أَفَحَسِبْتُمْ أَنَّمَا خَلَقْنَاكُمْ عَبَثًا وَأَنَّكُمْ إِلَيْنَا لَا تُرْجَعُونَ {المؤمنون/115} فَتَعَالَى اللَّهُ الْمَلِكُ الْحَقُّ لَا إِلَهَ إِلَّا هُوَ رَبُّ الْعَرْشِ الْكَرِيمِ {المؤمنون/116} وَمَن يَدْعُ مَعَ اللَّهِ إِلَهًا آخَرَ لَا بُرْهَانَ لَهُ بِهِ فَإِنَّمَا حِسَابُهُ عِندَ رَبِّهِ إِنَّهُ لَا يُفْلِحُ الْكَافِرُونَ {المؤمنون/117} وَقُل رَّبِّ اغْفِرْ وَارْحَمْ وَأَنتَ خَيْرُ الرَّاحِمِينَ {المؤمنون/118}

The Azamah of Allah ﷻ as mentioned فَتَعَالَى اللَّهُ الْمَلِكُ الْحَقُّ. One should really understand our limits that we are the creation and Allah ﷻ has the authority, discretion, and preference of whatever or however to implement according to the Divine Will. We don't have any power as miniscule beings. This is a reality. This may not be emphasized in our Western discourses due to the self-human imposed of problems of alienation from God. Yet, it is a reality for a person to adjust one's respectful attitudes, adab with Rabbul Alamin. الله اعلم.

---

295. 23:112 [And] He will ask [the doomed]: "What number of years have you spent on earth?" (23:113) They will answer: "We have spent there a day, or part of a day; but ask those who [are able to] count [time]..." 23:114 [Whereupon] He will say: "You have spent there but a short while: had you but known [how short it was to be]!
296. 23:117 Hence, he who invokes, side by side with God, any other deity [- a deity] for whose existence he has no evidence shall but find his reckoning with his Sustainer: [and,] verily, such deniers of the truth will never attain to a happy state! (23:118) Hence, [O believer,] say: "O my Sustainer! Grant [me] forgiveness and
bestow Thy mercy [upon me]: for Thou art the truest bestower of mercy!"

Sûrah Nûr

[3]²⁹⁷

الزَّانِي لَا يَنكِحُ إِلَّا زَانِيَةً أَوْ مُشْرِكَةً وَالزَّانِيَةُ لَا يَنكِحُهَا إِلَّا زَانٍ أَوْ مُشْرِكٌ وَحُرِّمَ ذَٰلِكَ عَلَى الْمُؤْمِنِينَ {النور/3}

One can review the Quranic ayahs with the values in our current contexts. A person in our society having multiple partners outside marriage is referred and expressed with the phrase as "sleeping around." This expression in informal and colloquial usage has a generally negative meaning to show the state of this person not to be trusted in a relationship. In other words, a person cannot establish a relationship with this person because this person does not have any sense of commitment and responsibility to his or her partner. Here, I don't want to use the word loyalty because in today's contemporary language, the word loyalty can represent some embedded negative meanings although it was considered a full positive word representing a virtuous trait until our recent Western history. Especially, it was considered as a positive word in traditional marriage ceremonies (39).

Secondly, with increasing epidemic diseases in gynecology, the notions of transmitted diseases display itself. So a person cannot risk his or her health due to a habit of a partner sleeping around and brink potential diseases.

In this perspective, the above ayah can allude that if someone makes a habit of sleeping around, at least he or she should have some ethical behavior to choose a similar person as a partner in order not to destroy the life of the other person. Alternatively, this person can choose to be committed and responsible to his or her partner in a sound relationship.

---

297. 24:3 [Both are equally guilty:] the adulterer couples with none other than an adulteress—that is, a woman who accords [to her own lust] a place side by side with God; and with the adulteress couples none other than an adulterer—that is, a man who accords (to his own lust) a place side by side with God: and this is forbidden unto the believers.

[10]²⁹⁸

{النور/10} وَلَوْلَا فَضْلُ اللَّهِ عَلَيْكُمْ وَرَحْمَتُهُ وَأَنَّ اللَّهَ تَوَّابٌ حَكِيمٌ

It is interesting to analyze the Name and Attribute of Allah حَكِيمٌ ﷻ. It comes in different places with similar and different meanings in many places in the Qurān. What should one really understand or immediately remember when this word or Name is mentioned?

It can possibly allude that when a person is doing anything and especially in the endeavors of good, one should pay very critical importance how one does it. In other words, one can call this as uslûb or method of delivery of the action. In our popular time, one can call this as wisdom. For example, in the case of adultery, slandering, or in the core of fitnahs, as mentioned in Sûrah Nûr, one should maintain the justice with hikmah or wisdom how correction is done. In other words, the legislation is the Qurān and interpretations of the Prophet ﷺ and fuqaha. In practice, the judiciary implements legislation with justice through the qadi. The execution and enforcement is done with hikmah. The Qurān is Hakim because the Qurān is revealed from Al-Hakìm. One can find the emphasis for this methodology of wisdom in deliverance of the divine message to people in the Qurān and in the teachings of the Prophet ﷺ. One can for example view in the delivery of the divine message to a child in the case of Luqman as :

وَلَقَدْ آتَيْنَا لُقْمَانَ الْحِكْمَةَ أَنِ اشْكُرْ لِلَّهِ وَمَن يَشْكُرْ فَإِنَّمَا يَشْكُرُ لِنَفْسِهِ وَمَن كَفَرَ فَإِنَّ اللَّهَ غَنِيٌّ حَمِيدٌ ²⁹⁹{لقمان/12} وَإِذْ قَالَ لُقْمَانُ لِابْنِهِ وَهُوَ يَعِظُهُ يَا بُنَيَّ لَا تُشْرِكْ بِاللَّهِ إِنَّ الشِّرْكَ لَظُلْمٌ عَظِيمٌ ³⁰⁰{لقمان/13} وَوَصَّيْنَا الْإِنسَانَ بِوَالِدَيْهِ حَمَلَتْهُ أُمُّهُ وَهْنًا عَلَى وَهْنٍ وَفِصَالُهُ فِي عَامَيْنِ أَنِ اشْكُرْ لِي وَلِوَالِدَيْكَ إِلَيَّ الْمَصِيرُ ³⁰¹{لقمان/14}

The words that he uses it يَا بُنَيَّ³⁰². It is very soft, gentle and kind.

---

298. 23:10 It is they, they who shall be the inheritors
299. And We had certainly given Luqmān wisdom [and said], "Be grateful to Allah جل جلاله." And whoever is grateful is grateful for [the benefit of] himself. And whoever denies [His favor]—then indeed, Allah جل جلاله is Free of need and Praiseworthy.
300. And [mention, O Muhammad], when Luqmān said to his son while he was instructing him, "O my son, do not associate [anything] with Allah جل جلاله. Indeed, association [with Him] is great injustice."
301. And We have enjoined upon man [care] for his parents. His mother carried him, [increasing her] in weakness upon weakness, and his weaning is in two years. Be grateful to Me and to your parents; to Me is the [final] destination.
302. O my son.

Similarly, in the cases of zina, the engagements of defamation, slander, offense, or insult, one should use hikmah, forgiveness, softness and gentleness as Allah ☀ mentions for the Divine Self as وَأَنَّ اللَّهَ تَوَّابٌ حَكِيمٌ {النور /10}[303].

Actions with Hikmah and without Hikmah

One can point the cases of actions with hikmah and without hikmah. For example, a person has a child and this child does something wrong. The parent knows the correct action instead of this wrong action of the child. This parent's nafs can immediately force him to yell, humiliate or be angry with this child but at the same tell the correct action to this child. Now, all the parts of this correct teaching can be victimized due to the anger, humiliating and yelling behavior of the parent towards their child.

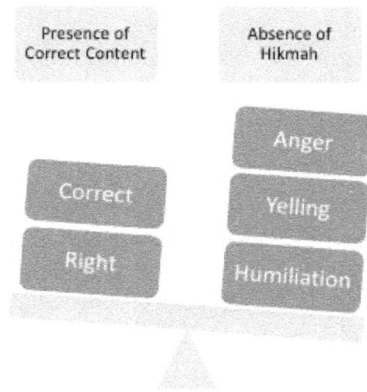

The above is a depiction of this case. In the above case, although there is a correct teaching, there is no positive outcome of this teaching due to absence of hikmah or wisdom in the delivery method. In other words, how we deliver a message or teaching can be as equally as, maybe more, important than the content of this teaching.

---

303. And because Allah جل جلاله is Accepting of repentance and Wise.

[11]304

إِنَّ الَّذِينَ جَاءُوا بِالْإِفْكِ عُصْبَةٌ مِّنكُمْ لَا تَحْسَبُوهُ شَرًّا لَّكُم بَلْ هُوَ خَيْرٌ لَّكُمْ لِكُلِّ امْرِئٍ مِّنْهُم مَّا اكْتَسَبَ مِنَ الْإِثْمِ وَالَّذِي تَوَلَّى كِبْرَهُ مِنْهُمْ لَهُ عَذَابٌ عَظِيمٌ {النور/11}

وَلَوْلَا فَضْلُ اللَّهِ عَلَيْكُمْ وَرَحْمَتُهُ فِي الدُّنْيَا وَالْآخِرَةِ لَمَسَّكُمْ فِي مَا أَفَضْتُمْ فِيهِ عَذَابٌ عَظِيمٌ {النور/14}

إِذْ تَلَقَّوْنَهُ بِأَلْسِنَتِكُمْ وَتَقُولُونَ بِأَفْوَاهِكُم مَّا لَيْسَ لَكُم بِهِ عِلْمٌ وَتَحْسَبُونَهُ هَيِّنًا وَهُوَ عِندَ اللَّهِ عَظِيمٌ {النور/15} وَلَوْلَا إِذْ سَمِعْتُمُوهُ قُلْتُم مَّا يَكُونُ لَنَا أَن نَّتَكَلَّمَ بِهَذَا سُبْحَانَكَ هَذَا بُهْتَانٌ عَظِيمٌ {النور/16}

إِنَّ الَّذِينَ يَرْمُونَ الْمُحْصَنَاتِ الْغَافِلَاتِ الْمُؤْمِنَاتِ لُعِنُوا فِي الدُّنْيَا وَالْآخِرَةِ وَلَهُمْ عَذَابٌ عَظِيمٌ {النور/23}

It is very interesting to note that one can overlook the importance of honor and reputation of a person through slandering and lies. SubhanAllah, Allah ﷻ repeats the grave seriousness with a very strong word عَظِيمٌ in the above ayahs. So, this offense, or sin is not something minor but severely and solemnly major. One can really measure the trembling of this word عَظِيمٌ that it is used constantly for one of the attributes of Allah ﷻ to allude to the greatness, majesty and grandeur of Allah ﷻ as subhana rabbiya al-azim in ruku position in every salah.

In other words, the greatness of this offense normally cannot be tolerated and immediately requires recompense. However, this does not happen immediately due to the Fadl and Rahmah of Allah ﷻ as mentioned in the below ayahs:

وَلَوْلَا فَضْلُ اللَّهِ عَلَيْكُمْ وَرَحْمَتُهُ وَأَنَّ اللَّهَ تَوَّابٌ حَكِيمٌ305 {النور/10}

وَلَوْلَا فَضْلُ اللَّهِ عَلَيْكُمْ وَرَحْمَتُهُ فِي الدُّنْيَا وَالْآخِرَةِ لَمَسَّكُمْ فِي مَا أَفَضْتُمْ فِيهِ عَذَابٌ عَظِيمٌ306 {النور/14}

---

304. (23:11) That will inherit the paradise; [and] therein shall they abide.
305. And if not for the favor of Allah upon you and His mercy...and because Allah جل جلاله is Accepting of repentance and Wise.
306. And if it had not been for the favor of Allah جل جلاله upon you and His mercy in this world and the Hereafter, you would have been touched for that [lie] in which you were involved by a great punishment.

{ وَلَوْلَا فَضْلُ اللَّهِ عَلَيْكُمْ وَرَحْمَتُهُ وَأَنَّ اللَّهَ رَؤُوفٌ رَحِيمٌ 307{النور/20}

وَلَوْلَا فَضْلُ اللَّهِ عَلَيْكُمْ وَرَحْمَتُهُ مَا زَكَا مِنكُم مِّنْ أَحَدٍ أَبَدًا وَلَكِنَّ اللَّهَ يُزَكِّي مَن يَشَاءُ وَاللَّهُ
سَمِيعٌ عَلِيمٌ 308{النور/21}

Therefore, the word عَظِيمٌ[309] is repeated to show the greatness of the offense, yet the expression وَلَوْلَا فَضْلُ اللَّهِ عَلَيْكُمْ وَرَحْمَتُهُ[310] is also repeated to show the greatness of the Fadl and Rahmah of Allah ﷻ that Allah ﷻ did not execute the required immediate recompense for this great offense, الله اعلم. As al-Mustafa ﷺ mentions (9) from Allah ﷻ that "My Mercy surpassed My Recompense." The word فضل[311] comes in different forms in the Qurān more than 100 times. In another hadith, Rasulullah ﷺ mentions that Allah ﷻ sent one percent of Divine Mercy, Rahmān on earth, remaining nine-percent out of 100 will in the akhirah, afterlife (9). This is a critical to analyze to situate the disposition of the person with his or her Creator, Rabbul A'lamin. All of us are existing with the Fadl of Allah ﷻ. It is also interesting to note the word فضل comes often in Sûrah Nisā. It is also interesting to note that the expressions عَذَابٌ عَظِيمٌ[312] and وَلَوْلَا فَضْلُ اللَّهِ عَلَيْكُمْ وَرَحْمَتُهُ occurs frequently in the Sûrah of Nûr than other surahs in the Qurān, الله اعلم.

---

307. And if it had not been for the favor of Allah جل جلاله upon you and His mercy…and because Alla جل جلاله h is Kind and Merciful.
308. And if not for the favor of Allah جل جلاله upon you and His mercy, not one of you would have been pure, ever, but Allah جل جلاله purifies whom He wills, and Allah جل جلاله is Hearing and Knowing.
309. Great.
310. And if not for the favor of Allah جل جلاله upon you and His mercy.
311. Favor.
312. Great punishment.

[30] ³¹³

قُل لِّلْمُؤْمِنِينَ يَغُضُّوا مِنْ أَبْصَارِهِمْ وَيَحْفَظُوا فُرُوجَهُمْ ذَلِكَ أَزْكَى لَهُمْ إِنَّ اللَّهَ خَبِيرٌ بِمَا يَصْنَعُونَ {النور/30}

It is interesting to focus on the word يَغُضُّوا as also mentioned in the ayah below

إِنَّ الَّذِينَ يَغُضُّونَ أَصْوَاتَهُمْ عِندَ رَسُولِ اللَّهِ أُوْلَئِكَ الَّذِينَ امْتَحَنَ اللَّهُ قُلُوبَهُمْ لِلتَّقْوَى لَهُم مَّغْفِرَةٌ وَأَجْرٌ عَظِيمٌ ³¹⁴{الحجرات/3}

In both cases of basar and sawt, there is a deliberate adjustment of the look and voice. Now as a technical legal term in fiqh, the following ayah explains it further what it means as a restriction.

On another level, as the word basar can also refer to heart, thoughts even emotions of understanding as mentioned in other parts of the Qurãn. In this case, this can mean not to have the embodiment of full nazar, looking or watching something but limiting and controlling oneself to have a very shallow and superficial interaction in order to prevent oneself in mind, heart and emotions related bad, sin, and evil induced renderings.

In our contemporary time, if for whatever reason, a person is in a situation of work, professional, or in need based relation such as in an hospital or market, then one should have this controlling relationship of one's physical organs and emotional faculties.

On another note, Allah ﷻ does not ask a person something he or she can handle as mentioned لاَ يُكَلِّفُ اللَّهُ نَفْسًا إِلاَّ وُسْعَهَا as mentioned in Sûrah Baqarah 286. This means that a person can inshAllah control oneself with the tawfiq of Allah ﷻ when it is mentioned as قُل لِّلْمُؤْمِنِينَ يَغُضُّوا مِنْ³¹⁵ أَبْصَارِهِمْ وَيَحْفَظُوا فُرُوجَهُمْ.

It is also interesting to note that the word غضب (gadab) has also the initial letters غ and ض. In Arabic morphology, the first two letters of a word can give some raw meaning of the word. In this case, as غض³¹⁶can

---

313. Tell the believing men to reduce [some] of their vision and guard their private parts. That is purer for them. Indeed, Allah جل جلاله is Acquainted with what they do.
314. Indeed, those who lower their voices before the Messenger of Allah جل جلاله—they are the ones whose hearts Allah جل جلاله has tested for righteousness. For them is forgiveness and great reward.
315. Tell the believing men to reduce [some] of their vision and guard their private parts.
316. Reduce.

refer to controlling and restricting as mentioned the ayahs for يَغُضُّ. In the case of غضب (gadab), one can understand the notion of controlling one's anger, الله اعلم.

<u>The word Gadab in the Qurān for people and for Allah ﷻ:</u>

For humans, gadab can have a meaning showing displeasure of someone with sadness and regret about something as mentioned for Musa as: وَلَمَّا رَجَعَ مُوسَى إِلَى قَوْمِهِ <u>غَضْبَانَ أَسِفًا</u> قَالَ بِئْسَمَا خَلَفْتُمُونِي مِن بَعْدِي أَعَجِلْتُمْ أَمْرَ رَبِّكُمْ وَأَلْقَى الأَلْوَاحَ وَأَخَذَ بِرَأْسِ أَخِيهِ يَجُرُّهُ إِلَيْهِ قَالَ ابْنَ أُمَّ إِنَّ الْقَوْمَ اسْتَضْعَفُونِي وَكَادُواْ يَقْتُلُونَنِي فَلاَ تُشْمِتْ بِيَ الأَعْدَاء وَلاَ تَجْعَلْنِي مَعَ الْقَوْمِ الظَّالِمِينَ {الأعراف/150}[317].

فَرَجَعَ مُوسَى إِلَى قَوْمِهِ <u>غَضْبَانَ أَسِفًا</u> قَالَ يَا قَوْمِ أَلَمْ يَعِدْكُمْ رَبُّكُمْ وَعْدًا حَسَنًا أَفَطَالَ عَلَيْكُمُ الْعَهْدُ أَمْ أَرَدتُّمْ أَن يَحِلَّ عَلَيْكُمْ غَضَبٌ مِّن رَّبِّكُمْ فَأَخْلَفْتُم مَّوْعِدِي {طه/86}[318]

Here, the word <u>غَضْبَانَ أَسِفًا</u> are together. In other words, being angry possibly with sadness and regret that gadab can lead to some undesired outcomes for humans, الله اعلم. Also, the ayah وَلَمَّا سَكَتَ عَن مُّوسَى الْغَضَبُ, أَخَذَ الأَلْوَاحَ وَفِي نُسْخَتِهَا هُدًى وَرَحْمَةٌ لِّلَّذِينَ هُمْ لِرَبِّهِمْ يَرْهَبُونَ {الأعراف/154}[319] shows that humans can have gadab with regret due to its outcomes and it is a transitory or temporary state. The Prophet ﷺ suggests to recite ta'wfiz at this temporary state of gadab to remove oneself from this state (9).

Also, for human renderings of gadab, Allah ﷻ mentions and encourages the believers not to act with the state of gadab but forgive people who put this person in the state of gadab as mentioned { وَالَّذِينَ يَجْتَنِبُونَ كَبَائِرَ الْإِثْمِ وَالْفَوَاحِشَ وَإِذَا مَا <u>غَضِبُوا هُمْ يَغْفِرُونَ</u> {الشورى/37}[320]

---

317. And when Moses returned to his people, angry and grieved, he said, "How wretched is that by which you have replaced me after [my departure]. Were you impatient over the matter of your Lord?" And he threw down the tablets and seized his brother by [the hair of] his head, pulling him toward him. [Aaron] said, "O son of my mother, indeed the people oppressed me and were about to kill me, so let not the enemies rejoice over me and do not place me among the wrongdoing people."

318. So Moses returned to his people, angry and grieved. He said, "O my people, did your Lord not make you a good promise? Then, was the time [of its fulfillment] too long for you, or did you wish that wrath from your Lord descend upon you, so you broke your promise [of obedience] to me?" ▯

319. And when the anger subsided in Moses, he took up the tablets; and in their inscription was guidance and mercy for those who are fearful of their Lord.

320. And those who avoid the major sins and immoralities, and when they are angry, they forgive.

For Allah ﷻ, gadab can mean the displeasure of Allah ﷻ for an evil act but not a deficient quality as in humans such as { وَمَن يَقْتُلْ مُؤْمِنًا مُتَعَمِّدًا فَجَزَآؤُهُ جَهَنَّمُ خَالِدًا فِيهَا وَغَضِبَ اللهُ عَلَيْهِ وَلَعَنَهُ وَأَعَدَّ لَهُ عَذَابًا عَظِيمًا 321{النساء/93}. When this word used for Allah ﷻ, the word أَسِفَ is not used because Allah ﷻ does not have human qualities of regret or sadness. Allah ﷻ has the displeasure of humans' renderings of evil, sins and oppression, yet Allah ﷻ is al-Hakim, executes the Divine Will with Wisdom and Patience.

Similarly, the words Kibir, or salawat has different connotations when it is used for humans compared to Allah ﷻ such as the salawat of angels, humans or Allah ﷻ on us or on the Prophet ﷺ have all different meanings.

Therefore, it is wrong to project completely the Transcendent Realities of Uluhiyah to the limited cases of creation. They should be different. These differences can be witnesses in the cases of intersecting points of the language. If one does not realize these differences, it may be a challenge and test for the person and lead the person to kufr, as ahlu-kitāb did in their full humanization of the divinity. May Allah ﷻ protect us, Amìn.

Sûrah Furqān

[3][322]

وَاتَّخَذُوا مِن دُونِهِ آلِهَةً لَّا يَخْلُقُونَ شَيْئًا وَهُمْ يُخْلَقُونَ وَلَا يَمْلِكُونَ لِأَنفُسِهِمْ ضَرًّا وَلَا نَفْعًا وَلَا يَمْلِكُونَ مَوْتًا وَلَا حَيَاةً وَلَا نُشُورًا

When the people get scared and have fear, stress and anxiety of anything other than Allah ﷻ, they may implicitly take those as their deities. The real imān requires detachment of everything and everyone in the heart and mind except Allah ﷻ. When the person is scared of the outcomes of his or her ventures, then this person can have some glitches in their imān.

---

321. But whoever kills a believer intentionally—his recompense is Hell, wherein he will abide eternally, and Allah جل جلاله has become angry with him and has cursed him and has prepared for him a great punishment.

322. 25:3 And yet, some choose to worship, instead of Him, [imaginary] deities that cannot create anything but are themselves created, and have it not within their power to avert harm from, or bring benefit to, themselves, and have no power over death, nor over life, nor over resurrection!

Sometimes, we rush for an outcome of something and yet, we don't follow the hikmah requiring patience as embodied by Rasulullah ﷺ. Sometimes, we follow the hikmah but we still have fears due to being overambitious of an outcome. Sometime, we mix our roles or responsibilities.

We cannot control the outcome of an action although we followed all the means or hikmah as mentioned وَقَالَ يَا بَنِيَّ لاَ تَدْخُلُواْ مِن بَابٍ وَاحِدٍ وَادْخُلُواْ مِنْ أَبْوَابٍ مُّتَفَرِّقَةٍ وَمَا أُغْنِي عَنكُم مِّنَ اللّهِ مِن شَيْءٍ إِنِ الْحُكْمُ إِلاَّ لِلّهِ عَلَيْهِ تَوَكَّلْتُ وَعَلَيْهِ فَلْيَتَوَكَّلِ الْمُتَوَكِّلُونَ ³²³ {يوسف/67}

When one analyzes this ayah the first part emphasizes the importance of following the means such as reasons, causality, mashwara-constultation or meetings with the experts on the matter, and making istikhara. Then, one should not mix their responsibility of fulfilling these means and expecting the outcome with certainty. Yet, Allah ﷻ endorses the outcome as mentioned ³²⁴وَمَا أُغْنِي عَنكُم مِّنَ اللّهِ مِن شَيْءٍ إِنِ الْحُكْمُ إِلاَّ لِلّهِ. If the person followed the means of making istikhara, inshAllah, this outcome will still be khayr for the person although the person can initially show some disappointments due to the outcome not being in his or her desired way. Although, these in essence should embody the person the real tawakkul to Allah ﷻ regardless of their expected outcomes as mentioned ³²⁵عَلَيْهِ تَوَكَّلْتُ وَعَلَيْهِ فَلْيَتَوَكَّلِ الْمُتَوَكِّلُونَ.

The real imān requires to fulfil everything as best one can in following the means, making istikhara, mashwara, and making tawakkul to Allah ﷻ in the beginning, during and at the end of any engagement while waiting the results of this process. As humans, we get scared for the outcomes of our engagements. Yet, when we make tawakkul to the One Who does not have any reserve from the outcome of any action as mentioned وَلَا يَخَافُ عُقْبَاهَا ³²⁶{الشمس/15}, then inshAllah, we can have the breezes of comfort and ease on our hearts and mind.

Fulfilling the requirement should not take the person to arrogance. If Allah ﷻ does not will something it does not happen regardless of

---

323. And he said, "O my sons, do not enter from one gate but enter from different gates; and I cannot avail you against [the decree of] Allah جل جلاله at all. The decision is only for Allah جل جلاله; upon Him I have relied, and upon Him let those who would rely [indeed] rely."
324. And I cannot avail you against [the decree of] Allah جلاله at all. The decision is only for Allah جل جلاله.
325. Upon Him I have relied, and upon Him let those who would rely [indeed] rely."
326. And He does not fear the consequence thereof.

the causalities. The expression له الملك و له الحمد ٣٢٧ can signify this that whatever is the outcome of an action, we should make hamd to Allah ﷻ.

On the other hand, sometimes we are fully aware that we did not fulfill the require means, reasons or causalities for an outcome. Yet, in these times, if we turn to Allah ﷻ humbly with ajz with spiritual and physical weakness and poverty, then Allah ﷻ can make the impossible possible.

[4-6]³²⁸

وَقَالَ الَّذِينَ كَفَرُوا إِنْ هَذَا إِلَّا إِفْكٌ افْتَرَاهُ وَأَعَانَهُ عَلَيْهِ قَوْمٌ آخَرُونَ فَقَدْ جَاؤُوا ظُلْمًا وَزُورًا

This verse can reflect some of the non-contextual and non-methodological approaches of some of the orientalists and some of the people who write about Islam in popular culture. Here, the word إِفْكٌ shows these uneducated or unscholarly approaches without a proper scientific and scholarly methodology of understanding and learning. The expression وَأَعَانَهُ عَلَيْهِ قَوْمٌ آخَرُونَ can show the problem when there is a wish and desire to terminate a concept or a message in a society regardless of its genuine or reasonable content then it becomes a group phenomenon when pointing to an enemy. In other words, the classical approaches of conspiracy theories (21) generally include a group as to make their ungrounded claims. They help each other in this uneducated and intolerant approach with an ungrounded bias.

وَقَالُوا أَسَاطِيرُ الْأَوَّلِينَ اكْتَتَبَهَا فَهِيَ تُمْلَى عَلَيْهِ بُكْرَةً وَأَصِيلًا

With the word اكْتَتَبَهَا, the Qurān brings and all their arguments to refute them what they may say to place doubts in people's minds.

قُلْ أَنزَلَهُ الَّذِي يَعْلَمُ السِّرَّ فِي السَّمَاوَاتِ وَالْأَرْضِ إِنَّهُ كَانَ غَفُورًا رَّحِيمًا

---

327. To him is the Kingdom and all praises is due to him.
328. 25:4 Moreover, those who are bent on denying the truth are wont to say, "This (Qur'an] is nothing but a lie which he (himself) has devised with the help of other people: who thereupon have perverted the truth and brought a falsehood into being." 25:5
And they say, "Fables of ancient times which he has caused to be written down,7 so that they might be read out to him at morn and evening!" (25:6) Say [O Muhammad]: "He who knows all the mysteries of the heavens and the earth has bestowed from on high this (Qur'an upon me)! Verily, He is much-forgiving, a dispenser of grace!"

After this, a very critical part comes and asks in the ayah as "Did you know who sent this Book? Tell them, the One Who knows all the secrets in the universe, skies, space, galaxies, earth, in the far points of earth, oceans sent this Book. Then, after this, leave your arrogance and bias and be open-minded and make repentance because Allah ☙is Much Forgiving and Very Merciful."

[7]329

وَقَالُوا مَالِ هَذَا الرَّسُولِ يَأْكُلُ الطَّعَامَ وَيَمْشِي فِي الْأَسْوَاقِ لَوْلَا أُنزِلَ إِلَيْهِ مَلَكٌ فَيَكُونَ مَعَهُ نَذِيرًا

This verse can show the unbalanced approach of some of the spiritual trainers to eliminate the food intake in order to increase the spiritual status of the person. Allah ☙created the humans with certain needs. As model humans, the prophets and messengers of Allah ☙ate and performed their daily and humanly activities and remained still as the people of God.

[11] 330

بَلْ كَذَّبُوا بِالسَّاعَةِ وَأَعْتَدْنَا لِمَن كَذَّبَ بِالسَّاعَةِ سَعِيرًا

The ones who don't believe with the traits of arrogance, and narrow-mindedness will also have problem with the belief in the afterlife and accountability. With the below verses, [12-14]

إِذَا رَأَتْهُم مِّن مَّكَانٍ بَعِيدٍ سَمِعُوا لَهَا تَغَيُّظًا وَزَفِيرًا 331{الفرقان/12} وَإِذَا أُلْقُوا مِنْهَا مَكَانًا ضَيِّقًا مُّقَرَّنِينَ دَعَوْا هُنَالِكَ ثُبُورًا 332{الفرقان/13} لَا تَدْعُوا الْيَوْمَ ثُبُورًا وَاحِدًا وَادْعُوا ثُبُورًا كَثِيرًا

---

329. 25:7 Yet they say: "What sort of apostle is this [man] who eats food (like all other mortals] and goes about in the market-places? Why has not an angel (visibly) been sent down unto him, to act as a warner together with him?"

330. 25:11 But nay! It is (the very coming of] the Last Hour to which they give the lie! However, for such as give the lie to [the announcement of] the Last Hour We have readied a blazing flame:

331. When it [i.e., the Hellfire] sees them from a distant place, they will hear its fury and roaring.

332. And when they are thrown into a narrow place therein bound in chains, they will cry out thereupon for destruction.

There is an inzar, a threat. If the person does not want to use their mind then the consequences are explained in the above verses.

[17]³³³

وَيَوْمَ يَحْشُرُهُمْ وَمَا يَعْبُدُونَ مِن دُونِ اللَّهِ فَيَقُولُ أَأَنتُمْ أَضْلَلْتُمْ عِبَادِي هَٰؤُلَاءِ أَمْ هُمْ ضَلُّوا السَّبِيلَ

The above verse explains that the person will face the accountability in the afterlife about what he or she did in the world. He or she will not be able to blame others about their wrong choices. To make this obvious, Allah ﷻ will ask in front of them of the ones who will be blamed.

[18]³³⁴

قَالُوا سُبْحَانَكَ مَا كَانَ يَنبَغِي لَنَا أَن نَّتَّخِذَ مِن دُونِكَ مِنْ أَوْلِيَاءَ وَلَٰكِن مَّتَّعْتَهُمْ وَآبَاءَهُمْ حَتَّىٰ نَسُوا الذِّكْرَ وَكَانُوا قَوْمًا بُورًا

The blamed ones will not get any blame on themselves.

[20]³³⁵

وَمَا أَرْسَلْنَا قَبْلَكَ مِنَ الْمُرْسَلِينَ إِلَّا إِنَّهُمْ لَيَأْكُلُونَ الطَّعَامَ وَيَمْشُونَ فِي الْأَسْوَاقِ وَجَعَلْنَا بَعْضَكُمْ لِبَعْضٍ فِتْنَةً أَتَصْبِرُونَ وَكَانَ رَبُّكَ بَصِيرًا {الفرقان/20}

It is important to recognize who we are. As humans, it is in our nature to eat and fulfill our human needs. In this perspective, when Allah ﷻ sends us messengers or prophets, it is normal and logical to expect someone to teach the people how to fulfill the human needs and at the same

---

333. 25:17 BUT [as for people who are oblivious of thy Sustainer's oneness12—] one Day He will gather them together with all that they [now] worship instead of God, and will ask [those to whom divinity was falsely ascribed]: "Was it you who led these My creatures astray, or did they by themselves stray from the right path?"
334. 25:18 They will answer: "Limitless art Thou in Thy glory! It was inconceivable for us to take for our masters anyone but Thyself! But [as for them—] Thou didst allow them and their forefathers to enjoy [the pleasures of] life to such an extent that they forgot all remembrance [of Thee]: for they were people devoid of all good."
335. 25:20 AND [even] before thee, [O Muhammad,] We never sent as Our message-bearers any but [mortal men,] who indeed ate food [like other human beings] and went about in the market-places: for [it is thus that] We cause you [human beings] to be a means of testing one another. Are you able to endure [this test] with patience? For [remember, O man,] thy Sustainer is truly all-seeing!

time please Allah ﷻ. The best teaching method in this case would be another human who could show this in his life practice as a role model. Therefore, in traditional ways of learning, people learn by observing by not through formal education of books or classroom teaching (39 & 40). There are a lot of incidents and reports that people learned from the Prophet صلى الله عليه وسلم by observing him ﷺ.

[21-23] [336]

وَقَالَ الَّذِينَ لَا يَرْجُونَ لِقَاءنَا لَوْلَا أُنزِلَ عَلَيْنَا الْمَلَائِكَةُ أَوْ نَرَى رَبَّنَا لَقَدِ اسْتَكْبَرُوا فِي أَنفُسِهِمْ وَعَتَوْ عُتُوًّا كَبِيرًا {الفرقان/21} يَوْمَ يَرَوْنَ الْمَلَائِكَةَ لَا بُشْرَى يَوْمَئِذٍ لِّلْمُجْرِمِينَ وَيَقُولُونَ حِجْرًا مَّحْجُورًا {الفرقان/22} وَقَدِمْنَا إِلَى مَا عَمِلُوا مِنْ عَمَلٍ فَجَعَلْنَاهُ هَبَاء مَّنثُورًا {الفرقان/23}

The above verses give the situation of people who run behind the useless arguments. The arguments which are doubtful, not clear and not purposeful although there is a clear Book and the Prophet, Rasul ﷺ. Then, they see the product and outcome of their perspectives as nothing. Everything is gone, as the word هَبَاء signifies.

This notion of a being, other than what Allah ﷻ created the person, presents itself with the expression لَوْلَا أُنزِلَ عَلَيْنَا الْمَلَائِكَةُ. Why do people want to be something or someone other than their own selves? Why do people not accept what is given or granted to them in the cases of things that they cannot control such as they are created as humans, man or woman, black or white, in China or in America or in Africa? Why do people not accept themselves to be humble and human? Why do people then not accept another human's or their species' advice? This person who is giving advice can be a friend, parent, teacher, messenger or prophet of God.

---

336. 25:21 But those who do not believe that they are destined to meet Us are wont to say, "Why have no angels been sent down to us?"—or, "Why do we not see our Sustainer?" Indeed, they are far too proud of themselves, having rebelled [against God's truth] with utter disdain!
25:22 [Yet] on that Day—the Day on which they shall see the angels- there will be no glad tiding for those who were lost in sin; and they will exclaim, "By a forbidding ban [are we from God's grace debarred]!"—(25:23) for We shall have turned towards all the [supposedly good] deeds they ever wrought, and shall have transformed them into scattered dust

All these above discourses and discussions can be related with لَقَد[337] اسْتَكْبَرُوا فِي أَنْفُسِهِمْ. That, this can be all due to the arrogance of the person not realizing his or her real self. The demagogies can extend with similar discourses and beyond such as نَرَى رَبَّنَا[338]. Before all the futile claims, demagogies and spiritual wanderings, the key for the person is to realize who he or she really is. This realization will happen eventually. But, if it happens with death, then it will be too late as mentioned in يَوْمَ يَرَوْنَ[339] الْمَلَائِكَةَ لَا بُشْرَى يَوْمَئِذٍ لِّلْمُجْرِمِينَ and may Allah protect us, amin. الله اعلم

[27][340]

وَيَوْمَ يَعَضُّ الظَّالِمُ عَلَى يَدَيْهِ يَقُولُ يَا لَيْتَنِي اتَّخَذْتُ مَعَ الرَّسُولِ سَبِيلًا {الفرقان/2}

This ayah shows the importance of following the Sunnah.

[29][341]

لَقَدْ أَضَلَّنِي عَنِ الذِّكْرِ بَعْدَ إِذْ جَاءنِي وَكَانَ الشَّيْطَانُ لِلْإِنسَانِ خَذُولًا {الفرقان/29}

The unbeneficial remorse, hasarah, of not following the Qurān is depicted.

[30][342]

The unfortunate reality of not following, recognizing and appreciating the Qurān is depicted in this ayah.

وَقَالَ الرَّسُولُ يَا رَبِّ إِنَّ قَوْمِي اتَّخَذُوا هَذَا الْقُرْآنَ مَهْجُورًا {الفرقان/30}

---

337. Indeed, they are far too proud of themselves.
338. Why do we not see our Sustainer.
339. The Day on which they shall see the angels—there will be no glad tiding for those who were lost in sin.
340. (25:27) and a Day on which the evildoer will bite his hands (in despair], exclaiming: "Oh, would that I had followed the path shown to me by the apostle!
341. (25:29) Indeed, he led me astray from the remembrance (of God) after it had come unto me!" For [thus it is:] Satan is ever a betrayer of man.
342. 25:30 AND (on that Day] the Apostle will say: "0 my Sustainer! Behold, [some of] my people have come to regard this Qur'an as something [that ought to be] discarded !"

[32]³⁴³

وَقَالَ الَّذِينَ كَفَرُوا لَوْلَا نُزِّلَ عَلَيْهِ الْقُرْآنُ جُمْلَةً وَاحِدَةً كَذَلِكَ لِنُثَبِّتَ بِهِ فُؤَادَكَ وَرَتَّلْنَاهُ
تَرْتِيلًا {الفرقان/32}

The tendency of humans going forward behind the unclear and unbeneficial arguments is present in the above ayahs. The people's arguments with demagogy while there is an existing phenomena and data. This phenomenon is clear, mubin, observable. This Books is provable and clear as Bayyinah. With all those explicit meanings, weaving into implicit and minute, not useful and unbeneficial arguments can show its face in this case. One day, a person comes to the Prophet ﷺ and asks about the time of yawmul qiyamah, then the Prophet directs and focuses the questioner by asking "what did you prepare for it?, (3)" The approach of relevance in learning is the key. Nowadays, the curriculum instruction increasingly emphasizing this notion of relevance in learning and teaching in all fields of disciplines (40). In addition, the Prophet ﷺ encourages one to focus on the knowledge that is going to be beneficial and relevant by saying "20) " (اللهم اني اعوذ بك من العلم لا ينفع) (hadith #250) "Oh, Allah ﷻ, I seek refuge in You from the unbeneficial useless knowledge."

The notion and teachings of sabab nuzûl, the revelation of the Qurān in pieces is today's curriculum approaches of relevancy in the fields of education and contextualization as in the fields of social sciences.

[33]³⁴⁴

وَلَا يَأْتُونَكَ بِمَثَلٍ إِلَّا جِئْنَاكَ بِالْحَقِّ وَأَحْسَنَ تَفْسِيرًا {الفرقان/33}

The above verse shows the clear stance of the Qurān. The Qurān is the truth, clear and there is no doubt.

---

343. 25:32 Now they who are bent on denying the truth are wont to ask, "Why has not the Qur'an been bestowed on him from on high in one single revelation?" (It has been revealed] in this manner so that We might strengthen thy heart thereby—for We have so arranged its component parts that they form one consistent whole.
344. (25:33) and [that] they [who deny the truth] might never taunt thee with any deceptive half-truth without Our conveying to thee the [full] truth and [providing thee] with the best explanation.

[34]³⁴⁵

الَّذِينَ يُحْشَرُونَ عَلَى وُجُوهِهِمْ إِلَى جَهَنَّمَ أُوْلَئِكَ شَرٌّ مَّكَانًا وَأَضَلُّ سَبِيلًا {الفرقان/34}

After the demagogy and baseless of their debate, the inzar comes for the accountability of the oppressors.

[35-40]³⁴⁶

وَلَقَدْ آتَيْنَا مُوسَى الْكِتَابَ وَجَعَلْنَا مَعَهُ أَخَاهُ هَارُونَ وَزِيرًا {الفرقان/35} فَقُلْنَا اذْهَبَا إِلَى الْقَوْمِ الَّذِينَ كَذَّبُوا بِآيَاتِنَا فَدَمَّرْنَاهُمْ تَدْمِيرًا {الفرقان/36} وَقَوْمَ نُوحٍ لَّمَّا كَذَّبُوا الرُّسُلَ أَغْرَقْنَاهُمْ وَجَعَلْنَاهُمْ لِلنَّاسِ آيَةً وَأَعْتَدْنَا لِلظَّالِمِينَ عَذَابًا أَلِيمًا {الفرقان/37} وَعَادًا وَثَمُودَ وَأَصْحَابَ الرَّسِّ وَقُرُونًا بَيْنَ ذَلِكَ كَثِيرًا {الفرقان/38} وَكُلًّا ضَرَبْنَا لَهُ الْأَمْثَالَ وَكُلًّا تَبَّرْنَا تَتْبِيرًا {الفرقان/39} وَلَقَدْ أَتَوْا عَلَى الْقَرْيَةِ الَّتِي أُمْطِرَتْ مَطَرَ السَّوْءِ أَفَلَمْ يَكُونُوا يَرَوْنَهَا بَلْ كَانُوا لَا يَرْجُونَ نُشُورًا {الفرقان/40}

The immediate ayah 35 then shows the importance of the following the teachings of the Book of Allah 🕮. Then, the examples are presented from the prior times.

[41]³⁴⁷

وَإِذَا رَأَوْكَ إِن يَتَّخِذُونَكَ إِلَّا هُزُوًا أَهَذَا الَّذِي بَعَثَ اللَّهُ رَسُولًا {الفرقان/41}

Here, some cases of people humiliating others are presented. These can be the signs of arrogance, not open-mindedness, unethical and insincere attitudes.

---

345. 25:34 [And so, tell those who are bent on denying the truth that] they who shall be gathered unto hell upon their faces—it is they who [in the life to come] will be worst in station and still farther astray from the path [of truth]!

346. 25:35 AND, INDEED, [long before Muhammad] We vouchsafed revelation unto Moses, and appointed his brother Aaron to help him to bear his burden;[(25:36) and We said, "Go you both unto the people who have given the lie to Our messages!"—and thereupon We broke those [sinners] to smithereens. 25:37 And [think of] the people of Noah: when they gave the lie to [one of] the apostles, We caused them to drown, and made them a symbol for all mankind: for, grievous suffering have We readied for all who [knowingly] do wrong! (25:38) And [remember how We punished the tribes of] 'Ad and Thamud, and the people of Ar-Rass, and many generations [of sinners] in-between: (25:39) and unto each of them did We proffer lessons, and each of them did We destroy with utter destruction.

347. (25:41) Hence, whenever they consider thee, [O Muhammad,] they but make thee a target of their mockery, [saying:] "Is this the one whom God has sent as an apostle?

[42]³⁴⁸

إِن كَادَ لَيُضِلُّنَا عَنْ آلِهَتِنَا لَوْلَا أَن صَبَرْنَا عَلَيْهَا وَسَوْفَ يَعْلَمُونَ حِينَ يَرَوْنَ الْعَذَابَ مَنْ
أَضَلُّ سَبِيلًا {الفرقان/42}

It is very interesting to realize that although there are a lot of blockage, a purposeful and evil propaganda against the message of the Qurān and Islam today, the message still has been affecting many people today as it affected in the past. That is their real fear as mentioned in the above ayah. When there is a logical message with practical implications to address the needs of humans and at the same time a message with full inclusivity then, it is very difficult to stop it unless there is a purposeful and ill-intentioned agenda to stop it. Therefore, the above verse shows this situation as an example of it today and as it happened in the past.

[43-44]³⁴⁹

أَرَأَيْتَ مَنِ اتَّخَذَ إِلَهَهُ هَوَاهُ أَفَأَنتَ تَكُونُ عَلَيْهِ وَكِيلًا {الفرقان/43}

أَمْ تَحْسَبُ أَنَّ أَكْثَرَهُمْ يَسْمَعُونَ أَوْ يَعْقِلُونَ إِنْ هُمْ إِلَّا كَالْأَنْعَامِ بَلْ هُمْ أَضَلُّ سَبِيلًا
{الفرقان/44}

These people don't have basar. Or, if they have basar with qishawah with blockage as mentioned in the 7th ayah in Sûrah Baqarah. Their curtain, qishawah is their hawa, their desires. Therefore, they don't interpret properly with their mind the meanings through their hearing. Their hawa make their interpretations empty, ungrounded, and demagogical similar to some of the philosophers and evolutionists. In these engagements, these theories are based on impossible probabilities whereas believing Allah ‌is easy, straightforward, and very logical.

On the other hand, they are like animals compared to humans. As animals can view at the things they may not have much meanings for them except that the animals can know things with their intrinsic

---

348. (25:42) Indeed, he would well-nigh have led us astray from our deities, had we not been [so] steadfastly attached to them!" But in time, when they see the suffering [that awaits them], they will come to know who it was that went farthest astray from the path [of truth]!
349. 25:43 Hast thou ever considered [the kind of man] who makes his own desires his deity? Couldst thou, then, [O Prophet,] be held responsible for him? (25:44) Or dost thou think that most of them listen [to thy message] and use their reason? Nay, they are but like cattle—nay, they are even less conscious of the right way!

properties, such as they know their Creator. So, in that sense, they are worse than the animals, as mentioned with إِنْ هُمْ إِلَّا كَالْأَنْعَامِ بَلْ هُمْ أَضَلُّ[350] سَبِيلًا.

[45-50][351]

أَلَمْ تَرَ إِلَى رَبِّكَ كَيْفَ مَدَّ الظِّلَّ وَلَوْ شَاءَ لَجَعَلَهُ سَاكِنًا ثُمَّ جَعَلْنَا الشَّمْسَ عَلَيْهِ دَلِيلًا {الفرقان/45} ثُمَّ قَبَضْنَاهُ إِلَيْنَا قَبْضًا يَسِيرًا {الفرقان/46} وَهُوَ الَّذِي جَعَلَ لَكُمُ اللَّيْلَ لِبَاسًا وَالنَّوْمَ سُبَاتًا وَجَعَلَ النَّهَارَ نُشُورًا {الفرقان/47} وَهُوَ الَّذِي أَرْسَلَ الرِّيَاحَ بُشْرًا بَيْنَ يَدَيْ رَحْمَتِهِ وَأَنْزَلْنَا مِنَ السَّمَاءِ مَاءً طَهُورًا {الفرقان/48} لِنُحْيِيَ بِهِ بَلْدَةً مَيْتًا وَنُسْقِيَهُ مِمَّا خَلَقْنَا أَنْعَامًا وَأَنَاسِيَّ كَثِيرًا {الفرقان/49} وَلَقَدْ صَرَّفْنَاهُ بَيْنَهُمْ لِيَذَّكَّرُوا فَأَبَى أَكْثَرُ النَّاسِ إِلَّا كُفُورًا {الفرقان/50}

Allah ﷻ mentions that how Allah ﷻ changes the sun, day, night, the wind, the rain, and the plants every day, seasons, months and years but still people, witnessing all these changes, don't turn to Allah ﷻ truly and don't logically think and still, most of the people are ungrateful to Allah ﷻ as mentioned فَأَبَى أَكْثَرُ النَّاسِ إِلَّا كُفُورًا[352].

[51-52][353]

وَلَوْ شِئْنَا لَبَعَثْنَا فِي كُلِّ قَرْيَةٍ نَذِيرًا {الفرقان/51} فَلَا تُطِعِ الْكَافِرِينَ وَجَاهِدْهُمْ بِهِ جِهَادًا كَبِيرًا {الفرقان/52}

And, remember, if Allah ﷻ wanted then Allah ﷻ would send all the places a specific nazir, a teacher and a reminder. But, still they would not

---

350. Nay, they are but like cattle—nay, they are even less conscious of the right way!
351. 45) ART THOU NOT aware of thy Sustainer (through His works)?—how He causes the shadow to lengthen [towards the night] when, had He so willed, He could indeed have made it stand still: but then, We have made the sun its guide; (25:46) and then, [after having caused it to lengthen,] We draw it in towards Ourselves with a gradual drawing-in. 25:47 And He it is who makes the night a garment for you, and [your] sleep a rest, and causes every [new] day to be a resurrection. (25:48) And He it is who sends forth the winds as a glad tiding of His coming grace; and [thus, too,] We cause pure water to descend from the skies, (25:49) so that We may bring dead land to life thereby, and give to drink thereof to many [beings] of Our creation, beasts as well as humans.
25:50 And, indeed, many times have We repeated [all] this unto men, so that they might take it to heart: but most men refuse to be aught but ingrate.
352. But most men refuse to be aught but ingrate.
353. (25:51) Now had We so willed, We could have [continued as before and] raised up a [separate] warner in every single community: (25:52) hence, do not defer to [the likes and dislikes of] those who deny the truth, but strive hard against them, by means of this [divine writ], with utmost striving.

believe. Therefore, do your best and don't be discouraged and move on with inviting to the way of Allah ﷻ as many as you can by taking the message to many as best as you can. Let them use their free will, and remember if Allah ﷻ wanted, Allah ﷻ made all of them as believers but let them use their free will. The ones who may not get a message properly will still be judged fair and just in the ways that you may not know or realize but still you focus on your own responsibility.

[53]³⁵⁴

وَهُوَ الَّذِي مَرَجَ الْبَحْرَيْنِ هَذَا عَذْبٌ فُرَاتٌ وَهَذَا مِلْحٌ أُجَاجٌ وَجَعَلَ بَيْنَهُمَا بَرْزَخًا وَحِجْرًا مَّحْجُورًا {الفرقان/35}

After this, remember, the imān and kufr do not mix as Allah ﷻ creates sweet and salty water as they do not mix.

[54-55]³⁵⁵

وَهُوَ الَّذِي خَلَقَ مِنَ الْمَاء بَشَرًا فَجَعَلَهُ نَسَبًا وَصِهْرًا وَكَانَ رَبُّكَ قَدِيرًا {الفرقان/54}
وَيَعْبُدُونَ مِن دُونِ اللَّهِ مَا لَا يَنفَعُهُمْ وَلَا يَضُرُّهُمْ وَكَانَ الْكَافِرُ عَلَى رَبِّهِ ظَهِيرًا {الفرقان/55}

And similarly, Allah ﷻ created humans from water. Then, Allah ﷻ enabled them to form family and kinship ties and created them in pairs of men and women. After this, they worship other things besides Allah ﷻ. These things do not give any benefit or harm. Even, they went to such an extent that they are supporting each other in this ideology and approach of false beliefs.

---

354. 25:53 AND HE it is who has given freedom of movement to the two great bodies of water—the one sweet and thirst-allaying, and the other salty and bitter—and yet has wrought between them a barrier and a forbidding ban.
355. (25:54) And He it is who out of this [very] water has created man, and has endowed him with [the consciousness of] descent and marriage-tie: for thy Sustainer is ever infinite in His power. 25:55 And yet, some people worship, instead of God things that can neither benefit them nor harm them: thus, he who denies the truth does indeed turn his back on his Sustainer!

[56]³⁵⁶

{وَمَا أَرْسَلْنَاكَ إِلَّا مُبَشِّرًا وَنَذِيرًا {الفرقان/56

Don't worry, continue on your path of invitation. In this invitation, give them the good news and warn them for the possible results, as the person of مُبَشِّرًا وَنَذِيرا³⁵⁷, good news giver and warner.

[57-58]³⁵⁸

قُلْ مَا أَسْأَلُكُمْ عَلَيْهِ مِنْ أَجْرٍ إِلَّا مَن شَاء أَن يَتَّخِذَ إِلَى رَبِّهِ سَبِيلًا {الفرقان/57} وَتَوَكَّلْ
{عَلَى الْحَيِّ الَّذِي لَا يَمُوتُ وَسَبِّحْ بِحَمْدِهِ وَكَفَى بِهِ بِذُنُوبِ عِبَادِهِ خَبِيرًا {الفرقان/58

When you tell them "we don't want anything from you for our advice and reminder," then, they still don't believe in you. When you tell them "I just want you to recognize and appreciate Allah ﷻ," then, they may not still rationalize and understand about it. But don't worry, make your tawakkul, reliance on Allah ﷻ.

[59]³⁵⁹

الَّذِي خَلَقَ السَّمَاوَاتِ وَالْأَرْضَ وَمَا بَيْنَهُمَا فِي سِتَّةِ أَيَّامٍ ثُمَّ اسْتَوَى عَلَى الْعَرْشِ الرَّحْمَنُ
{فَاسْأَلْ بِهِ خَبِيرًا {الفرقان/59

These unwise, irrational and inadvisable people do not know who the Rabbul Alamin is. Rabbul Alamin is the One Who created the skies, stars, planets, galaxies, universe and the earth and whatever in them or between them in all levels of microscopic and macroscopic scales.

---

356. (25:56) Yet [withal, O Prophet,] we have sent thee only as a herald of glad tidings and a warner.
357. Glad tidings and a warner.
358. (25:57) say: "For this, no reward do I ask of you [- no reward] other than that he who so wills may unto his Sustainer find a way!"
25:58 Hence, place thy trust in the Living One who dies not, and extol His limitless glory and praise: for one is as aware of His creatures' sins as He
359. (25:59) He who created the heavens and the earth and what is between them in six days and then established Himself above the Throne—the Most Merciful, so ask about Him one well informed [i.e., the Prophet (ﷺ)].

[63]³⁶⁰

وَعِبَادُ الرَّحْمَنِ الَّذِينَ يَمْشُونَ عَلَى الْأَرْضِ هَوْنًا وَإِذَا خَاطَبَهُمُ الْجَاهِلُونَ قَالُوا سَلَامًا {الفرقان/63}

Don't worry and move forward by saying "Salam", peace.

[64]³⁶¹

وَالَّذِينَ يَبِيتُونَ لِرَبِّهِمْ سُجَّدًا وَقِيَامًا {الفرقان/64}

Continue on your salah, especially don't miss your night prayers.

[65]³⁶²

وَالَّذِينَ يَقُولُونَ رَبَّنَا اصْرِفْ عَنَّا عَذَابَ جَهَنَّمَ إِنَّ عَذَابَهَا كَانَ غَرَامًا {الفرقان/65}

Continue on your istighfār, duas and especially don't miss your protection duas from Jahannam.

[70-71]³⁶³

إِلَّا مَن تَابَ وَآمَنَ وَعَمِلَ عَمَلًا صَالِحًا فَأُولَٰئِكَ يُبَدِّلُ اللَّهُ سَيِّئَاتِهِمْ حَسَنَاتٍ وَكَانَ اللَّهُ غَفُورًا رَّحِيمًا {الفرقان/70}

Whoever makes tawbah, turns to Allah ﷻ, and has imān with good actions, Allah ﷻ promises to transform this person's past bad and evil actions to the good actions, resulting in great and pleasant rewards from Allah ﷻ.

وَمَن تَابَ وَعَمِلَ صَالِحًا فَإِنَّهُ يَتُوبُ إِلَى اللَّهِ مَتَابًا {الفرقان/71}

---

360. (25:63) And the servants of the Most Merciful are those who walk upon the earth easily, and when the ignorant address them [harshly], they say [words of] peace ⊠
361. (25:64) And those who spend [part of] the night to their Lord prostrating ⊠and standing [in prayer].
362. (25:65) And those who say, "Our Lord, avert from us the punishment of Hell. Indeed, its punishment is ever adhering.
363. 25:70 Excepted, however, shall be they who repent and attain to faith and do righteous deeds: for it is they whose [erstwhile] bad deeds God will transform into good ones—seeing that God is indeed much-forgiving, a dispenser of grace, (25:71) and seeing that he who repents and [thenceforth] does what is right has truly turned unto God by [this very act of] repentance.

After this make your tawba and do good deeds and actions and return to Allah ﷻ as the person who is rewarded and accepted, pleased and forgiven by Allah ﷻ. The similar expression in 70 comes with general but repeats itself with specific emphasis and encouragement at a personal level to the person from Allah ﷻ, الله اعلم.

It is interesting to note that Rasulullah ﷺ mentions that he ﷺ at least makes 70 times istighfār daily (3) (hadith # 5948). The number of this ayah and previous one with ayah number 70 explains making constant tawbah, and istighfār to Allah ﷻ.

[72]³⁶⁴

وَالَّذِينَ لَا يَشْهَدُونَ الزُّورَ وَإِذَا مَرُّوا بِاللَّغْوِ مَرُّوا كِرَامًا {الفرقان/72}

If the people don't accept the message and make tawba don't worry, move on and turn away from their demagogy.

[73]³⁶⁵

وَالَّذِينَ إِذَا ذُكِّرُوا بِآيَاتِ رَبِّهِمْ لَمْ يَخِرُّوا عَلَيْهَا صُمًّا وَعُمْيَانًا {الفرقان/73}

And you are the person when you hear Our signs and verses, you take it seriously. You don't act like them. They act as if they did not hear it and act indifferently to them.

[77]³⁶⁶

قُلْ مَا يَعْبَأُ بِكُمْ رَبِّي لَوْلَا دُعَاؤُكُمْ فَقَدْ كَذَّبْتُمْ فَسَوْفَ يَكُونُ لِزَامًا {الفرقان/77}

Continue making dua.

رَبَّنَا لَا تُزِغْ قُلُوبَنَا بَعْدَ إِذْ هَدَيْتَنَا وَهَبْ لَنَا مِن لَّدُنكَ رَحْمَةً إِنَّكَ أَنتَ الْوَهَّابُ³⁶⁷

---

364. 25:72 And [know that true servants of God are only] those who never bear witness to what is false, and [who], whenever they pass by [people engaged in] frivolity, pass on with dignity;

365. (25:73) And who, whenever they are reminded of their Sustainer's messages, do not throw themselves upon them [as if] deaf and blind.

366. 25:77 SAY [unto those who believe]: "No weight or value would my Sustainer attach to you were it not for your
faith [in Him]!" [And say unto those who deny the truth:] "You have indeed given the lie [to God's message], and in time this [sin] will cleave unto you!"

367. Our lord do not turn our hearts away after you have guided us and grant us from you mercy, for you are the provider.

19

Sûrah Shuãrãh

[1]³⁶⁸

This book is clear without any doubt.

[2]³⁶⁹

Do not destroy yourself by putting too much pressure on yourself while you are doing the work of invitation, dawah.

[10-13]³⁷⁰

وَإِذْ نَادَى رَبُّكَ مُوسَى أَنِ ائْتِ الْقَوْمَ الظَّالِمِينَ {الشعراء/10} قَوْمَ فِرْعَوْنَ أَلَا يَتَّقُونَ {الشعراء/11} قَالَ رَبِّ إِنِّي أَخَافُ أَن يُكَذِّبُونِ {الشعراء/12} وَيَضِيقُ صَدْرِي وَلَا يَنطَلِقُ لِسَانِي فَأَرْسِلْ إِلَى هَارُونَ {الشعراء/31}

Sometimes, a responsibility is given by Allah according to the level and capacity of the person. Dealing with the people of kufr, ingratitude, ignorance, and arrogance can make the people not to want to be in these environments. One can explain to that a person about the favors of Allah, about the need for adab, about the need for having respect for the Qurãn, the shiar of Allah, signs of Allah that they need to be respected. Yet, due to this person's ignorance, arrogance, demagogy, and lack of appreciation, the person may want to just argue. Interestingly, one may call this in our modern terms as "critical thinking" for this type of approach. The person can miss the point if the person does not have relevance of holistic approach of adab, respect and genuine intention to learn. Dealing with such people can be so much energy taking, depressing and self-tearing. Therefore, in the different parts of the Qurãn, as one of the utmost efforts and traits of the Prophet is

---

368. 26:1 Ta. Sin. Mim.
369. 26:2 THESE ARE MESSAGES of the divine writ, clear in itself and clearly showing the truth.
370. (26:10) HENCE, [remember how it was] when thy Sustainer summoned Moses: "Go unto those evildoing people, (26:11) the people of Pharaoh, who refuse to be conscious of Me!" (26:12) He answered: "O my Sustainer! Behold, I fear that they will give me the lie. (26:13) and then my breast will be straitened and my tongue will not be free: send, then, [this Thy command] to Aaron.

depicted as a person of not getting angry and but, still not giving up from his mission.

The Prophet ﷺ used to relate the message in such an extent that "Laallaka Bahihun nafsaka" can also show these avenues of the negative attitude of others to the genuine and original message of Allah ﷻ. It made and put the Prophet at a high state of concern for others. This argumentation, negativity, arrogance, not caring, and/or ignorance from the others was at such an extent that Allah ﷻ mentioned to console the Prophet ﷺ for the negative argumentation against the Prophet. Allah ﷻ mentioned that their argumentation is not towards to the Prophet himself because the Prophet ﷺ was only messenger of Allah ﷻ. Yet, the Prophet ﷺ embodied his responsibility as the messenger of Allah ﷻ when he was relating the message. Therefore, this full positive and distinctive embodiment of his role (ﷺ) as the messenger of Allah ﷻ distinguished him ﷺ from other prophets. Because, the other prophets at one point asked help from Allah ﷻ against the true oppression of their people to their messengers except the Prophet ﷺ.

One can understand this unique position of the Prophet ﷺ in the afterlife in his ﷺ relationship with Allah ﷻ because he ﷺ is the one who is still continuing that full embodiment of messengership in the afterlife as well. He will ask Allah ﷻ for the forgiveness of people, while all the Prophets are in full aware of that their messengership responsibility is over and it is time to be worried even about their own selves if they did their responsibility correctly or not. الله اعلم.

(سبحانك لا علم لنا الا ما علمتنا انك انت العليم الحكيم[371]).

In this case, Musa as knew their arrogant and ignorant attitude: قَالَ [372] رَبِّ إِنِّي أَخَافُ أَن يُكَذِّبُونِ

And, being with this people can possibly cause [373] وَيَضِيقُ صَدْرِي وَلاَ يَنطَلِقُ لِسَانِي فَأَرْسِلْ إِلَى هَارُونَ

One can review the methodology of Musa as for inviting the Firawn and others to tawhid. This can be interesting to see the expected staging in one's invitation to Allah ﷻ. First, the signs are shown. Then, the person

---

371. Glory be to you, we have no knowledge except what you taught us that you are the All-Knower, the Wise.

372. He answered: "O my Sustainer! Behold, I fear that they will give me the lie.

373. and then my breast will be straitened, and my tongue will not be free: send, then, [this Thy command] to Aaron.

is expected to think about these internal and external signs about Allah
ﷻ, about after life and about one's responsibility towards it. Finally, the
person is expected to make a choice and a decision.

[18]³⁷⁴

قَالَ أَلَمْ نُرَبِّكَ فِينَا وَلِيدًا وَلَبِثْتَ فِينَا مِنْ عُمُرِكَ سِنِينَ

It is interesting to note the usage of word rabb throughout the Sûrah of
Shuārāh. In the above verse, the pharaoh (Firawn) uses the word rabb
that he brought up Musa (as). Then, the Firawn continues asking, "if I
am not your lord who is yours then?" by saying [23]:

قَالَ فِرْعَوْنُ وَمَا رَبُّ الْعَالَمِينَ³⁷⁵

Then, the conversations continue with the word Rabb but Musa as
uses and presents it for the Real and True Rabb, Rabbul Ā'lamin. Then,
Firawn stops using this word for himself. One can realize some of these
usage in the ayahs below. [23-28]³⁷⁶

قَالَ فِرْعَوْنُ وَمَا رَبُّ الْعَالَمِينَ {الشعراء/23} قَالَ رَبُّ السَّمَاوَاتِ وَالْأَرْضِ وَمَا
بَيْنَهُمَا إِن كُنتُم مُوقِنِينَ {الشعراء/24} قَالَ لِمَنْ حَوْلَهُ أَلَا تَسْتَمِعُونَ {الشعراء/25} قَالَ
رَبُّكُمْ وَرَبُّ آبَائِكُمُ الْأَوَّلِينَ {الشعراء/26} قَالَ إِنَّ رَسُولَكُمُ الَّذِي أُرْسِلَ إِلَيْكُمْ لَمَجْنُونٌ
{الشعراء/27} قَالَ رَبُّ الْمَشْرِقِ وَالْمَغْرِبِ وَمَا بَيْنَهُمَا إِن كُنتُمْ تَعْقِلُونَ

---

374. (26:18) [But when Moses had delivered his message, Pharaoh] said: "Did we not bring
thee up among us when thou wert a child? And didst thou not spend among us years of thy
[later] life?
375. Said Pharaoh, "And what is the Lord of the worlds?"
376. 26:23 Said Pharaoh, "And what is the Lord of the worlds?" 26:24 [Moses] said, "The
Lord of the heavens and earth and that between them, if you should be convinced." 26:25
[Pharaoh] said to those around him, "Do you not hear?" 26:26 [Moses] said, "Your Lord and the
Lord of your first forefathers." 26:27 [Pharaoh] said, "Indeed, your 'messenger' who has been
sent to you is mad." 26:28 [Moses] said, "Lord of the east and the west and that between them,
if you were to reason."

[39-44][377]

{وَقِيلَ لِلنَّاسِ هَلْ أَنتُم مُّجْتَمِعُونَ {الشعراء/39}

لَعَلَّنَا نَتَّبِعُ السَّحَرَةَ إِن كَانُوا هُمُ الْغَالِبِينَ {الشعراء/40} فَلَمَّا جَاء السَّحَرَةُ قَالُوا لِفِرْعَوْنَ أَئِنَّ لَنَا لَأَجْرًا إِن كُنَّا نَحْنُ الْغَالِبِينَ {الشعراء/41} قَالَ نَعَمْ وَإِنَّكُمْ إِذًا لَّمِنَ الْمُقَرَّبِينَ {الشعراء/42} قَالَ لَهُم مُّوسَى أَلْقُوا مَا أَنتُم مُّلْقُونَ {الشعراء/43} فَأَلْقَوْا حِبَالَهُمْ وَعِصِيَّهُمْ وَقَالُوا بِعِزَّةِ فِرْعَوْنَ إِنَّا لَنَحْنُ الْغَالِبُونَ {الشعراء/44}

When one analyses the word الْغَالِبِينَ in the above verses, it comes three times consecutively. There is an emphasis to allude the intention of people why they are engaged in a social or public discourse. Although what they support may not make sense they don't want to be with the losers. The translation or meaning from وَقِيلَ لِلنَّاسِ هَلْ أَنتُم مُّجْتَمِعُونَ {الشعراء/39}[378]

لَعَلَّنَا نَتَّبِعُ السَّحَرَةَ إِن كَانُوا هُمُ الْغَالِبِينَ[379] {الشعراء/40} seems to be "we don't care who is right or who loses but we want to be with the winners" when they were ordered to get together as an audience to observe the challenge between Musa as and Pharaoh with his aristocrats as mentioned with وَقِيلَ لِلنَّاسِ هَلْ أَنتُم مُّجْتَمِعُونَ {الشعراء/39}. Similarly, one can see the position of magicians. They also want to be winners and get some benefit from Pharaoh as an opportunistic outcome.

In this case, we can review three groups: the higher class, Firawn and administration, then, the magicians and then, the people. Both magicians and people who are the majority are motivated to fulfill the order because of their desire to be at the winning side and getting something out of this opportunity. This shows that it is easy to manipulate the crowds when especially there is the representation of power and people or general public that do not want to be losers, الله اعلم.

---

377. (26:39) and the people were asked: "Are you all present, (26:40) so that we might follow [in the footsteps of] the sorcerers if it is they who prevail?"(26:41) Now when the sorcerers came, they said unto Pharaoh: "Verily, we ought to have a great reward if it is we who prevail."26:42 Answered he: "Yea—and, verily, in that case you shall be among those who are near unto me." (26:43) [And] Moses said unto them: "Throw whatever you are going to throw!" (26:44) Thereupon they threw their [magic] ropes and their staffs, and said: "By Pharaoh's might, behold, it is we indeed who have prevailed!"

378. And it was said to the people, "Will you congregate.

379. That we might follow the magicians if they are the predominant?"

[46]

{380 فَأُلْقِيَ السَّحَرَةُ سَاجِدِينَ {46/الشعراء}

The above ayah shows the expected attitude of submission and surrender with humbleness when there is an order or miracle from Allah ﷻ. Magicians immediately embody their true position of being 'abd of Allah ﷻ and they make sajdah to Allah ﷻ.

A similar case presents itself in the case of angels as:

{فَسَجَدَ الْمَلَائِكَةُ كُلُّهُمْ أَجْمَعُونَ 381}ص/73{

The understanding or going behind the reasons should come after not before for the true attitude of a person with adab towards Allah ﷻ. This adab can be called taqwa. Oppositely in the case of shaytan, he immediately uses reason instead of the adab of submission and surrender as mentioned: [73-76][382]

{فَسَجَدَ الْمَلَائِكَةُ كُلُّهُمْ أَجْمَعُونَ {73/ص} إِلَّا إِبْلِيسَ اسْتَكْبَرَ وَكَانَ مِنَ الْكَافِرِينَ {74/ص}
{قَالَ يَا إِبْلِيسُ مَا مَنَعَكَ أَن تَسْجُدَ لِمَا خَلَقْتُ بِيَدَيَّ أَسْتَكْبَرْتَ أَمْ كُنتَ مِنَ الْعَالِينَ {75/ص}
{قَالَ أَنَا خَيْرٌ مِّنْهُ خَلَقْتَنِي مِن نَّارٍ وَخَلَقْتَهُ مِن طِينٍ {76/ص}

[51][383]

إِنَّا نَطْمَعُ أَن يَغْفِرَ لَنَا رَبُّنَا خَطَايَانَا أَن كُنَّا أَوَّلَ الْمُؤْمِنِينَ

It is interesting to analyze the word الْمُؤْمِنِينَ in the Qurān. It seems that it is the level of imān confirmed in the heart. Especially, this confirmation comes with difficulties and tests. May Allah جل جلاله give us a'fiyah, Amîn. The above verse is with the context of magicians who are put in a trial and threatened by death by the Pharaoh, Firawn. Yet, they still confirmed and held on to their belief, imān. Therefore, they make the

---

380. (26:46) And down fell the sorcerers, prostrating themselves in adoration,
381. So the angels prostrated—all of them entirely.
382. 38:73 So the angels prostrated—all of them entirely. 38:74 Except Iblees; he was arrogant and became among the disbelievers. 38:75 [Allah جل جلاله] said, "O Iblees, what prevented you from prostrating to that which I created with My hands? Were you arrogant [then], or were you [already] among the haughty?" 38:76 He said, "I am better than him. You created me from fire and ⊠created him from clay."
383. (26:51) Behold, we [but] ardently desire that our Sustainer forgive us our faults in return for our having been foremost among the believers!"

statement that "we hope that Allah ﷻ forgives us because of becoming as the first believers, muminin." It is also interesting to note that the word الْمُؤْمِنِينَ, al-mumin, the real believer comes frequently in the chapter of Ahzāb, the trials of confederations. As one can know that this chapter discusses the harsh trial of believers.

[84]384

وَاجْعَل لِّي لِسَانَ صِدْقٍ فِي الْآخِرِينَ {الشعراء/84}

Ibrahim as makes dua to be remembered well in the later generations and to be from the ones that Allah ﷻ is pleased with. Allah ﷻ accepts his dua and as we make in every salah in tahiyyāt reciting his name, also outside the salah making salawāt, and reading his name constantly in the Qurān and hadith.

In this case, who will remember the person? The angels or the people? Allah ﷻ knows everything as we don't use the word "to remember" for Allah ﷻ. So, it is important to ask the best way of remembrance. If some people have not good remembrance as mentioned in the Qurān with la'nah or lu'inah, with curse, then this may be the opposite of this case, similar to Shaytan.

There are other people when they leave a place, job, town or when they die they want to leave with a good remembrance. A person leaving their job with a good remembrance may want to go back to that job again. A person leaving a town with good remembrance may want to visit that town again. A person with good remembrance by angels will want to meet with angels. A person who Allah ﷻ is pleased with, then will definitely want to meet with Allah اعلم الله, ﷻ.

[108-110]385

فَاتَّقُوا اللَّهَ وَأَطِيعُونِ {الشعراء/108} وَمَا أَسْأَلُكُمْ عَلَيْهِ مِنْ أَجْرٍ إِنْ أَجْرِيَ إِلَّا عَلَى رَبِّ الْعَالَمِينَ {الشعراء/109} فَاتَّقُوا اللَّهَ وَأَطِيعُونِ {الشعراء/110}

---

384. (26:84) and grant me the power to convey the truth unto those who will come after me,
385. (26:108) Be, then, conscious of God, and pay heed unto me! 26:109 "And no reward whatever do I ask of you for it: my reward rests with none but the Sustainer of all the worlds. (26:110) Hence, remain conscious of God, and pay heed unto me!"

In this Sûrah and others, there are very interesting points for the methods of tabligh, outreach, characters of the Prophets and messengers. The expected attitude or the reasons of loss and the reasons of rejection are mentioned. Since the above expression is repeated in this Sûrah five times with Nûh as, Hûd as, Sālih as, Lut as and Shuayb as. The above expression is not mentioned with Musa as and Ibrahim as.

الله اعلم this can signify that Musa as and Ibrahim as were both in in an open method of making tabligh. Their methods and possibly characters were very fearless and challenged the authorities openly without any self-consequence. Therefore, the lives of both Musa and Ibrahim as were much action based. They changed their life conditions. They did migration and looked more opportunities in different contexts, places and times with different people and circumstances to invite them to Allah ﷻ. These actions were either related with tabligh or learning knowledge. One can look Musa as's life in different places with his, qawm, people and learning the knowledge for example with Khidr as. Similarly, Ibrahim as changed his living conditions, challenged his own people where his father lived. Then, he moved to another place and challenged another king, Nimrod without any fear. Besides, Ibrahim as inquired to learn from Allah ﷻ about how Allah ﷻ creates, and the case of creation of the birds with the witness of Ibrahim as is mentioned in the Qurān in this context. In this case of learning and knowledge, Allah ﷻ taught Ibrahim as directly as the Khalilullah, the Friend of Allah جل جلاله. On the other hand, Allah ﷻ sent Musa as to Khidr as to learn from him, SubhanAllah. There are different levels of the prophets. In this perspective, our Prophet Mustafa ﷺ, has the title of Khalilullah because as an ummi, Allah ﷻ teaches him ﷺ all the knowledge. In addition, al-Mustafa ﷺ gets the title of Habibullah, the one who is Loved by Allah ﷻ. In this perspective, our Prophet ﷺ have all the intrinsic qualities of other prophets as the final messenger and prophet صلى الله عليه وسلم of Allah ﷻ and as their imam. In his life time, the Prophet showed the representation of the hass, essence of these qualities. Although the Prophet referred Ibrahim as the Khalilullah, one can say that the Prophet ﷺ had all the attributes of Khalilullah, Kalimullah, Ruhullah, Safiyullah and all. Rasulullah ﷺ is cami'u, collector of all these qualitites.

اللهم صلي علي سيدنا محمد و علي سيدنا المرسلين امين٣٨٦

Comparatively, one can review the lives of Nûh as, Hûd as, Sālih as, Lut as and Shuayb. Their softness and gentleness with their people was notable. They did not move or migrate to any other location but dedicated all their lives to their people.

The expression taqwa can signify the main reason of these people's loss due to having no adequate taqwa.

The case of Yûnus as is also interesting. It has a unique category.

[149-151³⁸⁷]

{ وَتَنْحِتُونَ مِنَ الْجِبَالِ بُيُوتًا فَارِهِينَ {الشعراء/149} فَاتَّقُوا اللَّهَ وَأَطِيعُونِ {الشعراء/150}
وَلَا تُطِيعُوا أَمْرَ الْمُسْرِفِينَ {الشعراء/151} الَّذِينَ يُفْسِدُونَ فِي الْأَرْضِ وَلَا يُصْلِحُونَ

The power, responsibility, and authority should bring justice, and peace-making as mentioned in the word, يُصْلِحُونَ. If the power or authority is not used in this manner, then, يُفْسِدُونَ فِي الْأَرْضِ, fasad, mischief occurs. As power increases as mentioned in the part, وَتَنْحِتُونَ مِنَ الْجِبَالِ بُيُوتًا فَارِهِينَ, a person or groups can become arrogant and self-promoting.

[165]³⁸⁸

أَتَأْتُونَ الذُّكْرَانَ مِنَ الْعَالَمِينَ

The word الذُّكْرَانَ³⁸⁹ can possibly show that (الله اعلم) the case of LGBT is mainly a problem of men not women. In other words, the problem or unnatural tendency of man is due to his spiritual sickness. In that perspective, each spiritual sickness such as arrogance, backbiting, jealousy, anger or others are all sins. This issue is a sin itself.

A woman's tendency with the same gender is not mentioned. This shows in essence that the women may not have this problem like men. I think (الله اعلم) the expression of women in the cases of LGBT can be

---

386. Oh Allah جل جلاله, send blessings on our master Muhammad (ﷺ) and upon our Master of the Messengers.
387. (26:149) And that you will [always be able to] hew dwellings out of the mountains with [the same] great skill? 26:150 "Be, then, conscious of God, and pay heed unto me, (26:151) And pay no heed to the counsel of those who are given to excesses—
388. (26:165) "Must you, of all people, [lustfully] approach men.
389. Men.

deeply rooted as a reaction of women to the issues of subjugation of men.

In other words, as one of contemporary gynecologists mentions that "these women who claim to be partner with another woman in essence, they don't want to do anything with men. (41)". This could be due to an oppression, abuse, divorce, or other maltreatment of these women by men in their past history.

In other perspective, this can be another perspective or outcome of the Western discourse of feminism as a reaction to gender oppression or patriarchal dominance.

[166][390]

الْعَادُونَ

If one reviews and focuses on the word الْعَادُونَ, there are three places in the Qurān that this word comes. In each case, the word is used to explain what is normal, natural and within the limits of human spousal relationship. It is important to protect and use what Allah ﷻ gave to us as mentioned with the word, حَافِظُونَ. Yes, there may be some illicit, haram, temptations and feelings but the person is expected to control himself or herself. As always, Allah ﷻ shows us the halal, the ways of natural, clean and best ways of directing human needs for food, spousal relationships, ethics, justice and belief.

[5-7][391]

{ وَالَّذِينَ هُمْ لِفُرُوجِهِمْ حَافِظُونَ {المؤمنون/5} إِلَّا عَلَى أَزْوَاجِهِمْ أَوْ مَا مَلَكَتْ أَيْمَانُهُمْ فَإِنَّهُمْ غَيْرُ مَلُومِينَ {المؤمنون/6} فَمَنِ ابْتَغَى وَرَاءَ ذَلِكَ فَأُوْلَئِكَ هُمُ الْعَادُونَ {المؤمنون/7} }

---

390. (26:166) Keeping yourselves aloof from all the [lawful] spouses whom your Sustainer has created for you? Nay, but you are people who transgress all bounds of what is right!"
391. 23:5 And they who guard their private parts. 23:6 Except from their wives or those their right hands possess, for indeed, they will not be blamed. 23:7 But whoever seeks beyond that, then those are the transgressors.

[165-166]³⁹²

أَتَأْتُونَ الذُّكْرَانَ مِنَ الْعَالَمِينَ {الشعراء/165} وَتَذَرُونَ مَا خَلَقَ لَكُمْ رَبُّكُمْ مِنْ أَزْوَاجِكُم
بَلْ أَنْتُمْ قَوْمٌ عَادُونَ {الشعراء/166}

[29-31]³⁹³

وَالَّذِينَ هُمْ لِفُرُوجِهِمْ حَافِظُونَ {المعارج/29} إِلَّا عَلَى أَزْوَاجِهِمْ أَوْ مَا مَلَكَتْ أَيْمَانُهُمْ فَإِنَّهُمْ
غَيْرُ مَلُومِينَ {المعارج/30} فَمَنِ ابْتَغَى وَرَاء ذَلِكَ فَأُوْلَئِكَ هُمُ الْعَادُونَ {المعارج/31}

In Sûrah shuarah as mentioned above (166), Imam Bagawi (Rh) (36), describes this word, الْعَادُونَ, as mixing Halal with Haram. Zamahshari (43) describes the word الْعَادُونَ, transgressing the limits. In other words, Allah ﷻ shows the person an azimah in the fiqh terminology, the preferred way, but the person follows and does something else similar to other sins.

[171]³⁹⁴

إلَّا عَجُوزًا فِي الْغَابِرِينَ

The above verse comes repeatedly in the Qurān. I think (الله اعلم) that there is a possible hint in a families' private life. Because if it is not necessary, the Qurān does not describe the evils or batil explicitly not to fill the minds with temptations, urges or wrong renderings. In this case, a lady who is menopause in old ages can have painful experience with the relationships with her spouse (42).

Therefore, legitimization an action from her perspective, as in the case of the wife of Lut as, can be a wrong rendering, (الله اعلم). In a private relationship of spouses, the couples can have relations as long as it is not haram but taking this and applying it in different contexts in the case of الذُّكْرَانَ³⁹⁵ becomes haram, sin and not natural as the way that Allah ﷻ created the spouses and established the guidelines fitting into fitrah,

---

392. 26:165 Do you approach males among the worlds. 26:166 And leave what your Lord has created for you as mates? But you are a people transgressing."
393. 70:29 And those who guard their private parts. 70:30 Except from their wives or those their right hands possess, for indeed, they are not to be blamed. 70:31 But whoever seeks beyond that, then they are the transgressors.
394. (26:171) all but an old woman, who was among those that stayed behind.
395. Men.

natural disposition. Unnatural relationships and dispositions can spread disease (42). [192-197][396]

The below verses once again establish the authenticity and personal relevance of the Qurān.

{وَإِنَّهُ لَتَنزِيلُ رَبِّ الْعَالَمِينَ {الشعراء/192} نَزَلَ بِهِ الرُّوحُ الْأَمِينُ {الشعراء/193}
عَلَى قَلْبِكَ لِتَكُونَ مِنَ الْمُنذِرِينَ {الشعراء/194} بِلِسَانٍ عَرَبِيٍّ مُبِينٍ {الشعراء/195}
وَإِنَّهُ لَفِي زُبُرِ الْأَوَّلِينَ {الشعراء/196} أَوَلَمْ يَكُن لَّهُمْ آيَةً أَن يَعْلَمَهُ عُلَمَاءُ بَنِي إِسْرَائِيلَ
{الشعراء/197}

The below verse shows with emphasize and takīd multiple times that Allah ﷻ revealed the Qurān.

{وَإِنَّهُ لَتَنزِيلُ رَبِّ الْعَالَمِينَ {الشعراء/192}

One can realize multitude of emphasis in the expression وَإِنَّهُ لَتَنزِيلُ[397] with the phrases waw, innahu, and lam. Then, a similar emphasis comes after a few ayahs as {وَإِنَّهُ لَفِي زُبُرِ الْأَوَّلِينَ {الشعراء/196} that for sure this Book, the Qurān was mentioned in the previous books.

This ayah and similar ones in the Qurān show that the message of the Qurān and the Prophet is not new. Allah ﷻ sent the same message and guidance since the time of the creation of Adam as and the message with the Qurān will remain until the Day of Qiyamah. In this regard, Islam is not new, but a continuation of the previous messages. All the Divine Books show the continuation of one to another. Therefore, there is a mention in each scripture for the upcoming next scripture. All the messengers and prophets of Allah ﷻ show the continuation of one to another. Therefore, there is a mention in the sayings of the prophets for the next prophet or messenger of Allah ﷻ. Therefore, proclamation of faith in Islamic creed as mentioned in the last verses of Sûrah Baqarah and others necessitate that a believer is required to believe in all the Books and Prophets sent by Allah ﷻ. If someone embraces only their

---

396. (26:192) NOW, BEHOLD, this [divine writ] has indeed been bestowed from on high by the Sustainer of all the worlds: (26:193) trustworthy divine inspiration has alighted with it from on high (26:194) upon thy heart, [O Muhammad] so that thou mayest be among those who preach (26:195) in the clear Arabic tongue. 26:196 And, verily, [the essence of] this [revelation] is indeed found in the ancient books of divine wisdom [as well]. 26:197 Is it not evidence enough for them that [so many] learned men from among the children of Israel have recognized this [as true]?

397. This [divine writ) has indeed been bestowed.

own prophet or book and says "I only believe my prophet or book." This can be in other means alluding against to the Just Attribute of Allah ﷻ.

In other words, thinking that Allah ﷻ did not send a message, prophet or guidance at other times to other people is a wrong construction or Aqedah about Allah ﷻ implying that there were no divine guidance before Islam. Allah ﷻ is Just, Merciful and Caring. Allah ﷻ does not leave people without guidance. But it is the person's choice to decide, to accept and to follow. This establishes a true, robust and genuine authenticity in rational and mindful methodology of Islam.

Another level of authenticity and assurance comes with the statement نَزَلَ بِهِ الرُّوحُ الْأَمِينُ[398]. During process of delivery of the divine message to humans, there was no misinterpretation or a personal spiritual experience as this notion is common in Western engagements of religion.

In other words, we hear a lot of assertions from different religious groups, the statements of "I am inspired," or, "God inspired me." Although these personal inspirations can be relevant and genuine, but there is still the possibility of deception. So, Allah ﷻ places another level of authenticity and assurance that the Qurān is not a personal interpretation or experience. But there is a process of delivery similar to other books or scriptures.

Another level of experiential authenticity عَلَى قَلْبِكَ لِتَكُونَ مِنَ الْمُنْذِرِينَ[399] so that when you experience this with your own heart then you would invite others as well. After one experiences the divine messages in this case the revelation, the next stage of embodiment follows. As one of the titles of the Prophet was the "Walking Qurān" (9) (hadith#746). This title shows the full embodiment of the Qurān in the life of the Prophet (ﷺ). This embodiment is called Sunnah or hadith in tradition.

Therefore, the full human embodiment of the revelation, the Qurān, is the life and practices of the Prophet ﷺ. This is called Sunnah or hadith. Therefore, the hadith or Sunnah is as important as the Qurān. The Prophet (ﷺ) demonstrated as a human in his life span the Divine Will as revealed to us with the Qurān. Some people may call this the application of the theory. But calling the Qurān with this referral may not be correct and respectful in genuine Islamic discourses.

---

398. Trustworthy divine inspiration has alighted with it from on high.
399. Upon thy heart, [O Muhammad] so that thou mayest be among those who preach.

Another level of authenticity is بِلِسَانٍ عَرَبِيٍّ مُبِينٍ[400] the Qurān is in Arabic and translations are not the Qurān but interpretations. This phrase is repeated in various places in the Qurān to emphasize and underline this notion. When any text is translated, then it is not the original text anymore but interpreted meanings of the text in that language. This means that there is a room for error. The text should be understood in the original language with its context.

Another level of authenticity is[401] وَإِنَّهُ لَفِي زُبُرِ الْأَوَّلِينَ {الشعراء/196} that the Qurān was mentioned in the previous scriptures sent by Allah and if you don't believe it, then you can review the scholarship in other books as also testified by their scholars أَوَلَمْ يَكُن لَّهُمْ آيَةً أَن يَعْلَمَهُ عُلَمَاء بَنِي إِسْرَائِيلَ {الشعراء/197}[402]. The scholars of other scriptures know it. Therefore, the Qurān strongly criticizes these scholars. They know it, but they don't reveal it and inform about it.

One can also see the symmetry in the below ayahs: [192-194][403]

وَإِنَّهُ لَتَنزِيلُ رَبِّ الْعَالَمِينَ {الشعراء/192} نَزَلَ بِهِ الرُّوحُ الْأَمِينُ {الشعراء/193} عَلَى قَلْبِكَ لِتَكُونَ مِنَ الْمُنذِرِينَ {الشعراء/194}

With the following below ayahs: [210-214][404]

وَمَا تَنَزَّلَتْ بِهِ الشَّيَاطِينُ {الشعراء/210} وَمَا يَنبَغِي لَهُمْ وَمَا يَسْتَطِيعُونَ {الشعراء/211} إِنَّهُمْ عَنِ السَّمْعِ لَمَعْزُولُونَ {الشعراء/212} فَلَا تَدْعُ مَعَ اللَّهِ إِلَهًا آخَرَ فَتَكُونَ مِنَ الْمُعَذَّبِينَ {الشعراء/213} وَأَنذِرْ عَشِيرَتَكَ الْأَقْرَبِينَ {الشعراء/214}

In the ayahs 192-194, Allah establishes repetitively the authenticity of the Qurān with the وَإِنَّهُ لَتَنزِيلُ رَبِّ الْعَالَمِينَ[405], then, gauging the reader about the people's ungrounded thoughts and ideas opposing

---

400. In the clear Arabic tongue.
401. And, verily, [the essence of] this [revelation] is indeed found in the ancient books of divine wisdom [as well].
402. Is it not evidence enough for them[84] that [so many] learned men from among the children of Israel have recognized this [as true]?
403. (26:192) NOW, BEHOLD, this [divine writ] has indeed been bestowed from on high by the Sustainer of all the worlds: (26:193) trustworthy divine inspiration has alighted with it from on high (26:194) upon thy heart, [O Muhammad] so that thou mayest be among those who preach.
404. 26:210 And the devils have not brought it [i.e., the revelation] down. 26:211 It is not allowable for them, nor would they be able. 26:212 Indeed they, from [its] hearing, are removed. 26:213 So do not invoke with Allah جل جلاله another deity and [thus] be among the punished. 26:214 And warn, [O Muhammad], your closest kindred.
405. This [divine writ] has indeed been bestowed from on high by the Sustainer of all the worlds.

them with the same wording of وَمَا تَنَزَّلَتْ بِهِ الشَّيَاطِينُ[406]. Humans, jinn and shaytan are given free choice and acting accordingly but this free choice has also its limits. One of the places of their limit is that shaytan, people or jinn do not have access and freedom to interfere with the true revelation of Allah as mentioned: [211-212][407]

وَمَا يَنبَغِي لَهُمْ وَمَا يَسْتَطِيعُونَ {الشعراء/211} إِنَّهُمْ عَنِ السَّمْعِ لَمَعْزُولُونَ {الشعراء/212}

There are many perspectives of the above verses such as: [9][408]

إِنَّا نَحْنُ نَزَّلْنَا الذِّكْرَ وَإِنَّا لَهُ لَحَافِظُونَ {الحجر/9}

[7-10][409]

وَحِفْظًا مِّن كُلِّ شَيْطَانٍ مَّارِدٍ {الصافات/7} لَا يَسَّمَّعُونَ إِلَى الْمَلَإِ الْأَعْلَى وَيُقْذَفُونَ مِن كُلِّ جَانِبٍ {الصافات/8} دُحُورًا وَلَهُمْ عَذَابٌ وَاصِبٌ {الصافات/9} إِلَّا مَنْ خَطِفَ الْخَطْفَةَ فَأَتْبَعَهُ شِهَابٌ ثَاقِبٌ {الصافات/10}

Allah does not give the ability, means and free choice to these beings in the realms of claiming the Qurān sent by anyone else but except from Allah and since it is the last Book of Allah. In other words, being the last scripture from Allah necessitates that it should remain same until the End of Days. Therefore, these beings will not be given permission, willpower, and ability to alter the Qurān even though they may want to change it. Here is a place where the free will of humans, jinn and all creation is blocked.

Besides the above discussion, it may be interesting to view below ayahs with the expression إِنَّا نَحْنُ[410] to see and understand the limits of human's free will:

---

406. And the devils have not brought it [i.e., the revelation] down.
407. 26:211 It is not allowable for them, nor would they be able. 26:212 Indeed they, from [its] hearing, are removed.
408. Indeed, it is We who sent down the message [i.e., the Qurān], and indeed, We will be its guardian.
409. 37:7 And as protection against every rebellious devil. 37:8 [So] they may not listen to the exalted assembly [of angels] and are pelted from every side. 37:9 Repelled; and for them is a constant punishment. 37:10 Except one who snatches [some words] by theft, but they are pursued by a burning flame, piercing [in brightness].
410. Indeed, it is We.

إِنَّا نَحْنُ نَرِثُ الْأَرْضَ وَمَنْ عَلَيْهَا وَإِلَيْنَا يُرْجَعُونَ[411]{مريم/40}

إِنَّا نَحْنُ نُحْيِي الْمَوْتَى وَنَكْتُبُ مَا قَدَّمُوا وَآثَارَهُمْ وَكُلَّ شَيْءٍ أَحْصَيْنَاهُ فِي إِمَامٍ مُبِينٍ {يس/[412]12}

إِنَّا نَحْنُ نُحْيِي وَنُمِيتُ وَإِلَيْنَا الْمَصِيرُ[413]{ق/43}

إِنَّا نَحْنُ نَزَّلْنَا عَلَيْكَ الْقُرْآنَ تَنزِيلًا[414]{الإنسان/23}

عَلَى قَلْبِكَ لِتَكُونَ مِنَ الْمُنذِرِينَ[415]{الشعراء/194} Lastly, when one reviews the ayah then Allah ﷻ explains who should be the inzār for. After a few ayahs, later as {وَأَنذِرْ عَشِيرَتَكَ الْأَقْرَبِينَ[416]{الشعراء/214} that it is important to give and start informing about the message with the close ones who have kinship, الله اعلم.

[198-200][417]

وَلَوْ نَزَّلْنَاهُ عَلَى بَعْضِ الْأَعْجَمِينَ {الشعراء/198} فَقَرَأَهُ عَلَيْهِم مَّا كَانُوا بِهِ مُؤْمِنِينَ {الشعراء/199} كَذَلِكَ سَلَكْنَاهُ فِي قُلُوبِ الْمُجْرِمِينَ {الشعراء/200}

The person will always hear arguments as we hear today: why was the Qurān revealed to an Arab? Even, the Qurān was revealed to another person, non-Arab, they would still not want to genuinely understand, review and believe in it. The reason is due to the diseases in their heart: arrogance leading to stubbornness.

---

411. Indeed, it is We who will inherit the earth and whoever is on it, and to Us they will be returned.
412. Indeed, it is We who bring the dead to life and record what they have put forth and what they left behind, and all things We have enumerated in a clear register.
413. Indeed, it is We who give life and cause death, and to Us is the destination.
414. Indeed, it is We who have sent down to you, [O Muhammad], the Qurān progressively.
415. Upon your heart, [O Muhammad]—that you may be of the warners.
416. And warn, [O Muhammad], your closest kindred.
417. (26:198) But [even] had We bestowed it from on high upon any of the non-Arabs, (26:199) and had he recited it unto them [in his own tongue], they would not have believed in it. (26:200) Thus have We caused this [message] to pass [unheeded] through the hearts of those who are lost in sin:

[201]⁴¹⁸

لَا يُؤْمِنُونَ بِهِ حَتَّى يَرَوُا الْعَذَابَ الْأَلِيمَ {الشعراء/201}

And don't worry, these are the type of people that don't genuinely approach to learn from the Qurān and change themselves. They don't want to remove the arrogance within themselves unless they see the realities of accountability. It is similar to a student if one tells them if you don't study you will fail. This student studies not because of genuine learning but due to the fear of failing.

[202-209]⁴¹⁹

فَيَأْتِيَهُم بَغْتَةً وَهُمْ لَا يَشْعُرُونَ {الشعراء/202} فَيَقُولُوا هَلْ نَحْنُ مُنظَرُونَ {الشعراء/203} أَفَبِعَذَابِنَا يَسْتَعْجِلُونَ {الشعراء/204} أَفَرَأَيْتَ إِن مَّتَّعْنَاهُمْ سِنِينَ {الشعراء/205} ثُمَّ جَاءَهُم مَّا كَانُوا يُوعَدُونَ {الشعراء/206}

مَا أَغْنَى عَنْهُم مَّا كَانُوا يُمَتَّعُونَ {الشعراء/207} وَمَا أَهْلَكْنَا مِن قَرْيَةٍ إِلَّا لَهَا مُنذِرُونَ {الشعراء/208} ذِكْرَى وَمَا كُنَّا ظَالِمِينَ {الشعراء/209}

After, all the cases of the Prophets presented in this Sûrah, Allah ﷻ sent them genuine, honest, and caring prophets but they denied and they made fun of them. Then remember, فَيَأْتِيَهُم بَغْتَةً وَهُمْ لَا يَشْعُرُونَ {الشعراء/202} that Allah ﷻ can end life of a person at any time. At the time of dying, the person cries out "Oh Allah, give me some time, give me another chance and I promise I will be good, humble and appreciative." But Allah ﷻ mentions that they were the ones, who were saying and making fun that they were saying أَفَبِعَذَابِنَا يَسْتَعْجِلُونَ {الشعراء/204} "if what you were saying is right and show it to us". Allah ﷻ gives a person years of life as mentioned أَفَرَأَيْتَ إِن مَّتَّعْنَاهُمْ سِنِينَ {الشعراء/205}. In this life span, the person has free will, and opportunities to change, and to think about one's relationship with Allah ﷻ. In these

---

418. (26:201) They will not believe in it till they behold the grievous suffering
419. (26:202) That will come upon them [on resurrection,] all of a sudden, without their being aware [of its approach]; (26:203) And then they will exclaim, "Could we have a respite?" 26:204 Do they, then, [really] wish that Our chastisement be hastened on? (26:205) But hast thou ever considered [this]: If We do allow them to enjoy [this life] for some years, (26:206) and thereupon that [chastisement] which they were promised befalls them—(26:207) of what avail to them will be all their past enjoyments?
(26:208) And withal, never have We destroyed any community unless it had been warned (26:209) and reminded: for, never do We wrong [anyone].

years of life, a person has prospects to choose and to decide. But, with his or her philosophical or demagogical attitude of self-denial, this person finds alternative reasoning by ignoring the internal voice of conscience. The person then builds a wall of artificial deities to escape to and to refuge in through reason, guided with arrogance, and self-denial. The worst problem is that the person does not know him or herself through self-denial. The emotions, and the spiritual faculties are all crying but this person shuts down all the screams of the conscience and threatens them with "lowliness, backwardness, or lack of confidence." Therefore, Allah then mentions {الشعراء/207} مَا أَغْنَى عَنْهُم مَّا كَانُوا يُمَتَّعُونَ, these false artificial deities of attachments, mind, world, friends, positions, and wealth were not helpful when the person was dying and screaming. And after all, Allah is Just and does not oppress. Allah sends constantly internal and external signs, messengers, and opportunities to each person in order them to realize their real self and their needs. So that, one can realize the Creator, Allah as mentioned وَمَا أَهْلَكْنَا مِن قَرْيَةٍ إِلَّا لَهَا مُنذِرُونَ {الشعراء/208} ذِكْرَى وَمَا كُنَّا ظَالِمِينَ {الشعراء/209}. Therefore, at the end, no one has the right to blame others or Allah about any consequence, but their own selves because Allah is the Most Merciful and the Most Just and the Most Fair.

[214-220][420]

وَأَنذِرْ عَشِيرَتَكَ الْأَقْرَبِينَ {الشعراء/214} وَاخْفِضْ جَنَاحَكَ لِمَنِ اتَّبَعَكَ مِنَ الْمُؤْمِنِينَ {الشعراء/215} فَإِنْ عَصَوْكَ فَقُلْ إِنِّي بَرِيءٌ مِّمَّا تَعْمَلُونَ {الشعراء/216} وَتَوَكَّلْ عَلَى الْعَزِيزِ الرَّحِيمِ {الشعراء/217} الَّذِي يَرَاكَ حِينَ تَقُومُ {الشعراء/218} وَتَقَلُّبَكَ فِي السَّاجِدِينَ {الشعراء/219} إِنَّهُ هُوَ السَّمِيعُ الْعَلِيمُ {الشعراء/220}

Don't worry after you complete your responsibility inviting others and concentrate on your close kinship relations to invite them to Allah. When you spend time with the believers, be kind and caring to them. It is a reality that even if they may hurt you by engaging in evil with lack of adab with Allah, then still be patient. At that time, the person is

---

420. 26:214 And warn [whomever thou canst reach, beginning with] thy kinsfolk, (26:215) and spread the wings of thy tenderness over all of the believers who may follow thee; (26:216) but if they disobey thee, say, "I am free of responsibility for aught that you may do!"—(26:217) and place thy trust in the Almighty, the Dispenser of Grace, (26:218) who sees thee when thou standest [alone], (26:219) and (sees) thy behaviour among those who prostrate themselves [before Him]: (26:220) for, verily, He alone is all-hearing, all-knowing!

expected to make one's stance clear that he or she does not agree with their evil and disrespect of the shā"ir as they are the respected items and the signs designated by Allah ﷻ.

At that time, when the person feels lonely by himself or herself, it is important to rely, make tawakkul only to Allah ﷻ. Because, Allah ﷻ sees the person, knows the person's intention, real effort and the one's efforts of praying to Allah ﷻ asking for patience.

[218]⁴²¹

الَّذِي يَرَاكَ حِينَ تَقُومُ {الشعراء/218}

Allah ﷻ is aware of all the person's engagements.

[221-222]⁴²²

هَلْ أُنَبِّئُكُمْ عَلَى مَن تَنَزَّلُ الشَّيَاطِينُ {الشعراء/221} تَنَزَّلُ عَلَى كُلِّ أَفَّاكٍ أَثِيمٍ {الشعراء/222}

For sure, the people who are engaged in sin, backbiting, slander, evil and destruction will always be accompanied by the shaytans. Shaytans will give them the temptations, stress and anxiety. At the end, shaytan will pomp-up their arrogance by claiming that they are on the right path.

[223]⁴²³

يُلْقُونَ السَّمْعَ وَأَكْثَرُهُمْ كَاذِبُونَ {الشعراء/223}

Here, the word يُلْقُون can mean that these people are listening to the temptations of the shayateen (43). Or, the shayateen are listening to malail a'la and the people. Then, these shayateen take a word or a sound, and mix with lies and take it others to cause more fitnah and destruction, الله اعلم.

---

421. Who sees you when you arise.
422. (26:221) [And] shall I tell you upon whom it is that those evil spirits descend? (26:222) They descend upon all sinful self-deceivers
423. (26:223) who readily lend ear [to every falsehood], and most of whom lie to others as well.

20

Sûrah Naml

[7]⁴²⁴

إِذْ قَالَ مُوسَى لِأَهْلِهِ إِنِّي آنَسْتُ نَارًا سَآتِيكُم مِّنْهَا بِخَبَرٍ أَوْ آتِيكُم بِشِهَابٍ قَبَسٍ لَّعَلَّكُمْ تَصْطَلُونَ {النمل/7}

فَلَمَّا قَضَى مُوسَىالْأَجَلَ وَسَارَ بِأَهْلِهِ آنَسَ مِن جَانِبِ الطُّورِ نَارًا قَالَ لِأَهْلِهِ امْكُثُوا إِنِّي آنَسْتُ نَارًا لَّعَلِّي آتِيكُم مِّنْهَا بِخَبَرٍ أَوْ جَذْوَةٍ مِنَ النَّارِ لَعَلَّكُمْ تَصْطَلُونَ ⁴²⁵{القصص/29}

When one reviews the words تَصْطَلُونَ in the above two ayahs, other than their apparent meanings as mentioned in tafasir, one can also try to understand the inner meanings. In other words, as physical warmness brings the person comfort, the spiritual warmness with imān brings the person comfort as well, الله اعلم. In this case, warmness is a positive state or maqam. When one compares the case of Musa as with the Prophet ﷺ, Musa as went to get this maqam from Allah ﷻ yet the Prophet ﷺ was already in the state of warmness given by Allah ﷻ as mentioned يَا أَيُّهَا الْمُدَّثِّرُ{المدثر/1}⁴²⁷, الله اعلم, and يَا أَيُّهَا الْمُزَّمِّلُ⁴²⁶{المزمل/1}. In both cases, Allah ﷻ instructs them to give warmness of revelation with tabligh to people through the Qurān and Tawrah, الله اعلم.

---

424. 27:7 LO! (While lost in the desert,] Moses said to his family: "Behold, I perceive a fire (far away]; I may bring you from there some tiding [as to which way we are to pursue], or bring you tat least] a burning brand so that you might warm yourselves."
425. And when Moses had completed the term and was traveling with his family, he perceived from the direction of the mount a fire. He said to his family, "Stay here; indeed, I have perceived a fire. Perhaps I will bring you from there [some] information or burning wood from the fire that you may warm yourselves."
426. O you who wraps himself [in clothing].
427. O you who covers himself [with a garment].

[91-93]⁴²⁸

إِنَّمَا أُمِرْتُ أَنْ أَعْبُدَ رَبَّ هَذِهِ الْبَلْدَةِ الَّذِي حَرَّمَهَا وَلَهُ كُلُّ شَيْءٍ وَأُمِرْتُ أَنْ أَكُونَ مِنَ الْمُسْلِمِينَ {النمل/91} وَأَنْ أَتْلُوَ الْقُرْآنَ فَمَنِ اهْتَدَى فَإِنَّمَا يَهْتَدِي لِنَفْسِهِ وَمَن ضَلَّ فَقُلْ إِنَّمَا أَنَا مِنَ الْمُنذِرِينَ {النمل/92} وَقُلِ الْحَمْدُ لِلَّهِ سَيُرِيكُمْ آيَاتِهِ فَتَعْرِفُونَهَا وَمَا رَبُّكَ بِغَافِلٍ عَمَّا تَعْمَلُونَ {النمل/93}

In the above verses, reading the Qurān as tilawah is mentioned as وَأَنْ أَتْلُوَ الْقُرْآنَ⁴²⁹ as an order. As the Qurān, comes from the word qar'a and tilawah is another word. So, reading the Qurān is explicitly mentioned as a word. One can understand that the Qurān should be recited as a form of main dhikr, remembrance of Allah (الله اعلم ,) ﷻ.

On another note, the Qurān guides people as one can see وَأَنْ أَتْلُوَ⁴³⁰ الْقُرْآنَ فَمَنِ اهْتَدَى, that if person does tilawah, the recitation of the Qurān then, the expected result is guidance from Allah ﷻ. However, the free will and choice of the person is still there and present, and Allah ﷻ does not force. Still, the person needs to make the choice as it immediately follows with the expression فَمَنِ اهْتَدَى⁴³¹ in the ayah:

وَأَنْ أَتْلُوَ الْقُرْآنَ فَمَنِ اهْتَدَى فَإِنَّمَا يَهْتَدِي لِنَفْسِهِ وَمَن ضَلَّ فَقُلْ إِنَّمَا أَنَا مِنَ الْمُنذِرِينَ.⁴³²

SubhanAllah, yet, the person should continue doing inzar, inviting people to the religion and warning them the outcomes of their engagement whether people accept it or not as mentioned فَقُلْ إِنَّمَا أَنَا مِنَ⁴³³ الْمُنْذِرِينَ that "I am just a messenger relating you the message and warning you about the outcomes of your engagement."

---

428. 27:91 [SAY, O Muhammad:] "I have been bidden to worship the Sustainer of this City— Him who has made it sacred, and unto whom all things belong; and I have been bidden to be of those who surrender themselves to Him, (27:92) and to convey this Qur'an [to the world]." Whoever, therefore, chooses to follow the right path, follows it but for his own good; and if any wills to go astray, say [unto him]: "I am only a warner!"
27:93 And say: "All praise is due to God! In time He will make you see [the truth of] His messages, and then you shall know them [for what they are]." And thy Sustainer is not unmindful of whatever you all may do.
429. And to convey this Qur'an [to the world]."
430. And to convey this Qur'an [to the world]." Whoever, therefore, chooses to follow the right path."
431. Whoever, therefore, chooses to follow the right path.
432. And to convey this Qur'an [to the world]." Whoever, therefore, chooses to follow the right path, follows it but for his own good; and if any wills to go astray, say [unto him]: "I am only a warner!"
433. Say [unto him]: "I am only a warner!"

After all this, when you recognize, appreciate, have gratitude and imān for Allah ﷻ, then say Alhamdulillah as mentioned [434]وَقُلِ الْحَمْدُ لِلَّهِ because it is from the Fadl, Grace, and Rahmah, Mercy, of Allah ﷻ that you have imān and you should not brag about it. Having imān necessitates another Hamd which requires constant gratitude to Allah ﷻ. The ayah ends with the expression [435]سَيُرِيكُمْ آيَاتِهِ فَتَعْرِفُونَهَا as Allah ﷻ will constantly show internal and external, implicit and explicit signs, ayahs for each person in one's life span. In this perspective, Allah ﷻ knows the reality of everyone's engagements as mentioned [436]وَمَا رَبُّكَ بِغَافِلٍ عَمَّا تَعْمَلُونَ so that the observer should not be fooled with any type of evil or good-seeming incidents in life for others and deduce wrong meanings from them, الله اعلم. Everyone in life has individualized signs from Allah ﷻ as individualized education is especially promoted today.

Sûrah Qasas

All the narratives (stories about other nations) can also serve the purpose of comforting the person in a story or case format. The implicit and third person narrative styles can have a lighter, implicit and calmer effect on the person due the power and essence of the verse compared to the direct renderings of the verses straightforwardly talking with the person. In this case, a genuine person can be crashed into pieces due to overpowering effects of the words of Allah ﷻ as the months in their real and genuine understanding can crash as mentioned لَوْ أَنزَلْنَا هَذَا الْقُرْآنَ عَلَى جَبَلٍ لَّرَأَيْتَهُ خَاشِعًا مُّتَصَدِّعًا مِّنْ خَشْيَةِ اللَّهِ وَتِلْكَ الْأَمْثَالُ نَضْرِبُهَا لِلنَّاسِ لَعَلَّهُمْ يَتَفَكَّرُونَ [437]{الحشر/21}

---

434. And say: "All praise is due to God!
435. He will make you see [the truth of] His messages.
436. And thy Sustainer is not unmindful of whatever you all may do.
437. If We had sent down this Qurān upon a mountain, you would have seen it humbled and splitting from fear of Allah جل جلاله. And these examples We present to the people that perhaps they will give thought.

One can easily be overpowered, lose consciousness, and even die if there are no stories or narratives with calming effects due to weak and limited human realities when they encounter the Azamah of Allah ﷻ with the Qurān. Therefore, the stories or narratives can serve the purpose of tuning this frequency of Azamah according to the weak wavelengths of humans, الله اعلم.

[15]⁴³⁸

وَدَخَلَ الْمَدِينَةَ عَلَى حِينِ غَفْلَةٍ مِّنْ أَهْلِهَا فَوَجَدَ فِيهَا رَجُلَيْنِ يَقْتَتِلَانِ هَذَا مِن شِيعَتِهِ وَ هَذَا مِنْ عَدُوِّهِ فَاسْتَغَاثَهُ الَّذِي مِن شِيعَتِهِ عَلَى الَّذِي مِنْ عَدُوِّهِ فَوَكَزَهُ مُوسَى فَقَضَى عَلَيْهِ قَالَ هَذَا مِنْ عَمَلِ الشَّيْطَانِ إِنَّهُ عَدُوٌّ مُّضِلٌّ مُّبِينٌ

If the statement غَفْلَةٍ مِّنْ أَهْلِهَا⁴³⁹ can show that the people could have been resting at night-time. The accident of killing happens without the will of Musa (as) at these night times. Therefore, Musa as admits that this was the عَمَلِ الشَّيْطَانِ⁴⁴⁰. This الله اعلم, Allah ﷻ knows the best, can indicate that at night times the person should not be outside unnecessarily due to the dominance of different creation of Allah ﷻ and the possibility of doing evil as mentioned {القصص/1} قَالَ هَذَا مِنْ عَمَلِ الشَّيْطَانِ إِنَّهُ عَدُوٌّ مُّضِلٌّ مُّبِينٌ. As mentioned by the Prophet ﷺ that the different creations of Allah ﷻ spread on earth at night time.

---

438. And he entered the city at a time of inattention by its people and found therein two men fighting: one from his faction and one from among his enemy. And the one from his faction called for help to him against the one from his enemy, so Moses struck him and [unintentionally] killed him. [Moses] said, "This is from the work of Satan. Indeed, he is a manifest, misleading enemy."
439. At a time of inattention by its people.
440. The work of Satan.

[18-31]⁴⁴¹

فَأَصْبَحَ فِي الْمَدِينَةِ خَائِفًا يَتَرَقَّبُ فَإِذَا الَّذِي اسْتَنصَرَهُ بِالْأَمْسِ يَسْتَصْرِخُهُ قَالَ لَهُ مُوسَى إِنَّكَ لَغَوِيٌّ مُّبِينٌ {القصص/18}

فَخَرَجَ مِنْهَا خَائِفًا يَتَرَقَّبُ قَالَ رَبِّ نَجِّنِي مِنَ الْقَوْمِ الظَّالِمِينَ {القصص/21}

فَجَاءَتْهُ إِحْدَاهُمَا تَمْشِي عَلَى اسْتِحْيَاءٍ قَالَتْ إِنَّ أَبِي يَدْعُوكَ لِيَجْزِيَكَ أَجْرَ مَا سَقَيْتَ لَنَا فَلَمَّا جَاءَهُ وَقَصَّ عَلَيْهِ الْقَصَصَ قَالَ لَا تَخَفْ نَجَوْتَ مِنَ الْقَوْمِ الظَّالِمِينَ {القصص/25}

---

441. (28:18) And next morning he found himself in the city, looking fearfully about him, when lo! the one who had sought his help the day before [once again] cried out to him [for help—whereupon] Moses said unto him: "Behold, thou art indeed, most clearly, deeply in the wrong!" 28:19 But then, as soon as he was about to lay violent hands on the man who was their [common] enemy, the latter exclaimed: "O Moses, dost thou intend to slay me as thou didst slay another man yesterday? Thy sole aim is to become a tyrant in this land, for thou dost not care to be of those who would set things to rights!" 28:20 And [then and there] a man came running from the farthermost end of the city, and said: "O Moses! Behold, the great ones [of the kingdom] are deliberating upon thy case with a view to killing thee! Begone, then: verily, I am of those who wish thee well!" (28:21) So he went forth from thence, looking fearfully about him, and prayed: "O my Sustainer! Save me from all evildoing folk!" 28:22 And as he turned his face towards Madyan, he said [to himself]: "It may well be that my Sustainer will [thus] guide me onto the right path!" 28:23 NOW WHEN he arrived at the wells of Madyan, he found there a large group of men who were watering [their herds and flocks]; and at some distance from them he came upon two women who were keeping back their flock. He asked [them]: "What is the matter with you?" They answered: "We cannot water [our animals] until the herdsmen drive [theirs] home—for [we are weak and] our father is a very old man. 28:24 So he watered [their flock] for them; and then he withdrew into the shade and prayed: "O my Sustainer! Verily, in dire need am I of any good which Thou mayest bestow upon me!" (28:25) [Shortly] afterwards, one of the two [maidens] approached him, walking shyly, and said: "Behold, my father invites thee, so that he might duly reward thee for thy having watered [our flock] for us." And as soon as [Moses] came unto him and told him the story [of his life], he said: "Have no fear! Thou art now safe from those evildoing folk!" (28:26) Said one of the two [daughters]: "O my father! Hire him: for, behold, the best [man] that thou couldst hire is one who is [as] strong and worthy of trust [as he]!" 28:27 [After some time, the father] said: "Behold, I am willing to let thee wed one of these two daughters of mine on the understanding that thou wilt remain eight years in my service; and if thou shouldst complete ten [years], that would be [an act of grace] from thee, for I do not want to impose any hardship on thee: [on the contrary,] thou wilt find me, if God so wills, righteous in all my dealings." 28:28 Answered [Moses]: "Thus shall it be between me and thee! Whichever of the two terms I fulfil, let there be no ill-will against me. And God be witness to all that we say!" 28:29 AND WHEN Moses had fulfilled his term, and was wandering with his family [in the desert], he perceived a fire on the slope of Mount Sinai: [and so] he said to his family: "Wait here. Behold, I perceive a fire [far away]; perhaps I may bring you from there some tiding, or [at least] a burning brand from the fire, so that you might warm yourselves." 28:30 But when he came close to it, a call was sounded from the right-side bank of the valley, out of the tree [burning] on blessed ground: "O Moses! Verily, I am God, the Sustainer of all the worlds!" 28:31 And [then He said]: "Throw down thy staff!" But as soon as [Moses] saw it move rapidly, as if it were a snake, he drew back [in terror], and did not [dare to] return. [And God spoke to him again:] "O Moses! Draw near, and have no fear for, behold, thou art of those who are secure [in this world and in the next]!

وَأَنْ أَلْقِ عَصَاكَ فَلَمَّا رَآهَا تَهْتَزُّ كَأَنَّهَا جَانٌّ وَلَّى مُدْبِرًا وَلَمْ يُعَقِّبْ يَا مُوسَى أَقْبِلْ وَلَا تَخَفْ إِنَّكَ مِنَ الْآمِنِينَ {القصص/31}

[33-35][442]

قَالَ رَبِّ إِنِّي قَتَلْتُ مِنْهُمْ نَفْسًا فَأَخَافُ أَن يَقْتُلُونِ {القصص/33} وَأَخِي هَارُونُ هُوَ أَفْصَحُ مِنِّي لِسَانًا فَأَرْسِلْهُ مَعِيَ رِدْءًا يُصَدِّقُنِي إِنِّي أَخَافُ أَن يُكَذِّبُونِ {القصص/34}

As one view above ayahs, the ayahs follow each other very closely in the same Sûrah. They all have the common theme of fear, khawf depicted by Musa as. So, Musa as lived part of his life around fear. But, after the assurance of Allah ﷻ with the ayah

قَالَ سَنَشُدُّ عَضُدَكَ بِأَخِيكَ وَنَجْعَلُ لَكُمَا سُلْطَانًا فَلَا يَصِلُونَ إِلَيْكُمَا بِآيَاتِنَا أَنتُمَا وَمَنِ اتَّبَعَكُمَا الْغَالِبُونَ {القصص/35}

then, there was no fear mentioned in the Sûrah for Musa as. Although now Musa as was openly and face to face challenging firawn, Musa as embodied makhāfah only from Allah ﷻ because Allah ﷻ supported him as mentioned سَنَشُدُّ عَضُدَكَ[443].

[19][444]

فَلَمَّا أَنْ أَرَادَ أَن يَبْطِشَ بِالَّذِي هُوَ عَدُوٌّ لَّهُمَا قَالَ يَا مُوسَى أَتُرِيدُ أَن تَقْتُلَنِي كَمَا قَتَلْتَ نَفْسًا بِالْأَمْسِ إِن تُرِيدُ إِلَّا أَن تَكُونَ جَبَّارًا فِي الْأَرْضِ وَمَا تُرِيدُ أَن تَكُونَ مِنَ الْمُصْلِحِينَ {القصص/19}

In the above case, the Qurān depicts as a prototype of some people and characters hiding behind the ethical and good but in essence, they are doing and engaged in evil. This person is involved with evil but his

---

442. 28:33 He said, "My Lord, indeed I killed from among them someone, and I fear they will kill me. 28:34 And my brother Aaron is more fluent than me in tongue, so send him with me as support, verifying me. Indeed, I fear that they will deny me." 28:35 [Allah جل جلاله] said, "We will strengthen your arm through your brother and grant you both supremacy so they will not reach you. [It will be] through Our signs; you and those who follow you will be the predominant."

443. We will strengthen your arm.

444. And when he wanted to strike the one who was an enemy to both of them, he said, "O Moses, do you intend to kill me as you killed someone yesterday? You only want to be a tyrant in the land and do not want to be of the amenders."

argument is for the مِنَ الْمُصْلِحِينَ[445] that he is defending for peace. This is a very interesting psychology and phenomena that the Qurān depicts.

In another viewpoint, it is important not to act with the urges of immediate fear in especially complex situations. When Musa as was involved in an unintended accident of death then there was a fear developed due to complexity of the situation as mentioned فَأَصْبَحَ فِي الْمَدِينَةِ خَائِفًا يَتَرَقَّبُ فَإِذَا الَّذِي اسْتَنصَرَهُ بِالْأَمْسِ يَسْتَصْرِخُهُ قَالَ لَهُ مُوسَى إِنَّكَ لَغَوِيٌّ مُبِينٌ {القصص/18}[446]. Then, Musa as took as action as mentioned فَلَمَّا أَنْ أَرَادَ أَن يَبْطِشَ بِالَّذِي هُوَ عَدُوٌّ لَّهُمَا قَالَ يَا مُوسَى أَتُرِيدُ أَن تَقْتُلَنِي كَمَا قَتَلْتَ نَفْسًا بِالْأَمْسِ إِن تُرِيدُ إِلَّا أَن تَكُونَ جَبَّارًا فِي الْأَرْضِ وَمَا تُرِيدُ أَن تَكُونَ مِنَ الْمُصْلِحِينَ {القصص/19}. This made the situation more complex because of this person's publicizing Musa as's unintended accident. One can always view all as the qadar of Allah ﷻ and the preparations for Musa as mission. That is right.

However, as the Qurān depicts everything in detail, then we should think how to deduce meanings and benefits from each verse of the Qurān for our practical lives. The Qurān is an active book. As Imam Ghazali mentions, for each ayah there are more than sixty thousand meanings (44).

[29][447]

فَلَمَّا قَضَى مُوسَى الْأَجَلَ وَسَارَ بِأَهْلِهِ آنَسَ مِن جَانِبِ الطُّورِ نَارًا قَالَ لِأَهْلِهِ امْكُثُوا إِنِّي آنَسْتُ نَارًا لَّعَلِّي آتِيكُم مِّنْهَا بِخَبَرٍ أَوْ جَذْوَةٍ مِنَ النَّارِ لَعَلَّكُمْ تَصْطَلُونَ {القصص/29}

The word تَصْطَلُونَ can have an interesting and critical stance when one analyzes what it may mean beyond the immediate understandings of this word such as getting warm from the heat of fire. A similar case is also presented in إِذْ قَالَ مُوسَى لِأَهْلِهِ إِنِّي آنَسْتُ نَارًا سَآتِيكُم مِّنْهَا بِخَبَرٍ أَوْ آتِيكُم بِشِهَابٍ قَبَسٍ لَّعَلَّكُمْ تَصْطَلُونَ {النمل/7}[448].

---

445. Of the amenders.
446. And he became inside the city fearful and anticipating [exposure], when suddenly the one who sought his help the previous day cried out to him [once again]. Moses said to him, "Indeed, you are an evident, [persistent] deviator."
447. AND WHEN Moses had fulfilled his term, and was wandering with his family [in the desert], he perceived a fire on the slope of Mount Sinai: [and so] he said to his family: "Wait here. Behold, I perceive a fire [far away]; perhaps I may bring you from there some tiding, or [at least] a burning brand from the fire, so that you might warm yourselves."
448. [Mention] when Moses said to his family, "Indeed, I have perceived a fire. I will bring you from there information or will bring you a burning torch that you may warm yourselves."

As the person can get the heat of imān, Musa as communication with Allah ﷻ by receiving the official Prophethood is a huge boost and light and ignition of his state. Similarly, in other scales, a person for a few minutes being with the Prophet صلى الله عليه وسلم and being called as sahabah or a person visiting his or her shaykh and getting light of imān can be other examples of this spiritual heating or boost of imān or ignition as mentioned with the word تَصْطَلُونَ, الله اعلم. In this perspective, mirāj can be considered as another highest level boost for the Prophet ﷺ.

[48-50][449]

فَلَمَّا جَاءهُمُ الْحَقُّ مِنْ عِندِنَا قَالُوا لَوْلَا أُوتِيَ مِثْلَ مَا أُوتِيَ مُوسَى أَوَلَمْ يَكْفُرُوا بِمَا أُوتِيَ مُوسَى مِن قَبْلُ قَالُوا سِحْرَانِ تَظَاهَرَا وَقَالُوا إِنَّا بِكُلٍّ كَافِرُونَ {القصص/48} قُلْ فَأْتُوا بِكِتَابٍ مِّنْ عِندِ اللَّهِ هُوَ أَهْدَى مِنْهُمَا أَتَّبِعْهُ إِن كُنتُمْ صَادِقِينَ {القصص/49}

فَإِن لَّمْ يَسْتَجِيبُوا لَكَ فَاعْلَمْ أَنَّمَا يَتَّبِعُونَ أَهْوَاءهُمْ وَمَنْ أَضَلُّ مِمَّنِ اتَّبَعَ هَوَاهُ بِغَيْرِ هُدًى مِّنَ اللَّهِ إِنَّ اللَّهَ لَا يَهْدِي الْقَوْمَ الظَّالِمِينَ {القصص/50}

The above set of ayah can shed light on the discourses of debate about the authenticity of the scriptures. After the conversations, if they cannot say anything as mentioned فَإِن لَّمْ يَسْتَجِيبُوا لَكَ, then what should the person deduce for the other party? The expression فَاعْلَمْ[450] immediately follows as فَإِن لَّمْ يَسْتَجِيبُوا لَكَ فَاعْلَمْ. This can show that they lost this debate.

Similar to above ayahs, below is similar debate and challenge to ahlu kitāb as: [12-14][451]

فَلَعَلَّكَ تَارِكٌ بَعْضَ مَا يُوحَى إِلَيْكَ وَضَائِقٌ بِهِ صَدْرُكَ أَن يَقُولُواْ لَوْلاَ أُنزِلَ عَلَيْهِ كَنزٌ أَوْ جَاء مَعَهُ مَلَكٌ إِنَّمَا أَنتَ نَذِيرٌ وَاللّهُ عَلَى كُلِّ شَيْءٍ وَكِيلٌ {هود/12}

---

449. 28:48 And yet, now that the truth has come unto them from Us, they say, "'Why has he not been vouchsafed the like of what Moses was vouchsafed?" But did they not also, before this, deny the truth of what Moses was vouchsafed? [For] they do say, "Two examples of delusion, [seemingly] supporting each other!" And they add, "Behold, we refuse to accept either of them as true!"

450. So know.

451. 11:12 Then would you possibly leave [out] some of what is revealed to you, or is your breast constrained by it because they say, "Why has there not been sent down to him a treasure or come with him an angel?" But you are only a warner. And Allah جل جلاله is Disposer of all things. 11:13 Or do they say, "He invented it"? Say, "Then bring ten surahs like it that have been invented and call upon [for assistance] whomever you can besides Allah جل جلاله, if you should be truthful." 11:14 And if they do not respond to you—then know that it [i.e., the Qurān] was revealed with the knowledge of Allah جل جلاله and that there is no deity except Him. Then, would you [not] be Muslims?

أَمْ يَقُولُونَ افْتَرَاهُ قُلْ فَأْتُواْ بِعَشْرِ سُوَرٍ مِّثْلِهِ مُفْتَرَيَاتٍ وَادْعُواْ مَنِ اسْتَطَعْتُم مِّن دُونِ اللّهِ إِن كُنتُمْ صَادِقِينَ {هود/13} فَإِن لَّمْ يَسْتَجِيبُواْ لَكُمْ فَاعْلَمُواْ أَنَّمَا أُنزِلِ بِعِلْمِ اللّهِ وَأَن لاَّ إِلَهَ إِلاَّ هُوَ فَهَلْ أَنتُم مُّسْلِمُونَ{هود/14}

In above both cases of فَإِن لَّمْ يَسْتَجِيبُوا لَكَ فَاعْلَمْ, the topic is about the authenticity of the scriptures. In the debate, the person can hit the essence of their standpoint as mentioned:

قُلْ فَأْتُواْ بِعَشْرِ سُوَرٍ مِّثْلِهِ مُفْتَرَيَاتٍ وَادْعُواْ مَنِ اسْتَطَعْتُم مِّن دُونِ اللّهِ إِن كُنتُمْ صَادِقِينَ {هود/13}

قُلْ فَأْتُوا بِكِتَابٍ مِّنْ عِندِ اللّهِ هُوَ أَهْدَى مِنْهُمَا أَتَّبِعْهُ إِن كُنتُمْ صَادِقِينَ 452{القصص/49}

Again, this can show that they lost this debate.

At the same time, if they left some traces of doubt while challenging this person of imān then this mumin should remember that:

فَاعْلَمُواْ أَنَّمَا أُنزِلَ بِعِلْمِ اللّهِ وَأَن لاَّ إِلَهَ إِلاَّ هُوَ فَهَلْ أَنتُم مُّسْلِمُونَ{هود/14}

فَاعْلَمْ أَنَّمَا يَتَّبِعُونَ أَهْوَاءهُمْ وَمَنْ أَضَلُّ مِمَّنِ اتَّبَعَ هَوَاهُ بِغَيْرِ هُدًى مِّنَ اللَّهِ إِنَّ اللَّهَ لَا يَهْدِي الْقَوْمَ الظَّالِمِينَ 453{القصص/50}

[71-73]454

قُلْ أَرَأَيْتُمْ إِن جَعَلَ اللَّهُ عَلَيْكُمُ اللَّيْلَ سَرْمَدًا إِلَى يَوْمِ الْقِيَامَةِ مَنْ إِلَهٌ غَيْرُ اللَّهِ يَأْتِيكُم بِضِيَاء أَفَلَا تَسْمَعُونَ {القصص/71} قُلْ أَرَأَيْتُمْ إِن جَعَلَ اللَّهُ عَلَيْكُمُ النَّهَارَ سَرْمَدًا إِلَى يَوْمِ الْقِيَامَةِ

---

452. Say, "Then bring a scripture from Allah جل جلاله which is more guiding than either of them that I may follow it, if you should be truthful."

453. But if they do not respond to you—then know that they only follow their [own] desires. And who is more astray than one who follows his desire without guidance from Allah جل جلاله? Indeed, Allah جل جلاله does not guide the wrongdoing people.

454. 28:71 Say: "Have you ever considered [this]: If God had willed that there should always be night about you, without break, until the Day of Resurrection—is there any deity other than God that could bring you light? Will you not, then, listen [to the truth]?"

28:72 Say: "Have you ever considered [this]: If God had willed that there should always be daylight about you, without break, until the Day of Resurrection—is there any deity other than God that could bring you [the darkness of] night, wherein you might rest? Will you not, then, see [the truth]?"28:73 For it is out of His grace that He has made for you the night and the day, so that you might rest therein as well as seek to obtain [what you need] of His bounty: and [He gave you all this] so that you might have cause to be grateful.

مَنْ إِلَٰهٌ غَيْرُ اللَّهِ يَأْتِيكُم بِلَيْلٍ تَسْكُنُونَ فِيهِ أَفَلَا تُبْصِرُونَ {القصص/72} وَمِن رَّحْمَتِهِ جَعَلَ لَكُمُ اللَّيْلَ وَالنَّهَارَ لِتَسْكُنُوا فِيهِ وَلِتَبْتَغُوا مِن فَضْلِهِ وَلَعَلَّكُمْ تَشْكُرُونَ {القصص/73}

It is interesting to review the above ayahs through the teachings of the current modern science. At this time, we have timetables for sunset and sunrise for all different places in the world. There are places in the world which have very limited sunlight in certain times of the year. One can survey the psychology of the people who appreciate the limited sunlight in those days. They may try to achieve what they need to at those times. The modern concept of daylight savings arrangement of global change of times allude to this fact that the people try to use the sunlight and benefit from it. So, Allah ﷻ alludes this global current practice of changing nights and daylight. In this regard, although it is very clear, a lot of people can take this as granted like other nimahs, bounties, of Allah ﷻ and be in the category of not appreciating. As mentioned in وَمِن رَّحْمَتِهِ جَعَلَ لَكُمُ اللَّيْلَ وَالنَّهَارَ لِتَسْكُنُوا فِيهِ وَلِتَبْتَغُوا مِن فَضْلِهِ وَلَعَلَّكُمْ تَشْكُرُونَ {القصص/73}, these are all from the Rahmah and Fadl of Allah ﷻ that a person realizes it, appreciates it and makes shukr as mentioned in وَلَعَلَّكُمْ تَشْكُرُونَ[455].

One can also analyze this ayah with [61-62][456]

تَبَارَكَ الَّذِي جَعَلَ فِي السَّمَاءِ بُرُوجًا وَجَعَلَ فِيهَا سِرَاجًا وَقَمَرًا مُّنِيرًا {الفرقان/61} وَهُوَ الَّذِي جَعَلَ اللَّيْلَ وَالنَّهَارَ خِلْفَةً لِّمَنْ أَرَادَ أَن يَذَّكَّرَ أَوْ أَرَادَ شُكُورًا {الفرقان/62}

It is important to realize that change is a n'imah from Allah ﷻ. When a person observes this change in the nature and in oneself with the correct tools of imān, then the person can constantly increase their connection and marifah of Allah ﷻ as mentioned with أَن يَذَّكَّرَ. Once the person realizes and recognizes this constant change as a ni'mah, then the person is expected to make shukr as mentioned شُكُورًا {الفرقان/62}[457].

One can analyze the above ayahs around the different types of light and how we benefit them, and how the change of light in their intensity, color and frequency can affect us. One can observe with different types of lights emitted or encountered from stars, sun and reflected from

---

455. So that you might have cause to be grateful.
456. 25:61 Blessed is He who has placed in the sky great stars and placed therein a [burning] lamp and luminous moon. 25:62 And it is He who has made the night and the day in succession for whoever desires to remember or desires gratitude.
457. Gratitude.

تَبَارَكَ الَّذِي جَعَلَ فِي السَّمَاءِ بُرُوجًا وَجَعَلَ فِيهَا سِرَاجًا وَقَمَرًا مُنِيرًا
{الفرقان/61}⁴⁵⁸ .

One can analyze change of type and intensity of light with the change of day and night as mentioned وَهُوَ الَّذِي جَعَلَ اللَّيْلَ وَالنَّهَارَ خِلْفَةً.⁴⁵⁹

On the other hand, one can analyze today's light industry detailing all these for our daily applications as soft light, white light, day light, blue light, or yellow light. There are studies showing the effect of different types of light with their intensity and color effecting human psychology, and physiology (45). One can also analyze why or how our spiritual faculties are affected by different types of light with their intensity causing bright, gloomy, dark and other possibilities.

In all above ayahs, one of the common themes with a similar context is the necessary embodiment of shukr and hamd as mentioned شُكُورًا {الفرقان/62} and وَلَعَلَّكُمْ تَشْكُرُونَ {القصص/73}.

[85-88]⁴⁶⁰

إِنَّ الَّذِي فَرَضَ عَلَيْكَ الْقُرْآنَ لَرَادُّكَ إِلَى مَعَادٍ قُل رَّبِّي أَعْلَمُ مَن جَاءَ بِالْهُدَى وَمَنْ هُوَ فِي ضَلَالٍ مُّبِينٍ {القصص/85} وَمَا كُنتَ تَرْجُو أَن يُلْقَى إِلَيْكَ الْكِتَابُ إِلَّا رَحْمَةً مِّن رَّبِّكَ فَلَا تَكُونَنَّ ظَهِيرًا لِّلْكَافِرِينَ {القصص/86} وَلَا يَصُدُّنَّكَ عَنْ آيَاتِ اللَّهِ بَعْدَ إِذْ أُنزِلَتْ إِلَيْكَ وَادْعُ إِلَى رَبِّكَ وَلَا تَكُونَنَّ مِنَ الْمُشْرِكِينَ {القصص/87} وَلَا تَدْعُ مَعَ اللَّهِ إِلَهًا آخَرَ لَا إِلَهَ إِلَّا هُوَ كُلُّ شَيْءٍ هَالِكٌ إِلَّا وَجْهَهُ لَهُ الْحُكْمُ وَإِلَيْهِ تُرْجَعُونَ {القصص/88}

In the above ayahs, a person who is given the knowledge of the Book, the Qurān or other scriptures, is on guidance as long as the person practices genuinely what is given to this person. And it is a Rahmah and

---

458. Blessed is He who has placed in the sky great stars and placed therein a [burning] lamp and luminous moon.

459. And it is He who has made the night and the day in succession.

460. 28:85 VERILY, [O believer,] He who has laid down this Qur'an in plain terms, making it binding on thee, will assuredly bring thee back [from death] to a life renewed. Say [unto those who reject the truth]: "My Sustainer knows best as to who is right-guided and who is obviously lost in error!" 28:86

Now [as for thyself, O believer,] thou couldnt never foresee that this divine writ would [one day] be offered to thee: but [it did come to thee] by thy Sustainer's grace. Hence, never uphold those who deny the truth [of divine guidance], (28:87) and never let them turn thee away from God's messages after they have been bestowed upon thee from on high: instead,99 summon [all men] to thy Sustainer. And never be of those who ascribe divinity to aught but Him, (28:88) and never call upon any other deity side by side with God. There is no deity save Him. Everything is bound to perish, save His [eternal] Self. With Him rests all judgment; and unto Him shall you all be brought back.

Fadl from Allah ﷻ as mentioned وَمَا كُنتَ تَرْجُو أَن يُلْقَى إِلَيْكَ الْكِتَاب [461] that you were not expecting this guidance with the Book but إِلاَّ رَحْمَةً مِّن رَّبِّكَ [462] it is the Rahmah and Fadl, Mercy and Grace of Allah ﷻ to you.

Once the person has the knowledge of the book, scripture and enjoys about it in one's self practices, there is always the possibility of not implementing these Divine teachings correctly as mentioned by فَلاَ تَكُونَنَّ ظَهِيرًا لِّلْكَافِرِينَ [463]. A person can think that I am using the book of Allah ﷻ but in reality he or she can be helping to the ones who are against the revelation, the Qurān. Or, by misinterpreting the verses and the original teachings as mentioned وَلاَ يَصُدُّنَّكَ عَنْ آيَاتِ اللَّهِ بَعْدَ إِذْ أُنزِلَتْ إِلَيْكَ [464], the person with this action can do shirk but not kufr as mentioned وَلاَ تَكُونَنَّ مِنَ الْمُشْرِكِينَ [465]. As one can remember, the saying of the Prophet ﷺ, the smallest shirk is "riyā" for a believer (21) (hadith #429). After having the knowledge and experience of the Book, the Qurān, these above discourses can occur especially in the cases of outreach, dawah, or tabligh as mentioned وَادْعُ إِلَى رَبِّكَ [466]. This disposition can be true with the scholars and people of other scriptures as well. There are numerous verses in the Qurān addressing the ulamā-u bani Israil.

In the expression إِنَّ الَّذِي فَرَضَ عَلَيْكَ الْقُرْآنَ لَرَادُّكَ إِلَى مَعَادٍ [467], there is a meaning that when Allah ﷻ honors a person with the Qurān reading and enjoying, then Allah ﷻ is not going to leave the person for sure, inshAllah.

---

461. Now [as for thyself, O believer,] thou couldst never foresee98 that this divine writ would [one day] be offered to thee.
462. But [it did come to thee] by thy Sustainer's grace.
463. Never uphold those who deny the truth [of divine guidance].
464. And never let them turn thee away from God's messages after they have been bestowed upon thee.
465. And never be of those who ascribe divinity to aught but Him.
466. Instead, summon [all men] to thy Sustainer.
467. VERILY, [O believer,] He who has laid down this Qur'an in plain terms, making it binding on thee,95 will assuredly bring thee back [from death] to a life renewed.

21

Sûrah Ankabût

As the name of this Sûrah is ankabût, the ayahs among this Sûrah can have interesting links and connections similar to the threads in a spider web, الله اعلم. The word web or spider web is defined in Oxford dictionary as: "a network of fine threads" or "a complex system of interconnected elements" (22).

[2][468]

أَحَسِبَ النَّاسُ أَن يُتْرَكُوا أَن يَقُولُوا آمَنَّا وَهُمْ لَا يُفْتَنُونَ {العنكبوت/2}

On another note, the word fitnah can indicate the trials or mess of conflicts if the person is involved with it, similar to touching a spider web, then it is very difficult to get out of it. May Allah protect us from them.

[5][469]

مَن كَانَ يَرْجُو لِقَاءَ اللَّهِ فَإِنَّ أَجَلَ اللَّهِ لَآتٍ وَهُوَ السَّمِيعُ الْعَلِيمُ {العنكبوت/5}

To show, the interconnected of the elements such as words, if we take the word لِقَاء in the above ayah, the same word comes after some ayahs as: **[23]**[470]

وَالَّذِينَ كَفَرُوا بِآيَاتِ اللَّهِ وَلِقَائِهِ أُولَٰئِكَ يَئِسُوا مِن رَّحْمَتِي وَأُولَٰئِكَ لَهُمْ عَذَابٌ أَلِيمٌ {العنكبوت/23}

When one analyzes this key word لِقَاء[471] in the light of above two verses, one realizes that one of the essences of imān is to desire to meet with Allah . In other words, a person should not view death as

---

468. DO MEN THINK that on their [mere] saying, "We have attained to faith", they will be left to themselves, and will not be put to a test?

469. (29:5) Whoever looks forward [with hope and awe] to meeting God [on Resurrection Day, let him be ready for it]: for, behold, the end set by God [for everyone's life] is bound to come— and He alone is all-hearing, all-knowing!

470. And the ones who disbelieve in the signs of Allah جل جلاله and the meeting with Him— those have despaired of My mercy, and they will have a painful punishment.

471. Meeting.

something ugly but something sweet, beautiful and desired because the person is going to meet with Allah ﷻ. As the hadith mentions, the real imān necessitates loving Allah ﷻ and the Prophet ﷺ more than yourself and everything. In this perspective, the person would really want to meet with Allah ﷻ if the person has the essence of imān. The opposite is also mentioned as وَالَّذِينَ كَفَرُوا بِآيَاتِ اللَّهِ وَلِقَائِهِ[472] that kufr necessitates not meeting with Allah ﷻ but being scared. May, Allah ﷻ make us from the one who has the real imān, Amin.

[6][473]

وَمَن جَاهَدَ فَإِنَّمَا يُجَاهِدُ لِنَفْسِهِ إِنَّ اللَّهَ لَغَنِيٌّ عَنِ الْعَالَمِينَ {العنكبوت/6}

When a person makes a struggle to please Allah ﷻ in different means, there is no benefit of this struggle to Allah ﷻ but there is benefit to the person. Allah ﷻ is Al-Ghaniyy[474].

[25][475]

وَقَالَ إِنَّمَا اتَّخَذْتُم مِّن دُونِ اللَّهِ أَوْثَانًا مَّوَدَّةَ بَيْنِكُمْ فِي الْحَيَاةِ الدُّنْيَا ثُمَّ يَوْمَ الْقِيَامَةِ يَكْفُرُ بَعْضُكُم بِبَعْضٍ وَيَلْعَنُ بَعْضُكُم بَعْضًا وَمَأْوَاكُمُ النَّارُ وَمَا لَكُم مِّن نَّاصِرِينَ {العنكبوت/25}

In this ayah, there is the critical word مَّوَدَّةَ. People establish relationships to expect benefit and love one another. In its true essence, this can also be called as attachment. If it is not done for the sake of Allah ﷻ, the person can suffer in this dunya and in the akhirah. Therefore, true relationship with anyone comes after passing the filter of pleasure of Allah ﷻ. In other words, engagement or not, loving or not, and all others follow if and when Allah ﷻ is pleased. Then, this is not called as attachment although the outsiders may not know the inner dynamics of the person.

---

472. And the ones who disbelieve in the signs of Allah جلاله and the meeting with Him.
473. 29:6 Hence, whoever strives hard [in God's cause] does so only for his own good: for, verily, God does not stand in need of anything in all the worlds!
474. The independent.
475. 29:25 And [Abraham] said: "You have chosen to worship idols instead of God for no other reason than to have a bond of love, in the life of this world, between yourselves [and your forebears]: but then, on Resurrection Day, you shall disown one another and curse one another—for the goal of you all will be the fire, and you will have none to succour you.

[26-27]⁴⁷⁶

فَآمَنَ لَهُ لُوطٌ وَقَالَ إِنِّي مُهَاجِرٌ إِلَى رَبِّي إِنَّهُ هُوَ الْعَزِيزُ الْحَكِيمُ {العنكبوت/26} وَوَهَبْنَا
لَهُ إِسْحَقَ وَيَعْقُوبَ وَجَعَلْنَا فِي ذُرِّيَّتِهِ النُّبُوَّةَ وَالْكِتَابَ وَآتَيْنَاهُ أَجْرَهُ فِي الدُّنْيَا وَإِنَّهُ فِي
الْآخِرَةِ لَمِنَ الصَّالِحِينَ {العنكبوت/27}

With their other many meanings, the above ayah can allude to notions and dynamics of student-teacher and parent-children relationships. Ibrahim as was like a teacher for Lut as as mentioned ⁴⁷⁷فَآمَنَ لَهُ لُوطٌ although it is reported that there was some kinship relationship between them. The student-teacher relationship continues although the student may leave the teacher. For example, when the angels came to Ibrahim as for the people of Lut as, Ibrahim as immediately was in the protection of his student, Lut as. His student was on a mission for dawah. Therefore, it is important to check on one's students, الله اعلم.

In the other case, Ibrahim as was in a parent-children relationship with his sons and offspring as mentioned وَوَهَبْنَا لَهُ إِسْحَقَ وَيَعْقُوبَ⁴⁷⁸. The parent-children relationship can entail more direct language due to the rights of parents on the children. One can analyze the ayahs in the Qurān about Ibrahim as giving wasiyyah for his children not to associate anything or anyone to Allah ﷻ or in the case of Luqman as giving advice to his son. One can analyze the language in these dialogues which have for example the motifs of rahmah, love, directness, explicitness, openness, and concern.

Yet, at certain levels as reported for the lives of the salaf that there may not be a really clear distinction about these relationships, teacher-student compared to parent-children. There may be some converging points.

---

476. 29:26 Thereupon [his brother's son] Lot came to believe in him and said: "Verily, I [too] shall forsake the domain of evil (and turn) to my Sustainer: for, verily, He alone is almighty, truly wise!" (29:27) And [as for Abraham,] We bestowed upon him Isaac and [Isaac's son] Jacob, and caused prophethood and revelation to continue among his offspring. And We vouchsafed him his reward in this world: and, verily, in the life to come [too] he shall find himself among the righteous.

477. Thereupon [his brother's son] Lot came to believe in him.

478. And [as for Abraham,] We bestowed upon him Isaac and [Isaac's son] Jacob.

[45]479

اتْلُ مَا أُوحِيَ إِلَيْكَ مِنَ الْكِتَابِ وَأَقِمِ الصَّلَاةَ إِنَّ الصَّلَاةَ تَنْهَى عَنِ الْفَحْشَاء وَالْمُنكَرِ وَلَذِكْرُ
اللَّهِ أَكْبَرُ وَاللَّهُ يَعْلَمُ مَا تَصْنَعُونَ {العنكبوت/45}

In this ayah اتْلُ مَا أُوحِيَ إِلَيْكَ مِنَ الْكِتَابِ وَأَقِمِ الصَّلَاةَ إِنَّ الصَّلَاةَ تَنْهَى عَنِ الْفَحْشَاء
وَالْمُنكَرِ وَلَذِكْرُ اللَّهِ أَكْبَرُ وَاللَّهُ يَعْلَمُ مَا تَصْنَعُونَ {العنكبوت/45}, the expression اللَّهِ أَكْبَرُ
وَلَذِكْرُ أَكْبَرُ can show this ultimate constant and regular connection more than
the five-times prayers. The goal of fardh prayers is to instill the notion
of regular connection with Allah ﷻ but the ideal state is to spread this
in one's all daily minutes and seconds with notion of presence in front
of Allah ﷻ. Ahlu tasawwuf can call this khudur, the presence, readiness
and awareness in one's relationship with Allah ﷻ.

On another perspective, when the person is need of constant
intervention in one's life, the Names of Allah ﷻ الْحَيُّ الْقَيُّومُ saves the person
from the oppression and darkness of each second. Therefore, the dua of
the Prophet ﷺ as "يا حي يا قيوم برحمتك أستغيث يا ، أصلح لي شأني كله ، ولا تكلني
إلى نفسي طرفة عين480" (27), shows the need of constant connection with
Allah ﷻ at the level of each second or even each less time quantities. On
another perspective, this shows that the person should be constantly,
every second, self-dealing with him or herself to check the existence of
this connection and to refresh this connection that if the person is at
that second connected to Allah ﷻ. Each disconnection is a darkness, a
black hole, and a seed for depression, darkness and anxiety. Then, other
duas of the Prophet ﷺ as "اللهم ثبت قلبي على دينك481," complements this
important notion.

---

479. 29:45 CONVEY [unto others] whatever of this divine writ has been revealed unto thee,
and be constant in prayer: for, behold, prayer restrains [man] from loathsome deeds and from
all that runs counter to reason; and remembrance of God is indeed the greatest [good]. And
God knows all that you do.
480. Oh The Ever-Lasting, O The Sustainer & Protector of all that exists. I seek aid through Your
Mercy, correct all my matters for me & do not entrust me to my own self even for the blink of
an eye.
481. Oh Allah جل جلاله, set my heart firm on your religion.

[46]⁴⁸²

وَلَا تُجَادِلُوا أَهْلَ الْكِتَابِ إِلَّا بِالَّتِي هِيَ أَحْسَنُ إِلَّا الَّذِينَ ظَلَمُوا مِنْهُمْ وَقُولُوا آمَنَّا بِالَّذِي
أُنزِلَ إِلَيْنَا وَأُنزِلَ إِلَيْكُمْ وَإِلَهُنَا وَإِلَهُكُمْ وَاحِدٌ وَنَحْنُ لَهُ مُسْلِمُونَ {العنكبوت/46}

The importance of good interaction and exchange is mentioned by هِيَ
أَحْسَنُ.

In this ayah, Allah ﷻ gives the main guideline of the interaction
with Ahlu-kitāb. That is, to have a nice and humanly argumentation,
debate, agreements and disagreements. In other words, the way should
be always nice, humanly and civilized in the cases of conflicts and
disagreements. Especially, at our times of the notion of religion being
abused by different stakeholders, this attitude is critical.

The words in Sûrah Fath as

مُّحَمَّدٌ رَّسُولُ اللَّهِ وَالَّذِينَ مَعَهُ أَشِدَّاءُ عَلَى الْكُفَّارِ رُحَمَاءُ بَيْنَهُمْ تَرَاهُمْ رُكَّعًا سُجَّدًا يَبْتَغُونَ
فَضْلًا مِّنَ اللَّهِ وَرِضْوَانًا سِيمَاهُمْ فِي وُجُوهِهِم مِّنْ أَثَرِ السُّجُودِ ذَلِكَ مَثَلُهُمْ فِي التَّوْرَاةِ
وَمَثَلُهُمْ فِي الْإِنجِيلِ كَزَرْعٍ أَخْرَجَ شَطْأَهُ فَآزَرَهُ فَاسْتَغْلَظَ فَاسْتَوَى عَلَى سُوقِهِ يُعْجِبُ
الزُّرَّاعَ لِيَغِيظَ بِهِمُ الْكُفَّارَ وَعَدَ اللَّهُ الَّذِينَ آمَنُوا وَعَمِلُوا الصَّالِحَاتِ مِنْهُم مَّغْفِرَةً وَأَجْرًا
عَظِيمًا⁴⁸³ {الفتح/29}

أَهْلَ الْكِتَابِ إِلَّا بِالَّتِي⁴⁸⁶ as رُحَمَاءُ بَيْنَهُمْ⁴⁸⁵ and أَشِدَّاءُ عَلَى الْكُفَّارِ⁴⁸⁴ complements
هِيَ أَحْسَنُ. In other words, three types of treatment are expected: very
soft and gentle with the believers as mentioned in رُحَمَاءُ بَيْنَهُمْ, then with
unbending principles as mentioned in أَشِدَّاءُ عَلَى الْكُفَّارِ, and in a good
manner with people of the book as mentioned أَهْلَ الْكِتَابِ إِلَّا بِالَّتِي هِيَ أَحْسَنُ.

---

482. 29:46 And do not argue with the followers of earlier revelation otherwise than in a most
kindly manner—unless it be such of them as are bent on evildoing—and say: "We believe
in that which has been bestowed from on high upon us, as well as that which has been
bestowed upon you: for our God and your God is one and the same, and it is unto Him that
We [all] surrender ourselves."
483. Muhammad is the Messenger of Allah جل جلاله; and those with him are forceful against
the disbelievers, merciful among themselves. You see them bowing and prostrating [in
prayer], seeking bounty from Allah جل جلاله and [His] pleasure. Their mark [i.e., sign] is on their
faces [i.e., foreheads] from the trace of prostration. That is their description in the Torah. And
their description in the Gospel is as a plant which produces its offshoots and strengthens
them so they grow firm and stand upon their stalks, delighting the sowers—so that He [i.e.,
Allah جل جلاله] may enrage by them the disbelievers. Allah جل جلاله has promised those who
believe and do righteous deeds among them forgiveness and a great reward.
484. Are forceful against the disbelievers.
485. Merciful among themselves.
486. The followers of earlier revelation otherwise than in a most kindly manner.

But, the ones who have hate towards the believers among ahlu kitāb is mentioned as اِلَّا الَّذِينَ ظَلَمُوا مِنْهُمْ[487] that they can be treated with unbending principles as mentioned above for the other category الله اعلم.

[40][488]

فَكُلًّا أَخَذْنَا بِذَنبِهِ فَمِنْهُم مَّنْ أَرْسَلْنَا عَلَيْهِ حَاصِبًا وَمِنْهُم مَّنْ أَخَذَتْهُ الصَّيْحَةُ وَمِنْهُم مَّنْ خَسَفْنَا بِهِ الْأَرْضَ وَمِنْهُم مَّنْ أَغْرَقْنَا وَمَا كَانَ اللَّهُ لِيَظْلِمَهُمْ وَلَٰكِن كَانُوا أَنفُسَهُمْ يَظْلِمُونَ {العنكبوت/40}

One can realize the effects of sins causing retribution as mentioned فَكُلًّا أَخَذْنَا بِذَنبِهِ[489], may Allah ﷻ protect us.

[41][490]

مَثَلُ الَّذِينَ اتَّخَذُوا مِن دُونِ اللَّهِ أَوْلِيَاءَ كَمَثَلِ الْعَنكَبُوتِ اتَّخَذَتْ بَيْتًا وَإِنَّ أَوْهَنَ الْبُيُوتِ لَبَيْتُ الْعَنكَبُوتِ لَوْ كَانُوا يَعْلَمُونَ {العنكبوت/41}

One of the main themes of this ayah is only having Allah ﷻ as the real Waliyy, Protector, Friend, and Helper as also mentioned in وَمَا أَنتُم بِمُعْجِزِينَ فِي الْأَرْضِ وَلَا فِي السَّمَاءِ وَمَا لَكُم مِّن دُونِ اللَّهِ مِن وَلِيٍّ وَلَا نَصِيرٍ[491] {العنكبوت/22}.

There is no comparison of Allah جل جلاله with anyone. The example وَمَا أَنتُم بِمُعْجِزِينَ فِي الْأَرْضِ وَلَا فِي السَّمَاءِ وَمَا لَكُم مِّن دُونِ اللَّهِ مِن وَلِيٍّ of spider وَلَا نَصِيرٍ {العنكبوت/22}makes the person to embody this notion. It is interesting to see that there are certain kind of spiders which just stay in their built webs, homes and just wait, hoping to get what it wants. In reality, it is very thin and weak quickly destroyed. One can see a lot of spiders death or eating each other due to not finding proper food. They stay in their places, webs or homes hoping to get benefit but they

---

487. Unless it be such of them as are bent on evildoing.
488. (29:40) For, every one of them did We take to task for his sin: and so, upon some of them We let loose a deadly storm-wind; and some of them were overtaken by a [sudden] blast; and some of them We caused to be swallowed by the earth; and some of them We caused to drown. And it was not God who
wronged them, but it was they who had wronged themselves.
489. For, every one of them did We take to task for his sin.
490. 29:41 THE PARABLE of those who take [beings or forces] other than God for their protectors is that of the spider which makes for itself a house: for, behold, the frailest of all houses is the spider's house. Could they but understand this!
491. And you will not cause failure [to Allah جل جلاله] upon the earth or in the heaven. And you have not other than Allah جل جلاله any protector or any helper.

die and waste their life. Similarly, our expectations and sheltering in beings other than Allah ﷻ lead the person in full frustration and in a self-destructive outcome due to the person's choice.

[57]⁴⁹²

{57/العنكبوت} كُلُّ نَفْسٍ ذَائِقَةُ الْمَوْتِ ثُمَّ إِلَيْنَا تُرْجَعُونَ

{35/الأنبياء}⁴⁹³ كُلُّ نَفْسٍ ذَائِقَةُ الْمَوْتِ وَنَبْلُوكُم بِالشَّرِّ وَالْخَيْرِ فِتْنَةً وَإِلَيْنَا تُرْجَعُونَ

It is interesting in the above ayahs death is mentioned with the word ذَائِقَةُ, to taste. In this perspective, death is not something to be scared of as humans fear and depressed. Yet, it is presented something to be opposite in the wording zaikah, to taste it, الله اعلم.

Sûrah Rûm

[1-5]⁴⁹⁴

{1/الروم} الم {2/الروم} غُلِبَتِ الرُّومُ {2/الروم} فِي أَدْنَى الْأَرْضِ وَهُم مِّن بَعْدِ غَلَبِهِمْ سَيَغْلِبُونَ {3/الروم} فِي بِضْعِ سِنِينَ لِلَّهِ الْأَمْرُ مِن قَبْلُ وَمِن بَعْدُ وَيَوْمَئِذٍ يَفْرَحُ الْمُؤْمِنُونَ {4/الروم} بِنَصْرِ اللَّهِ يَنصُرُ مَن يَشَاءُ وَهُوَ الْعَزِيزُ الرَّحِيمُ {5/الروم}

It is interesting to reflect on the hikmah of why this case is mentioned other than it is immediate sababi-nuzûl reasons at the time of the Prophet. ﷺ In other words, what is the hukm or implications of these ayahs until end of days? As the Qurān does not have only sabab nuzûl meanings but it bears meanings for all times, what are their meanings today and in the future?

One possibility, الله اعلم can be that the country or societies of Rum at the time can reflect today's Europeans or Westerns, or the Christian majority population. In this perspective, one can reflect under rule of

---

492. (29:57) Every human being is bound to taste death, [and] in the end unto Us shall all be brought back:

493. Every soul will taste death. And We test you with evil and with good as trial; and to Us you will be returned.

494. 30:1 Alif. Lam. Mim. 30:2 DEFEATED have been the Byzantines (30:3) in the lands close-by; yet it is they who, notwithstanding this their defeat, shall be victorious (30:4) within a few years: [for with God rests all power of decision, first and last. And on that day will the believers [too, have cause to] rejoice (30:5) In God's succour: [for] He gives succor to whomever He wills, since He alone is almighty, a dispenser of grace.

Westerns or Europeans with majority of Christian population, believers maintain their religion in peace as mentioned فِي بِضْعِ سِنِينَ لِلَّهِ الْأَمْرُ مِن قَبْلُ وَمِن بَعْدُ وَيَوْمَئِذٍ يَفْرَحُ الْمُؤْمِنُونَ {الروم/4}.

In other words, establishing justice or structure as a power representation should not be the main goal of believers in life. Yet, it is important to serve and work for justice and peace. Yet, there is an order and priority with everything. In Mecca, when Muslims were facing all the full injustice treatment, Rasulullah ﷺ did encourage people to migrate to the societies where the justice and peace had been established although these societies were not Muslims (46). Yet, the ayahs in Makkah mostly focused on tawhid and accountability. One can talk about justice and peace if the person does not have a reference point of accountability and belief in Allah ﷻ. Tawhid requires justice and peace in all cases of hidden and public engagements because the person beliefs in Allah ﷻ and Allah ﷻ is al-Rakeeb.

In other words, if the establishment of justice is implemented by whomever Allah ﷻ wills that is important accept as mentioned بِنَصْرِ اللَّهِ يَنصُرُ مَن يَشَاء وَهُوَ الْعَزِيزُ الرَّحِيمُ {الروم/5}. This ayah also alludes to this possible notion as mentioned in the ayah as:

إِذْ قَالَ اللَّهُ يَا عِيسَى إِنِّي مُتَوَفِّيكَ وَرَافِعُكَ إِلَيَّ وَمُطَهِّرُكَ مِنَ الَّذِينَ كَفَرُواْ وَجَاعِلُ الَّذِينَ اتَّبَعُوكَ فَوْقَ الَّذِينَ كَفَرُواْ إِلَى يَوْمِ الْقِيَامَةِ ثُمَّ إِلَيَّ مَرْجِعُكُمْ فَأَحْكُمُ بَيْنَكُمْ فِيمَا كُنتُمْ فِيهِ تَخْتَلِفُونَ [495] {آل عمران/55}

What is important is that to establish a proper genuine relationship with Allah ﷻ and the rest then can follow. This also can be seen in the life of the Prophet ﷺ. In Makkah, the Prophet ﷺ did not have much concern of establishing a structured society but he ﷺ had concern of instilling the teachings of tawhid and imān. The first important, is the teachings of true tawhid, comes first in the period of Makkah. Later, in Madinah due to a need and qadar of Allah جل جلاله a structure and society is established with the later revealed ayahs of the Qurān.

When one reviews the hadith of the Prophet ﷺ during the end of days about fitnahs, killing, and mischief, the Prophet ﷺ mentions that

---

495. [Mention] when Allah جل جلاله said, "O Jesus, indeed I will take you and raise you to Myself and purify [i.e., free] you from those who disbelieve and make those who follow you [in submission to Allah جل جلاله alone] superior to those who disbelieve until the Day of Resurrection. Then to Me is your return, and I will judge between you concerning that in which you used to differ.

Muslims, in spite of their enormous numbers that there would be in turmoil, fitnah and fasad. This can again be due to misplacing the desire to establish structured society with power over the real concerns of imān or tawhid, الله اعلم. In other words, this can be similar to placing Madinah period first over Makkah period.

In this perspective, الله اعلم, Madinah period, true ruling of Muslims, may not come again. This is fine as long as it is justly and fully fulfilled by others. The real focus can or may be to have the Makkah period of instilling to souls the real teachings of imān and tawhid, الله اعلم.

On another note, one can ask why most of the Prophets who are mentioned in the Qurān in the area of East of Middle East? Even, the Western dominant Christianity has its roots in the Middle East with Isa as. One can approach this question in many ways. One way can be from cultural perspective. The Eastern cultures have intrinsic qualities that dictates respect with the teachers, parents, elders and other wisdom-based notions in their cultures. When one analyzes at the Western societies of today, mostly mind and intellect-based approaches are dominant. Both are good qualities. Yet, belief requires humbleness, humility and submission with respect. الله اعلم.

يَعْلَمُونَ ظَاهِرًا مِّنَ الْحَيَاةِ الدُّنْيَا وَهُمْ عَنِ الْآخِرَةِ هُمْ غَافِلُونَ {الروم/7}

Along with the interpretations of ayahs 1-5 in above, this ayah [7] can indicate that the events that we encounter in daily life in the world has also other dimensions, meanings and purposes than how we see and interpret. In this perspective, the creation that we see in our daily lives such as trees, stones, sky, clouds, sun, moon, hot, cold, and all the animals and others can have some other meanings. As mentioned, looking at everything with their connection to Allah ﷻ, and with their connections to akhirah afterlife, can have other meanings compared to how we interpret in their immediate literal meanings, الله اعلم.

[54][496]

اللهُ الَّذِي خَلَقَكُم مِّن ضَعْفٍ ثُمَّ جَعَلَ مِن بَعْدِ ضَعْفٍ قُوَّةً ثُمَّ جَعَلَ مِن بَعْدِ قُوَّةٍ ضَعْفًا
وَشَيْبَةً يَخْلُقُ مَا يَشَاءُ وَهُوَ الْعَلِيمُ الْقَدِيرُ {الروم/54}

One can ask what is the hikmah/wisdom of these phenomena, incidents or events that are mentioned in the Qurān as in this ayah and yet, these are clearly observable changes and realities by humans? In other words, the above process of change is observable by almost all humans. Why does the Qurān mention for us? There can be many reasons. Among many, here are some possibilities.

Normalization: If we take the above ayah as an example, a person witnesses and experiences this change of weakness and needy disposition as a baby, then acquiring strength and independent stance in the ages of youth and adulthood and becoming again weak and needy in the old age of senility. What does this mean? If the person does not know or acquire a proper meaning of this reality, then it is very easy and possible that the person can become depressed, anxious and miserable.

There are some changes happening in one's body and faculties of mind yet, the person is only observing it but cannot do anything about it and does not have any control over it. The ayah normalizes that Allah ﷻ created this process and it is normal. It is something out of the control of humans. There are a lot of things in our lives that are out of our control although we may claim that we own it. For example, we are not in control of biological cells with how they are working and what they are doing in our body. We are not in control of our organs made up by these cells with how they are working and what they are doing such as our liver, kidney, gallbladder, spleen and others in our body. We are not in control of physiological systems made up by these organs with how they are working and what they are doing such as our nervous system, circulatory system hormonal glands, and others in our body. Yet, we all claim to own them as our body. Allah ﷻ as the Rabbul Alamin maintains them. Similarly, changes in our body as we age is something out of our control. Allah ﷻ mentions in the Qurān that this is a reality as part of our creation.

---

496. 30:54 IT IS GOD who creates you [all in a state] of weakness, and then, after weakness, ordains strength [for you], and then, after [a period of] strength, ordains [old-age] weakness and grey hair.[48] He creates what He wills; and He alone is all-knowing, infinite in His power.

Once, the person expects and knows that this is coming, then there are minimal feelings of depression, anxiety and misery so that we don't feel that we are losing something that we own such as our strength, our hair, out teeth, our sight, our movement abilities and others.

At our present time, the cases of scheduling, or preparations for the events are the means of human psychology in order to establish a life style with a minimum stress levels in order to prevent stressful random, immediate, or instant occurrences of changes. Therefore, unexpected losses in one's life such as death, accidents, or others have a very devastating effects because the person is not prepared for it. In this regard of preparation, Allah ﷻ explains these observable and scheduled events in a human's life so that the person should be ready for these changes mentally, and spiritually, الله اعلم. Accordingly, they should make preparation for it.

Accessibility of Common Observable Events: The other important point is that Allah ﷻ gives these normalization points with common observable events by everyone in the Qurān. In this stance, one can be deceived and take these observable events as granted and move on in their life. Or another can realize these meanings and purpose, and he or she may not take those as granted. For example, the cases of rain, wind, air, trees, stones, sky, earth, seas, mountains, spouses, social incidents and many other observable events by humans mentioned in the Qurān in many places. Yet, one can take the disposition of stating that everything is explainable with science. In this case, the person is being curtained by the immediate layer but not going through the essence or purpose. Therefore, the Qurān or a scripture sent by Allah ﷻ is not a technical or expert book in their immediate meanings but accessible to everyone although the scholars can derive a lot of meanings with their expertise. The religion is accessible to everyone.

Need for a True Authority of Meanings: There should be an authority who should explain these meanings. If there are more than five billion people on the earth, everyone can have an idea about these meanings. Yet, an Authority but not in our dimension or realm should tell us as the consolidating, true and objective meanings. This authority is the Qurān revealed by our Creator, Rabbul A'lamin.

Different Meanings of the Qurãn for Different Stakeholders/ Human Types:

Each ayah of the Qurãn can have different meanings for each person with different age, social, ethnic, cultural and economic backgrounds in different times of the human history.

For example, this specific ayah اللَّهُ الَّذِي خَلَقَكُم مِّن ضَعْفٍ ثُمَّ جَعَلَ مِن بَعْدِ can ضَعْفٍ قُوَّةً ثُمَّ جَعَلَ مِن بَعْدِ قُوَّةٍ ضَعْفًا وَشَيْبَةً يَخْلُقُ مَا يَشَاء وَهُوَ الْعَلِيمُ الْقَدِيرُ {الروم/54} mean for a person the following meanings.

Before you die, you will be again in your weak state of mental and physical faculties. This is a last chance for you to be humble in front of your Creator if you are a kãfir before you meet with your Creator. This last stage of weakness is a hope and glad tidings for a believer that you will soon meet with your Creator that you have been longing for all your life.

Sûrah Luqmãn

[1-3]⁴⁹⁷

الم {لقمان/1} تِلْكَ آيَاتُ الْكِتَابِ الْحَكِيمِ {لقمان/2} هُدًى وَرَحْمَةً لِّلْمُحْسِنِينَ {لقمان/3}

It is interesting to analyze and try understand the Name and Attribute of Allah حَكِيمٌ ﷻ. It comes in different places with similar and different meanings in many places in the Qurãn. What should one really understand or immediately remember when this word or Name is mentioned?

It can possibly allude that when a person is doing anything and especially in the endeavors of good, one should pay very critical importance how one does it. In other words, one can call this as uslub or method of delivery of the action. In our popular time, one can call this as wisdom. For example, in the case of adultery, slandering, or in the core of fitnahs, as mentioned in Sûrah Nûr, one should maintain the justice with hikmah or wisdom how correction is done. In other words, the legislation is the Qurãn and interpretations of the Prophet صلى الله عليه وسلم and fuqaha.

---

497. 31:1 Alif. Lam. Mim. 31:2 THESE ARE MESSAGES of the divine writ, full of wisdom, (31:3) providing guidance and grace unto the doers of good.

In practice, the judiciary is implements legislation with justice through the qadi, the judge. The execution and enforcement is done with hikmah. The Qurān is Hakim because the Qurān is revealed from Al-Hakim. The applications of the Qurān is all with hikmah, wisdom.

One can find the emphasis for this methodology of wisdom in deliverance of the divine message to people in the Qurān and in the teachings of the Prophet ﷺ. One can for example view in the delivery of the divine message to a child in the case of Luqman as : [12-14][498]

وَلَقَدْ آتَيْنَا لُقْمَانَ الْحِكْمَةَ أَنِ اشْكُرْ لِلَّهِ وَمَن يَشْكُرْ فَإِنَّمَا يَشْكُرُ لِنَفْسِهِ وَمَن كَفَرَ فَإِنَّ اللَّهَ غَنِيٌّ حَمِيدٌ {لقمان/12} وَإِذْ قَالَ لُقْمَانُ لِابْنِهِ وَهُوَ يَعِظُهُ يَا بُنَيَّ لَا تُشْرِكْ بِاللَّهِ إِنَّ الشِّرْكَ لَظُلْمٌ عَظِيمٌ {لقمان/13} وَوَصَّيْنَا الْإِنسَانَ بِوَالِدَيْهِ حَمَلَتْهُ أُمُّهُ وَهْنًا عَلَى وَهْنٍ وَفِصَالُهُ فِي عَامَيْنِ أَنِ اشْكُرْ لِي وَلِوَالِدَيْكَ إِلَيَّ الْمَصِيرُ {لقمان/14}

The words that he uses it for example, يَا بُنَيَّ[499], is very soft, gentle and kind. When a person delivers the message with hikmah then the person can be taking the steps towards being a muhsin as mentioned تِلْكَ آيَاتُ الْكِتَابِ الْحَكِيمِ {لقمان/2}[500] هُدًى وَرَحْمَةً لِّلْمُحْسِنِينَ {لقمان/3}[501], الله اعلم.

[3]

هُدًى وَرَحْمَةً لِّلْمُحْسِنِينَ {لقمان/3}

The full state of ihsān defined by the hadith of Jibril as (3) is embodied by Rasulullah ﷺ. In his life ﷺ, when even he ﷺ was sleeping, his heart ﷺ was not sleeping (3). In other words, the purpose and mission of creation and humans is to be in this state of recognition, ليعبدون, as the state of worship mentioned in different parts of the Qurān. In this Sūrah,

---

498. 31:12 And We had certainly given Luqman wisdom [and said], "Be grateful to Allah جل جلاله." And whoever is grateful is grateful for [the benefit of] himself. And whoever denies [His favor]—then indeed, Allah جلاله جل is Free of need and Praiseworthy. 31:13 And [mention, O Muhammad], when Luqman said to his son while he was instructing him, "O my son, do not associate [anything] with Allah جلاله جل. Indeed, association [with Him] is great injustice." 3:14 And We have enjoined upon man [care] for his parents. His mother carried him, [increasing her] in weakness upon weakness, and his weaning is in two years. Be grateful to Me and to your parents; to Me is the [final] destination.

499. O my son.

500. These are verses of the wise Book.

501. As guidance and mercy for the doers of good.

especially the attitudes of two groups presented: muhsinûn, shakirûn, and humble versus mocking, arrogance, and kafirûn.

[6] & [21]⁵⁰²

وَمِنَ النَّاسِ مَن يَشْتَرِي لَهْوَ الْحَدِيثِ لِيُضِلَّ عَن سَبِيلِ اللَّهِ بِغَيْرِ عِلْمٍ وَيَتَّخِذَهَا هُزُوًا أُولَئِكَ لَهُمْ عَذَابٌ مُهِينٌ {لقمان/6}

وَإِذَا قِيلَ لَهُمُ اتَّبِعُوا مَا أَنزَلَ اللَّهُ قَالُوا بَلْ نَتَّبِعُ مَا وَجَدْنَا عَلَيْهِ آبَاءنَا أَوَلَوْ كَانَ الشَّيْطَانُ يَدْعُوهُمْ إِلَى عَذَابِ السَّعِيرِ {لقمان/21}

It is very important not to befriend todays popular so-called intellectual discourses which lack genuine understanding of the methodology of Islamic sciences, usûl. They knowingly or unknowingly distract people from genuine learning of Allah ﷻ as mentioned لِيُضِلَّ عَن سَبِيلِ اللَّهِ بِغَيْرِ عِلْمٍ⁵⁰³. In these gatherings, one may find people making fun of the sacred and generating jokes about them in order to humanize them according to their understanding. One can see the similar psychology of an attitude in ayah 21 as well with the traces of arrogance.

[12] & [22]⁵⁰⁴

وَلَقَدْ آتَيْنَا لُقْمَانَ الْحِكْمَةَ أَنِ اشْكُرْ لِلَّهِ وَمَن يَشْكُرْ فَإِنَّمَا يَشْكُرُ لِنَفْسِهِ وَمَن كَفَرَ فَإِنَّ اللَّهَ غَنِيٌّ حَمِيدٌ {لقمان/12}

وَمَن يُسْلِمْ وَجْهَهُ إِلَى اللَّهِ وَهُوَ مُحْسِنٌ فَقَدِ اسْتَمْسَكَ بِالْعُرْوَةِ الْوُثْقَى وَإِلَى اللَّهِ عَاقِبَةُ الْأُمُورِ {لقمان/22}

---

502. (31:6) But among men there is many a one that prefers a mere play with words [to divine guidance], so as to lead [those] without knowledge astray from the path of God, and to turn it to ridicule: for such there is shameful suffering in store. (31:21) and when such [people] are told to follow that which God has bestowed from on high, they answer, "Nay, we shall follow that which we found our forefathers believing in and doing!" Why—[would you follow your forefathers] even if Satan had invited them unto the suffering of the blazing flame?
503. So as to lead [those] without knowledge astray from the path of God.
504. 31:12 AND, INDEED, We granted this wisdom unto Luqman: "Be grateful unto God—for he who is grateful [unto Him] is but grateful for the good of his own self; whereas he who chooses to be ungrateful [ought to know that], verily, God is self-sufficient, ever to be praised!" 31:22 Now whoever surrenders his whole being unto God, and is a doer of good withal, has indeed taken hold of a support most unfailing: for with God rests the final outcome of all events.

One of the ways to communicate with the people, and invite them to Allah ﷻ is with hikmah, not being angry but still holding the calm and nice stand and delivering the message. This method of delivery can be shukr itself, the person knows and delivers to others with hikmah. The opposite of kufr is shukr. Kufr covers but shukr reveals and delivers the message.

The humble attitude is always this key disposition in all renderings as mentioned وَمَن يُسْلِمْ وَجْهَهُ إِلَى اللَّهِ وَهُوَ مُحْسِنٌ in وَمَن يُسْلِمْ وَجْهَهُ إِلَى اللَّهِ وَهُوَ مُحْسِنٌ. فَقَدِ اسْتَمْسَكَ بِالْعُرْوَةِ الْوُثْقَى وَإِلَى اللَّهِ عَاقِبَةُ الْأُمُورِ {22/لقمان}. This humble attitude is the safest position as mentioned فَقَدِ اسْتَمْسَكَ بِالْعُرْوَةِ الْوُثْقَى505.

Also, the person needs to be in the state of shukr due to the trait of hikmah given to this person by Allah ﷻ. In addition, due to the context of his dialogue, having a child as a sadaqa jariyah (9) (hadith # 1631) as mentioned by the Prophet ﷺ can require shukr. Sometimes having children, teaching and raising them can have its own difficulties and challenges. Yet, a person with the correct intention should make shukr for all the bounties of Allah ﷻ including having children.

In the expression وَمَن يَشْكُرْ فَإِنَّمَا يَشْكُرُ لِنَفْسِهِ وَمَن كَفَرَ فَإِنَّ اللَّهَ غَنِيٌّ حَمِيدٌ {12/لقمان}506, when a person makes shukr to Allah ﷻ, this attitude is benefitting to the person but not Allah ﷻ as mentioned فَإِنَّ اللَّهَ غَنِيٌّ507. Allah ﷻ does not need our gratitude or thanking. When a person thanks and shows gratitude to Allah ﷻ initially by recognizing it, and then thanking in the form of prayers, dhikr, and finally, by having always the disposition of gratitude, then this can bring immediate benefit to the person with more blessings from Allah ﷻ in this world and after.

One can also project this attitude in human relations as well. When a person recognizes others' service to them and thanks them, this attitude can encourage others to help and give more service to this person.

---

505. Has indeed taken hold of a support most unfailing.
506. And We had certainly given Luqman wisdom [and said], "Be grateful to Allah جل جلاله."
And whoever is grateful is grateful for [the benefit of] himself. And whoever denies [His favor]—then indeed, Allah جل جلاله is Free of need and Praiseworthy.
507. Allah جل جلاله is Free of need.

[23]⁵⁰⁸

وَمَن كَفَرَ فَلَا يَحْزُنكَ كُفْرُهُ إِلَيْنَا مَرْجِعُهُمْ فَنُنَبِّئُهُم بِمَا عَمِلُوا إِنَّ اللَّهَ عَلِيمٌ بِذَاتِ الصُّدُورِ
{لقمان/23}

But, after all these two positions of two groups, shakirun and kafirun, don't worry about the kafirun because you are doing your best to invite them with hikmah.

[30]⁵⁰⁹

ذَلِكَ بِأَنَّ اللَّهَ هُوَ الْحَقُّ وَأَنَّ مَا يَدْعُونَ مِن دُونِهِ الْبَاطِلُ وَأَنَّ اللَّهَ هُوَ الْعَلِيُّ الْكَبِيرُ
{لقمان/30}

One needs to remember that Allah ﷻ sends the Qurān and the Prophet ﷺ. All these teachings are the truth, pure and guidance as mentioned ذَلِكَ بِأَنَّ اللَّهَ هُوَ الْحَقُّ⁵¹⁰. The people's own renderings can be batil, not necessarily true, pure and considered as guidance as mentioned with وَأَنَّ مَا يَدْعُونَ مِن دُونِهِ الْبَاطِلُ⁵¹¹. After this, it is up to you what you want to do, and make your choice accordingly, and remember that Allah ﷻ is الْعَلِيُّ الْكَبِيرُ⁵¹².

[33]⁵¹³

يَا أَيُّهَا النَّاسُ اتَّقُوا رَبَّكُمْ وَاخْشَوْا يَوْمًا لَّا يَجْزِي وَالِدٌ عَن وَلَدِهِ وَلَا مَوْلُودٌ هُوَ جَازٍ عَن وَالِدِهِ شَيْئًا إِنَّ وَعْدَ اللَّهِ حَقٌّ فَلَا تَغُرَّنَّكُمُ الْحَيَاةُ الدُّنْيَا وَلَا يَغُرَّنَّكُم بِاللَّهِ الْغَرُورُ {لقمان/33}

Everyone's attitude of partial or full lacking appreciation of Allah ﷻ can be there. After all the signs from Rabbul Alamin such as skies, earth, seas, or sailing and all others, presented in this Sûrah, then the source of

---

508. (31:23) But as for him who is bent on denying the truth—let not his denial grieve thee: unto Us they must return, and then We shall make them [truly] understand all that they were doing [in life]: for, verily, God has full knowledge of what is in the hearts [of men].

509. 31:30 Thus it is, because God alone is the Ultimate Truth, so that all that men invoke instead of Him is sheer falsehood, and because God alone is exalted, truly great!

510. Thus it is, because God alone is the Ultimate Truth.

511. So that all that men invoke instead of Him is sheer falsehood.

512. Exalted and truly great.

513. 31:33 O MEN! Be conscious of your Sustainer, and stand in awe of the Day on which no parent will be of any avail to his child, nor a child will in the least avail his parent! Verily, God's promise [of resurrection] is true indeed: let not, then, the life of this world delude you, and let not [your own] deceptive thoughts about God delude you!

deceptions are presented for each individual to self-reflect about signs of Allah ﷻ. As a final and concluding emphasis on this deception that humans fall into, the expression فَلاَ تَغُرَّنَّكُمُ الْحَيَاةُ الدُّنْيَا وَلاَ يَغُرَّنَّكُم بِاللَّهِ الْغَرُورُ[514] is very critical.

In the above ayah, again the individual accountability in front of Allah ﷻ reveals itself. Even with the most loved and close ones, such as a child and a parent, the accountability of an individual will be separate, independent, singular and impartial.

Sûrah Sajdah

[16-17][515]

تَتَجَافَى جُنُوبُهُمْ عَنِ الْمَضَاجِعِ يَدْعُونَ رَبَّهُمْ خَوْفًا وَطَمَعًا وَمِمَّا رَزَقْنَاهُمْ يُنفِقُونَ {السجدة/16}

فَلَا تَعْلَمُ نَفْسٌ مَّا أُخْفِيَ لَهُم مِّن قُرَّةِ أَعْيُنٍ جَزَاء بِمَا كَانُوا يَعْمَلُونَ {السجدة/17}

For the sabab nuzûl of this ayah, there are different narrations. It can be praying magrib and waiting until Isha and at the same time, praying salatul abwabin (36). It can be also the any qiyam at night (47)

The importance of tahajjuh is mentioned in تَجَافَى جُنُوبُهُمْ عَنِ الْمَضَاجِعِ يَدْعُونَ رَبَّهُمْ خَوْفًا وَطَمَعًا وَمِمَّا رَزَقْنَاهُمْ يُنفِقُونَ {السجدة/16}. Especially for this prayer, there is a special reward prepared for the person that person cannot imagine as mentioned in فَلَا تَعْلَمُ نَفْسٌ مَّا أُخْفِيَ لَهُم مِّن قُرَّةِ أَعْيُنٍ جَزَاء بِمَا كَانُوا يَعْمَلُونَ {السجدة/17}. The adab of sleeping on the side is mentioned with the word جُنُوبُهُمْ as practiced by Rasulullah ﷺ.

---

514. let not, then, the life of this world delude you, and let not [your own] deceptive thoughts about God delude you.
515. (30:16) but as for those who refused to acknowledge the truth and gave the lie to Our messages—and [thus] to the announcement of a life to come—they will be given over to suffering. (30:17) EXTOL, then, God's limitless glory when you enter upon the evening hours, and when you rise at morn;

Sûrah Ahzâb

[1-4][516]

يَا أَيُّهَا النَّبِيُّ اتَّقِ اللَّهَ وَلَا تُطِعِ الْكَافِرِينَ وَالْمُنَافِقِينَ إِنَّ اللَّهَ كَانَ عَلِيمًا حَكِيمًا {الأحزاب/1}
وَاتَّبِعْ مَا يُوحَى إِلَيْكَ مِن رَّبِّكَ إِنَّ اللَّهَ كَانَ بِمَا تَعْمَلُونَ خَبِيرًا {الأحزاب/2} وَتَوَكَّلْ
عَلَى اللَّهِ وَكَفَى بِاللَّهِ وَكِيلًا {الأحزاب/3} مَّا جَعَلَ اللَّهُ لِرَجُلٍ مِّن قَلْبَيْنِ فِي جَوْفِهِ وَمَا
جَعَلَ أَزْوَاجَكُمُ اللَّائِي تُظَاهِرُونَ مِنْهُنَّ أُمَّهَاتِكُمْ وَمَا جَعَلَ أَدْعِيَاءَكُمْ أَبْنَاءَكُمْ ذَلِكُمْ قَوْلُكُم
بِأَفْوَاهِكُمْ وَاللَّهُ يَقُولُ الْحَقَّ وَهُوَ يَهْدِي السَّبِيلَ {الأحزاب/4}

It is important to do your best with taqwa and follow what is the haqq and then make tawakkul to Allah 🙵. When someone follows وَاتَّبِعْ {[517] مَا يُوحَى إِلَيْكَ مِن رَّبِّكَ then Allah 🙵 knows your best effort of your actions. During these stages and after, making tawakkul is the key.

In Sûrah Ahzab, one can witness the importance of taking Allah 🙵 as the sole and only Waliyy when compared to other things in life. In this perspective, trials or tests can visit the person to remind this notion as the themes of this Sûrah alludes. The notion of waliyy is mentioned in the beginning of this Sûrah as {الأحزاب/3}[518] وَتَوَكَّلْ عَلَى اللَّهِ وَكَفَى بِاللَّهِ وَكِيلًا. Then, another level or explanation of why Allah 🙵 should be the only Waliyy of the person is explained مَّا جَعَلَ اللَّهُ لِرَجُلٍ مِّن قَلْبَيْنِ فِي جَوْفِهِ [519]. The reality of having only one heart, the essence in one's body, can signify having only one essence and waliyy should be the key in one's life. This essence symbolized with the heart is Allah 🙵 for each individual. La ilaha illa Allah is a key stance simply reminding the person repetitively this essence, الله اعلم.

Sometimes, a person can be attached to another person or thing. Yet, Allah 🙵 mentions that the real attachment is only with Allah 🙵. As humans, we tend to think that "I can't live without this person." Yet,

---

516. 33:1 O PROPHET! Remain conscious of God, and defer not to the deniers of the truth and the hypocrites: for God is truly all-knowing, wise. (33:2) And follow [but] that which comes unto thee through revelation from thy Sustainer:1 for God is truly aware of all that you do, [O men]. (33:3) And place thy trust in God [alone]: for none is as worthy of trust as God. 33:4 NEVER has God endowed any man with two hearts in one body:2 and [just as] He has never made your wives whom you may have declared to be "as unlawful to you as your mothers' bodies" [truly] your mothers, so, too, has He never made your adopted sons [truly] your sons:4 these are but [figures of] speech uttered by your mouths—whereas God speaks the [absolute] truth:5 and it is He alone who can show [you] the right path.
517. And follow [but] that which comes unto thee through revelation from thy Sustainer.
518. And place thy trust in God [alone]: for none is as worthy of trust as God.
519. NEVER has God endowed any man with two hearts in one body.

when a test or trial comes as a teaching point, we realize that "I can't
live without Allah ﷻ. Yet, I can live without any person." This ayah and
others remind this reality.

As humans, we tend to take refuge in things other than Allah ﷻ.
These things implicitly or by not knowingly can be our spouses, children,
friends, sometimes our teachers, positions, wealth, fame, recognition or
our ownselves-nafs. As everything in life starts betraying to us one by
one, we then realize the Real Who is the Real Friend, As-Shakur, Who
appreciates and does not leave the person, Allah ﷻ.

Rasulullah ﷺ embodied this full refuge in Allah ﷻ in his life time
ﷺ. He ﷺ was raised without his parents. In his life time, he lost his
uncle who used to shelter him ﷺ. He lost his wife who used to give all
emotional, financial, and physical support to him ﷺ. At one point, he ﷺ
was ordered by Allah ﷻ to sleep at night without any guardian that Allah
ﷻ is sufficient for him ﷺ as a guardian.

[39]⁵²⁰

الَّذِينَ يُبَلِّغُونَ رِسَالَاتِ اللَّهِ وَيَخْشَوْنَهُ وَلَا يَخْشَوْنَ أَحَدًا إِلَّا اللَّهَ وَكَفَى بِاللَّهِ حَسِيبًا

There will be people who would spread fear and threats but Allah ﷻ is
sufficient in all cases.

[41-43 & 56] ⁵²¹

يَا أَيُّهَا الَّذِينَ آمَنُوا اذْكُرُوا اللَّهَ ذِكْرًا كَثِيرًا {الأحزاب/41} وَسَبِّحُوهُ بُكْرَةً وَأَصِيلًا
{الأحزاب/42}

هُوَ الَّذِي يُصَلِّي عَلَيْكُمْ وَمَلَائِكَتُهُ لِيُخْرِجَكُم مِّنَ الظُّلُمَاتِ إِلَى النُّورِ وَكَانَ بِالْمُؤْمِنِينَ
رَحِيمًا {الأحزاب/43}

---

520. (30:39) And [remember:] whatever you may give out in usury so that it might increase
through [other] people's possessions will bring [you] no increase in the sight of God—whereas
all that you give out in charity, seeking God's countenance, (will be blessed by Him:] for it is
they, they (who thus seek His countenance] that shall have their recompense multiplied!
521. 33:41 O you who have believed, remember Allah جل جلاله with much remembrance.
33:42 And exalt Him morning and afternoon. (33:43) It is He who confers blessing upon you,
and His angels [ask Him to do so] that He may bring you out from darknesses into the light.
And ever is He, to the believers, Merciful.
33:56 Indeed, Allah جل جلاله confers blessing upon the Prophet, and His angels [ask Him to do
so]. O you who have believed, ask [Allah جل جلاله to confer] blessing upon him and ask [Allah
جل جلاله to grant him] peace.

إِنَّ اللَّهَ وَمَلَائِكَتَهُ يُصَلُّونَ عَلَى النَّبِيِّ يَا أَيُّهَا الَّذِينَ آمَنُوا صَلُّوا عَلَيْهِ وَسَلِّمُوا تَسْلِيمًا {الأحزاب/56}

When one compares the ayahs in the above case in Sûrah Ahzab, Allah ﷻ mentions the value of the Prophet in a separate ayah comparing him to all humanity. In other words, the Prophet ﷺ in essence is the seed of all humanity. He is a perfect role model for all humans.

In this perspective, ta'kid, إِنَّ comes when the salawat is mentioned to the Prophet صلى الله عليه وسلم

إِنَّ اللَّهَ وَمَلَائِكَتَهُ يُصَلُّونَ عَلَى النَّبِيِّ يَا أَيُّهَا الَّذِينَ آمَنُوا صَلُّوا عَلَيْهِ وَسَلِّمُوا تَسْلِيمًا {الأحزاب/56},

whereas ta'kid is not used for other believers when Allah ﷻ sends the Divine blessings as salawat as mentioned in هُوَ الَّذِي يُصَلِّي عَلَيْكُمْ وَمَلَائِكَتُهُ لِيُخْرِجَكُم مِّنَ الظُّلُمَاتِ إِلَى النُّورِ وَكَانَ بِالْمُؤْمِنِينَ رَحِيمًا {الأحزاب/٤٣}, الله اعلم.

[47-48][522]

وَبَشِّرِ الْمُؤْمِنِينَ بِأَنَّ لَهُم مِّنَ اللَّهِ فَضْلًا كَبِيرًا {الأحزاب/47} وَلَا تُطِعِ الْكَافِرِينَ وَالْمُنَافِقِينَ وَدَعْ أَذَاهُمْ وَتَوَكَّلْ عَلَى اللَّهِ وَكَفَى بِاللَّهِ وَكِيلًا {الأحزاب/48}

For making proper tawakkul, a few steps are the key:

▶ Following the proper teachings of Allah ﷻ and Rasulullah ﷺ with وَلَا تُطِعِ الْكَافِرِينَ وَالْمُنَافِقِينَ [523]
▶ Ignoring the evil of others and being patient with وَدَعْ أَذَاهُمْ

[53][524]

وَمَا كَانَ لَكُمْ أَن تُؤْذُوا رَسُولَ اللَّهِ وَلَا أَن تَنكِحُوا أَزْوَاجَهُ مِن بَعْدِهِ أَبَدًا إِنَّ ذَلِكُمْ كَانَ عِندَ اللَّهِ عَظِيمًا {الأحزاب/53}

Above can be a proof that the Prophet ﷺ is aware of his ummah, and he is being informed about their situation even after his death, that the expression مِن بَعْدِهِ أَبَدًا can signify, الله اعلم.

---

522. 33;47 And give good tidings to the believers that they will have from Allah جل جلاله great bounty. (33:48) And do not obey the disbelievers and the hypocrites but do not harm them, and rely upon Allah جل جلاله. And sufficient is Allah جل جلاله as Disposer of affairs.
523. And do not obey the disbelievers and the hypocrites.
524. (33:53) And it is not [conceivable or lawful] for you to harm the Messenger of Allah or to marry his wives after him, ever. Indeed, that would be in the sight of Allah جل جلاله an enormity.

[56]⁵²⁵

إِنَّ اللَّهَ وَمَلَائِكَتَهُ يُصَلُّونَ عَلَى النَّبِيِّ يَا أَيُّهَا الَّذِينَ آمَنُوا صَلُّوا عَلَيْهِ وَسَلِّمُوا تَسْلِيمًا
{الأحزاب/56}

This is one of the key verses in the Qurān in the formation of the phrases of the different types of salawat for Rasulullah ﷺ. The scholars used different formations of the above wordings to construct different versions of salawat for the Prophet ﷺ.

---

525. 33:56 Indeed, Allah جل جلاله confers blessing upon the Prophet, and His angels [ask Him to do so]. O you who have believed, ask [Allah جل جلاله to confer] blessing upon him and ask [Allah جل جلاله to grant him] peace.

22

Sûrah Sab'a

[14][526]

فَلَمَّا قَضَيْنَا عَلَيْهِ الْمَوْتَ مَا دَلَّهُمْ عَلَى مَوْتِهِ إِلَّا دَابَّةُ الْأَرْضِ تَأْكُلُ مِنسَأَتَهُ فَلَمَّا خَرَّ تَبَيَّنَتِ الْجِنُّ أَن لَّوْ كَانُوا يَعْلَمُونَ الْغَيْبَ مَا لَبِثُوا فِي الْعَذَابِ الْمُهِينِ {سبأ/14}

This is an interesting ayah which shows a human is in charge of the unseen beings where in most cases people are scared of these unseen beings. In this perspective, Allah ﷻ shows that a small worm shows that the reality of knowns and unknowns to the creation. In other words, these unseen beings are not aware about the death of Sulayman as. Because, in most human engagements with the jinn, the deception of humans reveal itself that the jinn know the future, and unseen but Allah ﷻ mentions as أَن لَّوْ كَانُوا يَعْلَمُونَ الْغَيْبَ مَا لَبِثُوا فِي الْعَذَابِ الْمُهِينِ {سبأ/14}, that they don't know about the future, الله اعلم. Here is a case that Allah ﷻ shows that jinns are creation that they are limited like humans.

[37][527]

[40-41][528]

وَيَوْمَ يَحْشُرُهُمْ جَمِيعًا ثُمَّ يَقُولُ لِلْمَلَائِكَةِ أَهَٰؤُلَاء إِيَّاكُمْ كَانُوا يَعْبُدُونَ {سبأ/40} قَالُوا سُبْحَانَكَ أَنتَ وَلِيُّنَا مِن دُونِهِم بَلْ كَانُوا يَعْبُدُونَ الْجِنَّ أَكْثَرُهُم بِهِم مُّؤْمِنُونَ {سبأ/41}

---

526. 34:14 Yet [even Solomon had to die; but] when We decreed that he should die, nothing showed them that he was dead except an earthworm that gnawed away his staff. And when he fell to the ground, those invisible beings [subservient to him] saw clearly that, had they but understood the reality which was beyond the reach of their perception, they would not have continued [to toil] in the shameful suffering [of servitude].

527. (34:37) For, it is neither your riches nor your children that can bring you nearer to Us: only he who attains to faith and does what is right and just [comes near unto Us]; and it is [such as] these whom multiple recompense awaits for all that they have done; and it is they who shall dwell secure in the mansions [of paradise]

528. (34:40) And [as for those who now deny the truth,] one Day He will gather them all together, and will ask the angels, "Was it you that they were wont to worship?"34:41 They will answer: "Limitless art Thou in Thy glory! Thou [alone] art close unto us, not they! Nay, [when they thought that they were worshipping us,] they were but [blindly] worshipping forces concealed from theirsenses; most of them believed in them."

It is very interesting to see the evil renderings of slander of humans even blaming angels. Then, at this point, to execute full justice, Allah ﷻ asks angels in front these humans, although Allah ﷻ knows the reality. One can see the azamah, seriousness, of yawmul qiyamah that even angels are not safe, comfortable, and secure for their positions. They declare how they spent all their responsibilities as either executing the orders of Allah ﷻ or being in ibadah to Allah ﷻ and they mention قَالُوا سُبْحَانَكَ أَنتَ[529] وَلِيُّنَا مِن دُونِهِم. Then, they mention since they did not see us and witness us but they take jinn بَلْ كَانُوا يَعْبُدُونَ الْجِنَّ أَكْثَرُهُم بِهِم مُّؤْمِنُونَ[530] as their attached beings, الله اعلم. After Sûrah sabah, it is interesting to see Sûrah Fâtir immediately follows, explaining the creation of angels.

Sûrah Fâtir

[9][531]

وَاللَّهُ الَّذِي أَرْسَلَ الرِّيَاحَ فَتُثِيرُ سَحَابًا فَسُقْنَاهُ إِلَى بَلَدٍ مَّيِّتٍ فَأَحْيَيْنَا بِهِ الْأَرْضَ بَعْدَ مَوْتِهَا كَذَٰلِكَ النُّشُورُ {فاطر/9}

The winds or the wind?

The word الرِّيَاحَ[532] is plural that in the Qurān when it is plural as winds then it signifies a blessing but when it is singular that it is not a blessing but punishment. In that perspective, one can understand the view of zawj, couples and in the winds as coupling with plural form الرِّيَاحَ of a blessing, الله اعلم. The verses can also have implicit meanings other than their literal meanings. In that perspective, Allah ﷻ can transform people, فَأَحْيَيْنَا بِهِ[533], with the breeze and winds of the Divine favor, Fadl of Allah ﷻ, from the darkness of kufr, بَلَدٍ مَّيِّتٍ[534] pessimism to the light of imān, Nûr, and light اللهم جعلنا منهم[535].

---

529. They will answer: "Limitless art Thou in Thy glory! Thou [alone] art close unto us, not they!

530. But [blindly] worshipping forces concealed from their senses; most of them believed in them."

531. 35:9 AND [remember:] it is God who sends forth the winds, so that they raise a cloud, whereupon We drive it towards dead land and thereby give life to the earth after it had been lifeless: even thus shall resurrection be!

532. Wind.

533. Thereby give life to the earth.

534. Dead land.

535. Oh Allah جل جلاله, make us from them.

[10][536]

مَن كَانَ يُرِيدُ الْعِزَّةَ فَلِلَّهِ الْعِزَّةُ جَمِيعًا إِلَيْهِ يَصْعَدُ الْكَلِمُ الطَّيِّبُ وَالْعَمَلُ الصَّالِحُ يَرْفَعُهُ
وَالَّذِينَ يَمْكُرُونَ السَّيِّئَاتِ لَهُمْ عَذَابٌ شَدِيدٌ وَمَكْرُ أُولَئِكَ هُوَ يَبُورُ {فاطر/10}

When Allah ❀ raises people from kufr to imān and give the livelihood both in this dunya and akhirah, the person can claim izzah, nobility. But one should remember that the Noble and the Exalted and the Glorified is only Allah ❀ only. If you want to please Allah ❀ with good words such as the words of dhikr and the Qurān, and i'lm, as mentioned in الْكَلِمُ[537] الطَّيِّبُ and with وَالْعَمَلُ الصَّالِحُ[538] which can mean good work and action, then the person can be inshAllah placed at a high place with honor and nobility as mentioned with the words يَرْفَعُهُ[539] and الْعِزَّةَ الله اعلم[540].

[27][541]

أَلَمْ تَرَ أَنَّ اللهَ أَنزَلَ مِنَ السَّمَاءِ مَاء فَأَخْرَجْنَا بِهِ ثَمَرَاتٍ مُخْتَلِفًا أَلْوَانُهَا وَمِنَ الْجِبَالِ جُدَدٌ
بِيضٌ وَحُمْرٌ مُخْتَلِفٌ أَلْوَانُهَا وَغَرَابِيبُ سُودٌ {فاطر/27}

The Rain with its implicit meanings:

Again if one reviews the meaning of rain, that Allah ❀ gives life with it أَلَمْ تَرَ أَنَّ اللهَ أَنزَلَ مِنَ السَّمَاء مَاء[542].

---

536. 35:10 He who desires might and glory [ought to know that] all might and glory belong to God [alone]. Unto Him ascend all good words, and the righteous deed does He exalt. But as for those who cunningly devise evil deeds—suffering severe awaits them; and all their devising is bound to come to nought.7
537. All good words.
538. And the righteous deed.
539. He exalt.
540. Might and glory.
541. 35:27 ART THOU NOT aware that God sends down water from the skies, whereby We bring forth fruits of many hues—just as in the mountains there are streaks of white and red of various shades, as well as [others] ravenblack,
542. ART THOU NOT aware that God sends down water from the skies.

23

Sûrah Yāsîn

[11]543

{يس/11} إِنَّمَا تُنذِرُ مَنِ اتَّبَعَ الذِّكْرَ وَخَشِيَ الرَّحْمَن بِالْغَيْبِ فَبَشِّرْهُ بِمَغْفِرَةٍ وَأَجْرٍ كَرِيمٍ

One can also view the gist of belief is to have taqwa and khashyah of
Allah ﷻ when there is no one, the person has genuine relationship with
Allah ﷻ:

وَسَوَاء عَلَيْهِمْ أَأَنذَرْتَهُمْ أَمْ لَمْ تُنذِرْهُمْ لاَ يُؤْمِنُونَ وَسَوَاء عَلَيْهِمْ أَأَنذَرْتَهُمْ أَمْ لَمْ تُنذِرْهُمْ لاَ
يُؤْمِنُونَ 544{يس/10} إِنَّمَا تُنذِرُ مَنِ اتَّبَعَ الذِّكْرَ وَخَشِيَ الرَّحْمَن بِالْغَيْبِ فَبَشِّرْهُ بِمَغْفِرَةٍ
وَأَجْرٍ كَرِيمٍ {يس/11}

The reality of imān and one's relationship with Allah ﷻ reveals one's
true disposition when one is alone.

[52]545

قَالُوا يَا وَيْلَنَا مَن بَعَثَنَا مِن مَّرْقَدِنَا هَذَا مَا وَعَدَ الرَّحْمَنُ وَصَدَقَ الْمُرْسَلُونَ

The initial moments in waking up is very critical and important. When
a person wakes up in the morning everything is fresh. All the physical
and spiritual faculties are fresh. Therefore, using this energy to increase
one's imān and closeness to Allah ﷻ is important. Then this person can
get pleasure from his or her sleep, from the food, and from the silence.
If a person makes an intention for every dealing that he or she will use it
to get close to Allah ﷻ, then everything becomes tasty, without any side
effects, and pain.

---

543. 36:11 Thou canst [truly] warn only him who is willing to take the reminder to heart,
and who stands in awe of the Most Gracious although He is beyond the reach of human
perception: unto such, then, give the glad tiding of [God's] forgiveness and of a most excellent
reward.

544. And it is all the same for them whether you warn them or do not warn them—they will
not believe.

545. 36:52 They will say: "Oh, woe unto us! Who has roused us from our sleep [of death]?"
[Whereupon they will be told:] "This is what the Most Gracious has promised! And His
message-bearers spoke the truth!"

[55]^546

إِنَّ أَصْحَابَ الْجَنَّةِ الْيَوْمَ فِي شُغُلٍ فَاكِهُونَ

In its implicit meaning, the Jannah can be both in this world and afterlife. A person also can be in a pleasure with the help, humbleness and guidance from Allah ﷻ. Seeing and relating everything with and from Allah ﷻ, taking a meaning, not rushing, making reliance, tawakkul to Allah جل جلاله can form a Jannah in this world for the person.

[68]^547

وَمَنْ نُعَمِّرْهُ نُنَكِّسْهُ فِي الْخَلْقِ أَفَلَا يَعْقِلُونَ {يس/68}

One can find in the above ayah, the rules of opposites. If one specializes in the worldly matters time and effort then, this person can lack in the matters of akhirah. When a person is young physically, this person's wisdom and spiritual tendencies can be weak compared to the physical weakness of old age but with spiritual strength and experiential wisdom, الله اعلم.

[78-79]^548

وَضَرَبَ لَنَا مَثَلًا وَنَسِيَ خَلْقَهُ قَالَ مَنْ يُحْيِي الْعِظَامَ وَهِيَ رَمِيمٌ {يس/78} قُلْ يُحْيِيهَا
الَّذِي أَنْشَأَهَا أَوَّلَ مَرَّةٍ وَهُوَ بِكُلِّ خَلْقٍ عَلِيمٌ {يس/79}

Allah ﷻ presents a logic according to our understanding. If someone is trained in something, then this person can achieve it with his or her prior training compared to the person having no experience or training. Similarly, Allah ﷻ gives an example about creation and recreation. Allah ﷻ created in the beginning from nothing. After death, there will be

---

546. 36:55 "Behold, those who are destined for paradise shall today have joy in whatever they do.
547. (36:68) But [let them always remember that] if We lengthen a human being's days, We also cause him to decline in his powers [when he grows old]: will they not, then, use their reason?
548. (36:78) And [now] he [argues about Us, and] thinks of Us in terms of comparison, and is oblivious of how he himself was created! [And so] he says, "Who could give life to bones that have crumbled to dust?"
36:79 Say: "He who brought them into being in the first instance will give them life [once again], seeing that He has full knowledge of every act of creation:

recreation where there was already a sample that Allah ‎﷽‎ created before. For Allah ‎﷽‎, there is no notion of easiness versus difficulty.

Sûrah Saffãt

[83-85]⁵⁴⁹

وَإِنَّ مِن شِيعَتِهِ لَإِبْرَاهِيمَ {الصافات/83} إِذْ جَاء رَبَّهُ بِقَلْبٍ سَلِيمٍ {الصافات/84} إِذْ قَالَ لِأَبِيهِ وَقَوْمِهِ مَاذَا تَعْبُدُونَ {الصافات/85}

There are different narrations about Ibrahim as and his upbringing. One is that he was raised in a household of an idol maker. It is interesting to note that the devout exposure of religious life whether it is bãtil or haq can lead a person at the end to the correct and the true path of Allah ‎﷽‎.

In other words, a person who has an experience of religious life, can already have the desire of seeking for the unknown and for the not immediately apparent. Therefore, one can see a lot of new convert Muslims coming from devout prior religious backgrounds. Sometimes, piety and dedication in one religion can have disadvantages due to upholding strong group identities but not being open-minded. But overall, a person with a trait of the true concern of fear of unknown beyond this life with an attitude of humility, sincerity, and open-mindedness would be guided inshAllah to the genuine path, الله اعلم.

[102] ⁵⁵⁰

فَلَمَّا بَلَغَ مَعَهُ السَّعْيَ قَالَ يَا بُنَيَّ إِنِّي أَرَى فِي الْمَنَامِ أَنِّي أَذْبَحُكَ فَانظُرْ مَاذَا تَرَى قَالَ يَا أَبَتِ افْعَلْ مَا تُؤْمَرُ سَتَجِدُنِي إِن شَاء اللَّهُ مِنَ الصَّابِرِينَ {الصافات/102}

The expression فَلَمَّا بَلَغَ مَعَهُ السَّعْيَ⁵⁵¹ can show that parents can be attached to their kids when these parents see that these children are helping them and taking care of their needs. At this point, the parents are not

---

549. 37:83 AND, BEHOLD, of his persuasion was Abraham, too, (37:84) when he turned to his Sustainer with a heart free of evil, (37:85) and [thus] spoke to his father and his people: "What is it that you worship?

550. 37:102 And [one day,] when [the child] had become old enough to share in his [father's] endeavours, the latter said: "O my dear son! I have seen in a dream that I should sacrifice thee: consider, then, what would be thy view!" [Ishmael] answered: "O my father! Do as thou art bidden: thou wilt find me, if God so wills, among those who are patient in adversity!

551. And [one day,] when [the child] had become old enough to share in his [father's] endeavours.

fully taking care of these children anymore but on the contrary, these children are helping and taking care the needs of their parents. This can be similar to a planted garden when it gives its fruits. It is difficult to sell this garden or detach oneself from this worldly attachment as this thing benefits the person and the person witnesses this and tastes its fruits. At this point, Allah ﷻ asks Ibrahim as to detach himself from his son, الله اعلم.

Sûrah Sâd

Ulul-Albab Surahs: Sâd, Zumar and Ghāfir.

Now with the start of the three consecutive surahs, the expression أُولُوا[552] الْأَلْبَابِ is mentioned in the Sûrah Sâd twice, in Sûrah Zumar three times, and Sûrah Ghāfir once. Then, in the Qurān lastly, it was mentioned once in Sûrah Talaq. This key term أُولُوا الْأَلْبَابِ can mean the people or individuals who think, reason, learn, and apply these teachings in their lives.

[18-19][553]

إِنَّا سَخَّرْنَا الْجِبَالَ مَعَهُ يُسَبِّحْنَ بِالْعَشِيِّ وَالْإِشْرَاقِ {ص/18} وَالطَّيْرَ مَحْشُورَةً كُلٌّ لَّهُ أَوَّابٌ {ص/19}

فَفَهَّمْنَاهَا سُلَيْمَانَ وَكُلًّا آتَيْنَا حُكْمًا وَعِلْمًا وَسَخَّرْنَا مَعَ دَاوُودَ الْجِبَالَ يُسَبِّحْنَ وَالطَّيْرَ وَكُنَّا فَاعِلِينَ[554] {الأنبياء/79}

أَلَمْ تَرَ أَنَّ اللَّهَ يُسَبِّحُ لَهُ مَن فِي السَّمَاوَاتِ وَالْأَرْضِ وَالطَّيْرُ صَافَّاتٍ كُلٌّ قَدْ عَلِمَ صَلَاتَهُ وَتَسْبِيحَهُ وَاللَّهُ عَلِيمٌ بِمَا يَفْعَلُونَ[555] {النور/41}

---

552. The righteous people.
553. (38:18) [and for this,] behold, We caused20 the mountains to join him in extolling Our limitless glory at eventide and at sunrise, (38:19) and [likewise] the birds in their assemblies: [together] they all would turn again and again unto Him [who had created them].
554. And We gave understanding of it [i.e., the case] to Solomon, and to each [of them] We gave judgement and knowledge. And We subjected the mountains to exalt [Us], along with David and [also] the birds. And We were doing [that].
555. Do you not see that Allah جل جلاله is exalted by whomever is within the heavens and the earth and [by] the birds with wings spread [in flight]? Each [of them] has known his [means of] prayer and exalting [Him], and Allah جل جلاله is Knowing of what they do.

وَلَقَدْ آتَيْنَا دَاوُودَ مِنَّا فَضْلًا يَا جِبَالُ أَوِّبِي مَعَهُ وَالطَّيْرَ وَأَلَنَّا لَهُ الْحَدِيدَ {سبأ/10}[556]

When one analyses the above ayahs around the theme of the birds, الطَّيْر, one can reveal the phenomena of the dhikr of birds to be possibly witnessed by humans. Especially, if one observes the times of fajr when everyone is sleeping in silence, the birds from nowhere as if they get a command start chirping with their melodious sounds and dhikrs. If one joins them in dhikr there is a huge pleasure that one can possibly feel and experience at those times. In fact, these are the special times suggested by the Qurān and the Sunnah that one should engage with dhikr.

[34&35][557]

وَلَقَدْ فَتَنَّا سُلَيْمَانَ وَأَلْقَيْنَا عَلَى كُرْسِيِّهِ جَسَدًا ثُمَّ أَنَابَ {ص/34} قَالَ رَبِّ اغْفِرْ لِي وَهَبْ لِي مُلْكًا لَّا يَنبَغِي لِأَحَدٍ مِّنْ بَعْدِي إِنَّكَ أَنتَ الْوَهَّابُ {ص/35}

One can ask the question, if a person is given a lot of blessings from Allah ﷻ and the person still wants to die in the state of imān as a Muslim, what should be the disposition of the person in one's relationship with Allah ﷻ?

The answer for this can be the continuous gratitude, appreciation, hamd, tawba and istighfār to Allah ﷻ and not having the feelings of security and safety due to the blessings but thinking that at any time a test of Allah ﷻ can come in any form. In this case, as in the above ayah, one of the examples is Sulayman as. One can see his disposition as mentioned above that when something unusual happens he as shows his disposition as وَلَقَدْ فَتَنَّا سُلَيْمَانَ وَأَلْقَيْنَا عَلَى كُرْسِيِّهِ جَسَدًا ثُمَّ أَنَابَ {ص/34} قَالَ رَبِّ اغْفِرْ لِي[558]. He immediately asks forgiveness.

---

556. And We certainly gave David from Us bounty. [We said], "O mountains, repeat [Our] praises with him, and the birds [as well]." And We made pliable for him iron.
557. 38:24 And We certainly tried Solomon and placed on his throne a body; then he returned. (38:35) He prayed: "O my Sustainer! Forgive me my sins, and bestow upon me the gift of a kingdom which may not suit anyone after me: verily, Thou alone art a giver of gifts!"
558. He prayed: "O my Sustainer! Forgive me my sins."

Similarly, one can see the same disposition for the father of Sulayman as, Dawud as:

قَالَ لَقَدْ ظَلَمَكَ بِسُؤَالِ نَعْجَتِكَ إِلَى نِعَاجِهِ وَإِنَّ كَثِيرًا مِّنَ الْخُلَطَاءِ لَيَبْغِي بَعْضُهُمْ عَلَى بَعْضٍ إِلَّا الَّذِينَ آمَنُوا وَعَمِلُوا الصَّالِحَاتِ وَقَلِيلٌ مَّا هُمْ وَظَنَّ دَاوُودُ أَنَّمَا فَتَنَّاهُ فَاسْتَغْفَرَ رَبَّهُ وَخَرَّ رَاكِعًا وَأَنَابَ (سجدة مستحبة)559 {ص/24}

When a test or trial comes, he as was on alert and immediately says: وَظَنَّ دَاوُودُ أَنَّمَا فَتَنَّاهُ فَاسْتَغْفَرَ رَبَّهُ وَخَرَّ رَاكِعًا وَأَنَابَ560.

One can see their clear disposition as father and son:

وَلَقَدْ آتَيْنَا دَاوُودَ وَسُلَيْمَانَ عِلْمًا وَقَالَا الْحَمْدُ لِلَّهِ الَّذِي فَضَّلَنَا عَلَى كَثِيرٍ مِّنْ عِبَادِهِ الْمُؤْمِنِينَ {النمل/15}561that they make hamd وَقَالَا الْحَمْدُ لِلَّهِ562.

On another note, Sulayman as mentions that increased nimahs can increase his shukr and hamd for Allah ﷻ. When again an unusual nimah of Allah ﷻ reveals itself for Sulayman as he hears the conversations of the ant he immediately thanks to Allah ﷻ: [18-19]563

حَتَّى إِذَا أَتَوْا عَلَى وَادِ النَّمْلِ قَالَتْ نَمْلَةٌ يَا أَيُّهَا النَّمْلُ ادْخُلُوا مَسَاكِنَكُمْ لَا يَحْطِمَنَّكُمْ سُلَيْمَانُ وَجُنُودُهُ وَهُمْ لَا يَشْعُرُونَ {النمل/18} فَتَبَسَّمَ ضَاحِكًا مِّن قَوْلِهَا وَقَالَ رَبِّ أَوْزِعْنِي أَنْ أَشْكُرَ نِعْمَتَكَ الَّتِي أَنْعَمْتَ عَلَيَّ وَعَلَى وَالِدَيَّ وَأَنْ أَعْمَلَ صَالِحًا تَرْضَاهُ وَأَدْخِلْنِي بِرَحْمَتِكَ فِي عِبَادِكَ الصَّالِحِينَ {النمل/1}

---

559. [David] said, "He has certainly wronged you in demanding your ewe [in addition] to his ewes. And indeed, many associates oppress one another, except for those who believe and do righteous deeds—and few are they." And David became certain that We had tried him, and he asked forgiveness of his Lord and fell down bowing [in prostration] and turned in repentance [to Allah جل جلاله].
560. And David became certain that We had tried him, and he asked forgiveness of his Lord and fell down bowing [in prostration] and turned in repentance [to Allah جل جلاله].
561. And We had certainly given to David and Solomon knowledge, and they said, "Praise [is due] to Allah جل جلاله, who has favored us over many of His believing servants."
562. They said, "Praise [is due] to Allah جل جلاله.
563. 27:18 Until, when they came upon the valley of the ants, an ant said, "O ants, enter your dwellings that you not be crushed by Solomon and his soldiers while they perceive not." 27:19 So [Solomon] smiled, amused at her speech, and said, "My Lord, enable me to be grateful for Your favor which You have bestowed upon me and upon my parents and to do righteousness of which You approve. And admit me by Your mercy into [the ranks of] Your righteous servants."

Another example is the unusual appearance of the throne of Balqis and how immediately it is brought and the response of Sulayman as

قَالَ الَّذِي عِندَهُ عِلْمٌ مِّنَ الْكِتَابِ أَنَا آتِيكَ بِهِ قَبْلَ أَن يَرْتَدَّ إِلَيْكَ طَرْفُكَ فَلَمَّا رَآهُ مُسْتَقِرًّا عِندَهُ قَالَ هَذَا مِن فَضْلِ رَبِّي لِيَبْلُوَنِي أَأَشْكُرُ أَمْ أَكْفُرُ وَمَن شَكَرَ فَإِنَّمَا يَشْكُرُ لِنَفْسِهِ وَمَن كَفَرَ فَإِنَّ رَبِّي غَنِيٌّ كَرِيمٌ [564]{النمل/40}. Sulayman as immediately says this is from Fadl of Allah ﷻ. The test here is again about the disposition of the person if he would make shukr, and hamd to Allah ﷻ or just move on and not care, اللهم احفظنا من هذا و جعلنا من الشاكرين، امين[565]

[69][566]

مَا كَانَ لِي مِنْ عِلْمٍ بِالْمَلَإِ الْأَعْلَى إِذْ يَخْتَصِمُونَ {ص/69}

وَأَنَّا لَا نَدْرِي أَشَرٌّ أُرِيدَ بِمَن فِي الْأَرْضِ أَمْ أَرَادَ بِهِمْ رَبُّهُمْ رَشَدًا [567]{الجن/10}

Sometimes, some events can happen in one's life. It can be ibtilā, a test, or a guidance from Allah ﷻ. Therefore, Jinns are trying to understand these unseen realities in this ayah. Jinns may have more interaction tools about matters concerning the unseen events about humans. In this above ayah, they try to rationalize what is happening with the events if they are a test or not for humans as mentioned وَأَنَّا لَا نَدْرِي أَشَرٌّ أُرِيدَ بِمَن فِي الْأَرْضِ أَمْ أَرَادَ بِهِمْ رَبُّهُمْ رَشَدًا {الجن/10}.

Also, a discussion happens among them concerning angels, as mentioned in مَا كَانَ لِي مِنْ عِلْمٍ بِالْمَلَإِ الْأَعْلَى إِذْ يَخْتَصِمُونَ [568]{ص/69}.

Humans are most far or another level interpreting the events depending on their connection with Allah ﷻ. The level connection with unseen realities in their real meaning can increase in the below order as:

---

564. Said one who had knowledge from the Scripture, "I will bring it to you before your glance returns to you." And when [Solomon] saw it placed before him, he said, "This is from the favor of my Lord to test me whether I will be grateful or ungrateful. And whoever is grateful—his gratitude is only for [the benefit of] himself. And whoever is ungrateful—then indeed, my Lord is Free of need and Generous."
565. Oh Allah جلاله protect us from this, and make us from those who are grateful.
566. (38:69) [Say, O Muhammad:] "No knowledge would I have had of [what passed among] the host on high when they argued [against the creation of man].
567. And we do not know [therefore] whether evil is intended for those on earth or whether their Lord intends for them a right course.
568. I had no knowledge of the exalted assembly [of angels] when they were disputing [the creation of Adam].

1. Humans
2. Jinn
3. Angels

One can call this the worlds of shadah of humans, and the worlds of malakut, hakikah. Therefore, the story of Khidr and Musa as is the interaction of members of two different worlds. The world of jinn is in between shadah and malakut as they may interact with both worlds negatively or positively. The case of Shaytan as a jinn being among angels, the case of stoning of the jinns by angels as mentioned in Sûrah Saff, and the case of jinns interacting with humans are all some examples.

[78]⁵⁶⁹

وَإِنَّ عَلَيْكَ لَعْنَتِي إِلَى يَوْمِ الدِّينِ {ص/78}

The expression يَوْمِ الدِّينِ⁵⁷⁰ is also mentioned in Sûrah Fâtiha as the Day of Judgment.

[79]⁵⁷¹

قَالَ رَبِّ فَأَنْظِرْنِي إِلَى يَوْمِ يُبْعَثُونَ {ص/79}

Then, shaytan is asking permission until يَوْمِ يُبْعَثُونَ⁵⁷². Here, shaytan was informed about the yawmal hashr. Another point is whether يَوْمِ الدِّينِ and يَوْمِ يُبْعَثُونَ are referring to the same or different concepts, one can look further into it. We may refer them as the same. Yet, one can analyze if there are different events happening with these two different expressions.

---

569. (38:78) and My rejection shall be thy due until the Day of Judgment!"
570. Day of judgment.
571. (38:79) Said [Iblis]: "Then, O my Sustainer, grant me a respite till the Day when all shall be raised from the dead!"
572. Day when all shall be raised from the dead!

[80]⁵⁷³

قَالَ فَإِنَّكَ مِنَ الْمُنظَرِينَ {ص/80}

Allah ﷻ gives shaytan the respite, the delay due to his request with a wisdom. With all the other teachings of this ayah, this can also teach us the adab when or how one should apply patience, wisdom and delay the recompense even with one's most evil enemy.

Allah ﷻ knows shaytan, the future, the present and the past. Allah ﷻ does not punish shaytan but delays and holds it until a certain time that only Allah ﷻ knows. Within the context of this ayah, one who has authority and power to hurt others should really ponder and think their engagements within the context of this ayah, الله اعلم.

Immediately punishing someone for their wrong doings can be a problematic approach. Even, an example of this, the case of zulqarnayn as the holder of the authority and power, is mentioned in the Qurān as a person who gives people options to think and reconsider their position with their wrongdoings but does not immediately punish as mentioned: [86-88]⁵⁷⁴

حَتَّى إِذَا بَلَغَ مَغْرِبَ الشَّمْسِ وَجَدَهَا تَغْرُبُ فِي عَيْنٍ حَمِئَةٍ وَوَجَدَ عِندَهَا قَوْمًا قُلْنَا يَا ذَا الْقَرْنَيْنِ إِمَّا أَن تُعَذِّبَ وَإِمَّا أَن تَتَّخِذَ فِيهِمْ حُسْنًا {الكهف/86} قَالَ أَمَّا مَن ظَلَمَ فَسَوْفَ نُعَذِّبُهُ ثُمَّ يُرَدُّ إِلَى رَبِّهِ فَيُعَذِّبُهُ عَذَابًا نُّكْرًا {الكهف/87} وَأَمَّا مَنْ آمَنَ وَعَمِلَ صَالِحًا فَلَهُ جَزَاء الْحُسْنَى وَسَنَقُولُ لَهُ مِنْ أَمْرِنَا يُسْرًا {الكهف/88}

Sûrah Zumar

One of the key terms in this Sûrah is أُوْلُوا الْأَلْبَابِ to think, to reason, to learn and to apply. This expression is mentioned three times in this Sûrah and mentioned consecutively in surahs Zumar, Sād, and Ghāfir. Then, in the Qurān, it was mentioned one time in Sûrah Talaq.

---

573. 38:80 Answered He: "Verily, so [be it:] thou shalt be among those who are granted respite.
574. 18:86 Until, when he reached the setting of the sun [i.e., the west], he found it [as if] setting in a spring of dark mud, and he found near it a people. We [i.e., Allah جل جلاله] said, "O Dhul-Qarnayn, either you punish [them] or else adopt among them [a way of] goodness." 18:87 He said, "As for one who wrongs, we will punish him. Then he will be returned to his Lord, and He will punish him with a terrible punishment [i.e., Hellfire]. 18:88 But as for one who believes and does righteousness, he will have a reward of the best [i.e., Paradise], and we [i.e., Dhul-Qarnayn] will speak to him from our command with ease."

[1-2]⁵⁷⁵

تَنزِيلُ الْكِتَابِ مِنَ اللَّهِ الْعَزِيزِ الْحَكِيمِ {الزمر/1} إِنَّا أَنزَلْنَا إِلَيْكَ الْكِتَابَ بِالْحَقِّ فَاعْبُدِ اللَّهَ مُخْلِصًا لَّهُ الدِّينَ

It is important to note that there is a difference between the word تَنزِيل and أَنزَلَ although they have the same root word. Tanzil is the revelation of the Qurān at one time from Allah ﷻ to the place of Nubuwwah. After, revelation in pieces in 23 years to Rasulullah (ﷺ) to the world of humans can be called inzal.

The first ayah of Zumar starts with the expression as tanzil of the Book. The second ayah emphasizes the ikhlas, sincerity for Allah ﷻ by mentioning مُخْلِصًا in the expression فَاعْبُدِ اللَّهَ مُخْلِصًا لَّهُ الدِّينَ. The word مُخْلِصًا is a very critical word and comes in various places in the Qurān. It is an emphasis. It is the essence and gist of the Tawhid and belief in Allah ﷻ. The same word again comes in the 11ᵗʰ verse

[5]⁵⁷⁶

خَلَقَ السَّمَاوَاتِ وَالْأَرْضَ بِالْحَقِّ يُكَوِّرُ اللَّيْلَ عَلَى النَّهَارِ وَيُكَوِّرُ النَّهَارَ عَلَى اللَّيْلِ وَسَخَّرَ الشَّمْسَ وَالْقَمَرَ كُلٌّ يَجْرِي لِأَجَلٍ مُسَمًّى أَلَا هُوَ الْعَزِيزُ الْغَفَّارُ

It is also important to note that after the Kitāb, the revelation of the Qurān, the themes are directed to a focus on the nature, science, earth, skies, and space. Therefore, some of the scholars triangulate the learning from the revelation, the Qurān with the knowledge from the sciences. There is a similar verse in the beginning of the chapter Ahqāf. The only difference is the حم (hāmìm). Sûrah Ahqāf has حم (ha-mim) in the beginning. In that chapter also, the theme of nature, science, earth, skies and space comes after the mention of the revelation of the Qurān.

---

575. 39:1 THE BESTOWAL from on high of this divine writ issues from God, the Almighty, the Wise: (39:2) for, behold, it is We who have bestowed this revelation upon thee from on high, setting forth the truth: so worship Him, sincere in thy faith in Him alone!
576. 39:5 He it is who has created the heavens and the earth in accordance with [an inner] truth.5 He causes the night to flow into the day; and causes the day to flow into the night; and He has made the sun and the moon subservient [to His laws], each running its course for a term set [by Him]. Is not He the Almighty, the All-Forgiving?

[8]⁵⁷⁷

وَإِذَا مَسَّ الْإِنسَانَ ضُرٌّ دَعَا رَبَّهُ مُنِيبًا إِلَيْهِ ثُمَّ إِذَا خَوَّلَهُ نِعْمَةً مِّنْهُ نَسِيَ مَا كَانَ يَدْعُو إِلَيْهِ
مِن قَبْلُ وَجَعَلَ لِلَّهِ أَندَادًا لِّيُضِلَّ عَن سَبِيلِهِ قُلْ تَمَتَّعْ بِكُفْرِكَ قَلِيلًا إِنَّكَ مِنْ أَصْحَابِ النَّارِ
{الزمر/8}

فَإِذَا مَسَّ الْإِنسَانَ ضُرٌّ دَعَانَا ثُمَّ إِذَا خَوَّلْنَاهُ نِعْمَةً مِّنَّا قَالَ إِنَّمَا أُوتِيتُهُ عَلَى عِلْمٍ بَلْ هِيَ
فِتْنَةٌ وَلَكِنَّ أَكْثَرَهُمْ لَا يَعْلَمُونَ ⁵⁷⁸{الزمر/49}

The above ayahs are very interesting, real, and heart breaking for humans when they witness their own realities. The teachings in these ayahs for humans can sometimes be difficult to realize and accept these realities.

In other words, Allah ﷻ gives all the avenues of knowing Allah ﷻ, and worshipping and appreciating Allah ﷻ as the Rabbul Alamin. If the person continues in the attitude of ignoring all these signs, then another sign can come in one's life that the person can feel and understand their own human reality.

The person is weak but nothing, composed of flesh, meat, blood and bones. With all this nothingness in front of Rabbul Alamin, claiming to be something, using the words against and outside the realms of respect and adab with the Creator of everything, the person puts oneself really in a position of mockery and humiliation.

So, in this perspective, the trials and sicknesses can hit the person to remind their own selves and their own realities. These times such as surgery, pain, cancer, death, imprisonment, loss of the attached values such as people's wealth or position and all evil-seeming incidents can be some of these examples and can hit the person hard. May Allah ﷻ protect us.

---

577. 39:8 NOW [thus it is:] when affliction befalls man, he is likely to cry out13 to his Sustainer, turning unto Him [for help]; but as soon as He has bestowed upon him a boon by His grace, he forgets Him whom he invoked before, and claims that there are other powers that could rival God—and thus leads [others] astray from His path. Say [unto him who sins in this way]: "Enjoy thyself for a while in this thy denial of the truth; [yet,] verily, thou art of those who are destined for the fire!

578. And when adversity touches man, he calls upon Us; then when We bestow on him a favor from Us, he says, "I have only been given it because of [my] knowledge." Rather, it is a trial, but most of them do not know.

At these times, like a cold shower, the person can reevaluate one's position, purpose and goal in life and can perhaps turn back to Allah ﷻ as mentioned by دَعَا رَبَّهُ. When others see this person in this calamity, everyone can feel bad for this person as a normal human response. It is also expected that observers of this person take some mindfulness from these incidents for their lives.

But, as soon as Allah ﷻ removes this calamity from this person either this person can be appreciative and change his or her previous life, perspective and attitude with Allah ﷻ. Or, the person can forget his or her difficult times as mentioned in نِعْمَةً مِّنْهُ نَسِيَ مَا كَانَ يَدْعُو إِلَيْهِ مِن قَبْلُ [579] and can go back to the old life style, attitude and habits.

Or, this person can claim that the medicine, doctors, or something helped to remove the evil that this person was in. With this attitude, this person can give credit to oneself because of their choice as mentioned in قَالَ إِنَّمَا أُوتِيتُهُ عَلَى عِلْمٍ [580].

One should realize both attitudes are the attachments of continuation of the prior same unappreciative behavior of Allah ﷻ as mentioned in تَمَتَّعْ بِكُفْرِكَ قَلِيلًا. But, this won't last long because life is short.

اللهم احفظنا من هذا آمين

فَأَمَّا الْإِنسَانُ إِذَا مَا ابْتَلَاهُ رَبُّهُ فَأَكْرَمَهُ وَنَعَّمَهُ فَيَقُولُ رَبِّي أَكْرَمَنِ {الفجر/15} [581] وَأَمَّا إِذَا مَا ابْتَلَاهُ فَقَدَرَ عَلَيْهِ رِزْقَهُ فَيَقُولُ رَبِّي أَهَانَنِ {الفجر/16} [582]

In the last category, one can also see people who are in good life have good relationship with Allah ﷻ. But when tested with the sustenance, their relationship spoils and these people go into the blame mode.

اللهم احفظنا من هذا آمين

---

579. But as soon as He has bestowed upon him a boon by His grace, he forgets Him whom he invoked before.
580. He says, "I have only been given it because of [my] knowledge.
581. And as for man, when his Lord tries him and [thus] is generous to him and favors him, he says, "My Lord has honored me."
582. But when He tries him and restricts his provision, he says, "My Lord has humiliated me."

[9]583

أَمَّنْ هُوَ قَانِتٌ آنَاءَ اللَّيْلِ سَاجِدًا وَقَائِمًا يَحْذَرُ الْآخِرَةَ وَيَرْجُو رَحْمَةَ رَبِّهِ قُلْ هَلْ يَسْتَوِي
الَّذِينَ يَعْلَمُونَ وَالَّذِينَ لَا يَعْلَمُونَ إِنَّمَا يَتَذَكَّرُ أُولُوا الْأَلْبَابِ {الزمر/9}

It is interesting to note the word قَانِتٌ is one of the highest levels
among the believers as mentioned in Sûrah Ahzab when different
categories of believers are mentioned as إِنَّ الْمُسْلِمِينَ وَالْمُسْلِمَاتِ وَالْمُؤْمِنِينَ
وَالْمُؤْمِنَاتِ وَالْقَانِتِينَ وَالْقَانِتَاتِ وَالصَّادِقِينَ وَالصَّادِقَاتِ وَالصَّابِرِينَ وَالصَّابِرَاتِ وَالْخَاشِعِينَ
وَالْخَاشِعَاتِ وَالْمُتَصَدِّقِينَ وَالْمُتَصَدِّقَاتِ وَالصَّائِمِينَ وَالصَّائِمَاتِ وَالْحَافِظِينَ فُرُوجَهُمْ وَالْحَافِظَاتِ
وَالذَّاكِرِينَ اللَّهَ كَثِيرًا وَالذَّاكِرَاتِ أَعَدَّ اللَّهُ لَهُم مَّغْفِرَةً وَأَجْرًا عَظِيمًا 584{الأحزاب/35}
Praying in tahajjud at night has a high status including the possible
prayers of Isha and Fajr. It is very interesting to note that SubhanAllah,
to be able to get up at night in tahajjud or fajr can be very difficult for
many. But, the ayah mentions that to achieve this هَلْ يَسْتَوِي الَّذِينَ يَعْلَمُونَ585
وَالَّذِينَ لَا يَعْلَمُونَ knowing and understanding can help the person to wake
up the person and disturb him or her from one's sleeping although it can
be difficult to leave one's comfort.

The Prophet ﷺ mentions "if you knew what I knew you would cry a
lot and laugh less," (9) (hadith# 2359) meaning that knowing something
changes everything. When a person knows with yaqin the notions of the
khashya of Allah ﷻ, yawmul qiyamah, the questioning in qabr, then, will
it be possible for this person to be able to sleep comfortably at night?
Besides, knowing people's situations and their relationship with Allah
ﷻ, and the concern of inviting the gafilûn, the heedless, then, will it be
possible for this person to be able to sleep comfortably at night?

Therefore, the verse very meaningfully ends with إِنَّمَا يَتَذَكَّرُ أُولُوا
الْأَلْبَابِ. This Sûrah especially emphasizes, knowing and using the mind
and accordingly increasing one's connection and mārifah, gnosis about

---

583. (39:9) Or [dost thou deem thyself equal to] one who devoutly worships [God]
throughout the night, prostrating himself or standing [in prayer], ever-mindful of the life to
come, and hoping for his Sustainer's grace?" Say: "Can they who know and they who do not
know be deemed equal?" [But] only they who are endowed with insight keep this in mind!
584. Indeed, the Muslim men and Muslim women, the believing men and believing women,
the obedient men and obedient women, the truthful men and truthful women, the patient
men and patient women, the humble men and humble women, the charitable men and
charitable women, the fasting men and fasting women, the men who guard their private
parts and the women who do so, and the men who remember Allah جل جلاله often and the
women who do so—for them Allah جل جلاله has prepared forgiveness and a great reward.
585. Can they who know and they who do not know be deemed equal?

لَّذِينَ يَسْتَمِعُونَ الْقَوْلَ فَيَتَّبِعُونَ أَحْسَنَهُ Allah , as mentioned in the 18th ayah as ٥٨٦ أُولَٰئِكَ الَّذِينَ هَدَاهُمُ اللَّهُ وَأُولَٰئِكَ هُمْ أُولُوا الْأَلْبَابِ.

In another perspective, one can also think about the preferred discourses of heart and mind during the night. In other words, how should one be in the state of worship by using different faculties of heart and mind? In this case, the ayah especially encourages to focus on two perspectives: the expected engagements of akhirah and the Rahmah of Allah as mentioned in ٥٨٧ يَحْذَرُ الْآخِرَةَ وَيَرْجُو رَحْمَةَ.

In other words, during the night especially if the person reflects on the accountability, grave, judgment day, yawmul qiyamah and reads the ayahs of the Qurān, one can really be in the frightened, terrified and panicked mode of heart and mind as mentioned يَحْذَرُ الْآخِرَةَ. To balance this disposition in the engagements of night worship, one can have an incessant and never-ending hope from the Rahmah and Fadl of Allah as mentioned in وَيَرْجُو رَحْمَةَ.

When one analyzes the night worships of Rasulullah those two perspectives can be witnessed. Either the Prophet was crying due to the first case worried about his ummah, or he was crying with the second case as in a famous hadith by Aisha radiyallahu anha , he mentioned this disposition as٥٨٨ "11-15](9) "أفلم أكون عبدا شكورا.[٥٨٩

قُلْ إِنِّي أُمِرْتُ أَنْ أَعْبُدَ اللَّهَ مُخْلِصًا لَّهُ الدِّينَ {الزمر/11} وَأُمِرْتُ لِأَنْ أَكُونَ أَوَّلَ الْمُسْلِمِينَ {الزمر/12} قُلْ إِنِّي أَخَافُ إِنْ عَصَيْتُ رَبِّي عَذَابَ يَوْمٍ عَظِيمٍ {الزمر/13} قُلِ اللَّهَ أَعْبُدُ مُخْلِصًا لَّهُ دِينِي {الزمر/14} فَاعْبُدُوا مَا شِئْتُم مِّن دُونِهِ قُلْ إِنَّ الْخَاسِرِينَ الَّذِينَ خَسِرُوا أَنفُسَهُمْ وَأَهْلِيهِمْ يَوْمَ الْقِيَامَةِ أَلَا ذَٰلِكَ هُوَ الْخُسْرَانُ الْمُبِينُ {الزمر/15}

إِنَّا أَنزَلْنَا إِلَيْكَ الْكِتَابَ بِالْحَقِّ فَاعْبُدِ اللَّهَ مُخْلِصًا لَّهُ الدِّينَ The second ayah emphasizes the ikhlas, sincerity for Allah by mentioning مُخْلِصًا in the

---

586. Who listen to speech and follow the best of it. Those are the ones Allah جل جلاله has guided, and those are people of understanding.

587. Fearing the Hereafter and hoping for the mercy of his Lord.

588. Should I not be a thankful servant.

589. 39:11 Say [O Muhammad]: "Behold, I am bidden to worship God, sincere in my faith in Him alone; (39:12) and I am bidden to be foremost among those who surrender themselves unto God." (39:13) Say: "Behold, I would dread, were I to rebel against my Sustainer, the suffering [which would befall me] on that awesome Day [of Judgment]."

39:14Say: "God alone do I worship, sincere in my faith in Him alone (39:15) and [it is up to you, O sinners, to]worship whatever you please instead of Him!" Say: "Behold, the [true] losers will be they who shall have lost their own selves and their kith and kin on Resurrection Day:18 for is not this, this, the [most] obvious loss?

expression فَاعْبُدِ اللَّهَ مُخْلِصًا لَّهُ الدِّينَ. The word مُخْلِصًا is a very critical word and it comes in various places in the Qurān. It is an emphasis. It is the essence and gist of the Tawhid and belief in Allah ﷻ. The same word again comes in the 11th verse as:

قُلْ إِنِّي أُمِرْتُ أَنْ أَعْبُدَ اللَّهَ مُخْلِصًا لَّهُ الدِّينَ

That the Prophet صلى الله عليه وسلم and all the messengers and prophets of Allah ﷻ show this example in their life of worshipping and establishing relation with Allah جل جلاله as mukhlas, the sincere ones.

When one compares the verses 11 and 14:

قُلْ إِنِّي أُمِرْتُ أَنْ أَعْبُدَ اللَّهَ مُخْلِصًا لَّهُ الدِّينَ {الزمر/11}

قُلِ اللَّهَ أَعْبُدُ مُخْلِصًا لَّهُ دِينِي {الزمر/14}

One ayah is an order to the Prophets to be sincere and the other is an order for all other humans.

Alternatively, the teaching of the Prophets to the people is to be sincere.

After these advices, the free will comes in and

فَاعْبُدُوا مَا شِئْتُم مِّن دُونِهِ قُلْ إِنَّ الْخَاسِرِينَ الَّذِينَ خَسِرُوا أَنفُسَهُمْ وَأَهْلِيهِمْ يَوْمَ الْقِيَامَةِ أَلَا ذَلِكَ هُوَ الْخُسْرَانُ الْمُبِينُ {الزمر/15}

It is up to you what you want to do. But remember at the end, you will ruin your own life and afterlife as well as the life of the ones who follow you such as your family members.

[16]590

لَهُم مِّن فَوْقِهِمْ ظُلَلٌ مِّنَ النَّارِ وَمِن تَحْتِهِمْ ظُلَلٌ ذَلِكَ يُخَوِّفُ اللَّهُ بِهِ عِبَادَهُ يَا عِبَادِ فَاتَّقُونِ {الزمر/16}

Some people can ask the purpose of the fear for punishment. The answer for this can be taqwa. Some people can have taqwa due to fear although

---

590. (39:16) Clouds of fire will they have above them, and [similar] clouds beneath them...." In this way does God imbue His servants with fear. O you servants of Mine! Be, then, conscious of Me—

this may not be the highest motivation of doing things but still it is an acceptable level. A person may not want to displease Allah ﷻ by injustice to oneself and others due to this fear as mentioned يَا عِبَادَهُ بِهِ اللهُ يُخَوِّفُ ذَلِكَ عِبَادِ فَاتَّقُونِ.

Or, some people can have a higher level of motivation of doing or not doing things such as to please or not to displease Allah ﷻ because they love Allah ﷻ and they don't want to displease Allah ﷻ.

They want to appreciate all that Allah ﷻ did and is doing constantly for them. Then, Allah ﷻ will give them more when they follow the teachings and guidelines set by Allah ﷻ either due to fear or love.

[17-18]591

وَالَّذِينَ اجْتَنَبُوا الطَّاغُوتَ أَن يَعْبُدُوهَا وَأَنَابُوا إِلَى اللهِ لَهُمُ الْبُشْرَى فَبَشِّرْ عِبَادِ {الزمر/17}

[18]

لَّذِينَ يَسْتَمِعُونَ الْقَوْلَ فَيَتَّبِعُونَ أَحْسَنَهُ أُوْلَئِكَ الَّذِينَ هَدَاهُمُ اللهُ وَأُوْلَئِكَ هُمْ أُوْلُوا الْأَلْبَابِ

The disposition of listening when the message comes but not ignoring and applying it requires and entails the people of أُولُوا الْأَلْبَابِ.

[21]592

أَلَمْ تَرَ أَنَّ اللهَ أَنزَلَ مِنَ السَّمَاء مَاء فَسَلَكَهُ يَنَابِيعَ فِي الْأَرْضِ ثُمَّ يُخْرِجُ بِهِ زَرْعًا مُخْتَلِفًا أَلْوَانُهُ ثُمَّ يَهِيجُ فَتَرَاهُ مُصْفَرًّا ثُمَّ يَجْعَلُهُ حُطَامًا إِنَّ فِي ذَلِكَ لَذِكْرَى لِأُوْلِي الْأَلْبَابِ {الزمر/21}

Again, the expression لِأُوْلِي الْأَلْبَابِ is mentioned to indicate the importance of using the mind, learning and knowing the realities.

---

591. (39:17) seeing that for those who shun the powers of evil lest they [be tempted to] worship them, and turn unto God instead, there is the glad tiding [of happiness in the life to come]. Give, then, this glad tiding to [those of] My servants (39:18) who listen [closely] to all that is said, and follow the best of it: [for] it is they whom God has graced with His guidance, and it is they who are [truly] endowed with insight!
592. 39:21 ART THOU NOT aware that it is God who sends down water from the skies, and then causes it to travel through the earth in the shape of springs? And then He brings forth thereby herbage of various hues; and then it withers, and thou canst see it turn yellow; and in the end He causes it to crumble to dust. Verily, in [all] this there is indeed a reminder to those who are endowed with insight!

[38]593

وَلَئِن سَأَلْتَهُم مَّنْ خَلَقَ السَّمَاوَاتِ وَالْأَرْضَ لَيَقُولُنَّ اللَّهُ قُلْ أَفَرَأَيْتُم مَّا تَدْعُونَ مِن دُونِ اللَّهِ إِنْ
أَرَادَنِيَ اللَّهُ بِضُرٍّ هَلْ هُنَّ كَاشِفَاتُ ضُرِّهِ أَوْ أَرَادَنِي بِرَحْمَةٍ هَلْ هُنَّ مُمْسِكَاتُ رَحْمَتِهِ قُلْ
حَسْبِيَ اللَّهُ عَلَيْهِ يَتَوَكَّلُ الْمُتَوَكِّلُونَ

The above question can also be asked to a Muslim but not only necessarily
to a kāfir. If the person expects anything or fears from anything other
than Allah, then قُلْ أَفَرَأَيْتُم مَّا تَدْعُونَ مِن دُونِ اللَّهِ إِنْ أَرَادَنِيَ اللَّهُ بِضُرٍّ هَلْ هُنَّ, then
كَاشِفَاتُ ضُرِّهِ أَوْ أَرَادَنِي بِرَحْمَةٍ هَلْ هُنَّ مُمْسِكَاتُ رَحْمَتِهِ, the person asks these two
questions to one self as the verse asks. Then, if anything cannot do any
harm or benefit, then the person should expect, believe and connect
only to Allah with full sincerity as the remainder of the ayah mentions:
قُلْ حَسْبِيَ اللَّهُ عَلَيْهِ يَتَوَكَّلُ الْمُتَوَكِّلُونَ

[42]594

اللَّهُ يَتَوَفَّى الْأَنفُسَ حِينَ مَوْتِهَا وَالَّتِي لَمْ تَمُتْ فِي مَنَامِهَا فَيُمْسِكُ الَّتِي قَضَى عَلَيْهَا الْمَوْتَ
وَيُرْسِلُ الْأُخْرَى إِلَى أَجَلٍ مُسَمًّى إِنَّ فِي ذَلِكَ لَآيَاتٍ لِّقَوْمٍ يَتَفَكَّرُونَ {الزمر/42}

As the Qurān sets the main framework of teachings of Islam, Rasulullah
with the title of "walking Qurān" shows how this main framework is
embodied and practiced in a Muslim's life. For example, if one analyzes
this ayah and the dua of Rasulullah when he wakes up after
sleeping, he used to say 12) (الْحَمْدُ لِلَّهِ الَّذِي أَحْيَانَا بَعْدَ مَا أَمَاتَنَا وَإِلَيْهِ النُّشُور). This
is an example besides many others how to apply the teachings of the
Qurān in our lives as thought by Rasulullah.

The Prophet indicates the notion of death in sleeping and waking
up from death after sleeping as indicated in the ayah. The above ayah
instills and reminds this teaching to us in our lives as something we take

593. 39:38 And thus it is [with most people]: thou ask them, "Who is it that has created the
heavens and the earth?"—they Will surely answer, "God." Say: "Have you, then, ever considered
what it is that you invoke instead of God? If God wills that harm should befall me, could those
[imaginary powers] remove the harm inflicted by Him? Or, if He wills that grace should alight
on me, could they withhold His grace [from me]?" Say: "God is enough for me! In Him [alone]
place their trust all who have trust [in His existence]."
594. 39:42 It is God [alone that has this power—He] who causes all human beings to die at
the time of their [bodily] death, and [causes to be as dead], during their sleep, those that have
not yet died: thus, He withholds [from life] those upon whom He has decreed death, and lets
the others go free for a term set [by Him]. In [all] this, behold, there are messages indeed for
people who think!

it as granted. The Prophet ﷺ shows the teaching of this ayah how one can constantly apply and remind oneself the reality of this ayah.

[45]⁵⁹⁵

وَإِذَا ذُكِرَ اللَّهُ وَحْدَهُ اشْمَأَزَّتْ قُلُوبُ الَّذِينَ لَا يُؤْمِنُونَ بِالْآخِرَةِ وَإِذَا ذُكِرَ الَّذِينَ مِن دُونِهِ إِذَا هُمْ يَسْتَبْشِرُونَ {الزمر/45}

This ayah is interesting about using the word اشْمَأَزَّتْ to describe and portray the people's face and attitude. The change of attitude or facial expressions represent the inner dispositions of people. This change is due to the conversations about One and Unique Creator, Allah ﷻ.

In this perspective, the word وَحْدَهُ is emphasized as the attribute of Allah ﷻ. In this case, there would be people among Christians or other groups they would not be so pleased to engage oneself with true Oneness and Uniqueness of Allah ﷻ, which can be called true tawhid.

[53-54] ⁵⁹⁶

وَأَنِيبُوا إِلَى رَبِّكُمْ وَأَسْلِمُوا لَهُ مِن قَبْلِ أَن يَأْتِيَكُمُ الْعَذَابُ ثُمَّ لَا تُنصَرُونَ {الزمر/54}
وَاتَّبِعُوا أَحْسَنَ مَا أُنزِلَ إِلَيْكُم مِّن رَّبِّكُم مِّن قَبْلِ أَن يَأْتِيَكُمُ الْعَذَابُ بَغْتَةً وَأَنتُمْ لَا تَشْعُرُونَ {الزمر/55}

When one analyzes the above two ayahs the expression مِن قَبْلِ is repeated. The first مِن قَبْلِ sets a goal of the initial proper relationship of imān with Allah ﷻ at a personal level with humbleness, humility, and full submission with وَأَسْلِمُوا لَهُ and full turn to Allah ﷻ with وَأَنِيبُوا إِلَى رَبِّكُمْ. Then, the و in وَاتَّبِعُ can signify after this or at the same, the person is expected to peak and reach his or her zenith increasing, perfecting and embodying this imān as mentioned with وَاتَّبِعُوا أَحْسَنَ before one dies as mentioned with the second مِن قَبْلِ. In some of the tafāsir, the expression وَاتَّبِعُوا أَحْسَنَ can refer to the Qurān, the hadith or Islam.

---

595. 39:45 And yet, whenever God alone is mentioned, the hearts of those who will not believe in the life to come contract with bitter aversion—whereas, when those [imaginary powers] are mentioned side by side with Him, lo, they rejoice!

596. 39:53 SAY: "[Thus speaks God:] "O you servants of Mine who have transgressed against your own selves! Despair not of God's mercy: behold, God forgives all sins—for, verily, He alone is much-forgiving, a dispenser of grace!'"

39:54 Hence, turn towards your Sustainer [alone] and surrender yourselves unto Him ere the suffering [of death and resurrection] comes upon you, for then you will not be succoured.

So, from the above discussions, it is expected to have a positive change in one's life and increase this in change and meet with Allah ﷻ with the highest state of imān. In the dua of the Rasulullah ﷺ, he asks and teaches to ask from Allah ﷻ to be at the best state of imān an amal in the last part of one's life. Therefore, at a personal level, one should ask and check him or herself about this change in daily or spiritual schedules.

24

Sûrah Ghāfir

One of the key terms in this Sûrah is أُولُوا الْأَلْبَابِ to think, to reason, to learn and to apply. This expression is mentioned in the consecutively surahs Zumar, Sād, and Ghāfir. Then, in the Qurān, it was mentioned one time in Sûrah Talaq.

[1-2][597]

حم {غافر/1} تَنزِيلُ الْكِتَابِ مِنَ اللَّهِ الْعَزِيزِ الْعَلِيمِ {غافر/2}

Allah ﷻ emphasizes that this Book, the Qurān is from Allah ﷻ, Al-Aziz, Al-Al'im. There is no doubt about it.

---

597. 40:1 Ha; Mim. THE BESTOWAL from on high of this divine writ issues from God, the Almighty, the All-Knowing,

[1-14]⁵⁹⁸

All the narratives (stories about other nations) can also serve the purpose of comforting the person in a story or case format. The implicit and third person narrative styles can have a lighter, implicit and calmer effect on the person due the power and essence of the verse compared to direct renderings of the verses straightforwardly talking with the person. In this case, a genuine person can be crashed into pieces due to overpowering effects of Kalamullah, the Qurān due to being the words of Allah ﷻ as in their real and genuine understanding the mountains can

---

598. (40:3) forgiving sins and accepting repentance, severe in retribution, limitless in His bounty. There is no deity save Him: with Him is all journeys' end.
40:4 NONE BUT THOSE who are bent on denying the truth would call God's messages in question. But let it not deceive thee that they seem to be able to do as they please on earth: (40:5) to the truth gave the lie, before their time, the people of Noah and, after them, all those [others] who were leagued together [against God's message-bearers]; 2 and each of those cornmunities schemed against the apostle sent unto them, aiming to lay hands on him; and they contended [against his message) with fallacious arguments, so as to render void the truth thereby: but then I took them to task—and how awesome was My retribution! 40:6 And thus shall thy Sustainer's word come true against all who are bent on denying the truth: they shall find themselves in the fire [of hell]. 40:7 THEY WHO BEAR [within themselves the knowledge of] the throne of [God's] almightiness, as well as all who are near it, extol their Sustainer's limitless glory and praise, and have faith in Him, and ask forgiveness for all [others] who have attained to faith: "O our Sustainer! Thou embracest all things within [Thy] grace and knowledge: forgive, then, their sins unto those who repent and follow Thy path, and preserve them from suffering through the blazing fire! 40:8 "And, O our Sustainer, bring them into the gardens of perpetual bliss5 which Thou hast promised them, together with the righteous from among their forebears, and their spouses, and their offspring—for, verily, Thou alone art almighty, truly wise—(40:9) and preserve them from [doing] evil deeds: for anyone whom on that Day [of Judgment] Thou wilt have preserved from [the taint of] evil deeds, him wilt Thou have graced with Thy mercy: and that, that will be the triumph supreme!" 40:10 [But,] behold, as for those who are bent on denying the truth—[on that same Day] a voice will call out unto them:6 "Indeed, greater than your [present] loathing of yourselves7 was God's loathing of you [at the time] when you were called unto faith but went on denying the truth!"40:11 [Whereupon] they will exclaim: "O our Sustainer! Twice hast Thou caused us to die, just as twice Thou hast brought us to life! But now that we have acknowledged our sins, is there any way out [of this second death)?" (40:12) [And they will be told:] "This [has befallen you] because, whenever the One God was invoked, you denied this truth; whereas, when divinity was ascribed to aught beside Him, you believed [in it]! But all judgment rests with God, the Exalted, the Great!" 40:13 HE IT IS who shows you His Wonders [in all nature], and sends down sustenance for you from the sky: but none bethinks himself [thereof] save those who are wont to turn to God. (40:14) Invoke, then, God, sincere in your faith in Him alone, however hateful this may be to those who deny the truth!

599 لَوْ أَنزَلْنَا هَذَا الْقُرْآنَ عَلَى جَبَلٍ لَّرَأَيْتَهُ خَاشِعًا be crashed into pieces as mentioned
مُّتَصَدِّعًا مِّنْ خَشْيَةِ اللَّهِ وَتِلْكَ الْأَمْثَالُ نَضْرِبُهَا لِلنَّاسِ لَعَلَّهُمْ يَتَفَكَّرُونَ {الحشر/21}

One can easily be overpowered, lose consciousness, and even
die if there is no stories or narratives to calm down due to the weak
human realities when they encounter the Azamah of Allah 🕸 with the
Qurān. Therefore, the stories or narratives can serve the purpose of
decreasing or tuning this effect according to the weak human level,
الله اعلم. Especially, one can realize this type of analogy in frequency
and amplitude modulation in the sciences of radio or satellite related
broadcasting.

Here, is an example of meanings of the beginning of the verses in
this Sûrah related with the above discussion.

Allah 🕸 mentions that this book is coming from the One who knows
you, your needs and everything and accordingly reveals this Book.

Therefore, Allah 🕸 knows your zulm, oprresion, sins and everything
but remember one of the name of Allah 🕸 the One who forgives a lot, al-
Ghafir and at the same time accepts all the repentance. But, at the same,
don't take anything lightly, because Allah 🕸 is shadidul Iqab, then you
can turn to no one except Allah 🕸.

And remember, people who do not accept their mistakes, sins, and
argue about all these signs of Allah 🕸 are the ones who don't make tawba
to Allah 🕸 and don't appreciate Allah 🕸 and make kufr. Therefore, if you
see people constantly traveling and seem to be enjoying their time and
everything, don't be deceived by this.

There were a lot of examples of this from the people of Nûh as and
the people of Ahzab and all others. They did not accept their mistake but
constantly jadalu, did argumentation, to show their arrogance

Therefore, they ended naturally in the punishment.

And remember, the people who really know and have the khasyah
and fear, and respect of Allah جل جلاله such as the angels who hold
the Arsh constantly make tasbih to Allah 🕸 with Hamd with tasbih,
and believe in Allah جل جلاله and make tasbih and ask istighfār for the
ignorant ones of humans:

And the Most Merciful Allah 🕸 immediately responses and accepts
these sincere prayers and still protects them from evil

---

599. If We had sent down this Qurān upon a mountain, you would have seen it humbled and
splitting from fear of AllŒh. And these examples We present to the people that perhaps they
will give thought.

On the other hand, look at the ones who are arrogant!

Now, they are accepting what they did and ....!

And remember now, the essence of all these prayers (dua) is sincerity (ikhlas).

Sûrah Fussilat

[30]⁶⁰⁰

إِنَّ الَّذِينَ قَالُوا رَبُّنَا اللَّهُ ثُمَّ اسْتَقَامُوا تَتَنَزَّلُ عَلَيْهِمُ الْمَلَائِكَةُ أَلَّا تَخَافُوا وَلَا تَحْزَنُوا وَأَبْشِرُوا بِالْجَنَّةِ الَّتِي كُنتُمْ تُوعَدُونَ {فصلت/30}

The word اسْتَقَامُو is one of the key words. It is difficult to keep the values and beliefs and practice constantly with minimizing the wiggling on the desired path of Allah ﷻ.

[33-36]⁶⁰¹

وَمَنْ أَحْسَنُ قَوْلًا مِّمَّن دَعَا إِلَى اللَّهِ وَعَمِلَ صَالِحًا وَقَالَ إِنَّنِي مِنَ الْمُسْلِمِينَ {فصلت/33} وَلَا تَسْتَوِي الْحَسَنَةُ وَلَا السَّيِّئَةُ ادْفَعْ بِالَّتِي هِيَ أَحْسَنُ فَإِذَا الَّذِي بَيْنَكَ وَبَيْنَهُ عَدَاوَةٌ كَأَنَّهُ وَلِيٌّ حَمِيمٌ {فصلت/34} وَمَا يُلَقَّاهَا إِلَّا الَّذِينَ صَبَرُوا وَمَا يُلَقَّاهَا إِلَّا ذُو حَظٍّ عَظِيمٍ {فصلت/35} وَإِمَّا يَنزَغَنَّكَ مِنَ الشَّيْطَانِ نَزْغٌ فَاسْتَعِذْ بِاللَّهِ إِنَّهُ هُوَ السَّمِيعُ الْعَلِيمُ {فصلت/36}

Above ayahs can appeal the notion of easiness of being Muslim by verbal discourse as mentioned وَقَالَ⁶⁰² إِنَّنِي مِنَ الْمُسْلِمِينَ that this qawl, verbal discourse emerges also in وَمَنْ أَحْسَنُ قَوْلاً مِّمَّن دَعَا إِلَى اللَّهِ وَعَمِلَ صَالِحًا⁶⁰³.

---

600. 41:30 [But,] behold, as for those who say, "Our Sustainer is God," and then steadfastly pursue the right way—upon them do angels often descend, [saying:] "Fear not and grieve not, but receive the glad tiding of that paradise which has been promised to you!
601. 41:33 And who could be better of speech than he who calls [his fellow-men] unto God, and does what is just and right, and says, "Verily, I am of those who have surrendered themselves to God"? (41:34) But [since] good and evil cannot be equal, repel thou [evil] with something that is better—and lo! he between whom and thyself was enmity [may then become] as though he had [always] been close [unto thee], a true friend! 41:35 Yet [to achieve] this is not given to any but those who are wont to be patient in adversity: it is not given to any but those endowed with the greatest good fortune! (41:36) Hence, if it should happen that a prompting from Satan stirs thee up [to blind anger], seek refuge with God: behold, He alone is all-hearing, all-knowing!
602. And says, "Verily, I am of those who have surrendered themselves to God.
603. And who could be better of speech than he who calls [his fellow-men] unto God, and does what is just and right.

Then, the difficulties of tests, and trials can also emerge that one needs to adhere to the trait of patience as mentioned وَمَا يُلَقَّاهَا إِلَّا الَّذِينَ صَبَرُ[604]. The word يُلَقَّاهَا which can be translated with the verb "to reach" can allude to this embodiment of a real Muslim through patience as mentioned in وَمَا يُلَقَّاهَا إِلَّا الَّذِينَ صَبَرُ.

Even, this is not enough to make that as an embodiment unless there is a great struggle and a great fadl, tawfik and rahmah, blessing, ذُو حَظٍّ[605] عَظِيم , from Allah as mentioned وَمَا يُلَقَّاهَا إِلَّا ذُو حَظٍّ عَظِيم. One can see that the word يُلَقَّاهَا is mentioned again to allude to this difficulty and to the need of this active struggle as an action as presented in verb form يُلَقَّاهَا.

One can ask why this embodiment of patience is so difficult? Why does it need so much struggle? Here is a very practical example: وَلَا تَسْتَوِي الْحَسَنَةُ وَلَا السَّيِّئَةُ ادْفَعْ بِالَّتِي هِيَ أَحْسَنُ فَإِذَا الَّذِي بَيْنَكَ وَبَيْنَهُ عَدَاوَةٌ كَأَنَّهُ وَلِيٌّ حَمِيمٌ {فصلت/34}[606]. As from the meaning of this ayah, how many people can respond an evil action with something good? How many people can treat a person still good when the person is maltreated? These are realities and stations of patience. Yet, it is very very difficult to do it. So, verbal discourse of qawl وَقَالَ إِنَّنِي مِنَ الْمُسْلِمِينَ[607] is still good. Nevertheless, the real level of embodiment is achieved by being in the station of patience when facing the trials, difficulties and evil-seeming incidents, الله اعلم.

Then, Allah mentions and normalizes the difficulty of this state for weak humans like most of us by وَإِمَّا يَنزَغَنَّكَ مِنَ الشَّيْطَانِ نَزْغٌ فَاسْتَعِذْ بِاللهِ إِنَّهُ هُوَ السَّمِيعُ الْعَلِيمُ {فصلت/36}[608]. That, when we are not patient, we lose ourselves, we get angry, we become mean then, there is still a way to spiritually exit and to reset yourself by taking refuge to Allah from Shaytan and temptations of the nafs as mentioned وَإِمَّا يَنزَغَنَّكَ مِنَ الشَّيْطَانِ نَزْغٌ فَاسْتَعِذْ بِاللهِ إِنَّهُ هُوَ السَّمِيعُ الْعَلِيمُ. The Prophet used to take refuge to Allah in morning and night prayers (27).

---

604. Yet [to achieve] this is not given to any but those who are wont to be patient in adversity.
605. The greatest good fortune.
606. And not equal are the good deed and the bad. Repel [evil] by that [deed] which is better; and thereupon, the one whom between you and him is enmity [will become] as though he was a devoted friend.
607. And says, "Verily, I am of those who have surrendered themselves to God.
608. And if there comes to you from Satan an evil suggestion, then seek refuge in Allah جل جلاله. Indeed, He is the Hearing, the Knowing.

[52-53]⁶⁰⁹

قُلْ أَرَأَيْتُمْ إِن كَانَ مِنْ عِندِ اللهِ ثُمَّ كَفَرْتُم بِهِ مَنْ أَضَلُّ مِمَّنْ هُوَ فِي شِقَاقٍ بَعِيدٍ {فصلت/52}

سَنُرِيهِمْ آيَاتِنَا فِي الْآفَاقِ وَفِي أَنفُسِهِمْ حَتَّى يَتَبَيَّنَ لَهُمْ أَنَّهُ الْحَقُّ أَوَلَمْ يَكْفِ بِرَبِّكَ أَنَّهُ عَلَى كُلِّ شَيْءٍ شَهِيدٌ {فصلت/53}

The above two ayahs are very strong and freezes the person mind and all faculties with no choice. The first case is

قُلْ أَرَأَيْتُمْ إِن كَانَ مِنْ عِندِ اللهِ ثُمَّ كَفَرْتُم بِهِ مَنْ أَضَلُّ مِمَّنْ هُوَ فِي شِقَاقٍ بَعِيدٍ {فصلت/52}

In this case, the conversation of the Qurān with the person is as: what if the Qurān is from Allah ﷻ and the Prophet صلى الله عليه وسلم is sent by Allah ﷻ then after this, you still did not accept. What would be the finale of you in this world and after death except misguidance and an unpleasant accountability?

The second case is سَنُرِيهِمْ آيَاتِنَا فِي الْآفَاقِ وَفِي أَنفُسِهِمْ حَتَّى يَتَبَيَّنَ لَهُمْ أَنَّهُ الْحَقُّ أَوَلَمْ يَكْفِ بِرَبِّكَ أَنَّهُ عَلَى كُلِّ شَيْءٍ شَهِيدٌ {فصلت/53}

In this case, the ayah blocks all the remaining possibilities by engaging the same person with a dialogue as "let's assume you have a doubt. Then in this case, We are assuring you that We are going to show you many implicit & explicit, internal and external, rational and emotional, logical and experiential signs, openings and meanings in your life time that this Qurān is the truth and the Prophet ﷺ is the messenger of Allah ﷻ." SubhanAllah! These two ayahs with all others show the surrender of the weak person in front of Rabbul Alamin with the ijaz and balagah of the Qurān.

In this regards, for regular people like us, Allah ﷻ show all these signs in our life time as mentioned in the expression is ⁶¹⁰ سَنُرِيهِمْ آيَاتِنَا فِي الْآفَاقِ وَفِي أَنفُسِهِمْ. The person still has the free choice to accept these signs and follow. The person can still have an opening for the renderings of shaytan or through his or her ego if this person does not follow these signs although it is very clear. So, there is still the mystical opening of

---

609. (41:52) HAVE YOU given thought [to how you will fare] if this be truly [a revelation] from God, the while you deny its truth? Who could be more astray than one who places himself [so] deeply in the wrong? (41:53) In time We shall make them fully understand Our messages [through what they perceive] in the utmost horizons [of the universe] and within themselves.
610. In time We shall make them fully understand49 Our messages [through what they perceive] in the utmost horizons [of the universe].

a test for the person's free will because as the person is in a test in this world, the free will is the asset of the person and not taken from the person until he or she dies. Therefore, Allah ﷻ does not force the person to believe. If Allah ﷻ wanted everyone could be believer as mentioned in many ayahs of the Qurān [10:99]. Yet, the mystical part of this test is the choice or little inclination of the person with intention, struggle and humbleness, then Allah ﷻ guides with the Divine Fadl and Rahmah inshAllah.

As for the elect, the Prophets, Allah ﷻ shows the signs with another level called wahy as mentioned immediately in the following ayahs: [1-3 & 7][611]

حم {الشورى/1} عسق {الشورى/2} كَذَلِكَ يُوحِي إِلَيْكَ وَإِلَى الَّذِينَ مِن قَبْلِكَ اللَّهُ الْعَزِيزُ الْحَكِيمُ {الشورى/3}

وَكَذَلِكَ أَوْحَيْنَا إِلَيْكَ قُرْآنًا عَرَبِيًّا لِّتُنذِرَ أُمَّ الْقُرَى وَمَنْ حَوْلَهَا وَتُنذِرَ يَوْمَ الْجَمْعِ لَا رَيْبَ فِيهِ فَرِيقٌ فِي الْجَنَّةِ وَفَرِيقٌ فِي السَّعِيرِ {الشورى/7}

However, the signs or openings of the Prophets are called wahy as an exceptional case compared to other humans with certainty of following, closed to the renderings of shaytan and ego. The reason for this is that this responsibility is given to these elected messenger humans to deliver the message of Allah ﷻ to all humans as mentioned وَكَذَلِكَ أَوْحَيْنَا إِلَيْكَ قُرْآنًا عَرَبِيًّا لِّتُنذِرَ أُمَّ الْقُرَى وَتُنذِرَ يَوْمَ الْجَمْعِ لَا رَيْبَ فِيهِ. Therefore, this wahy necessitates to have no doubt even not a minor one. Because, the wahy is not due to the personal guidance of the messenger or prophet, but it is given to these messengers to guide others. Yet, Allah ﷻ guides and protect these messengers through this wahy and other means because they have the high title as "Messengers of Allah ﷻ."

---

611. 42:1 Hā, Meem. 42:2 'Ayn, Seen, Qāf. 42:3 Thus has He revealed to you, [O Muhammad], and to those before you—Allah جلاله جل, the Exalted in Might, the Wise. 42:7 And thus We have revealed to you an Arabic Qurān that you may warn the Mother of Cities [i.e., Makkah] and those around it and warn of the Day of Assembly, about which there is no doubt. A party will be in Paradise and a party in the Blaze.

25

Sûrah Shurã

[5-6]⁶¹²

{ تَكَادُ السَّمَاوَاتُ يَتَفَطَّرْنَ مِن فَوْقِهِنَّ وَالْمَلَائِكَةُ يُسَبِّحُونَ بِحَمْدِ رَبِّهِمْ وَيَسْتَغْفِرُونَ لِمَن فِي الْأَرْضِ أَلَا إِنَّ اللَّهَ هُوَ الْغَفُورُ الرَّحِيمُ {الشورى/5} وَالَّذِينَ اتَّخَذُوا مِن دُونِهِ أَولِيَاء اللَّهُ حَفِيظٌ عَلَيْهِمْ وَمَا أَنتَ عَلَيْهِم بِوَكِيلٍ {الشورى/6}

The skies are almost going to explode with the signs of thunder due to the humans non respectful behavior words, and attitude in their relationship with Rabbul Alamin. The disrespectful and unappreciative words that they engage when they talk about their Creator as all the beings witness this and take position against them. In that regards, the angels make dua to Allah ﷻ for the ignorance of humans for their words and attitudes. However, Allah ﷻ is aware and constantly watching them in their evil affairs, giving them chance, time and respite over and over..

[49]⁶¹³

لِلَّهِ مُلْكُ السَّمَاوَاتِ وَالْأَرْضِ يَخْلُقُ مَا يَشَاء يَهَبُ لِمَنْ يَشَاء إِنَاثًا وَيَهَبُ لِمَن يَشَاء الذُّكُورَ {الشورى/49}

One should really understand our limits that we are the creation and Allah ﷻ has the authority, discretion, and preference of whatever or however to implement according to the Divine Will. We don't have any power as miniscule beings. This is a reality. This may not be emphasized in our Western discourses due to the self-human imposed of problems of alienation from God. Yet, it is a reality for a person to adjust one's respectful attitudes, adab with Rabbul A'lamin. الله اعلم.

---

612. 42:5 The uppermost heavens are well-nigh rent asunder [for awe of Him]; and the angels extol their Sustainer's limitless glory and praise, and ask forgiveness for all who are on earth. Oh, verily, God alone is truly-forgiving, a dispenser of grace!
42:6 NOW AS FOR those who take aught beside Him for their protectors—God watches them, and thou art not responsible for their conduct.
613. 42:49 God's alone is the dominion over the heavens and the earth. He creates whatever He wills: He bestows the gift of female offspring on whomever He wills, and the gift of male offspring on whomever He wills;

[51]⁶¹⁴

وَمَا كَانَ لِبَشَرٍ أَن يُكَلِّمَهُ اللَّهُ إِلَّا وَحْيًا أَوْ مِن وَرَاء حِجَابٍ أَوْ يُرْسِلَ رَسُولًا فَيُوحِيَ بِإِذْنِهِ مَا يَشَاء إِنَّهُ عَلِيٌّ حَكِيمٌ {الشورى/51}

The above ayah alludes human reality. Humans, the creation of Allah ﷻ, has limits in their reflecting, knowing and deliberating about Allah ﷻ as well as humans have limits in, communicating with Allah ﷻ. Therefore, true knowledge about Allah ﷻ requires the Divine guidance, through scriptures and messengers. In this type of delivery process of the wahiy, revalation, Jibril as gives the message to the Prophet's heart.

قُلْ مَن كَانَ عَدُوًّا لِّجِبْرِيلَ فَإِنَّهُ نَزَّلَهُ عَلَى قَلْبِكَ بِإِذْنِ اللّهِ مُصَدِّقاً لِّمَا بَيْنَ يَدَيْهِ وَهُدًى وَبُشْرَى لِلْمُؤْمِنِينَ ⁶¹⁵{البقرة/97}

Yet, Allah ﷻ gives the means and makes the Qurān easy for humans to hold the Qurān in human's hearts through memorization. Millions of Muslims memorize the Qurān constantly. As insān, humans necessitate being heedless and forgetful, the Qurān's true embodiment in a person can explode the person as it explodes the mountains: لَوْ أَنزَلْنَا هَذَا الْقُرْآنَ عَلَى جَبَلٍ لَّرَأَيْتَهُ خَاشِعًا مُتَصَدِّعًا مِّنْ خَشْيَةِ اللهِ وَتِلْكَ الْأَمْثَالُ نَضْرِبُهَا لِلنَّاسِ لَعَلَّهُمْ يَتَفَكَّرُونَ ⁶¹⁶{الحشر/21}

Sûrah Zukhruf

[36]⁶¹⁷

وَمَن يَعْشُ عَن ذِكْرِ الرَّحْمَنِ نُقَيِّضْ لَهُ شَيْطَانًا فَهُوَ لَهُ قَرِينٌ {الزخرف/36}

In themes of this Sûrah, there are some key words mentioned and one of them is the importance of ذِكْر. This is a famous ayah to underline there is

---

614. 42:51 And it is not given to mortal man that God should speak unto him otherwise than through sudden52 inspiration, or [by a voice, as it were,] from behind a veil, or by sending an apostle to reveal, by His leave, whatever He wills [to reveal]: for, verily, He is exalted, wise.
615. Say, "Whoever is an enemy to Gabriel—it is [none but] he who has brought it [i.e., the Qurān] down upon your heart, [O Muhammad], by permission of Allah جل جلاله, confirming that which was before it and as guidance and good tidings for the believers."
616. If We had sent down this Qurān upon a mountain, you would have seen it humbled and splitting from fear of Allah جل جلاله. And these examples We present to the people that perhaps they will give thought.
617. 43:36 But as for anyone who chooses to remain blind to the remembrance of the Most Gracious, to him We assign an [enduring] evil impulse, to become his other self:

either Allah ﷻ to remember with dhikr or to be in company of Shaytan if one does not remember Allah ﷻ. There is nothing in between, either one or the other. If the person believes in Allah ﷻ then the person should be constantly in the dhikr of Allah جل جلاله through fard prayers, recitation of the Qurān, tasbih and others etc.

[43]⁶¹⁸

فَاسْتَمْسِكْ بِالَّذِي أُوحِيَ إِلَيْكَ إِنَّكَ عَلَى صِرَاطٍ مُسْتَقِيمٍ {الزخرف/43}

One of the other themes that comes in this Sûrah is holding tight to the book of Allah ﷻ, the Qurān as mentioned فَاسْتَمْسِكْ بِالَّذِي أُوحِيَ إِلَيْكَ⁶¹⁹. In other words, in order to establish true dhikr holding tight to the Qurān is the key.

Then, the person can be on sirat mustaqim inshAllah. This is another key word that comes in this Sûrah as صِرَاطٍ مُسْتَقِيمٍ⁶²⁰.

[61]⁶²¹

وَإِنَّهُ لَعِلْمٌ لِّلسَّاعَةِ فَلَا تَمْتَرُنَّ بِهَا وَاتَّبِعُونِ هَذَا صِرَاطٌ مُسْتَقِيمٌ {الزخرف/61}

This key word صِرَاطٌ مُسْتَقِيمٍ is also in the above ayah.

[89]⁶²²

فَاصْفَحْ عَنْهُمْ وَقُلْ سَلَامٌ فَسَوْفَ يَعْلَمُونَ {الزخرف/89}

When people do any type of evil rendering to the person through words, looks or thoughts, it is very difficult to move on. Yet, the most fruitful position is to move on both in this dunya and akhirah. Sometimes challenging the people against their faces about their negative and ill attitudes cause more damage if the person knows how and when to

---

618. (43:43) So hold fast to all that has been revealed to thee: for, behold, thou art on a straight way.
619. So hold fast to all that has been revealed to thee.
620. Straight way.
621. 43:61 AND, BEHOLD, this [divine writ] is indeed a means to know [that] the Last Hour [is bound to come]; 48 hence, have no doubt whatever about it, but follow Me: this [alone] is a straight way.
622. 43:89 Yet bear thou with them, and say, "Peace [be upon you]!"—for in time they will come to know [the truth].

apply the rule of "فَاصْفَحْ عَنْهُمْ وَقُلْ سَلَامٌ[623]." Rasulullah ﷺ was challenged the most, and had the most difficulties, yet, he ﷺ had the best way of implementing this teaching of فَاصْفَحْ عَنْهُمْ وَقُلْ سَلَامٌ, as this ayah initially referring to him and to us in its teachings who face similar situations. The following Sûrah Jasiyah, ayahs 14-15 explains this theme further.

Sûrah Jathiyah

[14-15][624]

قُل لِّلَّذِينَ آمَنُوا يَغْفِرُوا لِلَّذِينَ لا يَرْجُونَ أَيَّامَ اللَّهِ لِيَجْزِيَ قَوْمًا بِما كَانُوا يَكْسِبُونَ {الجاثية/14} مَنْ عَمِلَ صَالِحًا فَلِنَفْسِهِ وَمَنْ أَسَاءَ فَعَلَيْهَا ثُمَّ إِلَى رَبِّكُمْ تُرْجَعُونَ {الجاثية/15}

As one review the previous Sûrah's ending as فَاصْفَحْ عَنْهُمْ وَقُلْ سَلَامٌ فَسَوْفَ يَعْلَمُونَ{الزخرف/89}[625], these ayahs explain why the person should implement the teaching of فَاصْفَحْ عَنْهُمْ وَقُلْ سَلَامٌ although it is difficult. When the people don't have the understanding of accountability in front of Allah ﷻ as mentioned لِلَّذِينَ لا يَرْجُونَ أَيَّامَ اللَّهِ لِيَجْزِيَ قَوْمًا بِما كَانُوا يَكْسِبُونَ, then they can get in evil engagements but these are against their own selves as mentioned وَمَنْ أَسَاءَ فَعَلَيْهَا. They will get the result of their engagement but the person should move on as mentioned and forgive the ones as mentioned قُل لِّلَّذِينَ آمَنُوا يَغْفِرُوا لِلَّذِينَ لا يَرْجُونَ أَيَّامَ اللَّهِ. However, they will be accountable in front of Allah ﷻ as mentioned فَسَوْفَ يَعْلَمُونَ {الزخرف/89}. Our ideal expected position is to move one and forgive. Yet, their hasab and accountability is with Allah ﷻ and we don't involve ourselves with that part, الله اعلم.

---

623. Yet bear thou with them, and say, "Peace [be upon you]!"
624. (45:14) Tell all who have attained to faith that they should forgive those who do not believe in the coming of the Days of God,12 [since it is] for Him [alone] to requite people for whatever they may have earned.
45:15 Whoever does what is just and right, does so for his own good; and whoever does evil, does so to his own hurt; and in the end unto your Sustainer you all will be brought back.
625. So turn aside from them and say, "Peace." But they are going to know.

Sûrah Dukhan

[2]⁶²⁶

إِنَّا أَنزَلْنَاهُ فِي لَيْلَةٍ مُبَارَكَةٍ إِنَّا كُنَّا مُنذِرِينَ

[23]⁶²⁷

فَأَسْرِ بِعِبَادِي لَيْلًا إِنَّكُم مُّتَّبَعُونَ {الدخان/32}

In both of above ayahs, the word لَيْلَةٍ is used, to signify the importance of nights for different engagements. According to the hadith (#3397) (3), Allah ﷺ saved Musa as and with his people in the day of Ashura (الله اعلم). The word أَسْر is used for a night journey as mentioned also in Sûrah Isra.

---

626. 44:2 CONSIDER this divine writ, clear in itself and clearly showing the truth!
627. (44:23) And [God said]: "Go thou forth with My servants by night, for you will surely be pursued;

26

Sûrah Ahqāf

[1-2][628]

حم {الأحقاف/1} تَنْزِيلُ الْكِتَابِ مِنَ اللَّهِ الْعَزِيزِ الْحَكِيمِ {الأحقاف/2} مَا خَلَقْنَا السَّمَاوَاتِ وَالْأَرْضَ وَمَا بَيْنَهُمَا إِلَّا بِالْحَقِّ وَأَجَلٍ مُسَمًّى وَالَّذِينَ كَفَرُوا عَمَّا أُنْذِرُوا مُعْرِضُونَ

It is also important to note that after the Kitāb, the revelation, the Qurān, the themes are diverted to focus on the nature, science, earth, skies, and space. Therefore, some of the scholars triangulate the learning from the revelation, the Qurān with the knowledge from the sciences. There is a similar verse in the beginning of the chapter Zumar. The only difference is the حم (hāmìm). Sûrah Zumar does not have حم (hāmìm) in the beginning. In that chapter also, the theme of nature, science, earth, skies and space comes after the mention of the revelation of the Qurān.

Sûrah Muhammad

[1-3][629]

الَّذِينَ كَفَرُوا وَصَدُّوا عَن سَبِيلِ اللَّهِ أَضَلَّ أَعْمَالَهُمْ {محمد/1} وَالَّذِينَ آمَنُوا وَعَمِلُوا الصَّالِحَاتِ وَآمَنُوا بِمَا نُزِّلَ عَلَى مُحَمَّدٍ وَهُوَ الْحَقُّ مِن رَّبِّهِمْ كَفَّرَ عَنْهُمْ سَيِّئَاتِهِمْ وَأَصْلَحَ بَالَهُمْ {محمد/2} ذَلِكَ بِأَنَّ الَّذِينَ كَفَرُوا اتَّبَعُوا الْبَاطِلَ وَأَنَّ الَّذِينَ آمَنُوا اتَّبَعُوا الْحَقَّ مِن رَّبِّهِمْ كَذَلِكَ يَضْرِبُ اللَّهُ لِلنَّاسِ أَمْثَالَهُمْ {محمد/3}

The above verses open one of the mysteries of the attitude of kufr and imān. As mentioned in detail in the 6th verse of Sûrah Baqarah, the state of kufr implies not appreciation although the person does recognize all the blessings. In this case, the person can do some good and ethical

---

628. 46:1 Ha; Mim.46:2 THE BESTOWAL from on high of this divine writ issues from God, the Almighty, the Wise.
629. 47:1 AS FOR THOSE who are bent on denying the truth and on barring [others] from the path of God—all their [good] deeds will He let go to waste;' (47:2) whereas those who have attained to faith and do righteous deeds, and have come to believe in what has been bestowed from on high on Muhammad—for it is the truth from their Sustainer—[shall attain to God's grace:] He will efface their [past] bad deeds, and will set their hearts at rest.47:3 This, because they who are bent on denying the truth pursue falsehood, whereas they who have attained to faith pursue [but] the truth [that flows] from their Sustainer. In this way does God set forth unto man the parables of their true state.

behavior but the level of initial and real appreciation does not exist for the One, Allah ﷻ Who deserves the first, the utmost and the only appreciation in its true sense and reality.

Besides the real appreciation, the auxiliary appreciations in the forms of ethical and good behavior does not have much value compared to the main one as mentioned أَضَلَّ أَعْمَالَهُمْ[630]. On the other hand, when the person after recognition, appreciates Allah ﷻ with the teachings of Rasulullah ﷺ then Allah ﷻ appreciates, as one of the names of Allah جل جلاله is As-Shakur and immediately gives them another favor and blessing with كَفَّرَ عَنْهُمْ سَيِّئَاتِهِمْ وَأَصْلَحَ بَالَهُمْ[631]. In more detail, ذَلِكَ بِأَنَّ الَّذِينَ[632] كَفَرُوا اتَّبَعُوا الْبَاطِلَ وَأَنَّ الَّذِينَ آمَنُوا اتَّبَعُوا الْحَقَّ مِن رَّبِّهِمْ, with their free choice although they knew Allah ﷻ they did not appreciate it with kufr, being ungrateful, not in recognition but covering the realities. In this case, they chose to follow batil, falsehood.

Therefore, with this type of people of kufr, it is normal to expect evil. They can try to stop the people of imān as mentioned وَصَدُّوا عَن سَبِيلِ اللَّهِ[633].

[9, 26-29] [634]

ذَلِكَ بِأَنَّهُمْ قَالُوا لِلَّذِينَ كَرِهُوا مَا نَزَّلَ اللَّهُ سَنُطِيعُكُمْ فِي بَعْضِ الْأَمْرِ وَاللَّهُ يَعْلَمُ إِسْرَارَهُمْ {محمد/26} فَكَيْفَ إِذَا تَوَفَّتْهُمُ الْمَلَائِكَةُ يَضْرِبُونَ وُجُوهَهُمْ وَأَدْبَارَهُمْ {محمد/27} ذَلِكَ بِأَنَّهُمُ اتَّبَعُوا مَا أَسْخَطَ اللَّهَ وَكَرِهُوا رِضْوَانَهُ فَأَحْبَطَ أَعْمَالَهُمْ {محمد/28} أَمْ حَسِبَ الَّذِينَ فِي قُلُوبِهِم مَّرَضٌ أَن لَّن يُخْرِجَ اللَّهُ أَضْغَانَهُمْ {محمد/29}

In reality, they did not give importance to Ridwan of Allah ﷻ.

ذَلِكَ بِأَنَّهُمُ اتَّبَعُوا مَا أَسْخَطَ اللَّهَ وَكَرِهُوا رِضْوَانَهُ فَأَحْبَطَ أَعْمَالَهُمْ

---

630. All their [good] deeds will He let go to waste.
631. He will efface their [past] bad deeds, and will set their hearts at rest.
632. This, because they who are bent on denying the truth pursue falsehood, whereas they who have attained to faith pursue [but] the truth [that flows] from their Sustainer.
633. And who are bent on barring [others] from the path of God.
634. (47:9) this, because they hate [the very thought of] what God has bestowed from on highand thus He causes all their deeds to come to nought! (47:26) [they do turn their backs on it] inasmuch as they are wont to say unto those who abhor all that God has revealed, "We will comply with your views on some points." But God knows their secret thoughts: (47:27) hence, how [will they fare] when the angels gather them in death, striking their faces and their backs? (47:28) This, because they were wont to pursue what God condemns, and to hate [whatever would meet with] His goodly acceptance: and so He has caused all their [good] deeds to come to nought.
47:29 Or do they in whose hearts is disease think, perchance, that God would never bring their moral failings to light?

The opposite of rida, رِضْو[635], pleasure is suht, سُخَط[636], as mentioned in the munjid dictionary (49). If a person follows what Allah ﷻ has gadab on it then this can mean that the pleasure of Allah ﷻ is not (astagfirullah) important, and this person's deeds can become in vain, may Allah جل جلاله protect us, Amìn.

The word إِسْرَارَهُمْ[637] can signify the importance of not being consistent in sin and evil. Then, if the person becomes persistent then, the person can get سُخَط of Allah ﷻ, may Allah ﷻ protect me and everyone. The free choice of a person sometimes makes the person to do wrong even though he or she knows it as mentioned وَكَرِهُو[638]. And the result is إِذَا[639] تَوَفَّتْهُمُ الْمَلَائِكَةُ يَضْرِبُونَ وُجُوهَهُمْ وَأَدْبَارَهُمْ. May Allah ﷻ protect us from this aqibah, Amìn.

[19][640]

فَاعْلَمْ أَنَّهُ لَا إِلَهَ إِلَّا اللَّهُ وَاسْتَغْفِرْ لِذَنبِكَ وَلِلْمُؤْمِنِينَ وَالْمُؤْمِنَاتِ وَاللَّهُ يَعْلَمُ مُتَقَلَّبَكُمْ وَمَثْوَاكُمْ {محمد/19}

It is important to realize what Allah ﷻ wants from us. This is la ilaha illa Allah as opposed to kufr.

The expression of La ilaha illa Allah is worded in such a way that there is no room for interpretation as more than one deity. It is clear. It is precise.

As the ayah mentions شَهِدَ اللَّهُ أَنَّهُ لَا إِلَهَ إِلَّا هُوَ وَالْمَلَائِكَةُ وَأُولُوا الْعِلْمِ قَائِمًا بِالْقِسْطِ لَا إِلَهَ إِلَّا هُوَ الْعَزِيزُ الْحَكِيمُ[641]{آل عمران/18}, only Allah ﷻ can be witness of this in the true sense, then angels who are witnessing the seen and unseen relative to humans and then the people of knowledge. The people of the knowledge, real scholars if they objectively approach with their means

---

635. Pleasure.
636. Condemns.
637. Their secret thoughts.
638. And they disliked.
639. how [will they fare) when the angels gather them in death, striking their faces and their backs?
640. 47:19
Know, then, [O man,] that there is no deity save God, and [while there is yet time,] ask forgiveness for thy sins and for [the sins of] all other believing men and women: for God knows all your comings and goings as well as your abiding [at rest].
641. Allah جل جلاله witnesses that there is no deity except Him, and [so do] the angels and those of knowledge—[that He is] maintaining [creation] in justice. There is no deity except Him, the Exalted in Might, the Wise.

of intellect such as Aristotle (14) can deduce La ilaha illa Allah. This objectiveness or fairness can be implied with the word بِالْقِسْطِ.

In this regards, to emphasize this definite, sole and singular fact of لَا إِلَهَ إِلاَّ هُوَ, this very strong and vigorous ayah emphasizes twice within one ayah شَهِدَ اللّهُ أَنَّهُ لاَ إِلَهَ إِلاَّ هُوَ وَالْمَلاَئِكَةُ وَأُوْلُواْ الْعِلْمِ قَآئِمَاً بِالْقِسْطِ لاَ إِلَهَ إِلاَّ هُوَ الْعَزِيزُ الْحَكِيمُ {آل عمران/18}. The people of shu'ûr and i'lm, knowledge know and testify the oneness of Allah ﷻ. Even, they can testify and prove it. For example, Aristotle wrote a long book to prove this with logic and reason (14). Angels already know this as a reality. Yet, the most important is the emphasis and testify of Allah ﷻ on this certainty, truth and precision as شَهِدَ أَللهُ أَنَّهُ لَا إِلَهَ إِلاَّ هُوَ [642]. There is nothing more after this but only explosion of minds of weak creations and but submission and surrender to Allah ﷻ. Therefore, one makes as a habit of this testimony in the dua as mentioned in this ayah as practiced in the morning and night duas of the Prophet ﷺ (18).

[32-35][643]

إِنَّ الَّذِينَ كَفَرُوا وَصَدُّوا عَن سَبِيلِ اللّهِ وَشَاقُّوا الرَّسُولَ مِن بَعْدِ مَا تَبَيَّنَ لَهُمُ الْهُدَى لَن يَضُرُّوا اللّهَ شَيْئًا وَسَيُحْبِطُ أَعْمَالَهُمْ {محمد/32} يَا أَيُّهَا الَّذِينَ آمَنُوا أَطِيعُوا اللّهَ وَأَطِيعُوا الرَّسُولَ وَلَا تُبْطِلُوا أَعْمَالَكُمْ {محمد/33} إِنَّ الَّذِينَ كَفَرُوا وَصَدُّوا عَن سَبِيلِ اللّهِ ثُمَّ مَاتُوا وَهُمْ كُفَّارٌ فَلَن يَغْفِرَ اللّهُ لَهُمْ {محمد/34} فَلَا تَهِنُوا وَتَدْعُوا إِلَى السَّلْمِ وَأَنتُمُ الْأَعْلَوْنَ وَاللّهُ مَعَكُمْ وَلَن يَتِرَكُمْ أَعْمَالَكُمْ {محمد/35}

Again, similar to the beginning ayahs, in this Sûrah there is more detail about what is batil and haqq. Al haqq is following the way of Allah ﷻ through the teachings of the Prophet ﷺ.

Therefore, with the people of kufr, the person can expect evil. They can try to stop the people of imān from their practice and from doing good as mentioned وَصَدُّوا عَن سَبِيلِ اللّهِ [644].

---

642. Allah جل جلاله witnesses that there is no deity except Him.
643. 47:32 Indeed, those who disbelieved and averted [people] from the path of Allah جل جلاله and opposed the Messenger after guidance had become clear to them—never will they harm Allah جل جلاله at all, and He will render worthless their deeds. 47:33 O you who have believed, obey Allah جل جلاله and obey the Messenger and do not invalidate your deeds. 47:34 Indeed, those who disbelieved and averted [people] from the path of Allah جل جلاله and then died while they were disbelievers—never will Allah جل جلاله forgive them. 47:35 So do not weaken and call for peace while you are superior; and Alla جل جلاله h is with you and will never deprive you of [the reward of] your deeds.
644. And averted [people] from the path of Allah جل جلاله.

Sûrah Fath

مُحَمَّدٌ رَسُولُ اللهِ وَالَّذِينَ مَعَهُ اَشِدَّاءُ عَلَى الْكُفَّارِ رُحَمَاءُ بَيْنَهُمْ تَرَيْهُمْ رُكَّعًا سُجَّدًا يَبْتَغُونَ
فَضْلًا مِنَ اللهِ وَرِضْوَانًا سِيمَاهُمْ فِي وُجُوهِهِمْ مِنْ اَثَرِ السُّجُودِ ذَلِكَ مَثَلُهُمْ فِي التَّوْرَيةِ وَمَثَلُهُمْ
فِي الْاِنْجِيلِ كَزَرْعٍ اَخْرَجَ شَطْئَهُ فَاٰزَرَهُ فَاسْتَغْلَظَ فَاسْتَوٰى عَلَى سُوقِهِ يُعْجِبُ الزُّرَّاعَ لِيَغِيظَ
بِهِمُ الْكُفَّارَ وَعَدَ اللهُ الَّذِينَ اٰمَنُوا وَعَمِلُوا الصَّالِحَاتِ مِنْهُمْ مَغْفِرَةً وَاَجْرًا عَظِيمًا[645]

According to one interpretation (N. Lema), this ayah shows the khilafah of Abu Bakr ra with the expression of مَعَهُ وَالَّذِينَ[646], the khilafah of Omar ra with the expression of الْكُفَّارِ عَلَى اَشِدَّاءُ[647], the khilafah of Osman ra with the expression of بَيْنَهُمْ رُحَمَاءُ[648], and the khilafah of Ali ra with the expression of اللهِ مِنَ فَضْلًا يَبْتَغُونَ سُجَّدًا رُكَّعًا تَرَيْهُمْ[649] وَرِضْوَانًا respectively.

Sûrah Qāf

[33][650]

مَنْ خَشِيَ الرَّحْمَنَ بِالْغَيْبِ وَجَاءَ بِقَلْبٍ مُنِيبٍ {ق/33}

The reality of imān and one's relationship with Allah ﷻ reveals one's true disposition when one is alone. If someone wants to spend time in solitude to pray, worship to Allah ﷻ and makes this as the top priority in one's life and takes the most pleasure to be with Allah ﷻ, then this person can show the signs of being بِالْغَيْبِ الرَّحْمَنَ خَشِيَ مَنْ[651]. A person in this state then with the Fadl of Allah ﷻ can be in the steps of بِقَلْبٍ وَجَاءَ[652]

---

645. Muhammad is the Messenger of Allah جل جلاله; and those with him are forceful against the disbelievers, merciful among themselves. You see them bowing and prostrating [in prayer], seeking bounty from Allah جل جلاله and [His] pleasure. Their mark [i.e., sign] is on their faces [i.e., foreheads] from the trace of prostration. That is their description in the Torah. And their description in the Gospel is as a plant which produces its offshoots and strengthens them so they grow firm and stand upon their stalks, delighting the sowers—so that He [i.e., Allah جل جلاله] may enrage by them the disbelievers. Allah جل جلاله has promised those who believe and do righteous deeds among them forgiveness and a great reward.
646. And those with him.
647. Forceful against the disbelievers.
648. Merciful among themselves.
649. You see them bowing and prostrating [in prayer], seeking bounty from Allah جل جلاله and [His] pleasure.
650. (50:33) Who feared the Most Merciful unseen and came with a heart returning [in repentance].
651. Who feared the Most Merciful unseen.
652. And came with a heart returning [in repentance].

مُنِيبٍ. Here, the word مُنِيبٍ[653] is used instead of سليم[654] compared to other ayahs. This could be that when a person makes a habit of turning to Allah ﷻ constantly, and regularly in especially solitude with بِالْغَيْبِ then, this title of مُنِيبٍ, munib is given to this person, اللهم جعلنا منهم، امين.

In this regard, the word مُنِيبٍ can indicate the desired dynamic state to reach to the goal of station of سليم of the heart, الله اعلم.

[39][655]

فَاصْبِرْ عَلَى مَا يَقُولُونَ وَسَبِّحْ بِحَمْدِ رَبِّكَ قَبْلَ طُلُوعِ الشَّمْسِ وَقَبْلَ الْغُرُوبِ {ق/39}

The importance and easiness in the application of patience can be achieved if and when a person engages oneself with dhikr, tasbih with hamd before sunrise and sunset. These may be the times when a person can take the power of patience if the person engages herself or himself. The effect of قَبْلَ طُلُوعِ[656] can continue all day and the effect of وَقَبْلَ الْغُرُوبِ[657] can continue all night, الله اعلم(AA).

Similarly,

فَاصْبِرْ عَلَى مَا يَقُولُونَ وَسَبِّحْ بِحَمْدِ رَبِّكَ قَبْلَ طُلُوعِ الشَّمْسِ وَقَبْلَ غُرُوبِهَا وَمِنْ آنَاء اللَّيْلِ فَسَبِّحْ وَأَطْرَافَ النَّهَارِ لَعَلَّكَ تَرْضَى[658] {طه/130}

The pleasure of Allah ﷻ comes with Sabr.

---

653. Returning [in repentance].
654. Sound [heart].
655. 50:39 HENCE, [O believe,] bear thou with patience whatever they may say, and extol thy Sustainer's limitless glory and praise before the rising of the sun and before its setting;
656. Before the rising.
657. And before its setting.
658. So be patient over what they say and exalt [Allah جل جلاله] with praise of your Lord before the rising of the sun and before its setting; and during periods of the night [exalt Him] and at the ends of the day, that you may be satisfied.

27

Sûrah Zāriyāt

[49-50][659]

وَمِن كُلِّ شَيْءٍ خَلَقْنَا زَوْجَيْنِ لَعَلَّكُمْ تَذَكَّرُونَ {الذاريات/49} فَفِرُّوا إِلَى اللَّهِ إِنِّي لَكُم مِّنْهُ
نَذِيرٌ مُّبِينٌ {الذاريات/50}

Allah ﷻ mentions the creation of everything with their pairs as زَوْجَيْنِ.
One can realize that the benefits of complementary roles of each pair to
another. For example, the husband and wife relationship brings sakinah
to each other as mentioned وَمِنْ آيَاتِهِ أَنْ خَلَقَ لَكُم مِّنْ أَنفُسِكُمْ أَزْوَاجًا لَّتَسْكُنُوا إِلَيْهَا
وَجَعَلَ بَيْنَكُم مَّوَدَّةً وَرَحْمَةً إِنَّ فِي ذَلِكَ لَآيَاتٍ لِّقَوْمٍ يَتَفَكَّرُونَ {الروم/21}
Yet, this pair relationship does not replace one's relationship with
Allah ﷻ as mentioned immediately فَفِرُّوا إِلَى اللَّهِ[660]. One can witness this
especially in disputes between the spouses, the notion of فَفِرُّوا إِلَى اللَّهِ. If
a person has an excellent relationship with her or his spouse, and one
day if they had an argument, this can be super destroying mentally and
emotionally if the person does not know how to exit with فَفِرُّوا إِلَى اللَّهِ.

Sûrah Rahmān

[13][661]

This one chapter is in a unique style compared to other chapters.
This chapter is Sûrah Rahmān. One of the uniqueness is the constant
repetition and instilment of the ayah فَبِأَيِّ آلَاءِ رَبِّكُمَا تُكَذِّبَانِ {الرحمن/13}.
The main essence of this chapter is to underline the essence of
this ayah in creation. It is to emphasize this essence in one's imān, and
in ones' spiritual advancement in relationship with Allah ﷻ. This can
ultimately help reaching to the level of رَاضِيَةً مَّرْضِيَّةً[662] by embodying
an imān with the qualities of constant appreciation, thankfulness, and

---

659. (51:49) And in everything have We created opposites,33 so that you might bear in mind
[that God alone is One]
(51:50) And so, [O Muhammad, say unto them:] "Flee unto God [from all that is false and evil]!
Verily, I am
660. "Flee unto God [from all that is false and evil]!
661. (55:13) Which, then, of your Sustainer's powers can you disavow?
662. Well pleased and pleasing [to Him].

gratitude that the person becomes pleased with everything that Allah ﷻ gives. اللهم اجعلنا منهم، امين.

This Sûrah shows also how one can reach the highest level of imān as mentioned in Sûrah Fajr as mentioned above: [28-30][663]

ارْجِعِي إِلَى رَبِّكِ رَاضِيَةً مَّرْضِيَّةً {الفجر/28} فَادْخُلِي فِي عِبَادِي {الفجر/29} وَادْخُلِي جَنَّتِي {الفجر/30}

The above ayah ارْجِعِي إِلَى رَبِّكِ رَاضِيَةً مَّرْضِيَّةً has a critical stance in Islam. Here, the word ارْجِعِي[664] is used to possibly mentioned to attain the level of رَاضِيَةً مَّرْضِيَّةً in the world. With this state, then the person dies and goes to Allah ﷻ. In other words, a person can be filled fully with the light of imān that then the person becomes constantly appreciative, thankful, and pleased with everything of what Allah ﷻ gives and bestows on the person. With this guidance, this person can in real spiritual light, Nûr, peaceful, and happy state of imān in this world. This person can be so much happy with this light of increasing imān that the person constantly thanks, and appreciates everything but everything from Allah ﷻ. In this regards, Rasulullah ﷺ represents this at the highest level as the role mode and lead. Then, for others it is the level to attain and to reach to struggle in one's life radiyah and mardiyyah. The dua of رضيت بالله[665] رب وبالأسلم دين و بمحمد نبي و رسولا can truly show this state if one really can transfuse and embody the meanings of this dua constantly in one's life.

[60] [666]

When one looks at this Sûrah, one can understand that everything Allah ﷻ gives is a nimah. The most nimahs will be given in the afterlife. Therefore, a good portion of this Sûrah mentions about the upcoming nimahs of Allah ﷻ in the afterlife. Because, as one of the key expressions in this Sûrah:

هَلْ جَزَاء الْإِحْسَانِ إِلَّا الْإِحْسَانُ {الرحمن/60}

---

663. 89:28 Return to your Lord, well-pleased and pleasing [to Him], 89:29 And enter among My [righteous] servants, 89:30 And enter my paradise."
664. Return.
665. I am pleased with Allah جل جلاله as my Lord, Islām as my religion, and Muhammad (ﷺ) as the Messenger and Prophet.
666. (55:60) Could the reward of good be aught but good?

Allah ﷻ appreciates as Al-Shakur, all the efforts and struggles on the path of practicing the religion through one's life. Therefore, Allah ﷻ gives huge rewards and compensation for this struggle. One can say that "I did not deserve this much with my little effort", but one should remember, Allah ﷻ is the Rabbul Alamin. For the little but sincere and humble efforts, Allah ﷻ can reward in huge quantity and quality.

Sûrah Hadid

As one can review the periodic table, one of the isotopes of iron, hadìd in Arabic, corresponds to this Sûrah number with its atomic number. In chemistry (50), it is interesting to note that all the radioactive elements tend to be similar to iron as they want to radiate in their instable state. The case of formation of iron from outer space, as mentioned with the word anzalna, is interesting to encounter in the present scientific discussions (51).

[13] [667]

يَوْمَ يَقُولُ الْمُنَافِقُونَ وَالْمُنَافِقَاتُ لِلَّذِينَ آمَنُوا انظُرُونَا نَقْتَبِسْ مِن نُورِكُمْ قِيلَ ارْجِعُوا وَرَاءكُمْ فَالْتَمِسُوا نُورًا فَضُرِبَ بَيْنَهُم بِسُورٍ لَّهُ بَابٌ بَاطِنُهُ فِيهِ الرَّحْمَةُ وَظَاهِرُهُ مِن قِبَلِهِ الْعَذَابُ {الحديد/13}

Here, another interesting concept is the trend that when a person does not have a Nûr, he or she may benefit from the ones who has it. In this case, one can review this ayah with other the Quranic ayahs when Allah ﷻ mentions even in the scenes of akhirah as: يَوْمَ يَقُولُ الْمُنَافِقُونَ وَالْمُنَافِقَاتُ لِلَّذِينَ آمَنُوا انظُرُونَا نَقْتَبِسْ مِن نُورِكُمْ قِيلَ ارْجِعُوا وَرَاءكُمْ فَالْتَمِسُوا نُورًا فَضُرِبَ بَيْنَهُم بِسُورٍ لَّهُ بَابٌ بَاطِنُهُ فِيهِ الرَّحْمَةُ وَظَاهِرُهُ مِن قِبَلِهِ الْعَذَابُ {الحديد/13}. Munāfiqs in the dunya used to benefit from the Nûr, light, of the imān and its reflections. As the munafiqûn were and are living with the ahlu-imān, they have been getting some benefit of this imān. If an evil person sits and hangs around

---

667. 57:13 On that Day shall the hypocrites, both men and women, speak [thus] unto those who have attained to faith: "Wait for us! Let us have a [ray of] light from your light!" [But] they will be told: "Turn back, and seek a light [of your own]!" And thereupon a wall will be raised between them [and the believers], with a gate in it: within it will be grace and mercy, and against the outside thereof, suffering.

with good people, there will be some good effect on him or her even though he or she maintains the evilness. This ayah mentioned in Sûrah Hadîd shows that they want to continue with this attitude even in the akhirah, الله اعلم.

[16]⁶⁶⁸

أَلَمْ يَأْنِ لِلَّذِينَ آمَنُوا أَن تَخْشَعَ قُلُوبُهُمْ لِذِكْرِ اللَّهِ وَمَا نَزَلَ مِنَ الْحَقِّ وَلَا يَكُونُوا كَالَّذِينَ أُوتُوا الْكِتَابَ مِن قَبْلُ فَطَالَ عَلَيْهِمُ الْأَمَدُ فَقَسَتْ قُلُوبُهُمْ وَكَثِيرٌ مِّنْهُمْ فَاسِقُونَ {الحديد/16}

One should really focus and critically analyze this ayah what it means for me and you, the people of Islam. Allah ﷻ mentions that others before Islam received the scripture from Allah ﷻ. Yet, their hearts were still hard and not affected. In this sense, we have the diamond teachings of the Qurān. We have the pearl teachings of the Rasulullah ﷺ as the hadith. Yet, is this helping us to have khashya of Allah ﷻ as mentioned in تَخْشَعَ⁶⁶⁹ قُلُوبُهُمْ لِذِكْرِ اللَّهِ? Both the Qurān and hadith are the truth, authentic and from Allah ﷻ as mentioned وَمَا نَزَلَ مِنَ الْحَقِّ⁶⁷⁰. So, normalizing the learning without devotion but as a way of religious, academic, intellectual and identity life as mentioned وَلَا يَكُونُوا كَالَّذِينَ أُوتُوا الْكِتَابَ مِن قَبْلُ فَطَالَ عَلَيْهِمُ⁶⁷¹ الْأَمَدُ فَقَسَتْ قُلُوبُهُمْ is very but very dangerous. In this process, the hearts don't have the khasyah of Allah ﷻ. Then, they become lost wanderers as mentioned وَكَثِيرٌ مِّنْهُمْ فَاسِقُونَ⁶⁷². If you do the same, then similar end can happen, may Allah ﷻ protect us, Amîn.

---

668. (57:16) IS IT NOT time that the hearts of all who have attained to faith should feel humble at the remembrance of God and of all the truth that has been bestowed [on them] from on high,22 lest they become like those who were granted revelation aforetime, and whose hearts have hardened with the passing of time so that many of them are [now] depraved?
669. The hearts of all who have attained to faith should feel humble at the remembrance of God.
670. And of all the truth that has been bestowed [on them].
671. Lest they become like those who were granted revelation aforetime,23 and whose hearts have hardened with the passing of time.
672. Many of them are [now] depraved.

28

Sûrah Mujadalah

[7]673

أَلَمْ تَرَ أَنَّ اللَّهَ يَعْلَمُ مَا فِي السَّمَاوَاتِ وَمَا فِي الْأَرْضِ مَا يَكُونُ مِن نَّجْوَى ثَلَاثَةٍ إِلَّا هُوَ
رَابِعُهُمْ وَلَا خَمْسَةٍ إِلَّا هُوَ سَادِسُهُمْ وَلَا أَدْنَى مِن ذَلِكَ وَلَا أَكْثَرَ إِلَّا هُوَ مَعَهُمْ أَيْنَ مَا كَانُوا
ثُمَّ يُنَبِّئُهُم بِمَا عَمِلُوا يَوْمَ الْقِيَامَةِ إِنَّ اللَّهَ بِكُلِّ شَيْءٍ عَلِيمٌ {المجادلة/7}

One can find more detail explanations in the books of tafāsir of the pious salaf about why Allah ﷻ did not mention when there are two people or one person and Allah ﷻ is still there and All-Present and Watching.

In the case of two people, as the name of the Sûrah is al-mujādalah, Allah ﷻ can forgive the renderings between the couples when they ask forgiveness together as a one unit. Because Allah ﷻ is Al-Ghafûr674, Ar-Rahîm675, At-Tawwāb676 and Al-Sattār677.

In the case of one person, it may indicate that Allah ﷻ is al-Gûfur, Ar-Rahîm and At-Tawwāb that when a person makes a sin and ask forgiveness from Allah ﷻ, then Allah ﷻ can forgive it when it does not become fahishāh, public, especially.

Again, in the above cases of the possible hikmahs of why one or two were not mentioned as Allah ﷻ is al-Sattār, this can also allude the preference disposition of hiding the faults of others for Muslims as much as possible but not exposing them, الله اعلم.

---

673. 58:7 ART THOU NOT aware that God knows all that is in the heavens and all that is on earth? Never can there be a secret confabulation between three persons without His being the fourth of them, nor between five without His being the sixth of them; and neither between less than that, or more, without His being with them wherever they may be. But in the end, on Resurrection Day, He will make them truly understand what they did: for, verily, God has full knowledge of everything.

674. The Ever-Forgiving.

675. The Most Merciful.

676. The Ever-Returning.

677. The Hidden.

[22] ⁶⁷⁸

لَا تَجِدُ قَوْمًا يُؤْمِنُونَ بِاللَّهِ وَالْيَوْمِ الْآخِرِ يُوَادُّونَ مَنْ حَادَّ اللَّهَ وَرَسُولَهُ وَلَوْ كَانُوا آبَاءهُمْ أَوْ أَبْنَاءهُمْ أَوْ إِخْوَانَهُمْ أَوْ عَشِيرَتَهُمْ أُوْلَئِكَ كَتَبَ فِي قُلُوبِهِمُ الْإِيمَانَ وَأَيَّدَهُم بِرُوحٍ مِّنْهُ وَيُدْخِلُهُمْ جَنَّاتٍ تَجْرِي مِن تَحْتِهَا الْأَنْهَارُ خَالِدِينَ فِيهَا رَضِيَ اللَّهُ عَنْهُمْ وَرَضُوا عَنْهُ أُوْلَئِكَ حِزْبُ اللَّهِ أَلَا إِنَّ حِزْبَ اللَّهِ هُمُ الْمُفْلِحُونَ {المجادلة/22}

One of the key words in the above ayah is يُوَادُّون⁶⁷⁹ which can have very profound meanings depending on the context and its usage. As the Sûrah mentions discourses about family life, and its challenges, one can view this word with its context in kindship and social relations. In other words, although as humans we need each other, we need our family members, friends, and social engagements, this word puts forward the notion of priorities in one's life. In this perspective and the context of the Sûrah, there will be times the person will be left alone due to either isolation as a result of disputes or arguments or self-isolation due to not getting preferred attention from others. These are the times that can hit the person hard if he or she does not have priorities in one's life. Either the person can fall in deeper depressive states by blaming others and increase this isolation. Or, the person can use this time to focus on the priorities that are preferred by Allah ﷻ as mentioned with the word يُوَادُّون⁶⁸⁰.

Well, one can ask the question, why this should come at those times but not other times? Because, the person is distracted and heedless although he or she may claim the opposite. In other words, when the routine is broken with unexpected cases that the person depends on, then this case is referred as evil in our contemporary language. Yet, these are the times that can be opportunistic to boost one's relationship with Allah ﷻ. Especially, if the person humbly and logically performs self-

---

678. 58:22 Thou canst not find people who [truly) believe in God and the Last Day and [at the same time] love anyone who contends against God and His Apostle—even though they be their fathers, or their sons, or their brothers, or [others of] their kindred. (As for the true believers,] it is they in whose hearts He has inscribed faith, and whom He has strengthened with inspiration from Himself, and whom [in time] He will admit into gardens through which running waters flow, therein to abide. Well-pleased is God with them, and well-pleased are they with Him. They are God's partisans: oh, verily, it is they, the partisans of God, who shall attain to a happy state!

679. They love.

680. They love.

reflection of muraqaba. Therefore, constant muraqaba helps the person
to always keep this perspective of priorities one's life.

Lastly, as we always have the desire to belong somewhere, Allah ﷻ
shows the highest possible identity by mentioning حِزْبُ اللَّهِ[681]. Yet, this
identity is embodied through the notion of above discussion of one's
life priorities to coincide with the ones that are preferred by Allah ﷻ
as mentioned with the word يُوَادُّونَ. These people with these identities
will have the real happiness in this world and after as mentioned هُمُ[682]
الْمُفْلِحُونَ, الله اعلم.

Sûrah Hashir

[19[683]]

{وَلَا تَكُونُوا كَالَّذِينَ نَسُوا اللَّهَ فَأَنْسَاهُمْ أَنْفُسَهُمْ أُولَٰئِكَ هُمُ الْفَاسِقُونَ {الحشر/19}

When the person forgets about Allah نَسُوا اللَّهَ, ﷻ, then this can mean that
the person does not read and apply teachings of the Qurān and Sunnah.
Therefore, the person does not know who he or she is without reading
the Qurān and Sunnah.

In that perspective, the Qurān and Hadith constantly explain who
the person is in reality. The explanations of who created the person,
what one's purpose and goal should be, what the nature, sky, mountain,
animals mean, what death means, what evil and good means, what the
seen and unseen realities are, what the limits of the person are and what
the ethical and just ways in the relationship with the Creator, with other
humans, animals and other beings. If the person does not know, does
not learn and apply, then the person really can forget who he or she is.

In that perspective, Allah ﷻ is Just. If the person makes the choice for
his or her free will for engaging with these teachings of the Qurān and
Sunnah, then Allah ﷻ can create the means and possibilities what this
person wants in life. Then, this person can become the lost wanderer,
the fasiq, in his or her entire life. This person can think that he or she has

---

681. God's partisans.
682. They, who shall attain to a happy state!
683. (59:19) And be not like those who are oblivious of God, and whom He therefore causes
to be oblivious of [what is good for] their own selves: [for] it is they, they who are truly
depraved!

a purpose, goal and meaning but in reality, the person has wasted all his life as mentioned in Sûrah kahf: [103-106][684]

قُلْ هَلْ نُنَبِّئُكُمْ بِالْأَخْسَرِينَ أَعْمَالًا {الكهف/103} الَّذِينَ ضَلَّ سَعْيُهُمْ فِي الْحَيَاةِ الدُّنْيَا وَهُمْ يَحْسَبُونَ أَنَّهُمْ يُحْسِنُونَ صُنْعًا {الكهف/104} أُولَئِكَ الَّذِينَ كَفَرُوا بِآيَاتِ رَبِّهِمْ وَلِقَائِهِ فَحَبِطَتْ أَعْمَالُهُمْ فَلَا نُقِيمُ لَهُمْ يَوْمَ الْقِيَامَةِ وَزْنًا {الكهف/105} ذَلِكَ جَزَاؤُهُمْ جَهَنَّمُ بِمَا كَفَرُوا وَاتَّخَذُوا آيَاتِي وَرُسُلِي هُزُوًا {الكهف/106}

These people's situation in reality is so sad. They think that they are doing something good and logical. But in reality, unfortunately, they are wasting their time. The main reason is that when the message comes to them then, they are in the attitude of "I don't care." Or, they make fun and humiliation of the people of genuine practice such as the messengers, or they make can make fun of the teachings of the Prophet صلى الله عليه وسلم and the Qurān. May Allah ﷻ protect us. Amìn.

[22-24][685]

هُوَ اللَّهُ الَّذِي لَا إِلَهَ إِلَّا هُوَ عَالِمُ الْغَيْبِ وَالشَّهَادَةِ هُوَ الرَّحْمَنُ الرَّحِيمُ {الحشر/22} هُوَ اللَّهُ الَّذِي لَا إِلَهَ إِلَّا هُوَ الْمَلِكُ الْقُدُّوسُ السَّلَامُ الْمُؤْمِنُ الْمُهَيْمِنُ الْعَزِيزُ الْجَبَّارُ الْمُتَكَبِّرُ سُبْحَانَ اللَّهِ عَمَّا يُشْرِكُونَ {الحشر/23} هُوَ اللَّهُ الْخَالِقُ الْبَارِئُ الْمُصَوِّرُ لَهُ الْأَسْمَاءُ الْحُسْنَى يُسَبِّحُ لَهُ مَا فِي السَّمَاوَاتِ وَالْأَرْضِ وَهُوَ الْعَزِيزُ الْحَكِيمُ {الحشر/24}

---

684. 18:103 Say, [O Muhammad], "Shall we [believers] inform you of the greatest losers as to [their] deeds? 87:104 [They are] those whose effort is lost in worldly life, while they think that they are doing well in work." 87:105 Those are the ones who disbelieve in the verses of their Lord and in [their] meeting Him, so their deeds have become worthless; and We will not assign to them on the Day of Resurrection any weight [i.e., importance]. 87:106 That is their recompense—Hell—for what they denied and [because] they took My signs and My messengers in ridicule.
685. 59:22 GOD IS HE save whom there is no deity: the One who knows all that is beyond the reach of a created being's perception, as well as all that can be witnessed by a creature's senses or mind:~ He, the Most Gracious, the Dispenser of Grace. (59:23) God is He save whom there is no deity: the Sovereign Supreme, the Holy, the One with whom all salvation rests,28 the Giver of Faith, the One who determines what is true and false, the Almighty, the One who subdues wrong and restores right, the One to whom all greatness belongs! Utterly remote is God, in His limitless glory, from anything to which men may ascribe a share in His divinity! 59:24 He is God, the Creator, the Maker who shapes all forms and appearances! His [alone] are the attributes of perfection. All that is in the heavens and on earth extols His limitless glory: for He alone is almighty, truly wise!

[22]

هُوَ اللَّهُ الَّذِي لَا إِلَهَ إِلَّا هُوَ عَالِمُ الْغَيْبِ وَالشَّهَادَةِ هُوَ الرَّحْمَنُ الرَّحِيمُ {الحشر/22}

The expression عَالِمُ الْغَيْبِ[686] can indicate that the person is always in the fear of the unknowns, the future and the present. Allah ﷻ mentions this that Allah ﷻ knows and is in control of the all the unknowns and knowns for humans عَالِمُ الْغَيْبِ وَالشَّهَادَةِ[687]. Therefore, if the person makes real tawakkul to Allah ﷻ then, the person can be safe from the fears of with the Fadl, and Rahmah of Allah ﷻ as mentioned هُوَ الرَّحْمَنُ[688]. Allah ﷻ is especially merciful to ahlu-imān as mentioned الرَّحِيمُ[689].

Allah ﷻ knows the present and future but one should remember that Allah ﷻ is Merciful and Very Merciful as mentioned by هُوَ اللَّهُ الَّذِي لَا[690] إِلَهَ إِلَّا هُوَ عَالِمُ الْغَيْبِ وَالشَّهَادَةِ هُوَ الرَّحْمَنُ الرَّحِيمُ. With the Divine Knowledge of Allah ﷻ, Allah ﷻ has the Authority and control over everything as mentioned الْمَلِكُ[691]. With the Divine Knowledge and Authority, Allah ﷻ is the only One Who can give true security to the a'bd for their fears as mentioned by الْمُؤْمِنُ[692].

Why? Because Allah الْمُهَيْمِنُ[693] ﷻ can protect the person from all the evil. Allah ﷻ is الْعَزِيزُ الْجَبَّارُ الْمُتَكَبِّرُ[694], the Exalted One, the Powerful, the Real Authority of Control that no one can prevent Allah ﷻ from the Divine Execution of the Divine Will.

After this, leave all your doubts! and know! and say! "سُبْحَانَ اللَّهِ عَمَّا[695] يُشْرِكُونَ" that "I remove all the imperfect understandings about Allah ﷻ in my heart and mind and I know that Allah ﷻ is perfect. I don't want

---

686. The One who knows all that is beyond the reach of a created being's perception.
687. The One who knows all that is beyond the reach of a created being's perception, as well as all that can be witnessed by a creature's senses or mind.
688. He, the Most Gracious.
689. The Most Merciful.
690. GOD IS HE save whom there is no deity: the One who knows all that is beyond the reach of a created being's perception, as well as all that can be witnessed by a creature's senses or mind:~ He, the Most Gracious, the Dispenser of Grace.
691. The Sovereign.
692. The Giver of Faith.
693. The One who determines what is true and false.
694. The Almighty, the One who subdues wrong and restores right, the One to whom all greatness belongs!
695. Utterly remote is God, in His limitless glory, from anything to which men may ascribe a share in His divinity!

to be like those who have incorrect understandings about Allah ﷻ عَمَّا[696], "يُشْرِكُون"

And remember!, Allah ﷻ is constantly and continuously in action as mentioned هُوَ اللَّه الْخَالِقُ الْبَارِئُ الْمُصَوِّرُ[697]. It is not like as some others say about Allah ﷻ that, astagfirullah, God does not interfere.

Finally, remember! that these are only some of the names of Allah ﷻ there are countless perfect Names of Allah لَهُ الأَسْمَاءُ الْحُسْنَى[698] ﷻ.

After all this, remember! everything but everything on and between the earth, skies, galaxies, universes and in different dimensions recognize, appreciate, chant, glorify and pray to Allah ﷻ as mentioned يُسَبِّحُ لَهُ مَا فِي السَّمَاوَاتِ وَالأَرْض[699]. Allah ﷻ is the Exalted One. Allah ﷻ has the Full Wisdom with Full Authority.

As these ayahs are very critical as the topic is the Names and Attributes of Allah ﷻ and also advised to read it regularly by the Prophet ﷺ (27). Lastly, one of the interesting point to pay attention is the repetition of the phrase اللَّه هُوَ.

Sûrah Tahrìm

[8][700]

يَا أَيُّهَا الَّذِينَ آمَنُوا تُوبُوا إِلَى اللَّهِ تَوْبَةً نَصُوحًا عَسَى رَبُّكُمْ أَنْ يُكَفِّرَ عَنكُمْ سَيِّئَاتِكُمْ وَيُدْخِلَكُمْ جَنَّاتٍ تَجْرِي مِن تَحْتِهَا الأَنْهَارُ يَوْمَ لا يُخْزِي اللَّهُ النَّبِيَّ وَالَّذِينَ آمَنُوا مَعَهُ نُورُهُمْ يَسْعَى بَيْنَ أَيْدِيهِمْ وَبِأَيْمَانِهِمْ يَقُولُونَ رَبَّنَا أَتْمِمْ لَنَا نُورَنَا وَاغْفِرْ لَنَا إِنَّكَ عَلَى كُلِّ شَيْءٍ قَدِيرٌ

Every human has sin. Therefore, if Allah ﷻ forgives the person and covers his or her sins as mentioned أَنْ يُكَفِّرَ عَنكُمْ سَيِّئَاتِكُمْ[701] then the person can go to Jannah. When this fact is also recognized and admitted by humans as mentioned وَاغْفِرْ لَنَا[702] then the complete light, Nûr, of Allah

---

696. From anything to which men may ascribe a share in His divinity!
697. He is God, the Creator, the Maker who shapes all forms and appearances!
698. His [alone] are the attributes of perfection.
699. All that is in the heavens and on earth extols His limitless glory.
700. 66:8 O you who have attained to faith! Turn unto God in sincere repentance: it may well be that your Sustainer will efface from you your bad deeds, and will admit you into gardens through which running waters flow, on a Day on which God will not shame the Prophet and those who share his faith: their light will spread rapidly before them, and on their right; [and] they will pray: "O our Sustainer! Cause this our light to shine for us forever, and forgive our sins: for, verily, Thou hast the power to will anything!"
701. It may well be that your Sustainer will efface from you your bad deeds.
702. And forgive our sins.

☸ on humans can reveal as رَبَّنَا أَتْمِمْ لَنَا نُورَنَا [703]. No one can go to Jannah except or but with the Rahmah and Fadl of Allah ☸ as mentioned by the Prophet 9) (صلى الله عليه وسلم) (hadith# 2818). So, humans cannot claim a right to go to Jannah.

Sûrah Mumtahina

[1-3][704]

يَا أَيُّهَا الَّذِينَ آمَنُوا لَا تَتَّخِذُوا عَدُوِّي وَعَدُوَّكُمْ أَوْلِيَاء تُلْقُونَ إِلَيْهِم بِالْمَوَدَّةِ وَقَدْ كَفَرُوا بِمَا جَاءكُم مِّنَ الْحَقِّ يُخْرِجُونَ الرَّسُولَ وَإِيَّاكُمْ أَن تُؤْمِنُوا بِاللَّهِ رَبِّكُمْ إِن كُنتُمْ خَرَجْتُمْ جِهَادًا فِي سَبِيلِي وَابْتِغَاء مَرْضَاتِي تُسِرُّونَ إِلَيْهِم بِالْمَوَدَّةِ وَأَنَا أَعْلَمُ بِمَا أَخْفَيْتُمْ وَمَا أَعْلَنتُمْ وَمَن يَفْعَلْهُ مِنكُمْ فَقَدْ ضَلَّ سَوَاء السَّبِيلِ {الممتحنة/1} إِن يَثْقَفُوكُمْ يَكُونُوا لَكُمْ أَعْدَاء وَيَبْسُطُوا إِلَيْكُمْ أَيْدِيَهُمْ وَأَلْسِنَتَهُم بِالسُّوءِ وَوَدُّوا لَوْ تَكْفُرُونَ {الممتحنة/2} لَن تَنفَعَكُمْ أَرْحَامُكُمْ وَلَا أَوْلَادُكُمْ يَوْمَ الْقِيَامَةِ يَفْصِلُ بَيْنَكُمْ وَاللَّهُ بِمَا تَعْمَلُونَ بَصِيرٌ {الممتحنة/3}

The above verses mention the realities of the Muslim life. It happened in the past, happening today and will happen in the future. Therefore, it is important to know where everyone stands and accordingly control one's heart. A lot of times, Muslims don't understand why people have an attitude towards them. There are problems that are caused by Muslims because of not understanding true teachings of Islam. However, there are also realities and attitudes of others because of a person merely being a Muslim. These verses normalize this position, realities and differences. There can be possible reasons such as jealousy, group arrogance, fear of losing power and position and etc. for this.

---

703. O our Sustainer! Cause this our light to shine for us forever.
704. 60:1 O YOU who have attained to faith! Do not take My enemies—who are your enemies as well—for your friends, showing them affection even though they are bent on denying whatever truth has come unto you, [and even though] they have driven the Apostle and yourselves away, [only] because you believe in God, your Sustainer! If [it be true that] you have gone forth [from your homes] to strive in My cause, and out of a longing for My goodly acceptance, [do not take them for your friends,] inclining towards them in secret affection: for I am fully aware of all that you may conceal as well as of all that you do openly. And any of you who does this has already strayed from the right path. 60:2 If they could but overcome you, they would [still] remain your foes, and would stretch forth their hands and tongues against you with evil intent: for they desire that you [too] should deny the truth. But [bear in mind that] neither your kinsfolk nor

[4-6] 705

قَدْ كَانَتْ لَكُمْ أُسْوَةٌ حَسَنَةٌ فِي إِبْرَاهِيمَ وَالَّذِينَ مَعَهُ إِذْ قَالُوا لِقَوْمِهِمْ إِنَّا بُرَآء مِنكُمْ وَمِمَّا تَعْبُدُونَ مِن دُونِ اللَّهِ كَفَرْنَا بِكُمْ وَبَدَا بَيْنَنَا وَبَيْنَكُمُ الْعَدَاوَةُ وَالْبَغْضَاء أَبَدًا حَتَّى تُؤْمِنُوا بِاللَّهِ وَحْدَهُ إِلَّا قَوْلَ إِبْرَاهِيمَ لِأَبِيهِ لَأَسْتَغْفِرَنَّ لَكَ وَمَا أَمْلِكُ لَكَ مِنَ اللَّهِ مِن شَيْءٍ رَّبَّنَا عَلَيْكَ تَوَكَّلْنَا وَإِلَيْكَ أَنَبْنَا وَإِلَيْكَ الْمَصِيرُ {الممتحنة/4} رَبَّنَا لَا تَجْعَلْنَا فِتْنَةً لِّلَّذِينَ كَفَرُوا وَاغْفِرْ لَنَا رَبَّنَا إِنَّكَ أَنتَ الْعَزِيزُ الْحَكِيمُ {الممتحنة/5} لَقَدْ كَانَ لَكُمْ فِيهِمْ أُسْوَةٌ حَسَنَةٌ لِمَن كَانَ يَرْجُو اللَّهَ وَالْيَوْمَ الْآخِرَ وَمَن يَتَوَلَّ فَإِنَّ اللَّهَ هُوَ الْغَنِيُّ الْحَمِيدُ

Then, the Qurān gives Ibrahim as the example, قَدْ كَانَتْ لَكُمْ أُسْوَةٌ حَسَنَةٌ فِي706 إِبْرَاهِيمَ. Even this expression is mentioned in the beginning of the verse and mentioned after two verses, لَقَدْ كَانَ لَكُمْ فِيهِمْ أُسْوَةٌ حَسَنَةٌ707.

Ibrahim as puts a clear stance with his position. Although they, the group of believers, were a few against the majority, his approach was very wise, gentle and logical.

---

705. 60:4 Indeed, 'you have had a good example in Abraham and those who followed him, when they said unto their [idolatrous] people: "Verily, we are quit of you and of all that you worship instead of God: we deny the truth of whatever you believe; and between us and you there has arisen enmity and hatred, to last until such a time as you come to believe in the One God!" The only exception was Abraham's saying to his father "I shall indeed pray for [God's] forgiveness for thee,6 although I have it not in my power to obtain anything from God in thy behalf." [And Abraham and his followers prayed:] "O our Sustainer! In Thee have we placed our trust, and unto Thee do we turn: for unto Thee is all journeys' end. 60:5 O our Sustainer! Make us not a plaything for those who are bent on denying the truth! And forgive us our sins, O our sustainer: for Thou alone art, almighty, truly wise!" (60:6) In them, indeed, you have a good example for everyone who looks forward [with hope and awe] to God and the Last Day. And if any turns away, [let him know that] God is truly self-sufficient, the One to whom all praise is due."
706. Indeed, 'you have had a good example in Abraham.
707. In them, indeed, you have a good example for everyone.

[10][708]

يَا أَيُّهَا الَّذِينَ آمَنُوا إِذَا جَاءكُمُ الْمُؤْمِنَاتُ مُهَاجِرَاتٍ فَامْتَحِنُوهُنَّ اللَّهُ أَعْلَمُ بِإِيمَانِهِنَّ فَإِنْ
عَلِمْتُمُوهُنَّ مُؤْمِنَاتٍ

It is interesting to see that this verse establishes some credibility and
trust measures when new people join to Islam. It is recommended to
understand and test as mentioned فَامْتَحِنُوهُنَّ[709]. Even, the name of this
chapter comes from this concept. On the other hand, اعلم الله, it may
indicate that the women joiners can be more.

يَا أَيُّهَا النَّبِيُّ إِذَا جَاءكَ الْمُؤْمِنَاتُ يُبَايِعْنَكَ عَلَى أَن لَّا يُشْرِكْنَ بِاللَّهِ شَيْئًا وَلَا يَسْرِقْنَ وَلَا
يَزْنِينَ وَلَا يَقْتُلْنَ أَوْلَادَهُنَّ وَلَا يَأْتِينَ بِبُهْتَانٍ يَفْتَرِينَهُ بَيْنَ أَيْدِيهِنَّ وَأَرْجُلِهِنَّ وَلَا يَعْصِينَكَ
فِي مَعْرُوفٍ فَبَايِعْهُنَّ وَاسْتَغْفِرْ لَهُنَّ اللَّهَ إِنَّ اللَّهَ غَفُورٌ رَّحِيمٌ[710] {الممتحنة/12}

This verse shows the importance of taking promise from the new
joiners not to engage in evil. Because when a person promises something
not to do it, it is more difficult for one to go against oneself if the person
is ethical and will feel guilty about their promise. This is an extra internal
restraint due to conscience of the person.

---

708. 60:10 O YOU who have attained to faith! Whenever believing women come unto you,
forsaking the domain of evil, examine them, [although only] God is fully aware of their faith;
and if you have thus ascertained that they are believers, do not send them back to the deniers
of the truth, [since] they are [no longer] lawful to their erstwhile husbands, and these are [no
longer] lawful to them. None the less, you shall return to them whatever they have spent [on
their wives by way of dower]; and [then, O believers,] you will be committing no sin if you
marry them after giving them their dowers. On the other hand, hold not to the marriage-tie
with women who [continue to] deny the truth, and ask but for [the return of] whatever you
have spent [by way of dower]—just as they [whose wives have gone over to you] have the
right to demand [the return of] whatever they have spent. Such is God's judgment: He judges
between you [in equity]—for God is all-knowing, wise.
709. Examine them.
710. O Prophet, when the believing women come to you pledging to you that they will
not associate anything with Allah, nor will they steal, nor will they commit unlawful sexual
intercourse, nor will they kill their children, nor will they bring forth a slander they have
invented between their arms and legs, nor will they disobey you in what is right—then accept
their pledge and ask forgiveness for them of Allah. Indeed, Allah is Forgiving and Merciful.

[13]⁷¹¹

يَا أَيُّهَا الَّذِينَ آمَنُوا لَا تَتَوَلَّوْا قَوْمًا غَضِبَ اللَّهُ عَلَيْهِمْ قَدْ يَئِسُوا مِنَ الْآخِرَةِ كَمَا يَئِسَ الْكُفَّارُ مِنْ أَصْحَابِ الْقُبُورِ {الممتحنة/13}

The Sûrah ends again with the beginning theme of realities of being a Muslim. The verse also makes a psychological analysis of others.

Sûrah Saff

[4-6]⁷¹²

إِنَّ اللَّهَ يُحِبُّ الَّذِينَ يُقَاتِلُونَ فِي سَبِيلِهِ صَفًّا كَأَنَّهُم بُنيَانٌ مَّرْصُوصٌ {الصف/4} وَإِذْ قَالَ مُوسَى لِقَوْمِهِ يَا قَوْمِ لِمَ تُؤْذُونَنِي وَقَد تَّعْلَمُونَ أَنِّي رَسُولُ اللَّهِ إِلَيْكُمْ فَلَمَّا زَاغُوا أَزَاغَ اللَّهُ قُلُوبَهُمْ وَاللَّهُ لَا يَهْدِي الْقَوْمَ الْفَاسِقِينَ {الصف/5} وَإِذْ قَالَ عِيسَى ابْنُ مَرْيَمَ يَا بَنِي إِسْرَائِيلَ إِنِّي رَسُولُ اللَّهِ إِلَيْكُم مُّصَدِّقًا لِّمَا بَيْنَ يَدَيَّ مِنَ التَّوْرَاةِ وَمُبَشِّرًا بِرَسُولٍ يَأْتِي مِن بَعْدِي اسْمُهُ أَحْمَدُ فَلَمَّا جَاءهُم بِالْبَيِّنَاتِ قَالُوا هَذَا سِحْرٌ مُّبِينٌ {الصف/6}

The portion of the verse ⁷¹³إِنَّ اللَّهَ يُحِبُّ الَّذِينَ يُقَاتِلُونَ فِي سَبِيلِهِ صَفًّا mentions the importance of working together in groups or organizations for doing good. The first example is Musa as representing Jews, the second example is Isa as representing the Christians, and the last example is Muhammad ﷺ representing the Muslims. Then in the last part of the Sûrah:

---

711. 60:13 O YOU who have attained to faith! Be not friends with people whom God has condemned! They [who would befriend them] are indeed bereft of all hope of a life to come— just as those deniers of the truth are bereft of all hope of [ever again seeing] those who are [now] in their graves.

712. 61:4 Verily, God loves [only] those who fight in His cause in [solid] ranks, as though they were a building firm and compact.

61:5 Now when Moses spoke to his people, [it was this same truth that he had in mind:] "O my people! Why do you cause me grief, the while you know that I am an apostle of God sent unto you?" And so, when they swerved from the right way, God let their hearts swerve from the truth: for God does not bestow His guidance upon iniquitous folk.

61:6 And [this happened, too,] when Jesus, the son of Mary, said: "O children of Israel! Behold, I am an apostle of God unto you, [sent] to confirm the truth of whatever there still remains5 of the Torah, and to give [you] the glad tiding of an apostle who shall come after me, whose name shall be Ahmad." But when he [whose coming Jesus had foretold] came unto them7 with all evidence of the truth, they said: "This [alleged message of his] is [nothing but] spellbinding eloquence!"

713. Verily, God loves [only] those who fight in His cause in [solid] ranks.

[14]⁷¹⁴

يَا أَيُّهَا الَّذِينَ آمَنُوا كُونُوا أَنصَارَ اللَّهِ كَمَا قَالَ عِيسَى ابْنُ مَرْيَمَ لِلْحَوَارِيِّينَ مَنْ أَنصَارِي
إِلَى اللَّهِ قَالَ الْحَوَارِيُّونَ نَحْنُ أَنصَارُ اللَّهِ فَآمَنَت طَّائِفَةٌ مِّن بَنِي إِسْرَائِيلَ وَكَفَرَت طَّائِفَةٌ
فَأَيَّدْنَا الَّذِينَ آمَنُوا عَلَى عَدُوِّهِمْ فَأَصْبَحُوا ظَاهِرِينَ

Early Christians are shown as role models as an example of a group or a unit for Muslims in supporting each other for the good. These are some themes in the Qurān that come also to show that Allah ﷻ send at different times the same message. In this perspective, Islam and Muslims are not technical terms but the real and genuine followers of the religion of Allah ﷻ.

Sûrah Juma'

[2]⁷¹⁵

هُوَ الَّذِي بَعَثَ فِي الْأُمِّيِّينَ رَسُولًا مِّنْهُمْ يَتْلُو عَلَيْهِمْ آيَاتِهِ وَيُزَكِّيهِمْ وَيُعَلِّمُهُمُ الْكِتَابَ
وَالْحِكْمَةَ وَإِن كَانُوا مِن قَبْلُ لَفِي ضَلَالٍ مُّبِينٍ

Allah ﷻ sends the Prophet ﷺ to teach the people as mentioned الْأُمِّيِّينَ⁷¹⁶. In this case, the Prophet ﷺ is also ummi meaning the one who is natural, pure and genuine. Knowledge and i'lm is important as long as it is genuine, natural and pure and the person applies it as mentioned in the previous Sûrah Saff as baratul istilal, which is the methodology of an introduction to upcoming topics, as يَا أَيُّهَا الَّذِينَ آمَنُوا لِمَ تَقُولُونَ مَا لَا تَفْعَلُونَ {الصف/2}.

---

714. 61:14 O YOU who have attained to faith! Be helpers [in the cause of God—even as Jesus, the son of Mary, said unto the white-garbed ones,14 "Who will be my helpers in God's cause?"—whereupon the white-garbed [disciples] replied, "We shall be [thy] helpers [in the cause] of God!" And so [it happened that] some of the children of Israel came to believe [in the apostleship of Jesus], whereas others denied the truth.15 But [now] We have given strength against their foes unto those who have [truly] attained to faith:16 and they have become the ones that shall prevail.
715. 62:2 He it is who has sent unto the unlettered people an apostle from among themselves,1 to convey unto them His messages, and to cause them to grow in purity, and to impart unto them the divine writ as well as wisdom whereas before that they were indeed, most obviously, lost in error—; (62:3) and [to cause this message to spread] from them unto other people as soon as they come into contact with them: for He alone is almighty, truly wise!
716. The unlettered people.

Later, an opposite example of not using the il'm in its true sense is given:

مَثَلُ الَّذِينَ حُمِّلُوا التَّوْرَاةَ ثُمَّ لَمْ يَحْمِلُوهَا كَمَثَلِ الْحِمَارِ يَحْمِلُ أَسْفَارًا بِئْسَ مَثَلُ الْقَوْمِ الَّذِينَ كَذَّبُوا بِآيَاتِ اللَّهِ وَاللَّهُ لَا يَهْدِي الْقَوْمَ الظَّالِمِينَ 717﴿الجمعة/5﴾.

The Prophet ﷺ mentions the importance of useful knowledge in his dua that one should learn and increase knowledge in order to practice and act on it (9) (hadith# 2722). In this case, in Islam, learning or acquiring knowledge is not an intellectual entertainment but it is a need to excel in one's relationship with Allah ﷻ and to please Allah ﷻ.

[11]⁷¹⁸

وَإِذَا رَأَوْا تِجَارَةً أَوْ لَهْوًا انفَضُّوا إِلَيْهَا وَتَرَكُوكَ قَائِمًا قُلْ مَا عِندَ اللَّهِ خَيْرٌ مِّنَ اللَّهْوِ وَمِنَ التِّجَارَةِ وَاللَّهُ خَيْرُ الرَّازِقِينَ ﴿الجمعة/11﴾

Sometimes, our worldly engagements can especially allure to us very attractive. This attraction can be at such a degree that one can consider the pleasure received from them to be above of the pleasure in one's relationship with Allah ﷻ through ibadah, reading the Qurān and enjoying and being constantly with Allah ﷻ in khudur, in the Divine Presence. Yet, in the above ayah, Allah ﷻ mentions that the real pleasure of good is with Allah ﷻ as mentioned مَا عِندَ اللَّهِ خَيْرٌ مِّنَ اللَّهْوِ وَمِنَ التِّجَارَةِ.⁷¹⁹ As humans, we are constantly in the process of making choices. In this decision making, if the person embodies always the pleasure of Allah ﷻ then the benefit, joy, and happiness that the person gets from other means of fun and worldly engagements will be much less or trivial compared to the pleasure received through the pleasure of Allah ﷻ through constant connection of ihsan. Most of the time even the halal engagements leave traces of pain in the person. Yet, there are no traces of pain but happiness and tranquility when the person is engaged in ibadah and marifah, knowledge, of Allah ﷻ with ikhlas, الله اعلم.

---

717. The example of those who were entrusted with the Torah and then did not take it on is like that of a donkey who carries volumes [of books]. Wretched is the example of the people who deny the signs of Allah. And Allah does not guide the wrongdoing people.
718. 62:11 Yet [it does happen that] when people12 become aware of [an occasion for] worldly gain13 or a passing delight, they rush headlong towards it, and leave thee standing [and preaching]. Say: "That which is with God is far better than all passing delight ad all gain! And God is the best of providers!"
719. That which is with God is far better than all passing delight and all gain!

Sûrah Munafiqûn

[9]⁷²⁰

يَا أَيُّهَا الَّذِينَ آمَنُوا لَا تُلْهِكُمْ أَمْوَالُكُمْ وَلَا أَوْلَادُكُمْ عَن ذِكْرِ اللَّهِ وَمَن يَفْعَلْ ذَلِكَ فَأُولَئِكَ هُمُ
الْخَاسِرُونَ {المنافقون/9}

It is important to place everything in their proper place in one's relation
with Allah ﷻ. Even one's own children, family members and wealth
should be placed in their proper place in priority in one's relationship
with Allah ﷻ.

Sûrah Tahrim

[4-6]⁷²¹

إِن تَتُوبَا إِلَى اللَّهِ فَقَدْ صَغَتْ قُلُوبُكُمَا وَإِن تَظَاهَرَا عَلَيْهِ فَإِنَّ اللَّهَ هُوَ مَوْلَاهُ وَجِبْرِيلُ
وَصَالِحُ الْمُؤْمِنِينَ وَالْمَلَائِكَةُ بَعْدَ ذَلِكَ ظَهِيرٌ {التحريم/4} عَسَى رَبُّهُ إِن طَلَّقَكُنَّ أَن يُبْدِلَهُ
أَزْوَاجًا خَيْرًا مِّنكُنَّ مُسْلِمَاتٍ مُّؤْمِنَاتٍ قَانِتَاتٍ تَائِبَاتٍ عَابِدَاتٍ سَائِحَاتٍ ثَيِّبَاتٍ وَأَبْكَارًا
{التحريم/5} يَا أَيُّهَا الَّذِينَ آمَنُوا قُوا أَنفُسَكُمْ وَأَهْلِيكُمْ نَارًا وَقُودُهَا النَّاسُ وَالْحِجَارَةُ عَلَيْهَا
مَلَائِكَةٌ غِلَاظٌ شِدَادٌ لَا يَعْصُونَ اللَّهَ مَا أَمَرَهُمْ وَيَفْعَلُونَ مَا يُؤْمَرُونَ {التحريم/6}

The above ayahs are interesting to analyze in family life. The notion
of وَإِن تَظَاهَرَا عَلَيْهِ⁷²² can show that in family matters, there may be all
or some members grouping against one person. Today, it can be called
othering. In these cases, if the person is left alone and does not and

---

720. 63:9 O YOU who have attained to faith! Let not your worldly goods or your children make
you oblivious of the remembrance of God: for if any behave thus—it is they, they who are the
losers!
721. 66:4 [Say, O Prophet:] "Would that you two turn unto God in repentance, for the hearts of
both of you have swerved [from what is right]! And if you uphold each other against him [who
is God's message-bearer, know that] God Himself is his Protector, and [that,] therefore, Gabriel,
and all the righteous among the believers and all the [other] angels will come to his aid."
66:5 [O wives of the Prophet!] Were he to divorce [any of] you, God might well give him in
your stead spouses better than you—women who surrender themselves unto God, who truly
believe, devoutly obey His will, turn [unto Him] in repentance [whenever they have sinned]
worship [Him alone] and go on and on [seeking His goodly acceptance]9 —be they women
previously married or virgins.
66:6 O YOU who have attained to faith! Ward off from yourselves and those who are close
to you that fire [of the hereafter] whose fuel is human beings and stones: [lording] over it
are angelic powers awesome [and] severe, who do not disobey God in whatever He has
commanded them, but [always] do what they are bidden to do.
722. And if you uphold each other against him.

cannot defend him or herself and still maintains the relationship with Allah ﷻ, then Allah ﷻ mentions that فَإِنَّ اللَّهَ هُوَ مَوْلَاهُ وَجِبْرِيلُ وَصَالِحُ الْمُؤْمِنِينَ وَالْمَلَائِكَةُ بَعْدَ ذَلِكَ ظَهِيرٌ {التَّحريم/4}[723]. So, this person has a better group than the former one. This is especially important in the process of grief and to prevent any type of depression. However, the point is to protect the soundness of a family as mentioned [724]يَا أَيُّهَا الَّذِينَ آمَنُوا قُوا أَنْفُسَكُمْ وَأَهْلِيكُمْ نَارً. In other words, the problems and issues should be auxiliary and not destroy the main purpose of preparing yourself with your family members for akhirah, meeting with Allah ﷻ, الله اعلم.

In this regard, the expression وَإِن تَظَاهَرَا عَلَيْهِ can also allude to today's possible feminism trends especially in the context or in the discourses of women supporting other women due to shared commonality of gender.

In the family matters, man can be left out and can be more private in solving family problems. Compared to women, she can be more vocal and public trying to seek problems with the expression وَإِن تَظَاهَرَا عَلَيْهِ.

Yet, at the end, the ayah wants us to focus the real purpose and goal in family matters as يَا أَيُّهَا الَّذِينَ آمَنُوا قُوا أَنْفُسَكُمْ وَأَهْلِيكُمْ نَارً, الله اعلم.

---

723. God Himself is his Protector, and [that,] therefore, Gabriel, and all the righteous among the believers and all the [other] angels will come to his aid."
724. O YOU who have attained to faith! Ward off from yourselves and those who are close to you that fire [of the hereafter].

29

Sûrah Mulk

[10-11]⁷²⁵

وَقَالُوا لَوْ كُنَّا نَسْمَعُ أَوْ نَعْقِلُ مَا كُنَّا فِي أَصْحَابِ السَّعِيرِ {الملك/10} فَاعْتَرَفُوا بِذَنبِهِمْ فَسُحْقاً لِأَصْحَابِ السَّعِيرِ {الملك/11}

The importance of using the free choice in one's life as mentioned وَقَالُوا لَوْ كُنَّا نَسْمَعُ أَوْ نَعْقِلُ⁷²⁶ and then accepting this fact as mentioned فاعترفوا⁷²⁷.

May Allah protect us from this, Amìn.

Sûrah Qalam

[1-14]⁷²⁸

ن وَالْقَلَمِ وَمَا يَسْطُرُونَ {القلم/1} مَا أَنتَ بِنِعْمَةِ رَبِّكَ بِمَجْنُونٍ {القلم/2} وَإِنَّ لَكَ لَأَجْراً غَيْرَ مَمْنُونٍ {القلم/3} وَإِنَّكَ لَعَلى خُلُقٍ عَظِيمٍ {القلم/4} فَسَتُبْصِرُ وَيُبْصِرُونَ {القلم/5} بِأَيِّيكُمُ الْمَفْتُونُ {القلم/6} إِنَّ رَبَّكَ هُوَ أَعْلَمُ بِمَن ضَلَّ عَن سَبِيلِهِ وَهُوَ أَعْلَمُ بِالْمُهْتَدِينَ {القلم/7} فَلَا تُطِعِ الْمُكَذِّبِينَ {القلم/8} وَدُّوا لَوْ تُدْهِنُ فَيُدْهِنُونَ {القلم/9} وَلَا تُطِعْ كُلَّ حَلَّافٍ مَّهِينٍ {القلم/10} هَمَّازٍ مَّشَّاء بِنَمِيمٍ {القلم/11} مَنَّاعٍ لِّلْخَيْرِ مُعْتَدٍ أَثِيمٍ {القلم/12} عُتُلٍّ بَعْدَ ذَلِكَ زَنِيمٍ {القلم/13} أَن كَانَ ذَا مَالٍ وَبَنِينَ {القلم/14}

---

725. 67:10 And they will add: "Had we but listened [to those warnings], or [at least] used our own reason, we would not [now] be among those who are destined for the blazing flame!" (67:11) Thus will they come to realize their sins: but [by that time,] remote will have become all good from those who are destined for the blazing flame.
726. And they will add: "Had we but listened [to those warnings], or [at least] used our own reason.
727. Thus will they come to realize.
728. 68:1 Nun. CONSIDER the pen, and all that they write [therewith]! (68:2) Thou art not, by thy Sustainer's grace, a madman! (68:3) And, verily, thine shall be a reward neverending (68:4) for, behold, thou keepest indeed to a sublime way of life; (68:5) and [one day] thou shalt see, and they [who now deride thee] shall see, (68:6) which of you was bereft of reason. 68:7 Verily, thy Sustainer alone is fully aware as to who has strayed from His path, Just as He alone is fully aware of those who have found the right way. (68:8) Hence, defer not to [the likes and dislikes of] those who give the lie to the truth: (68:9) they would like thee to be soft [with them], so that they might be soft [with thee]. 68:10 Furthermore, defer not to the contemptible swearer of oaths, (68:11) [or to] the slanderer that goes about with defaming tales, (68:12) [or] the withholder of good, [or] the sinful aggressor. (68:13) Cruel, moreover, and an illegitimate pretender. (68:14) Because he is a possessor of wealth and children.

In this Sûrah, the possibility of people's blame for the da'i who is trying to invite people to Allah ﷻ is explained in the beginning, الله اعلم. If one thinks the ayah ن وَالْقَلَمِ وَمَا يَسْطُرُونَ {القلم/1} مَا أَنتَ بِنِعْمَةِ رَبِّكَ بِمَجْنُونٍ {القلم/2} from the opposite of these ayahs (mafûmu-mukhalif), then the possibilities of the tool of writing in the engagements of sihr, magic, can also be deduced. In this case, the negative writings with sihr can be countered with its positive writings of protection, tawfiz. In other words, if sihr is a poison, then tawfiz is its antidote, الله اعلم.

In each case of people's evil renderings through verbal, written and physical discourses, having patience to their attitude mentioned in the beginning of this Sûrah and at the end, it can be to imply the great reward from Allah ﷻ as mentioned وَإِنَّ لَكَ لَأَجْرًا غَيْرَ مَمْنُونٍ {القلم/3}.

On another perspective, sometimes with the effects of people's evils, plot and sihr the person can question him or herself. Therefore, Allah ﷻ mentions to the Prophet صلى الله عليه وسلم that وَإِنَّكَ لَعَلى خُلُقٍ عَظِيمٍ. They will see and the Prophet will see who is right and who is wrong, who has insanity, who is misguided as mentioned by فَسَتُبْصِرُ {القلم/4} وَيُبْصِرُونَ {القلم/5} بِأَيِّيِّكُمُ الْمَفْتُونُ {القلم/6} إِنَّ رَبَّكَ هُوَ أَعْلَمُ بِمَن ضَلَّ عَن سَبِيلِهِ وَهُوَ أَعْلَمُ بِالْمُهْتَدِينَ. Therefore, don't give attention to what they say and move on as mentioned by فَلَا تُطِعِ الْمُكَذِّبِينَ. They constantly talk, backbite, slander, humiliate people and laugh with this. Nothing positive, genuine, and respectful is there. They even prevent the good, the khayr as mentioned وَدُّوا لَوْ تُدْهِنُ فَيُدْهِنُونَ {القلم/9} وَلَا تُطِعْ كُلَّ حَلَّافٍ مَهِينٍ {القلم/10} هَمَّازٍ مَّشَّاء بِنَمِيم {القلم/11} مَنَّاعٍ لِّلْخَيْرِ مُعْتَدٍ أَثِيم {القلم/12}

Then, the rest of the Sûrah gives an example of attitude of some of these people who thought they were smart in their engagements treating the needy, but they were being stingy as narrated with the people of the garden.

[17-18][729]

إِنَّا بَلَوْنَاهُمْ كَمَا بَلَوْنَا أَصْحَابَ الْجَنَّةِ إِذْ أَقْسَمُوا لَيَصْرِمُنَّهَا مُصْبِحِينَ {القلم/17} وَلَا يَسْتَثْنُونَ {القلم/18}

---

729. (68:17) [As for such sinners,] behold, We [but] try them11 as We tried the owners of a certain garden who vowed that they would surely harvest its fruit on the morrow, (68:18) and made no allowance [for the will of God]:

This is very interesting that the whole azab and punishment is given to them due to وَلَا يَسْتَثْنُونَ. What does it mean? When a person excludes Allah ﷻ from the picture, then anything can happen. In other words, when the person thinks implicitly or explicitly that he or she is the creator, sustainer, nourisher or maker of everything, then those are the dispositions of breathing arrogance. The practical examples can be not saying inshAllah or la hawla wa la quwwata illa billah. The similar case of a person as in this Sûrah who is having wealth and gardens is presented also in Sûrah Kahf as

[23-24][730]

وَلَا تَقُولَنَّ لِشَيْءٍ إِنِّي فَاعِلٌ ذَلِكَ غَدًا {الكهف/23} إِلَّا أَن يَشَاءَ اللَّهُ وَاذْكُر رَّبَّكَ إِذَا نَسِيتَ وَقُلْ عَسَى أَن يَهْدِيَنِ رَبِّي لِأَقْرَبَ مِنْ هَذَا رَشَدًا {الكهف/24}

Then anything can happen to show the opposite to the person. May Allah ﷻ protects us from even one second of negligence and forgetfulness of this fact. In this perspective, the true state of Ihsan is the full state of imān and free of arrogance, shirk and kufr.

In this sense, ideally ihsan is a state of not optional but required state for a believer if he or she wants to be protected from the makr of Allah ﷻ, from the outcomes of the trials or tests in one's life.

[29] [731]

قَالُوا سُبْحَانَ رَبِّنَا إِنَّا كُنَّا ظَالِمِينَ {القلم/29}

As we see in this case, these people of imān learn their lesson but in a hard way. So, inshAllah to be protected from the hard way, the state of ihsan is the goal. After making a mistake, definitely it is a virtue and level to recognize the oppression of one's own self as presented in the case here.

---

730. 18:23 And never say of anything, "Indeed, I will do that tomorrow," 18:24 Except [when adding], "If Allah wills." And remember your Lord when you forget [it] and say, "Perhaps my Lord will guide me to what is nearer than this to right conduct."
731. 68:29 They answered: "Limitless in His glory is our Sustainer! Verily, we were doing wrong!"

[48-51] [732]

{ فَاصْبِرْ لِحُكْمِ رَبِّكَ وَلَا تَكُن كَصَاحِبِ الْحُوتِ إِذْ نَادَى وَهُوَ مَكْظُومٌ {القلم/48} لَّوْلَا أَن تَدَارَكَهُ نِعْمَةٌ مِّن رَّبِّهِ لَنُبِذَ بِالْعَرَاءِ وَهُوَ مَذْمُومٌ {القلم/49} فَاجْتَبَاهُ رَبُّهُ فَجَعَلَهُ مِنَ الصَّالِحِينَ {القلم/50} وَإِن يَكَادُ الَّذِينَ كَفَرُوا لَيُزْلِقُونَكَ بِأَبْصَارِهِمْ لَمَّا سَمِعُوا الذِّكْرَ وَيَقُولُونَ إِنَّهُ لَمَجْنُونٌ {القلم/51} وَمَا هُوَ إِلَّا ذِكْرٌ لِّلْعَالَمِينَ {القلم/52} }

Then the Sûrah ends with the case of Yûnus as. It starts with it with nun and ends with it, as the classical interpretation of nun is Yûnus as (8). The letter nun as a symbol can depict a ship carrying a person. It can be a barat-istidlal or introduction and conclusion as the theme mentions what is going to come at the end mentioning it at the beginning. This is مَا أَنتَ بِنِعْمَةِ رَبِّكَ بِمَجْنُونٍ{القلم/2} as mentioned in the beginning of the Sûrah then بِأَبْصَارِهِمْ لَمَّا سَمِعُوا الذِّكْرَ وَيَقُولُونَ إِنَّهُ لَمَجْنُونٌ {القلم/51} is mentioned later as the barat istidlal.

The case of patience and their evil eye, and sihr are mentioned explicitly here with وَإِن يَكَادُ الَّذِينَ كَفَرُوا لَيُزْلِقُونَكَ بِأَبْصَارِهِمْ لَمَّا سَمِعُوا الذِّكْرَ وَيَقُولُونَ إِنَّهُ لَمَجْنُونٌ {القلم/51} وَمَا هُوَ إِلَّا ذِكْرٌ لِّلْعَالَمِينَ {القلم/52}. The purpose of make sihr, evil eye and other arguments as mentioned in the beginning of the Sûrah was to give doubt to the person of dai' who is inviting people to Islam. But Allah again assures similar to the beginning that this Qurān is the truth and reminder for all the universe and Creation وَمَا هُوَ إِلَّا ذِكْرٌ لِّلْعَالَمِينَ {القلم/52}.

اللهم جعلنا من الذاكرين[733]

آمين

---

732. 68:48 BEAR THEN with patience thy Sustainer's will and be not like him of the great fish, who cried out [in distress] after having given in to anger.27 (68:49) [And remember:] had not grace from his Sustainer reached him, he would indeed have been cast forth upon that barren shore in a state of disgrace: (68:50) but [as it was,] his Sustainer had elected him and placed him among the righteous.

68:51 Hence, [be patient,] even though they who are bent on denying the truth would all but kill thee with their eyes whenever they hear this reminder, and [though] they say, "[As for Muhammad,] behold, most surely he is a madman!"

733. Oh Allah, make us among those who remember you.

Sûrah Muzammil

[10]⁷³⁴

{المزمل/10} وَاصْبِرْ عَلَى مَا يَقُولُونَ وَاهْجُرْهُمْ هَجْرًا جَمِيلًا

The initial meaning of the ayah can address to the Prophet صلى الله عليه
وسلم in the discourses of tabligh or dawah, invitation of others. The
implicit meaning is to everyone in the engagements of dawah and others.

One can have the difficulty of showing patience when the person is
disturbed constantly. Being disturbed with family members, children,
or any person can make one's life difficult. The notion of patience comes
in when the person still maintains one's rational human interactions but
does not yell, break hearts, curse or simply get angry or discharge this
potential energy in a destructive way on others. Leaving them in the
positive states of peace is important as mentioned وَاهْجُرْهُمْ هَجْرًا جَمِيلاً⁷³⁵
although one can him or herself may be disturbed.

اللهم اجعلنا من الذين يتبعون الحق⁷³⁶

Sûrah Jinn

[10]⁷³⁷

{الجن/10} وَأَنَّا لَا نَدْرِي أَشَرٌّ أُرِيدَ بِمَن فِي الْأَرْضِ أَمْ أَرَادَ بِهِمْ رَبُّهُمْ رَشَدًا

[69]⁷³⁸

{ص/69} مَا كَانَ لِي مِنْ عِلْمٍ بِالْمَلَإِ الْأَعْلَى إِذْ يَخْتَصِمُونَ

Sometimes the events can happen in one's life. It can be an ibtila, a test, or
a guidance from Allah ﷻ. Therefore, Jinns are trying to understand these
unseen realities to humans because they may have more interaction

---

734. (73:10) And endure with patience whatever people may say[against thee], and avoid
them with a comely avoidance.
735. And avoid them with a comely avoidance.
736. Oh Allah, make us from those who follow the truth.
737. 72:10 "'And [now we have become aware] that we [created beings] may not know
whether evil fortune is intended for [any of] those who live on earth, or whether it is their
Sustainer's will to endow them with consciousness of what is right.
738. I had no knowledge of the exalted assembly [of angels] when they were disputing [the
creation of Adam].

tools with the parts related of the unseen realms to humans. In this above ayah, they try to rationalize what is happening with these events if they are test or not وَأَنَّا لَا نَدْرِي أَشَرٌّ أُرِيدَ بِمَن فِي الْأَرْضِ أَمْ أَرَادَ بِهِمْ رَبُّهُمْ رَشَدًا {الجن/10}.

As discussion is happening among them, there is another level of discourse occurs among angels as mentioned in مَا كَانَ لِي مِنْ عِلْمٍ بِالْمَلَإِ الْأَعْلَى إِذْ يَخْتَصِمُونَ {ص/69}.

In this regard, there are possible renderings from above ayahs. Humans are the most far or in another level of understanding and interpreting the seen and unseen events depending on their connection with Allah .

The level of connection about unseen realities in their true and real meanings can increase from:

1. Humans
2. Jinns
3. Angels

One can call this the worlds of shadah of humans, seen and witnessed by human five senses, and the worlds of malakut, hakikah of angels. Therefore, in the story of Khidr and Musa as, there is the interaction of members from two worlds. Khidr as is from the worlds of malakut and Musa as is from the worlds of shadah. The world of jinn is in between shadah and malakut as they may interact with both worlds negatively or positively. The case of Shaytan as a jinn being among angels, the case of stoning the jinns with stars as mentioned in Sûrah Saffât by angels, and the case of jinns interacting with humans etc. can be some examples to support above taxonomy.

One can bring the question of Shaytan if he is/was a Jinn or angel. As one can remember the discourses in traditional scholarship that there are both opinions. One can ask if the Jinns have a limited time, then if shaytan is a Jinn why he is still alive and living? When Shaytan did not respect Adam as by not making sajdah, he said [739] ربي فانزني الي يوم يبعثونthat Shaytan is granted an exceptional lifespan until the end of days by Allah as mentioned in different verses of the Qurān.

---

739. Reprieve me until the Day they are resurrected.

[18]⁷⁴⁰

وَأَنَّ الْمَسَاجِدَ لِلَّهِ فَلَا تَدْعُوا مَعَ اللَّهِ أَحَدًا {الجن/18}

The masjid are not owned by anyone or entity. When a place is designated as masjid then, the person or the entities don't have right to implement individual or private or official ownership. These places become a place open to everyone and there is no exclusive treatment to any person, الله اعلم.

Sûrah Insãn

It is interesting to note that the word الإنسَان⁷⁴¹ is mentioned in the Qurãn ~ 63 times. The Prophet ﷺ died when he ﷺ was 63. Rasulullah ﷺ lived a life of insãn kamil for 63 years. He ﷺ showed us how can one be a true human being.

[8]⁷⁴²

وَيُطْعِمُونَ الطَّعَامَ عَلَى حُبِّهِ مِسْكِينًا وَيَتِيمًا وَأَسِيرًا

The word مِسْكِينًا⁷⁴³ is the first in the above sequencing of the ayah. This word also may mean a person who is disabilitated for different reasons although the person may have strength to work or access to work. A person who is traumatized due to losing someone. It can be a person overwhelmed with the accountability in front of Allah ﷺ and does not have any interest or physical power except worshipping to Allah ﷺ. In the classical sense, this word مِسْكِينًا is translated as the poor, yet the word فاكير has also the possibility of meaning poor financially compared to the word مِسْكِينًا as mentioned by some muffasirun.

---

740. 72:18 And [know] that all worship14 is due to God [alone]: hence, do not invoke anyone side by side with God!
741. Man.
742. (76:8) and who give food—however great be their own want of it—unto the needy, and the orphan, and the captive
743. The needy.

[9] 744

إِنَّمَا نُطْعِمُكُمْ لِوَجْهِ اللَّهِ لَا نُرِيدُ مِنكُمْ جَزَاءً وَلَا شُكُورًا

Especially, when someone feeds a person there should not be an expectation of جزاك اللهbecause the verse mentions that جَزَاء745 is not needed. There should not be an expectation of شكرن because the verse mentions شُكُورًا746 is not needed. The sole purpose should be لِوَجْهِ أَللهِ747, to please Allah ﷻ. Although a person may say it but there should not be any expectation for the one who gives and does something good. The intention is in the heart. Allah ﷻ knows everyone's real dealings.

Sûrah Muzammil

[20]748

It is important to realize that people benefit from the Qurān according to their needs. In this perspective, sometimes a letter, a word, a verse as a sentence, and a few verses as a paragraph can suffice in the daily, hourly or even sometimes minutely intakes from the Qurān. As the person is dynamically in non-stop thinking mode, except maybe in sleeping, the encounters of feelings, sadness, joys, and sometimes heedlessness moments can be disturbing. Yet, it can be balanced with the teachings of the Qurān. Therefore, the Qurān itself instructs as in Sûrah muzzamil,

إِنَّ رَبَّكَ يَعْلَمُ أَنَّكَ تَقُومُ أَدْنَى مِن ثُلُثَيِ اللَّيْلِ وَنِصْفَهُ وَثُلُثَهُ وَطَائِفَةٌ مِّنَ الَّذِينَ مَعَكَ وَاللَّهُ يُقَدِّرُ اللَّيْلَ وَالنَّهَارَ عَلِمَ أَن لَّن تُحْصُوهُ فَتَابَ عَلَيْكُمْ فَاقْرَءُوا مَا تَيَسَّرَ مِنَ الْقُرْآنِ عَلِمَ أَن

---

744. (9) [Saying, in their hearts,] "We feed you for the sake of God alone: we desire no recompense from you, nor thanks.
745. Recompense.
746. Thanks.
747. The sake of God alone.
748. 73:20 BEHOLD, [O Prophet,] thy Sustainer knows that thou keepest awake [in prayer] nearly two-thirds of the night, or one-half of it, or a third of it, together with some of those who follow thee.11 And God who determines the measure of night and day, is aware that you would never grudge it:12 and therefore He turns towards you in His grace. Recite, then, as much of the Qur'an as you may do with ease. He knows that in time there will be among you sick people, and others who will go about the land in search of God's bounty, and others who will fight in God's cause. Recite, then, [only] as much of it as you may do with ease, and be constant in prayer, and spend in charity, and [thus] lend unto God a goodly loan: for whatever good deed you may offer up in your own behalf, you shall truly find it with Godyea, better, and richer in reward. And [always] seek God's forgiveness: behold, God is much-forgiving, a dispenser of grace!

سَيَكُونُ مِنكُم مَّرْضَى وَآخَرُونَ يَضْرِبُونَ فِي الْأَرْضِ يَبْتَغُونَ مِن فَضْلِ اللَّهِ وَآخَرُونَ
يُقَاتِلُونَ فِي سَبِيلِ اللَّهِ فَاقْرَؤُوا مَا تَيَسَّرَ مِنْهُ وَأَقِيمُوا الصَّلَاةَ وَآتُوا الزَّكَاةَ وَأَقْرِضُوا
اللَّهَ قَرْضًا حَسَنًا وَمَا تُقَدِّمُوا لِأَنفُسِكُم مِّنْ خَيْرٍ تَجِدُوهُ عِندَ اللَّهِ هُوَ خَيْرًا وَأَعْظَمَ أَجْرًا
وَاسْتَغْفِرُوا اللَّهَ إِنَّ اللَّهَ غَفُورٌ رَّحِيمٌ {المزمل/20}

to read whatever you can. The expression فَاقْرَؤُوا مَا تَيَسَّرَ مِنَ الْقُرْآنِ[749] is
repeated twice in this Sûrah, chapter, in order to instruct us to hold the
portion of the Qurān in our daily and constant encounters as a regular
routine practice. And, Allah ﷻ mentions that everyone's schedule is
different but the key is the struggle of reading every day persistently.

Sûrah Mudassir

[1-7][750]

يَا أَيُّهَا الْمُدَّثِّرُ {المدثر/1} قُمْ فَأَنذِرْ {المدثر/2} وَرَبَّكَ فَكَبِّرْ {المدثر/3} وَثِيَابَكَ فَطَهِّرْ
{المدثر/4} وَالرُّجْزَ فَاهْجُرْ {المدثر/5} وَلَا تَمْنُن تَسْتَكْثِرُ {المدثر/6} وَلِرَبِّكَ فَاصْبِرْ
{المدثر/7}

Although the person may not want to engage with others, Allah ﷻ
mentions the etiquettes and the need of engaging with others due to the
reminding them about their real purpose in this life. As there are some
external etiquettes of this engagement as mentioned (4) وَثِيَابَكَ فَطَهِّرْ, there
are more in one's internal etiquettes of controlling, making tazkiya and
focusing in one's inner self with one's heart and mind as mentioned (3)
وَرَبَّكَ فَكَبِّرْ, (5) وَالرُّجْزَ فَاهْجُرْ, (6) وَلَا تَمْنُن تَسْتَكْثِرُ and (7) وَلِرَبِّكَ فَاصْبِرْ. One can
see as external has the coefficient of one, then the internal struggle can
have the coefficient of three or four. The real change even in the case of
delivering in one's message to others become fruitful in focusing one's
internal disposition mainly and then external renderings, الله اعلم.

---

749. Recite, then, as much of the Qur'an as you may do with ease.
750. 74:1 O THOU [in thy solitude] enfolded! (2) Arise and warn! (3) And thy Sustainer's
greatness glorify! (4) And thine inner self purify! (5) And all defilement shun! (6) And do not
through giving seek thyself to gain, (7) but unto thy Sustainer turn in patience.

30

Sûrah Naba

[19]⁷⁵¹

{وَفُتِحَتِ السَّمَاء فَكَانَتْ أَبْوَابًا {النبأ/19}

In our current time, the spaceships should be ejected at certain locations on the earth to go through and pierce the sky (52). The word أَبْوَابًا⁷⁵² can signify this notion, الله اعلم.

Sûrah Abasa

[1-12]⁷⁵³

{عَبَسَ وَتَوَلَّى {عبس/1} أَن جَاءهُ الْأَعْمَى {عبس/2} وَمَا يُدْرِيكَ لَعَلَّهُ يَزَّكَّى {عبس/3}
أَوْ يَذَّكَّرُ فَتَنفَعَهُ الذِّكْرَى {عبس/4} أَمَّا مَنِ اسْتَغْنَى {عبس/5} فَأَنتَ لَهُ تَصَدَّى {عبس/6}
وَمَا عَلَيْكَ أَلَّا يَزَّكَّى {عبس/7} وَأَمَّا مَن جَاءكَ يَسْعَى {عبس/8} وَهُوَ يَخْشَى {عبس/9}
فَأَنتَ عَنْهُ تَلَهَّى {عبس/10} كَلَّا إِنَّهَا تَذْكِرَةٌ {عبس/11} فَمَن شَاء ذَكَرَهُ {عبس/12}

According to some, the sabab nuzûl of this Sûrah is not for the Prophet but it is for another person (53). On the other hand, this Sûrah alludes to the difficult task of tabligh or dawah. As a human, we tend to make dawah differently with the people of different backgrounds of culture, age, gender, and social status. There are many reasons of hikmah for this perspective as witnessed in the lives of the Prophets and our beloved Prophet ﷺ, al-Mustafa. On the other hand, it is very difficult to keep the balance of the right disposition of heart, mind and the rulings established by Allah ﷻ and the Prophet ﷺ.

---

751. (78:19) and when the skies are opened and become [as wide-flung] gates;¹⁰
752. Gates.
753. 80:1 HE FROWNED and turned away (80:2) because the blind man approached him! 80:3 Yet for all thou didst know, [O Muhammad,] he might perhaps have grown in purity, (4) or have been reminded [of the truth], and helped by this reminder. (5) Now as for him who believes himself to be selfsufficient2 (6) to him didst thou give thy whole attention, (7) although thou art not accountable for his failure to attain to purity; (8) but as for him who came unto thee full of eagerness (9) and in awe [of God] (10) him didst thou disregard! 80:11 NAY, VERILY, these [messages] are but a reminder: (12) and so, whoever is willing may remember Him

In other words, as we are increasingly living in a society of different people with different value systems through culture, society, language, ethnicity, and others, it is sometimes very difficult to make the right decision to follow the guidelines appropriate to the context within the limits of the Qurān and Sunnah. This does not mean that the limits of the Qurān and Sunnah is narrow, na'uzu billah, they are vast. But making the right choice within this vast context can be challenging.

On a positive note, one can remember the hadith of Aisha ra about her question to the Prophet صلى الله عليه وسلم, the definition of muhsin or who has birr, the Prophet mentions that the ones who do good to please Allah ﷻ and be at a disposition of uncertainty if their good action is accepted by Allah ﷻ or not (27).

On the other hand, the terrifying part is being involved with a disposition with a good-seeming intention, but it is in reality receiving the gadab, saht, or displeasure of Allah ﷻ. The technical term for these types of dispositions can be bidah, or dalālah etc. In other words for tablihg or dawah purposes, the cases of gender mixing, opposite gender interactions, the rules of tahkfīf for the new comers of the religion are generally proposed to be present due to the need, time and context. One can see the reasons behind it, yet uncertainty of displeasing Allah ﷻ on the path of the struggles to please Allah ﷻ can really sometimes freeze, disable, and immobilize the person. Because if the intention is to please Allah ﷻ on all these struggles then, no one wants to end up displeasing Allah ﷻ due to wrong, ignorant, or improper choices.

The extreme cases of above examples can be witnessed when there are clear opposing rules of group movements. These examples can be claiming another Prophet after the Prophet Muhammad ﷺ, intermingling with opposite gender with no purpose, the authority of exiling a person from religion, new age movements of abandoning the faraid of prayers, rituals or etc. May Allah protect us, Amìn. رَبَّنَا لَا تُزِغْ [754] قُلُوبَنَا بَعْدَ إِذْ هَدَيْتَنَا وَهَبْ لَنَا مِن لَّدُنكَ رَحْمَةً إِنَّكَ أَنتَ الْوَهَّابُ

---

754. Our Lord, do not turn our hearts away after you have guided us, and grant us mercy, for you are the Most Merciful.

Sûrah Mutaffifin

[14]755

كَلَّا بَلْ رَانَ عَلَى قُلُوبِهِم مَّا كَانُوا يَكْسِبُونَ {المطففين/14}

The above ayah can signify the disconnection from imān through sins is a process but not a one day or instant event. If a person can think the scientific process of رَانَ, rusting, it needs time for chemical reaction to happen (54). Allah ﷻ mentions this exactly, the process of rusting on the hearts with the expression رَانَ عَلَى قُلُوبِهِم756.

This is exactly a literal translation of this expression. This rusting and detachment occur as a process due to the choices and actions of people as the word يَكْسِبُونَ757 can imply. In this regard, the word kasb is the person's acquirement and no one can blame, others or astaghfirullah and na'uzu billah, Allah ﷻ that the choice of disbelief or misguidance, kufr, is a force or compulsion.

It is interesting to note that one of the ways to prevent rusting is painting in chemistry. If the sins are like rust and painting can be the istighfār and refreshment of imān can be through tawba, i'lm, knowledge and ibadah, worship.

Therefore, one of the terms also mentioned in the Qurān is sibgah, صبغت758, as the painting or anointed. The one who is painted or anointed by Allah ﷻ is protected against these rusting136-138] :]759

قُولُواْ آمَنَّا بِاللّهِ وَمَا أُنزِلَ إِلَيْنَا وَمَا أُنزِلَ إِلَى إِبْرَاهِيمَ وَإِسْمَاعِيلَ وَإِسْحَقَ وَيَعْقُوبَ وَالأَسْبَاطِ وَمَا أُوتِيَ مُوسَى وَعِيسَى وَمَا أُوتِيَ النَّبِيُّونَ مِن رَّبِّهِمْ لاَ نُفَرِّقُ بَيْنَ أَحَدٍ مِّنْهُمْ وَنَحْنُ لَهُ مُسْلِمُونَ {البقرة/136} فَإِنْ آمَنُواْ بِمِثْلِ مَا آمَنتُم بِهِ فَقَدِ اهْتَدَواْ وَّإِن تَوَلَّوْاْ فَإِنَّمَا

---

755. (83: 14) Nay, but their hearts are corroded by all [the evil] that they were wont to do!

756. Their hearts are corroded by all [the evil].

757. They were wont to do!

758. Religion.

759. 2:136 Say, [O believers], "We have believed in Allah and what has been revealed to us and what has been revealed to Abraham and Ishmael and Isaac and Jacob and the Descendants [al-Asbāt] and what was given to Moses and Jesus and what was given to the prophets from their Lord. We make no distinction between any of them, and we are Muslims [in submission] to Him." 2:137 So if they believe in the same as you believe in, then they have been [rightly] guided; but if they turn away, they are only in dissension, and Allah will be sufficient for you against them. And He is the Hearing, the Knowing. 2:138 [And say, "Ours is] the religion of Allah. And who is better than Allah in [ordaining] religion? And we are worshippers of Him."

هُمْ فِي شِقَاقٍ فَسَيَكْفِيكَهُمُ اللَّهُ وَهُوَ السَّمِيعُ الْعَلِيمُ {البقرة/137} صِبْغَةَ اللَّ وَمَنْ أَحْسَنُ مِنَ اللَّهِ صِبْغَةً وَنَحْنُ لَهُ عَابِدُونَ {البقرة/138}

These are the first the Prophets of Allah ﷻ. In Christianity the term, the anointed or painted one is used for the Prophet Isa, Jesus as.

Sûrah Fajr

[28-30][760]

ارْجِعِي إِلَى رَبِّكِ رَاضِيَةً مَّرْضِيَّةً {الفجر/28} فَادْخُلِي فِي عِبَادِي {الفجر/29} وَادْخُلِي جَنَّتِي {الفجر/30}

The ayah ارْجِعِي إِلَى رَبِّكِ رَاضِيَةً مَّرْضِيَّةً has a critical stance in Islam. Here, the word ارْجِعِي[761] is used to possibly mentioned to attain the level of رَاضِيَةً مَّرْضِيَّةً[762] in the world. With this state, then the person dies and goes to Allah ﷻ. In other words, a person can be filled fully with the light of imãn that then the person becomes constantly appreciative, thankful, and pleased with everything that Allah ﷻ gives. As a guidance, this person is in real light, peaceful state, and happiness in this word. This person is so much happy with this light of increasing imãn that the person constantly thanks and appreciates everything but everything from Allah ﷻ.

In this regard, the name and title of Muhammad ﷺ represents this at the highest level as the role model and lead. Then, for others it is the level to attain, to reach, and to struggle in one's life to attain the level of radiyah and mardiyyah. The dua of رضيت بالله رب وبالأسلم دين و بمحمد[763] نبي و رسولا can truly show this state if one really can transfuse this dua's meanings constantly in one's life.

At another level, there is a chapter in a unique style compared to other chapters in the Qurãn. This chapter is Sûrah Rahmãn. One of the uniqueness is the constant repetition and instilment of the ayah فَبِأَيِّ آلَاءِ رَبِّكُمَا تُكَذِّبَانِ[764] {الرحمن/13}.

---

760. (89:28) Return thou unto thy Sustainer, well-pleased [and] pleasing [Him]: (29) enter, then, together with My [other true] servants (30) yea, enter thou My paradise!"
761. Return.
762. Well-pleased [and] pleasing [Him].
763. I am pleased with Allah as my Lord, Islãm as my religion, and Muhammad (ﷺ) as the messenger and prophet.
764. So which of your Lords sign do you deny?

The main essence of this chapter is to underline this essence in creation, the essence in imān, the essence in ones' spiritual advancement in relationship with Allah ﷻ to reach to the level رَاضِيَةٍ مَّرْضِيَّةٍ by embodying an imān with the qualities of constant appreciation, thankfulness, gratitude and being pleased with everything that Allah ﷻ gives.

اللهم اجعلنا منهم، امين

When a person in this world reaches the level of رَاضِيَةٍ مَّرْضِيَّةٍ then, the person is already in Jannah. So, Jannah is both here, in this world and after death. In other words, the person is constantly in Jannah. There is no change of position, before or after death. Once you are in that state or in that group as mentioned فَادْخُلِي فِي عِبَادِي then, inshAllah you are already in Jannah. When the person is in this state, there is not really much meaning of death. اللهم اجعلنا منهم، امين

Sûrah Duha

[4][765]

وَلَلْآخِرَةُ خَيْرٌ لَّكَ مِنَ الْأُولَى {الضحى/4}

When the person is struggling to increase his or her relationship with Allah ﷻ, there is always the fear that "Am I pleasing Allah ﷻ? What if my engagement is a test even though it may look positive with the amount of worship, reading the Qurān, righteous work and others? Will I lose what I have in my relationship with Allah ﷻ...etc." These along with other similar ones are all valid and important concerns. These concerns should be there as the Prophet ﷺ mentions in one hadith to Aisha radiyallahu anha that these concerns are the signs for the believers when they do a virtuous act but they are not sure if really it is something pleasing to Allah ﷻ or not (27).

On the other hand, if this goes to another extreme that the person becomes pessimist about his or her own disposition that he or she is a liar, munāfiq, the one using the religion of Allah ﷻ similar to selling to a cheap price as mentioned in the Qurān, the one who is showing

---

765. (93:4) for, indeed, the life to come will be better for thee than this earlier part [of thy life]!

off people through the Qurān and other means of religious duties and others then, this ayah as {الضحى/4} وَلَلْآخِرَةُ خَيْرٌ لَّكَ مِنَ الْأُولَى can be another balancing agent to calm this person down, to balance his or her disposition and to keep him or her moving encouragingly on the path. In other words, there should always be the uncertainty of the one's self with the relationship with Allah ﷻ although the person can be a great scholar and a worshipper. There are very devastating incidents reported by the Qurān and the Prophet ﷺ about the people using religious affairs but perhaps not realizing it and then, facing a very grave and shameful account in front of Allah ﷻ. As this disposition can freeze the person in their ability of self-check and self-control, the balancing agent always is the Rahmah and Fadl of Allah ﷻ as promised here in وَلَلْآخِرَةُ خَيْرٌ لَّكَ مِنَ الْأُولَى {الضحى/4}.

With Allah ﷻ's Rahmah and Fadl, one can expect that there is a linear increase in one's relationship with Allah ﷻ as this ayah وَلَلْآخِرَةُ خَيْرٌ لَّكَ مِنَ الْأُولَى {الضحى/4} can allude. In other words, one cannot expect any instantaneous or linear increase in one's self-correction or tazkiya if there is no Fadl and Rahmah of Allah ﷻ as mentioned very strongly in the Sûrah Nûr [21][766] as وَلَوْلَا فَضْلُ اللَّهِ عَلَيْكُمْ وَرَحْمَتُهُ مَا زَكَا مِنكُم مِّنْ أَحَدٍ أَبَدًا. Having a good zann from the Fadl and Rahmah of Allah ﷻ but carrying constantly the notion at the same that "anything at any time can be or become a test, trial or point of deviation" الله اعلم.... رَبَّنَا لَا تُزِغْ قُلُوبَنَا بَعْدَ إِذْ هَدَيْتَنَا وَهَبْ لَنَا مِن لَّدُنكَ رَحْمَةً إِنَّكَ أَنتَ الْوَهَّابُ [767]

Sûrah Qadir

[4][768]

تَنَزَّلُ الْمَلَائِكَةُ وَالرُّوحُ فِيهَا بِإِذْنِ رَبِّهِم مِّن كُلِّ أَمْرٍ {القدر/4}

This ayah can show that Allah ﷻ mentions the inzal of Jibril to earth as a phenomenon of significance. All the angels act with the permission of Allah ﷻ.

---

766. And if not for the favor of Allah upon you and His mercy, not one of you would have been pure, ever.

767. Our Lord, do not turn our hearts away after you have guided us, and grant us mercy, for you are The Most Merciful.

768. (97:4) In hosts descend in it the angels, 3 bearing divine inspiration4 by their Sustainer's leave; from all [evil] that may happen

Sûrah Asr

[1-3][769]

بِسْمِ اللَّهِ الرَّحْمَنِ الرَّحِيمِ

وَالْعَصْرِ {العص/2} إِنَّ الْإِنسَانَ لَفِي خُسْرٍ {العص/1} إِلَّا الَّذِينَ آمَنُوا وَعَمِلُوا الصَّالِحَاتِ وَتَوَاصَوْا بِالْحَقِّ وَتَوَاصَوْا بِالصَّبْرِ {العص/3}

As the word وَالْعَصْرِ can allude to the specific and long periods of time, this word also can allude to the constant times of struggles and tests that one faces in his or her life that requires patience. For example, a parent not losing her or himself and getting angry to their children can also take some lessons from this Sûrah. In this sense, a parent still continues his or her main duties with Allah ﷻ primarily. Yet at the same time, this parent can try to give advice about the truth, right disposition and taqwa of Allah ﷻ with patience as mentioned in this category.

In parental, spousal, personal, social or other engagements, standing in the right disposition without losing the right and correct disposition without doing zulm is very but very difficult. Therefore, if one reviews the life of the Rasulullah ﷺ, in the utmost cases of the urge of being angry, he ﷺ still controls himself and puts forward the correct disposition. [770] اللهم ثقلنا باخلاق رسول الله.

For the layman like us, the first is to preserve what we have, not endangering our imān, good actions and ibadah such as salah and others as mentioned إِلاَّ الَّذِينَ آمَنُوا وَعَمِلُوا الصَّالِحَاتِ[771]. Then, if the person is still at a sound level of preservation of the requirements of imān, then one can proceed to the next step by giving advice as mentioned وَتَوَاصَوْا بِالْحَقِّ وَتَوَاصَوْا بِالصَّبْرِ {العص/3}[772], الله اعلم. Patience in all these engagements is the key to maintain istiqamah, balance.

---

769. (103:1) By time, (103:2) Indeed, mankind is in loss. (103:3) Except for those who believed and done righteous deeds and advised each other to the truth and advised each other to patience.
770. Oh Allah bless us with the character of Rasulullah ﷺ.
771. Except for those who believed and done righteous deeds.
772. And advised each other to the truth and advised each other to patience.

Sûrah Ikhlãs

One should remember the learning process of a person. A person's learning skills mainly build up on the methodology of comparing and contrasting in increasing one's knowledge. In other words, a person looks around the objects, beings, incidents and experiences and deduce causalities, and results. This is the area where inclinations form. Then, the person intends to execute the inclinations with one's free choice and free will.

On the other hand, Allah ﷻ is not like humans. The person makes a mistake to fully deduce meanings about the Creator, Allah ﷻ by using same methodology of analogy and comparison. This is a major mistake of humans in executing the free will and free choice. In other words, the methodology of comparison and contrast cannot be fully executed with the unseen. It cannot be fully executed to have the true knowledge of Allah ﷻ. Therefore, there is a guidance needed. In this perspective, the scriptures from Allah ﷻ, the Qurãn and hadith serves as the key to implement the notion of "guided method of comparison and analogy." In other words, the person can have the true knowledge of Allah ﷻ with the same method of comparison and analogy with the guidance of the Qurãn and the hadith and by understanding and normalizing the limits of comparison for the unseen and for especially Allah ﷻ. The discussion here mainly underlines rationalizing of the limits of execution of free will and free choice. It also indicates the necessity of knowledge directly given by Allah ﷻ about the guidelines of knowing our Creator.

BIBLIOGRAPHY

1. Vahide, S. *The Collection of Light* . s.l.: ihlas nur publication, 2001.
2. Sirhindi, Ahmad. *Maktubat Imam Rabbani Shaykh Ahmad Sirhindi Faruqi.* s.l.: Maktabah Mujaddidiyah (www.maktabah.org), 2008.
3. Al-Bukhari, M. *The translation of the meanings of Sahih Al-Bukhari.* s.l.: Kazi Publications, 1986.
4. Demirci, Muhsin. *Tefsir Tarihi (History of Exegesis of Quran).* Istanbul: ifav, 2010. pp. 34–38.
5. As-Suyuti, Jalal ad-Din. *Gateway to the Qur'anic Sciences.* s.l.: Turath Publishing, 2017.
6. Kumek, Y. *The Noble Quran: Selected Passages From Al-Quran Al-Kareem With Interpreted Meanings.* Buffalo, New York: Medina House Publishing, 2020.
7. Kumek, Yunus J. *Practical Mysticism: Sufi Journeys of Heart and Mind.* Dubuque: Kendall Hunt, 2018.
8. Razi, M. *Mafatih al-Ghayb known as al-Tafsir al-Kabir.* Cairo: Dar Ibya al-Kutub al-Bahiyya, 1172.
9. Muslim, A. *Sahih Muslim (translated by Siddiqui, A.).* s.l.: Peace Vision, 1972.
10. Al-Ghazali, M. *Ihya 'Ulum al-Din* . s.l.: Dar al-Fikr, 2004.
11. Kasir, Ibn. *Tafsir al-Qur'an al-Azim.* Beirut: Dar al-Ilm, 1982.
12. Bukhari, Muhammad Ibn Ismail. *Moral Teachings of Islam: Prophetic Traditions from Al-Adab Al-mufrad.* s.l.: Rowman Altamira, 2003.
13. Taftazani, At. *Sharhu Taftazani.* p. 69.
14. Aristotle. *Aristotle's Metaphysics.*
15. Kumek, Yunus. *Revealing Pearls and Diamonds: Selected Duas of Rasulullah saw.* s.l.: Medina House Publishing, 2019.
16. Arabi, Ibn. *Al Futuhat Al Makkiya.* s.l.: Dar Al-Kotob Al-Ilmiyah.
17. Raymond D. Berendt, Edith L. R. Corliss, Morris S. Ojalvo. *Quieting A Practical Guide to Noise Control.* s.l.: University Press of the Pacific, 2000. pp. 1–2.

18. Dawud, Abu (Sulaiman bin Ash'ath). *Sunan Abu Dawud*. riyadh: Darussalam, 2008.

19. Laney, Marti Olsen. *The Introvert Advantage: How to Thrive in an Extrovert World*. s.l.: Workman Publishing Company, 2002. p. 41.

20. Majah, Ibn. *Sunan Ibn Majah*. s.l.: Darus-Salam, 2007.

21. G., Muhammad F. *Ijaz of the Quran*. s.l.: Nile, 2008.

22. Oxford, University Press. Oxford Dictionaries. [Online] 2016. [Cited: 2016.] http://www.oxforddictionaries.com/us/definition/american_english/say.

23. Hanbal, Ahmad B. *Musnad Imam Ahmad Ibn Hanbal*. s.l.: Dar-Us-Salam Publications, 2012.

24. Shafi, Muhammad. *Ma'ariful Qur'an*. s.l.: maktaba-e Darul-Uloom, 2005. pp. 129–131. Vol. 1.

25. Al-Marghinani, Burhan Uddin Abu Al-Hasan Ali Ibn Abu Bakr Ibn Abdul Jaleel Ar-Rashidani. *Al Hidayah Sharh Bidayat Al-Mubtadi*. Beirut, Lebanon: Dar Al Hadith.

26. Al-Wahidi, Imam Ali Ibn Ahmad. *Alwajizu fi tafsiriil kitabil Aziz*. s.l.: Darul Qalam & Dar Shamia.

27. Tirmizi, M. *Jami At-Tirmizi*. s.l.: Dar-us-Salam, 2007.

28. Al-Hakim. *Mustadrak*. p. 1/612.

29. Hibban, Ibn. *As-Sahih*. pp. 4/612, 6/411.

30. Bolelli, Nusraddin. *Balagatul Arabiyya*. s.l.: ifav, 2009.

31. Ibrahim Kalin, John L. Esposito. *Islamophobia The Challenge of Pluralism in the 21st Century*. s.l.: Oxford University Press, USA, 2011. p. 192.

32. Maturidi, Abu Mansur Al. *Ta'wilat Ahl As Sunnah*. s.l.: Dar al Kotob al ilmiyyah,.

33. Oxford, University Press. Oxford Dictionaries. [Online] 2016. [Cited: 2016.] http://www.oxforddictionaries.com/us/definition/american_english/.

34. Thalabi, Abu Ishaq. *Al-Kashaf wal bayab*. Beirut: DKI, 2004.

35. Mojaddedi, Jawid. *The Wiley Blackwell Companion to the Qur'an*. s.l.: Wiley, 2017. p. 120.

36. AbdulFadl, Muhammad. *Lectures on Quran*. 2019.

37. Baghawi, Husayn. *Tafsir al-Baghawi al-musamma Ma'alim al-tanzil*. Bayrut: Dar al-Ma'rifah, 1987.

38. Ehrman, Bart D. *Misquoting Jesus The Story Behind Who Changed the Bible and Why*. s.l.: HarperOne, 2009.

39. Janney, Rebecca Price. *Then Comes Marriage? A Cultural History of the American Family.* s.l.: Moody Publishers, 2010. p. 108.
40. Rebeca Mejía-Arauz, Barbara Rogoff. *Children Learn by Observing and Contributing to Family and Community Endeavors: A Cultural Paradigm.* s.l.: Elsevier Science, 2015. p. 54.
41. Cox, R.R. *Schutz's Theory of Relevance: A Phenomenological Critique.* s.l.: Springer Netherlands, 2012.
42. O., Dr. Meggie. *LBGT issue from the Perspective of a ObGyn Specialist.* [interv.] Y. Kumek. March 17, 2016.
43. Zamakhshari, Abu Kassim. *Tafsir al-Kashaf.* Beirut: DKI, .
44. 'Imadi, Abu Al-Su'Ud Muhammad Ibn Muhammad Ibn Mus. *Tafsir abi al-su'ud, aw, irshad al-'aql al-salim ila mazaya al-qur'an al-karim.* s.l.: Turath For Solutions, 2013.
45. al-Ghazali, Abu Hamid. *The Quran and Its Exegesis (translation by Helmut Gatie).* s.l.: Oxford: Oneworld, 1996.
46. *Psychology and Light: The Effects of Light on Mental Functions.* Muensterberg, Hugo. 1916, Scientific American, Vol. 82, p. 406.
47. Shaykh Muhammad Nazim Adil Al-Haqqani, Shaykh Muhammad Hisham Kabbani. *Muhammad, the Messenger of Islam His Life & Prophecy.* s.l.: Islamic Supreme Council of America, 2002. p. 141.
48. Nasafi, I. *Tafsirul Nasafi.*
49. Ma'lūf, Luwīs. *Al Munjid Arabic Dictionary.* s.l.: Dar Al mashriq, 2000.
50. Shushmaruk, Peter. *Magnetic Universe.* s.l.: Lulu.com. p. 62.
51. Hauck, Dennis William. *The Complete Idiot's Guide to Alchemy.* s.l.: Alpha Books, 2008. p. 201.
52. Bizony, Piers. *How to Build Your Own Spaceship The Science of Personal Space Travel.* 2009. p. chapter 3.
53. *Surah Abasa.* Yener, M. s.l.: New Hope.
54. Pinna, Simon de. *Chemical Reactions.* s.l.: Gareth Stevens Pub. p. 32.

AUTHOR BIO

Dr. Kumek had classical training in Islamic sciences from the respected Shuyûqh/Teachers of Turkey, India, Egypt, Yemen, Somalia, Morocco, Sudan, and the United States. He stayed and studied classical Islamic sciences in Egypt and Turkey as well.

In his Western training, education and teaching experience, Dr. Kumek has acted as the religious studies coordinator at State University of New York (SUNY) Buffalo State and taught undergraduate and graduate courses in religious studies at SUNY at Buffalo State, Niagara University, Daemen College and Harvard Divinity School. Dr. Kumek also pursued doctorate degree in physics at SUNY at Buffalo published academic papers in the areas of quantum physics and medical physics. Then, he decided to engage with the world of social sciences through social anthropology, education, and cultural anthropology in his doctorate studies and subsequently, spent a few years as a research associate in the anthropology department of the same university and subsequently, completed a postdoctoral fellowship at Harvard Divinity school. Some of his book titles include sociology through religion, religious literacy through ethnography, selected passages from the Qurãn, selected passages from the Hadith (titled as Rasulullah ﷺ) and selected prayers of the Prophet Muhammad ﷺ (titled as Pearls and Diamonds). Dr. M. Yunus Kumek is currently teaching on Muslim Ministry and Spiritual Care at Harvard Divinity School.

ACKNOWLEDGMENTS

I would like to thank all my unnamed teachers, friends, and students for their input, ideas, suggestions, help, and support during and before the preparation of this book.

I would like to thank Dr. David Banks, faculty of the Department of Anthropology, State University of New York (SUNY), Sister Toni Hajdaj, Sister Umm Aisha, Dr. AbdulAhad, Br. Ali Rifat and His wife Sister Yildiz at-Turki, Sheikh Dr. Omar of Maryland al-Hindi, Sheikh Tamer of Buffalo, and Sheikh Ali of Hartford Seminary, Sisters Asya Hamad, Amina Osman, and Fatima Samrodia of Darul-Ulum Madania of Buffalo, Mufti Hussain Memon of Darul-Ulum Canada and Imam Khalil Qadri of Islamic Center of Niagara Frontier (ISNF) for all their editing, suggestions and comments.

I want to also thank the team of Medina House Publishing in all their preparations and efforts at all stages of this book especially Br. Murat, Br. Khalid (Halit), Br. Mehmet (Matt) and Sister Karen.

Lastly, I would like to thank all of my family members for their patience with me during the preparation of this book.

We ask Allah ﷻ to accept all our efforts with the Divine Karam, Fadl, and Grace but not with our faulty and limited efforts deeming rejection. اللَّهُمَّ صلِّ عَلى سَيِّدِناَ وَ حَبِيْبَنَا وَ مَوْلَانَا مُحَمَّد.

Index